Davy Crockett, James

The story of the filibusters

Davy Crockett, James Jeffrey Roche

The story of the filibusters

ISBN/EAN: 9783337821210

Printed in Europe, USA, Canada, Australia, Japan

Cover: Foto ©ninafisch / pixelio.de

More available books at **www.hansebooks.com**

THE STORY OF THE FILIBUSTERS. BY JAMES JEFFREY ROCHE

TO WHICH IS ADDED THE LIFE OF COLONEL DAVID CROCKETT

ILLUSTRATED

LONDON: T. FISHER UNWIN. NEW YORK: MACMILLAN & CO. MDCCCXCI

To

L. I. G.

"The best-condition'd and unwearied spirit
In doing courtesies."

Merchant of Venice.

PREFACE TO "THE FILIBUSTERS."

THE rise and fall of the American Filibusters belong to the history of the Nineteenth Century. From time to time their deeds have been recounted by actors in the stirring scenes, by contemporary observers, and, incidentally, by travellers in Spanish America who lingered for a moment over the romantic legend of the modern Vikings.

Among the works consulted in the preparation of this volume are: "A History of Miranda's Attempt to Effect a Revolution in South America," by one of his officers; Yokum's "History of Texas"; Green's narrative of the Mier Expedition, and Kendall's of that to Santa Fe; Henri de la Madelaine's "Life of Raoussett-Boulbon"; Well's account of Walker's expeditions to Sonora and Nicaragua; Walker's "History of the War in Nicaragua"; and the several works relating to the latter country of Squier, Scherzer, Stout, Captain Pim, Chevalier Belly, M. Nicaisse, and many other travellers.

From such sources, as well as from the periodicals and official documents of the day, and from the lips or pens of living comrades in the more recent of those tragedies, have been gathered the facts told in the following pages. It has been no easy task to sift the grains of truth from the mountain of myth, prejudice, and fiction under which the actual deeds of the Filibusters long lay buried.

Thirty years ago it would have been well-nigh impossible, in the heated atmosphere of the slavery conflict, to view such a subject with philosophical impartiality. To-day we may study the Filibuster dispassionately, for he belongs to extinct species. The speculator has supplanted him without perceptibly improving the morality of the world. Even the word "filibuster," transformed to a verb, is degraded to the base uses of politics. It is time to write the history and the epitaph of the brave, lawless, generous anomaly on civilization.

BOSTON, U.S., *March*, 1891.

CONTENTS.

CHAPTER VII.

CHAPTER VIII.

CHAPTER IX.

CHAPTER X.

CHAPTER XI.

CHAPTER XII.

CHAPTER XIII.

CHAPTER XIV.

CHAPTER XV.

CHAPTER XVI.

CHAPTER XVII.

CHAPTER XVIII.

LIFE OF COLONEL DAVID CROCKETT.

LIST OF ILLUSTRATIONS.

MAP OF THE
REPUBLIC
OF
NICARAGUA
1850 – 1860
Scale of Miles
0 5 10 20 30 40
HONDURAS
NEW SEGOVIA
MATAGALPA
LEON
GRANADA
RIVAS
PACIFIC OCEAN
L. MANAGUA
LAKE NICARAGUA
R. Guascoran
Choluctecа R.
Rian
Nicara
New Segovia
R. Coco
Alaguina
Somolo Grande
Condega
Xinolega
Sebaco
Sacate Grande I.
Choluctecа
Tigre I.
Subannah Grande
San Juan
Matagalpa
Vol Suanacaire
San Jerinomo
Sta. Teresia
Sauce
R. Chocoyos
Vol Coseguina
Savana Grande
Trinidad
Vol Riejo
San Benito
Buenaventura
Delpochapa
Realejo
Vol Orota
Leon
Teustope
S. Benito
Boaca
Jiguilito
Pueblo Nueva
Nagarote
S. Lorenzo
Rita
Port of Tamarindo
Managua
Pa
Mt. Masaya
Masaya
Granada
Nandaime
San Rafael
Niquinomo
Zapatero
Playa Grande
Obraje
Ometepec
Rivas
Brito
San Jorge
San Juan del Sur
Virgin Bay
Naranjo
Salinas B.
Descartes Pt.
St. Elena B.
Sta Rosa
Liberto
Gua.
Murcialegos B.
CO
15
14
13
12
11
87
86
Longitude W

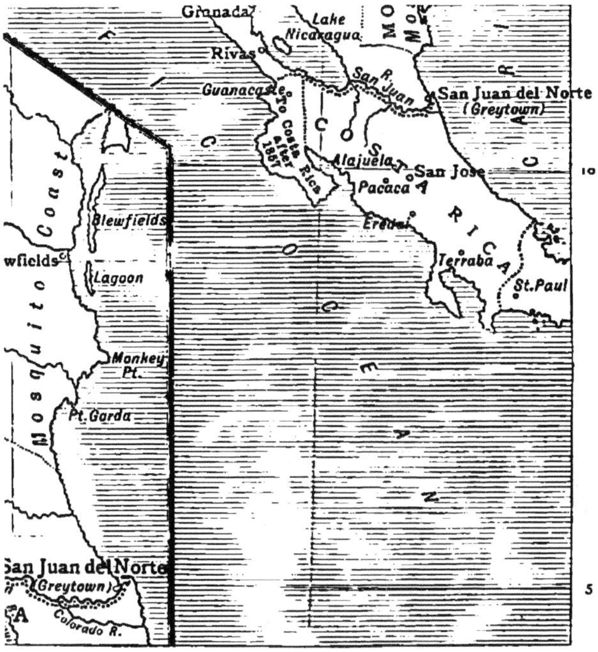

Longitude West 85 from Greenwich

T. FISHER UNWIN, PATERNOSTER SQUARE, LONDON, E.C.

THE STORY OF THE FILIBUSTERS.

CHAPTER I.

Etymology of the word Filibuster—Norse Adventurers—The Buccaneers—Miranda—Services under the Directory—First Expedition from the United States—Dr. Jenner and the King of Spain—Miranda's second expedition and death.

THE difference between a filibuster and a freebooter is one of ends rather than of means. Some authorities say that the words have a common etymology; but others, including Charlevoix, maintain that the filibuster derived his name from his original occupation, that of a cruiser in a "flibote," or "Vly-boat," first used on the river Vly, in Holland. Yet another writer says that the name was first given to the gallant followers of Dominique de Gourgues, who sailed from Finisterre, or Finibuster, in France, on the famous expedition against Fort Caroline in 1567.

The name, whatever its origin, was long current in the Spanish as "filibustero" before it became adopted into the English. So adopted, it has been used to describe a type of adventurer who occupied a curious place in American history during the decade from 1850 to 1860.

The citizen or subject of any country, who makes war upon a state with which his own is at peace, with intent to overrun and occupy it, not merely for the piratical ends of rapine and plunder, is a filibuster in the true sense of the term. Such act of war is, by the law of nations, a crime against both countries. Its morality, before the meaner court of popular judgment, will rest upon the measure of its success alone. So judged, as all invaders are judged at last, the bold adventurer draws but few prizes in the lottery of fame. Cortez and Houston are among the few successful filibusters of modern times.

In the shadowy chronicles of the Norsemen we find the first trace of that adventurous spirit which, during twelve centuries, gave the dominion of the ocean to the seafaring people of Northern Europe. The bold Vikings who, without chart or compass, sailed over unknown and dangerous seas, crossed the Atlantic and swept the Mediterranean, were the worthy fathers of the Drakes and Ansons of later years. History bespeaks them cruel, rapacious, daring; pirates when, as Wheaton says, the occupation of a pirate was considered not only lawful, but honourable. But they were not wholly destructive. Borrowing a lesson in natural history from their own lemming, they solved the troublesome problem, how to get rid of a surplus population, by sending the superfluous members forth to seek a new field. The lemming eats his way to the sea, in which he finds his grave; but his human imitator more wisely found there a pathway to fortune. They went forth mainly to conquer, incidentally to colonize and settle. Among themselves they were primitive republicans, though harsh tyrants to their vanquished foes. "Who is your king or leader?" asked the herald of King Charles the Simple, before the decisive battle on the banks of the Eure in A.D. 898. "We have no king, no chief, no master; but 'Rolf, the Walker,' leads us in war and on the day of battle," was the proud answer of Rolf's comrades and peers. That this was no idle boast, Rolf's own descendant, King John of England, learned to his sorrow when the sons of the sturdy Norse filibusters met him face to face at Runnymede. The Magna Charta is the written code of that fierce democracy, dreaded alike by its serfs and its kings. The Vikings stand alone as a race of warriors whose hardihood overcame even their native superstition, in leading them to defy the gods themselves. They were sceptics, because they knew not fear. Love was as yet an unknown power in their religion.

The Norsemen were suppressed only by absorption. Owing no fealty to their native land, they took possession of the conquered countries, in which they proved to be the strongest barrier against further aggressions from the dreaded North. But before this degree of safety was gained, all Europe had felt the scourge of the terrible Vikings, who had burned or put in vassalage London, Cologne, Treves, Paris, Tours, and Marseilles; carried their victorious arms to Portugal, Spain, Sicily, and Constantinople; and given dynasties of Norse blood to England, Russia, and France. Rolf married a natural daughter of King Charles, whence came the Norman dukes and the royal line of England. In brief, the Vikings held the western world at their mercy, overturning thrones, founding kingdoms, stabling their horses in the palaces of princes, and upholding on their hireling spears the crown of the fallen Cæsars.

With the rise of the powerful maritime nations of Europe filibusterism slumbered for several centuries. The immortal expedition of Cortes being, in so far as it lacked the sanction of his king, wholly that of a filibuster, needs but passing mention here. Its success has lifted it into the realms of history and made it a household story. Filibusterism was to awake on a new field and lead the van in the long warfare which, in two hemispheres and during three centuries, has followed the meeting of Northman and Southron. England, and also France, looked with jealous eyes upon the grasping policy of Spain in the New World. The fortune of discovery had given to the two former the apparently barren lots of Canada and the British colonies. Spain had drawn the rich prize of El Dorado. Not content with the spoils of Mexico and Peru, she grudged to the hardy hunters of the West Indies their petty trade with her colonies. She claimed the Mississippi. The epitaph of Columbus was read as a veritable bequest by Spanish greed. But avarice overreached itself. The persecutions heaped upon the "boucaniers" of the West Indies aroused a spirit of opposition, which success fanned into aggressive fires, and which the governments of England and France did nothing to extinguish. The cumbrous galleon with its golden freight was no match for the swift Vly-boat, manned by reckless adventurers in whom the appetite for gold was whetted by the memory of countless wrongs.

From unexpected successes by sea the Buccaneers made bold to attack the rich towns on the Spanish Main, which they held for heavy ransoms, or sacked with all the attendant cruelty of their ancestral Berserkers. Panama, Granada, Gibraltar, every town or fort of note, fell before the resistless buccaneers, until the names of Morgan, Portugues, Dampier, and Lolonois became words of terror to the Spanish colonists. Yet it must be borne in mind that the buccaneers were not pirates. They warred against one enemy, the same which had for years oppressed them and their brethren, while the countries to which they owed allegiance were too weak or too indifferent to protect their distant sons. When the buccaneer degenerated into the mere pirate, none were more prompt than his late comrades to follow up and punish the Ishmaelite. Buccaneer Morgan, knighted and made governor of Jamaica, was the terror of the West India pirates, though the virtue of his motives may fairly be questioned.

To her buccaneers England owes the birth of her great navy, whose first fame was won in the rout of the Spanish

Armada. They were buccaneers who first sailed around the world; they founded the East India Company, and were Britain's sword and shield for the defence of her nascent colonies. Neglect and indifference rewarded their deeds, until they had grown strong enough to protect themselves. Spain had her paid servants in the very cabinets of England and France, a policy which she has not forgotten how to employ in other lands and later days.

Because of a growing respect for the law of nations, filibusterism, during the grave changes of the eighteenth century and the lull before the storm of the American revolutions, slumbered once again.

The American revolution meant the people defending its rights; the French revolution meant the people avenging its wrongs. Each was successful; both taught an undying lesson to humanity. Free America, with wise selfishness, aimed to assure and bequeath her liberty; Republican France, with loftier if less practical aims, sought to carry the gospel of freedom to all nations. She failed only when she yielded her dearly won liberty to the seduction of martial glory. Napoleon, the child of the people, became a parricide, and usurped the place of the fallen trinity—Liberty, Equality, and Fraternity.

Among the ardent friends of liberty who rallied around the flag of the Directory was Don Francisco Miranda, a native of Venezuela, of which province his grandfather had been governor. He was well educated, and owned a large private fortune. On account of his revolutionary sentiments he was forced to fly his native country and the military service of Spain, in which he had gained the rank of colonel. The bulk of his property was made forfeit. With what he could save from the wreck he fled to the United States in 1783. He afterwards visited several European countries. The French revolution found him in Russia, whence he at once set out to offer his sword to the Directory. He held a command under Dumourier in the Holland campaign of 1783, in which he won a brave name but no serviceable laurels. The campaign was a failure. Dumourier deserted the cause, and Miranda was arrested and tried for treason. Although undoubtedly innocent, his political intrigues had aroused against him powerful enemies who procured his banishment from France. He removed to England, a country whose ministry he interested in his life-long scheme for the revolution of his native land. New York was chosen as the point of departure. With bills of exchange on London he bought there the ship *Leander*, with a formidable armament. On the 2nd of February, 1805, the first filibustering expedition from the United States, consisting of about two hundred men, "some of them gentlemen and persons of good standing in society, though mostly of crooked fortunes," set sail for Venezuela on a crusade of liberty. When eleven days at sea they were brought to by H.B.M. ship *Cleopatre*, and nineteen of the adventurers were impressed, in the ungracious fashion of the British navy of the period. The *Leander* was detained, notwithstanding her American clearance, until General Miranda produced some private papers, at sight of which the British captain not only allowed her to proceed unmolested, but also gave her a "protection paper," forbidding all other English cruisers to detain or search her. Apart from the *Leander's* questionable mission, this remarkable permit to travel on the high seas throws a striking light upon the construction of international law at the beginning of the nineteenth century.

Miranda received material aid and comfort from Admiral Cochrane, commanding the British squadron on the West India station, but although his force was swelled by two small vessels, it was, from its first advent on the Spanish Main, a wretched failure. Differences among the invaders, aggravated by the wayward temper of the leader, together with a total apathy or active hostility on the part of the very Venezuelans whom the filibusters had come so far to deliver, brought all their fond hopes to nought. Such of the adventurers as were not captured by the Spaniards surrendered to an English frigate and were carried to the West Indies, whence they made the best of their way home.

Whilst lacking in the heroism and splendid audacity of kindred later crusades, Miranda's expedition was a painful prototype in its ill fortune for subsequent ventures. The inevitable defeat, with its ghastly epilogue of butchery or lingering captivity; the rescue of the wretched survivors by a pitying English or American vessel of war; the world's merciless verdict upon the failure: such has been the dismal tragedy as acted on different stages, from the days of Miranda to that "last appearance" in Santiago de Cuba.

Of the prisoners taken, ten were hanged; some fifty others were condemned to terms of imprisonment varying from eight to ten years. Among the latter was Major Jeremiah Powell, whose father visited Spain in a vain effort to procure his release. Returning, in despair, by way of London, he bethought him of a novel expedient. It was that of getting a letter of introduction to the Spanish monarch from the great Doctor Jenner. Armed with this he returned to Madrid and presented himself before the Court. The student of Spanish, and notably of Spanish-American history, will find few instances of generous or tender instinct in its bloody annals. Let it be written, as a bright line on the dark page of Spanish cruelty, that the appeal of humanity's benefactor was not made in vain. Major Powell was at once set free. The conquest of deadly pestilence was hardly a greater victory than that won over the heart of a merciless despot. Two half-pay officers of the British army, an ex-colonel of the United States service, a chevalier of the Austrian Empire, and several adventurous young men of good families in the United

States formed the circle from which Miranda chose his officers. Among the latter was a youth named Smith, grandson of President Adams. It was rumoured that he was among the prisoners taken at Caracas. The Spanish minister at Washington, the Marquis de Casa Yrujo, fancying that he saw a good chance of serving his government, and, at the same time, getting credit for an humane act, wrote to a friend of young Smith's father at New York, offering to interest himself on behalf of the prisoner, who otherwise would probably be condemned to die with his companions. Respect for the exalted character of Mr. Adams, he said, prompted this step, but he must nevertheless stipulate that Colonel Smith should impart to him full and complete information about the plans of Miranda, and a list of the Spanish subjects who were concerned in them. The father, yet ignorant of the fact that his son was not among the unfortunate prisoners, at once replied thanking the noble Marquis for the interest he had shown, but adding with a dignity and fortitude worthy a Roman: "Do me the favour, my friend, to inform the Marquis, that were I in my son's place I would not comply with his proposals to save my life; and I will not cast so great an indignity on that son, my family, and myself, as to shelter him under the shield of disgrace."

What sympathy, if any, was given to the undertaking by the administration of President Jefferson, it is hard to determine. Miranda always claimed to have been in the confidence of the American Government, as he undoubtedly was in that of Great Britain. It is certain that the people of the United States already looked with brotherly feelings upon the misgoverned peoples of Spanish America. Some of the leaders were tried before the United States courts upon their return, but, defended with burning eloquence by Thomas Addis Emmett, himself an exiled patriot, they were promptly acquitted.

Failing in his attempt to free Venezuela from without, Miranda returned to the country in December, 1810, and was favourably received by the semi-independent colonial government. Obtaining a seat in the republican congress he soon rose to the vice-presidency of that body, and organized a more formidable scheme of revolution. On the 5th of July, 1811, he signed the act of independence, and was appointed commander-in-chief of the forces. On his staff was Simon Bolivar, who was destined to play a more fortunate part than that of his chief in the destinies of South America. For a time Miranda was successful in the field, but reverses were soon followed by treachery, and when, in pursuance of the authority of Congress, he signed the treaty of Victoria, restoring Venezuela to Spanish rule, on July 25, 1812, he was denounced as a traitor by his fellow revolutionists, who, with little consistency, delivered him up to the enemy in whose interest they pretended he had acted. His after fate sufficiently establishes his innocence of treason to the revolutionary cause. The Spaniards sent him a prisoner to Cadiz, where he lingered for four years, dying in a dungeon, with a chain around his neck.

Of all his deeds fame has preserved but one enduring memento, his name, carved with those of the other great soldiers of the Directory, on the Arc de Triomphe in Paris.

CHAPTER II.

Aaron Burr—Mina's expedition and fate—The Alamo massacre—Travis, Bowie, and Crockett—The tragedy of Goliad—Houston and Santa Ana—Victory of San Jacinto—The Sante Fe and Mier expeditions.

WHILE Miranda's ambitious schemes were drawing the notice of the State department towards the seaboard, a more serious filibustering scheme was quietly hatching in another quarter, in the brain of one of the boldest and ablest adventurers known to American history. The imperial crown of the Montezumas was the prize for which an ex-vice-president of the United States risked fame, fortune, everything—and lost! The story of Aaron Burr is a matter of familiar history. His demoralized forces surrendered at Bayou Pierre, on the Mississippi, on January 17, 1807. Acquitted of the charge of treason, for which he was tried, but condemned by the unanimous opinion of his contemporaries, the sober judgment of history must pause before endorsing either verdict. The relations of Spain and the United States were in a hopelessly tangled state. Burr proposed to settle the disputed question of territorial rights by conquering the whole of Spanish North America, a scheme which his countrymen might not have severely rebuked or discouraged; but, unfortunately for his fame, Burr's ambition was personal and selfish. He would conquer, but not for his country's sake—a distinction, even then, sufficient to constitute a grave offence against the sovereign people.

What are now known as the Gulf States—Florida, Louisiana, and Texas—were then held under the colonial sway of Spain. The first and second became absorbed by purchase. Texas, as early as 1812, had begun to invite the notice of the restless filibustering element, but its more immediate importance lay in its convenience as a field of operations for the Mexican revolutionists. Hidalgo and his compatriots unfurled the standard of independence in September, 1810. Their first attempt to enlist outside aid was made six months later, when Bernardo Guttierez de Lara, a native Mexican, was sent as a commissioner to Washington to invoke recognition for the new Republic. His mission failing, Guttierez went to New Orleans and began recruiting adventurers, with such success that he was able in February, 1812, to lead a force of 450 men across the border into Texas.

His success was brilliant from the outset, and, in spite of some serious reverses, he succeeded in making himself master of Leon and Texas. Then came into play the unfailing ally of tyranny, corruption. Alvarez de Toledo, who had been appointed the successor of Guttierez as commissioner to Washington, made use of his position to negotiate with the Spanish minister for the betrayal of his compatriot. Returning to Texas, he incited mutiny among the troops of Guttierez, who deposed their commander and appointed Alvarez to succeed him. Personal ambition, rather than treason to his country, must have been the motive influencing the latter; for when the Royalist general, Arredondo, marched with an overwhelming force against the patriots at San Antonio de Bexar, Alvarez boldly gave him battle. Guttierez, with noble patriotism, fought in the ranks of his late command and did not survive the defeat. His heroic devotion was imitated on the same spot by Barrett Travis, twenty-two years afterwards. The defeat and death of Guttierez occurred on March 15, 1814.

Among the Americans who took service under Guttierez was Augustus W. Magee, of Massachusetts, who laid down his commission as a lieutenant in the United States army to join the filibusters. His fate was peculiar. After several successes he found himself, as he supposed, so beset by Governor Salcedo that he made terms for the surrender of himself and followers and their transportation to the United States. But the men boldly refused to abide by the timid measures of their leader, disavowed the contract, and actually assailed and routed the enemy, who was awaiting their surrender. Magee, overcome with shame at the success of those whom he had proved himself unworthy to lead, blew out his brains on the night of the victory.

Reuben Kemper, of Virginia, was another of the American adventurers of a widely different type. He is described as a man of gigantic proportions, with a voice and a heart to match his stalwart frame, and a profanity that attracted attention even on that Homeric field. As early as 1808 he made an attempt to capture Baton Rouge, and was kidnapped for his pains by the Spaniards, who would have cut short his career summarily but for the intervention of the United States commander at Pointe Coupée. On attaining his liberty, Kemper vowed to devote his life to the extirpation of Spanish rule in America. In 1812 he led an abortive attempt to capture Mobile, but was more successful on receiving from Guttierez the command of six hundred Americans with whom he gained several victories. Dissensions in the patriot ranks at last sent him home in disgust. He afterwards served with distinction under Jackson at New Orleans, and survived to witness the final extinction of Spanish rule on the American continent.

Another stormy petrel blown from Europe to Mexican seas was Don Francisco Javier Mina, who managed to compress a world of adventure into his brief life. Born at Idocin in Spain in 1789, he won fame while a mere youth by leading his hardy mountaineers in many a guerrilla fight against the French. In his twenty-first year he had gained the rank of colonel, and was on the high road to preferment when the blind policy of King Ferdinand drove him into rebellion, along with his uncle, the brave General Espoz y Mina. A well-planned scheme of revolution having failed, he fled the country and made his way to England, where he was warmly welcomed. His talents and courage inspired the government of that country, which for reasons of its own wished to foment insurrection in Spanish America, to equip him for a renewal of warfare against Ferdinand on his transatlantic territory. He arrived in the United States well supplied with money and letters to the friends of the Mexican revolutionists, and on April 15, 1817, he landed a force of 270 men from New Orleans at Soto la Marina. Defeating a superior force of Royalists in several engagements, he made a junction with the revolutionary army, and speedily drove the enemy out of the Northern provinces.

It was a far harder task, however, to overcome the jealousy and incompetence of Torres, then in chief command; and Mina, betrayed by his allies, fell into the hands of Viceroy Apodaca, who had him immediately executed, with twenty-five of his followers, on November 11, 1817. Mina was but twenty-eight years old when he ended his career, but he had given proofs of rare worth as a soldier and a patriot.

Among the Americans who shared his fortunes was Colonel Perry, of New Orleans. Despairing of success, as soon as he discovered the worthlessness of the native leaders, he abruptly withdrew from the army and undertook, with only fifty followers, to cut his way back to the United States by land. In this attempt they partially succeeded, but were soon overtaken and surrounded by an overwhelming force. Perry rejected all demands to surrender until, the last of his band having fallen by his side, he put a pistol to his head and blew out his brains.

When Mexico at last won her freedom, her most northerly state, Texas, held an anomalous position. A large proportion of its people was made up of Americans who had borne their share in the battle for liberty. By birth and associations they were more closely allied with their Northern than with their Southern neighbours. It did not take them long to learn that Mexico, in changing her government had not changed her nature. The intolerance of the new rulers differed little from that of the old, while civil government was far less stable under the Republic than it had been while swayed by the Spaniard.

Upon the declaration of Texan independence in September, 1835, General Cos marched a large army into the rebellious state, determined to drive the rash intruders out of the country. In the first engagement, at Gonzales, the Texans routed their foes, and General Cos was forced to take refuge behind the walls of the Alamo, in San Antonio de Bexar. But the Texan blood was now fairly up, and General Burlison, with only 216 men, laid siege to the fortress. The garrison numbered 1,700, but in spite of the fearful odds, the Texans stormed the place and sent General Cos under parole to his astonished brother-in-law, the redoubtable Santa Ana. Colonel James Bowie, who had just defeated another large Mexican force, at the Mission Conception, joined Colonel Travis at the Alamo. Let Bowie live in story as the inventor of the celebrated "Bowie knife," though he had other and nobler claims to fame. At the battle of Gonzales he broke his sword while engaged in a hand-to-hand encounter; but fought desperately with the broken stump, and thence, it is said (having killed his man), drew the idea of the terrible blade that bears his name. The story, as well as the invention, may be apocryphal, but there is no doubt that Bowie was one of the bravest and coolest men that ever lived, even in Texas. To the Alamo presently also came David Crockett, of Tennessee, hunter, soldier, Congressman, unique in history.

Colonel Barrett Travis had 144 men with him in the Alamo when Santa Ana and 4,000 Mexicans sat down before it, demanding an unconditional surrender on February 23, 1836. Cos, heedless of his parole, was with the besiegers. Travis answered with a cannon shot, and the enemy hoisted the red flag, signifying "no quarter." In no spirit of bravado, but with a sincerity which the event only too fully confirmed, the Texan commander issued the following proclamation :—

"*To the People of Texas and all Americans in the World.*

"COMMANDANCY OF THE ALAMO, BEXAR,
"*February* 24, 1836.

"FELLOW CITIZENS AND COMPATRIOTS,—I am besieged by a thousand or more of the Mexicans under Santa Ana. I have sustained a continual bombardment and cannonade for twenty-four hours and have not lost a man. The enemy have demanded a surrender at discretion; otherwise the garrison is to be put to the sword if the fort is taken. I have answered the summons with a cannon shot, and our flag still waves proudly from the walls. I shall never surrender or retreat. Then I call on you in the name of liberty, patriotism, and everything dear to the American character, to come to our aid with all despatch. The enemy are receiving reinforcements daily, and will no doubt increase to three or four thousand in four or five days. Though this call may be neglected, I am determined to sustain myself as long as possible, and die like a soldier who never forgets what is due to his own honour and that of his country. Victory or death!

"(Signed), W. BARRETT TRAVIS,
"Lieut.-Col. Com't."

Houston, to whom Travis addressed an urgent call for reinforcements, could do nothing. On the 3rd of March, with death staring the little garrison in the face, Travis sent a despatch to the Revolutionary committee, calmly stating his position, reiterating his determination never to surrender, and dwelling with almost impersonal interest on the beneficial effect to follow such determined resistance as he and his men were making. "I will do the best I can under the circumstances," he says, "and I feel confident that the determined valour and desperate courage heretofore evinced by my men will not fail them in the last struggle; and although they may be sacrificed to the vengeance of a Gothic enemy, the victory will cost the enemy so dear that it will be worse for him than a defeat."

Day by day the toils were drawn closer around the doomed walls. Day by day the little garrison was thinned by wounds and sickness. Vainly they gazed northward across the plain for the invoked aid. The hungry eye beheld only a long train of Mexican recruits hastening like vultures to the feast of blood. Once they were gladdened by the sight of a little band of countrymen spurring towards the walls. But they were no forerunners of a relieving army. Thirty-two gallant Texans threw themselves into the fort, cutting their way through the besiegers, simply and solely that they might fight with their comrades; that they might be found, living or dead, by the side of David Crockett and Barrett Travis. Each morning a dwindling garrison answered to the roll-call, and the thin ranks were stretched a little wider apart along the crumbling ramparts which it had needed thrice their numbers to defend. They husbanded their scanty stores. They never wasted a shot. During that long and terrible fortnight it is said that nearly ten victims fell to each American rifle. With a thousand of his men shot down, and trembling in baffled wrath, Santa Ana on the fourteenth day, ordered another general assault. His officers drove their men to the breach at the sword's point.

When the smoke of battle had rolled away there was silence in the Alamo. The dead and dying strewed the ground. Santa Ana entered the fort. On the rampart, dead at his post, lay the commander, Travis, shot through the head. Beside him was the body of a Mexican officer, pierced to the heart by the sword still clutched in the dead hero's hand. They found Bowie in his own room. He was sick in bed when they broke into it, but his trusty rifle was with him, and four Mexicans died before he was reached. A fifth fell across his dead body, pierced through and through by the terrible knife. At the door of the magazine they shot Evans, ere he could touch a match and wreak a Samson vengeance on the foe.

Santa Ana stepped into the court-yard. There were six prisoners. His orders were that none should be taken. Nevertheless, David Crockett and five others had stoutly resisted, until his clubbed rifle broken in his sinewy hands, the dauntless backwoodsman listened to the promise of quarter. Santa Ana paused a moment before his unmoved captives. It was but for a moment. The next his hand sought the hilt of his sword. Crockett, divining his purpose, sprang at the traitor, but he was too late; a dozen blades had flashed at the sign and the hapless prisoners fell dead, the last of all the garrison.

These men of the Alamo were volunteers, simple citizens, bound by no tie save that of fealty to cause and comrades. Unsung of poet, all but unnamed in history, the brave men of the Alamo went to their certain death, with a sublime fortitude, beside which the obedient immolation of Balaklava's Six Hundred is but the triumph of disciplined machines. A monument raised to their memory bears the magnificent inscription:—

"Thermopylæ had its messenger of defeat; the Alamo had none."

It needs more than judicial impartiality to question the right of the Texan revolution while telling the story of the Alamo. Right and wrong are barred from consideration in recalling the tragedy of Goliad. Colonel Fannin and 330 of his men, who had surrendered to Santa Ana as prisoners of war, under a solemn promise that they should be returned to the United States, were marched out of the fort, on the morning of Palm Sunday, March 27, 1836, and, without a moment's warning, fired upon and murdered in cold blood. The outlaws to whom this fearful penalty was dealt out, without even the mockery of a Spanish trial, were all young men or lads, "the oldest not over thirty years of age." The world, freely as its soil is saturated with human blood, stood aghast at this horrible slaughter. Texas trembled at the Mexican's vengeance. Houston alone, husbanding his scanty means, animating his raw levies, working, planning, providing for all, laid his trap with such shrewd forethought, that in less than two months he had sprung it upon Santa Ana and all his army, and on the banks of the San Jacinto, dictated terms of peace to his captive, the butcher of the Alamo and Goliad. The victory was unstained by a single act of revenge. Thenceforth the world knew that Texas was free. The men who could use success with such forbearance were men worthy of self-government.

Texas striving for independence was to the nations of the world an object of keener interest than Texas sending her heroic filibusters to nameless graves. Lord Palmerston, anticipating with literal exactness the policy of a later administration dealing with Central America, threatened to send a ship of war to Texas "to demand payment of certain claims against the republic." The United States, with a similar foreshadowing of its future policy, at once took measures to insure the independence of Texas against all European meddlers. As usual, the people were in advance of their government, and Texas became a state of the American union, Mexico's attempt to hold it costing her the fairest part of her domain.

Before this happy end was reached, more than one bloody tragedy had been added to the gloomy history of Texas. In June, 1841, General McLeod led from Austin a party of 320 men, bound for Santa Fe, New Mexico, upon the ostensibly peaceful mission of opening up trade with that place. His real aim was to foment insurrection against the Mexican Government and annex the territory to Texas. After a long and painful journey through woods and desert, being attacked by Indians, and lost on the then mysterious waste of the "Llanos Estacados," the expedition reached the frontier in scattered parties which were promptly captured by Governor Armijo. It was not, however, until after they had given up their arms, under the false representations of a traitorous comrade and the promise of friendly treatment from Armijo, that they found out how grievous had been their error in trusting to the word of the Mexican. The whole party, with the exception of three or four who had been put to death in pure wantonness, were sent under a strong guard to the city of Mexico, making the long and painful journey on foot, exposed to the grossest outrages from their brutal guard. Many died on the way, and the survivors were thrown into prison, where they lingered for months, until the miserable remnant were at last set free at the motion of the British and American ministers.

Liberty was granted at the same time to the survivors of the Mier Expedition—an ill-starred band who, in December, 1842, had crossed the Rio Grande in pursuit of Mexican raiders. Colonel William Fisher headed the party, numbering about five hundred, their general, Somerville, having declined to lead them over the border. At the town of Mier they met and repulsed over two thousand Mexicans under General Ampudia, but their leader was wounded in the fight, and, against the protests of his chief officers, agreed to a conditional surrender. The terms, of course, were broken by the victor, and the unfortunate prisoners were hurried into the interior and buried in dungeons with the lowest convicts. Captain Ewin Cameron, one of the boldest in the band, foreseeing the fate before them, organized an attack on the guard before reaching their prison. They overpowered their armed escort, and made their way to the mountains, whence a few managed to reach Texas, but the greater part were recaptured, including their courageous leader. Santa Ana ordered them to be decimated. Cameron was lucky enough to draw a white bean in the fatal lottery, but it did not avail him. He was shot the next day. Few men would be found willing to increase the risks against them in such a terrible game of hazard; but there was one, a youth named George Bibb Crittenden, who, drawing a white bean, gave it to a comrade, with the self-sacrificing words, "You have a wife and children; I haven't, and I can afford to risk another chance." He did so, and fortunately again drew a safe lot. Crittenden survived to participate gallantly in the Mexican War, and attained the rank of brigadier-general on the Southern side in the Civil War. He was a son of the Kentucky statesman, John J. Crittenden.

The prisoners were scattered amongst various strongholds, where many sank under disease, starvation, and cruelty. The survivors when freed were turned adrift, penniless, to make the best of their way home to the United States. General Thomas J. Green was one of those who escaped by tunnelling the walls of the castle of Perote; the story of which exploit, with his subsequent adventures, he has told in a book little known but of vast interest.

It needs a Scott to tell to the world the story of our border romance, though no fiction ever surpassed the thrilling facts which were then of almost daily occurrence.

Fame is a curious gift of the gods. Colonel Crockett, the daring soldier, is all but forgotten, while the whimsical, semi-fabulous "Davy" Crockett, hero of a hundred wild stories, seems likely to live for ever. Few remember how heroically he "went ahead," to the last extremity, after first making sure of what was "right" and fit in a patriot. Knightly scutcheon never bore a nobler device than that of the simple backwoodsman, nor lived there ever a *preux chevalier* who set a higher value upon his plighted word.

There were brave men, too, before Agamemnon. Mexier and Perry and Nolan, names well known on the border, lived and fought, and died, alas, in vain, before the adopted son of an Indian, sturdy Sam Houston, crowned the long struggle with victory. Filibusters all, if you will, but every one a man, in an age when manliness is none too highly prized, and a country which is belied as the chosen home of dollars worshippers merely,

CHAPTER III.

The Lopez Expedition—Landing at Cardenas—Pickett's Fight—An Exciting Chase--Last Expedition—Execution of Lopez and Crittenden.

FILIBUSTERISM under that name, however, was unknown to the people of the United States, until the famous descents of Lopez upon Cuba in 1850 and 1851. Narciso Lopez was a countryman of Miranda, and, like him, an officer in the Spanish service. Born at Caracas in 1799, he entered the royal army at an early age, attained the rank of colonel in his twenty-first year, and distinguished himself so well in the first Carlist war that he was promoted to the rank of major-general, and made Governor of Valencia. He went to Cuba in 1843 with Governor-General Valdes, who took him into high favour, and loaded him with honours. But O'Donnell, the successor of Valdes, did not continue the vice-regal favours, and Lopez consequently retired to private life, and ere long was discovered to be conspiring against the Government. He fled to the United States, where he found hundreds of adventurous spirits ready and eager for any undertaking that bade fair to be spiced with danger.

His first attempt at invasion, in August, 1849, was checked at the outset by President Taylor, whose marshals captured the whole expedition as it was on the point of departure from New York. Nothing daunted by this mishap, Lopez travelled throughout the Southern and South-Western States, secretly enlisting men and making provision for their transportation to Cuba. At New Orlean he chartered a steamer and two barks and assembled his forces. From the valleys of the Ohio and Mississippi and the Gulf States they came, a hardy band of adventurers, three-fourths of whom had served in the Mexican War, the officers being men of known courage and ability. Colonel Theodore O'Hara commanded the first detachment, numbering 250, which sailed on the bark *Georgiana*, on the 25th of April, 1850, under orders to rendezvous at the island of Mujeres. Their colonel had won an honourable fame in the Mexican War and was not without greater distinction in the world of letters. He wrote the "Bivouac of the Dead," a lyric which will live at least as long as the memory of those whom it celebrated. Three weeks after their departure they were joined at the island of Contoy (for the *Georgiana* had not been able to make the rendezvous) by the steamer *Creole*, carrying Lopez and his fortunes and 450 followers. The whole command was then transferred to the *Creole* and sailed away for the shores of Cuba.

The little army was reviewed by their general, who made them a stirring harangue in Spanish (for he did not speak the tongue of his motley followers) promising them the co-operation of the Cubans the moment they should unfurl the Lone Star flag on the island, and the undying gratitude of a liberated people. More substantial rewards were also held out, in a bounty of four thousand dollars to every private soldier at the end of the first year's service, or sooner if the revolution should succeed within that time. In the meanwhile they were to receive the same pay, according to rank, as that of the army of the United States. It is not extravagant to say that hardly a man in the expedition gave a second thought to the money advantages contingent on success. The reckless dare-devils were content to enjoy a vagabond campaign seasoned with danger and hard fighting, while those of higher aims thirsted for the fame of Liberators. Among the men of education and lofty sentiments were Colonels O'Hara and John T. Pickett; the latter a bold and fertile organizer, who enjoyed the distinction of having a reward of 25,000 dollars offered for his head by the Captain-General of Cuba. The Adjutant-General, Gonzales, was a native Cuban, who had forsaken a promising career in the university to join the revolutionists. Many there were, too, of whom we shall hear again in Central America—Wheat, Titus, Kewen, Allen, and others.

Matanzas had been chosen as the first point of attack, but as they rightly judged that the Spaniards had been advised of their movements, it was decided to land at Cardenas, whither the *Creole's* bow was pointed, every eye turning to catch the first sight of the promised land. They entered the harbour about midnight, unchallenged by the over-confident enemy. So little were they expected by the good people of Cardenas, that not a boatman nor wharf watchman could be seen to take a line ashore, and the steamer lay a few yards from the pier until the first officer, Fayssoux, leaped overboard with a rope between his teeth and made her fast.

Pickett, upon landing, marched rapidly with fifty men of the Kentucky battalion through the city and seized the station of the railroad which connected Cardenas and Matanzas. The main body, consisting of four companies, formed upon the pier and marched towards the plaza, intending to surprise the garrison. Before reaching the plaza they were challenged and fired upon by a patrol. Instantly the alarm was sounded in the garrison, and volleys of musketry began to play about the ears of the invaders. Colonel O'Hara was wounded at the first discharge, but his men fought with cool bravery under the leadership of Lopez, who was constantly in the foremost rank, seeking to make himself known to the defenders. He was sure that upon recognizing him they would at once fraternize with the invaders. But the garrison made a stubborn resistance until their quarters were carried by assault, when they threw down their arms and shouted "Vivas!" for Lopez and Liberty. The governor, whose house was opposite the barracks, held out until it was in flames, when he surrendered, and the filibusters, after a three hours' battle, had won Cardenas.

Now was the time for the legions of revolutionists to fall in beside their liberators, and Lopez issued a strong appeal for volunteers. Not one native responded! Whether from apathy or cowardice, they showed no desire to risk their lives in the cause of liberty. The situation was becoming grave. Already the alarm had gone forth and the lancers of the enemy were beginning to appear in formidable numbers in the streets. Lopez saw that the capture of Cardenas was a barren victory. To carry out his intention of proceeding by rail to Matanzas in the face of the whole Spanish army, and without a single native adherent to welcome his appearance, would have been madness. Reluctantly he gave orders to embark, and recalled the detachment which had been guarding the railroad. The enemy seeing them retreat grew bolder, and made several determined efforts to prevent the embarkation, but the filibusters threw up a barricade of empty hogsheads and easily repelled the attack. After a final attempt to cut off the detachment from the railroad, in which Pickett drove them back with heavy loss, they offered no further opposition to the retreat. Cardenas had been won and lost within twelve hours. The *Creole* steamed out of the harbour at nine o'clock in the evening, but stuck fast on a sand-bank and lay there for five hours, until sufficiently lightened of her cargo to float again.

A council of war was held, and it was declared that no further attempts at a landing on the island were practicable, owing to the indecision of the native population. Lopez strove in vain to gainsay this determination, and even begged to be put ashore alone, or with the thirty

Spanish soldiers who had just joined his cause. His mad request being refused he resigned command, and the steamer was headed for Key West, coming to anchor at nightfall within forty miles of that port.

In the meantime, the authorities of Cuba had despatched a war steamer in search of the filibusters, and offered a reward of 50,000 dollars for the capture of Lopez. The *Pizarro* sped into Key West while the *Creole* was lying at anchor, and set out again in quest of her at daybreak. The people of the town were apprised of her mission and thronged the piers and hills to behold the issue. Soon they descried on the horizon the smoke of a steamer, which, as it drew near, was recognized as the *Creole*. Not far in her wake they also saw the huge *Pizarro* throwing out volumes of smoke and rapidly closing with her prey. As the pursued steamer approached the coast it was seen that her fuel was giving out, while the *Pizarro* was crowding on every pound of steam that her boilers could carry. A few minutes more and the guns of the Spaniard would have opened upon the devoted vessel, but at the critical moment the funnel of the *Creole* began to belch forth clouds of smoke and her wheels to revolve, as the wheels of a steamboat can when her Mississippi river captain begins to levy contributions on his cargo. The filibusters rolled barrels of bacon into the furnace-room, tore up the dry wood-work of the boat, and pulled the red shirts off their backs to feed the flames. Better a magnificent explosion and sudden death than capture and torture by the merciless Spaniard. The device succeeded. The *Creole* gallantly rounded the point, a few hundred yards ahead of her pursuer, and dropped anchor under the guns of Key West as the *Pizarro*, without even saluting the fort, came ploughing behind her and halted a few rods away, with port-holes open and broadsides grinning like the fangs of a bloodhound baulked of his prey. Her gunners stood by their pieces, match in hand, and ready at a word to blow the *Creole* to destruction. For a time it looked as though the word would be spoken; but, if such was the Spaniard's desire, he prudently forbore its gratification when he saw the United States officers take possession of the steamer, and a grim-looking array of filibusters swarm in the embrasures of the fort and sight the huge guns which were trained upon his deck.

Lopez and his followers made the best of their way from Key West; they to their homes and he to the custody of a United States marshal. The expedition had suffered a loss of fourteen killed and thirty wounded. Among the killed was their chaplain! The list of the enemy's loss was not officially published, but is supposed to have reached a hundred killed and as many wounded. Lopez was tried for his violation of the neutrality laws, but escaped conviction, and immediately set about preparing another expedition. His faith in the devotion of his American friends was better founded than the reliance which he placed on the promises of his native adherents.

In the following year, Aug. 12, 1851, he landed a force of 450 men at Bahia Honda, with the greater part of which he marched into the country, where he had been led to expect a general uprising the moment he should appear among the Creoles. Colonel W. S. Crittenden, a brave young soldier of the Mexican War, remained with the smaller body, awaiting reinforcements. But Lopez, as usual, had misjudged the spirit of his countrymen, who were not yet ripe for revolt. With his little band of 323 men he repulsed 1300 of the enemy, killing their general, Enna; but being forced to retreat into the interior, his forces dwindled away and the leader was at last captured and carried in chains to Havana. Fifty of his followers were shot at once. Lopez was strangled by the garrote on Sept. 1st. It pleased his enemies to add this pang of an ignominious death. The old hero met it without flinching. Spain had honoured him for facing death upon many a bloody field, and she could not dishonour him while dying for the adopted country which was not worthy of his love.

Meanwhile Crittenden and his detachment had been captured at sea and conveyed to Havana, where they were allowed the merest mockery of a trial. But one verdict was possible, where sentence had been already passed. Only a few hours elapsed between the trial and execution. The crowds of Havanese who flocked to the show, as to a national bull-baiting, saw them die with stoical fortitude. They saw Crittenden, with but twenty-eight years of life behind him, stand and face death with unflinching mien. They bade him kneel in the customary attitude, with his back to the firing party. "An American kneels only to his God," he answered, and so met his death.

CHAPTER IV.

The Count Raoussett-Boulbon—A father "de la vieille roche"—Raoussett's contract to garrison Sonora—Proclamations and pronunciamientos—Battle of Hermosillo—Negotiations with Santa Ana—Expedition to Guaymas—Engagement and defeat—Last words of a noble adventurer—Death of the Count.

TO Mexico the gift of liberty was as the boon of eternal life to the wandering Jew. Freed from the exactions of a despotic master, absolved by the bounty of nature from the stern, ceaseless struggle for physical life, stirred no longer by the warlike spirit of the conquerors, the Latin races in America seemed for a time to have fallen into a condition of hopeless lethargy. To those causes of decay must furthermore be added the amalgamation with inferior races. The Spaniard married with the Indian, the Indian with the Negro, the offspring of the hybrids intermarrying and each cross begetting a lower type, with all of the vices and few of the virtues of either parent.

To redeem this fair land, with its boundless mineral and agricultural wealth, from the hands of its slothful owners, was a dream which fired the ambition and, it may be added, the cupidity of many daring minds. With the decline and final overthrow of Spanish power the richest mines of Northern Mexico were abandoned for lack of strength to repel the never-subdued and ever-hostile Indian tribes. Mexico was weak, torn by strife, and disorganized. In her feeble hands the mines of Sonora and Arizona were literally "treasure hoarded in the ground."

There was in California, in 1852, a man of high birth and humble calling, a day labourer, with the proudest French ancestral blood in his veins—a soldier of Algiers, a count by birth and rank. Raousset-Boulbon, or, to give him his full name and title, Count Gaston Raoulx de Raousset-Boulbon, was a prodigal. He had squandered his substance in the riotous living of Paris and come to the land of gold to mend his fortunes. Unhappily for his peaceful aspirations, California, in 1852, offered a poor field to the man whose only gifts were education, the use of arms, nobility of soul, and a patrician title. Such endowments were neither rare nor deemed precious in that primitive community. The poet has sung, and the novelist painted, the wild contrasts of that marvellous period, but no flight of fancy could exaggerate the picture. San Francisco, the seaport, was a truly cosmopolitan city. There were two French newspapers published daily, so great were the attractions of El Dorado to the rarely migrating Gaul. Among the hundreds of his countrymen who, like himself, had failed to find a fortune in the golden state, Gaston judged that he might easily enroll a band of adventurers for any bold undertaking. He was not mistaken when the occasion offered itself. In the indescribable human medley of California the Count Raousset-Boulbon cannot be said to have been out of place. Nobody, nothing was that. He was discontented with a career hitherto fruitful only in misfortune.

He was the son of an *émigré* of the old stamp, a self-willed, fantastic old man, who carried the sternest rules of obedience into the most trifling domestic affairs, and might have adopted the motto, "L'état, c'est moi." His scheme of government may be inferred from a brief anecdote recounted by the biographer of Gaston. The latter, returning from Paris, appeared at home with two things distasteful to his sire—a beard and a cigar. "Madam," said the father to his wife, the stepmother of Gaston, "it would give me pain to argue with my son, and I could not brook opposition. The cigar I can overlook; but pray tell him that it pleases me not to see one of his age wear a beard like a 'moujik,' and that I shall be obliged to request its sacrifice." Gaston grudgingly obeyed the royal edict, for which he was formally thanked. Some days after the sire spoke again, "Madam, I authorize you to say to my son that he may let his beard grow again. Upon second thoughts I do not find it unbecoming." Compliance followed as before; but the tardy efforts of nature did not satisfy the old count, who gravely decided that "a beard does not become Gaston. Madam, I beg you to tell him once more that he must shave." Gaston, instead of obeying, packed his portmanteau and fled to Paris, and was forthwith disowned by his irate parent.

His life in Paris was that of a Bohemian, until the death of his father, in 1845, enabled him to carry out a dear ambition, that of founding a colony in Algiers; but the revolution of 1848 recalled him to France and to a political career. He conducted a newspaper, *La Liberté*, and was twice elected to the Assembly. Beaten in a third candidacy he forsook politics in disgust, and turned his eyes towards California. Paris in 1850 counted as many as twenty Californian societies for organized emigration. Gaston, restless, weary, and yet fired with the longing for some great deed, was almost penniless when, in his thirty-second year, he took a third-class passage for California, along with a dozen compatriots of various ranks.

Reaching the wondrous city, which his biographer aptly calls "the modern Babel, with the confusion of tongues," Gaston, with a manliness little to be expected in one of his training, betook himself to the stern duty of earning a livelihood by hard labour. He tried fishing, which barely earned him bread. As a lighterman he did better, until the building of a wharf ruined his business. A speculative enterprise for importing cattle from Lower California proved "more picturesque than profitable." At this juncture when, in his own words, "a gendarme would have charged on me at full gallop," so wretched was his appearance, his friend, M. Dillon, the French Consul at San Francisco, procured him letters of introduction to Señor Arista, President of Mexico, and Gaston repaired to the capital of that country, full of enthusiasm. The banking-house of Jecker, Torre and Co. acting as agents of the Government, signed a contract with Gaston, whereby the latter pledged himself to land at Guaymas, in Lower California, a company of five hundred French immigrants, armed and equipped for military duty, ostensibly and immediately for the protection of the Restauradora Mining Company against the incursions of the Arizona Indians, but really intended to serve as the nucleus of an extensive French colony, to be used as a barrier against the supposed encroachments of their American neighbours. Already the expansion of the United States in the direction of Mexico and the Pacific coast had aroused the jealousy of Europe. There is no doubt that Gaston's scheme for the protection of Mexico, befriended as it was by the representative of France in California and the French minister in Mexico, M. Levasseur, was not without substantial aid from the home government. The banker Jecker played a leading part, years afterwards, in the ill-starred attempt of Napoleon III. to found an empire in Mexico.

As a present reward for his services in protecting the Arizona mines, Gaston was to have a share in all their profits. He was yet to learn, as the royal Maximilian did later, that a bargain needs more than two parties to ensure its fulfilment, in Mexico. Arista was President of Mexico, but Governor Blanco ruled in Arizona. Arizona is a state of boundless mineral wealth, and little else. "Ruins of houses, ruins of churches, ruins of towns, and, above all, ruins of crouching men and of weeping women," is Gaston's graphic summary of Sonora and Arizona as he found them in 1852. Two hundred and sixty gallant Frenchmen landed at Guaymas on the 1st of June, and were warmly hailed as deliverers by the fickle populace. Governor Blanco, however, showed himself strangely lukewarm towards his new allies, whom he peremptorily forbade to leave Guaymas. The reason of his opposition was simple. He was interested in a rival company to the Restauradora. Vexatious delays followed. The recruits lost heart and hope. Gaston, chafing at the delay, had gone forward to Hermosillo, whither he brought his followers, after vainly awaiting the governor's leave to set out for Arizona. Blanco thereupon decided to offer these alternatives: "The Frenchmen shall renounce their nationality, or I shall compel them to leave the country." Gaston protested vainly in a letter to the French minister, and kept on his march to Arispe. He wrote also to Governor Blanco, who temporized and offered new conditions, denationalization of the company, their reduction to a maximum force of fifty, or a guaranty that they should not violate an ancient Mexican law forbidding foreigners to own real estate, mines, or other such property. These propositions were laid before the company by Gaston, who, at the same time, offered the means of departure to any who wished to avail themselves of them. Not a man was found willing to accept the opportunity. Gaston then, in a firm but temperate note, declined to accede to Blanco's terms, claiming for himself and his followers the fulfilment of their contract with the government of Mexico. Blanco threatened to treat the strangers as pirates and outlaws. To some of them he made secret offers of rich rewards if they would betray their comrades.

In these straits, harassed also by the savage Apaches, Gaston took up the line of march back to Hermosillo. On the 30th of September they encamped at the pueblo of La Madelaine. Here, as elsewhere in Mexico, the national gallantry of the adventurers, "half-heroes, half-bandits," as they were, won them immense favour with the fair Sonoriennes, though it is doubtful if the latter's graver brethren took so kind a view of "*fenêtres escaladeés, des maris infortunés, des duels, des processions, des bals, des representations theatrales,*" and the other exploits faithfully chronicled by the light-hearted chief.

A sterner welcome met them in another summons from Blanco: "Surrender your arms, or prepare to be treated as outlaws." Gaston, feeling that either choice promised little of mercy, proceeded to force the issue at once by hastening his march upon Hermosillo. By striking there a decisive blow he expected to rally around his standard the always numerous body of disaffected citizens, and so prepare the way for the independence of Sonora. Despatching an emissary to California for recruits, he set out, on the 6th of October, by the southerly road for Hermosillo. Fifty leagues from that city Blanco lay at Arispe, uncertain of his enemy's plans. Gaston's force numbered two hundred and fifty-three men, including forty-two horsemen and twenty-six marine veterans detailed to serve the four small cannon of the little army. Among them were many old soldiers of Africa and barricade veterans of Paris. Four or five months of sojourn in the Arizona deserts had not improved their looks. But with a good-natured patience truly French they made light of their troubles, jested at their sorry attire, and when their boots gave out made sandals of hides, or trudged along barefoot. In such guise and manner they marched to Hermosillo, but a few hours too late, for Blanco had distanced them by forced journeys, and thrown a body of twelve hundred men into the town. Gaston, without waiting to rest his weary followers, gave orders to attack. In less than an hour he was master of the place, and General Blanco was flying with the remnant of his command to Ures. Yet the latter could better spare his two hundred killed and wounded than the little band of adventurers could afford their loss of forty-two. To the filibuster there are no reserves.

But a greater calamity awaited the expedition. Gaston

was stricken down with sickness in the hour of victory, and, feeling the insecurity of his position, gave reluctant orders to march to Guaymas. His malady, dysentery, grew worse as they advanced. Within three leagues of Guaymas they halted at the rancho Jesus Maria. Envoys from Blanco met them there and treated for a parley between the two commanders, of which nothing came but a short-lived truce. That evening Gaston was delirious, nor were suspicions of poison wanting. The French camp became panic-stricken, so that M. Calvo, Vice-Consul of France at Guaymas, and himself a partner in Blanco's rival mining company, easily persuaded the subordinates to sign a treaty resigning the contract and agreeing to leave the country. Gaston awoke from a three-weeks' stupor to find himself without an army. He was permitted to leave the country, and returned to San Francisco with his ambition only whetted by his late trials.

There was to be no mistaking the nature of his future operations. The next expedition should be made up solely of Frenchmen and soldiers, its avowed end the independence of Sonora. "These men shall be fully warned that they go to Sonora to fight; that their fortunes rest on the points of their bayonets; that if they be conquered they shall infallibly perish as pirates; that it is for them a matter of victory or death."

His friend, President Arista, had resigned his office, in the face of civil war, on the 6th of January, 1853. Mexico was in worse than its normal state of anarchy. A dictatorship was proclaimed, and Santa Ana recalled to govern the wretched country. One of his first acts was to send for De Boulbon, who, upon promise of a safe conduct, visited the capital.

The interview was dramatic between the old, crafty, and cold-blooded butcher of the Alamo, and the young, romantic, hot-headed conqueror of Hermosillo. The latter was in the prime of manhood, of medium size, well-proportioned and graceful, erect, broad-browed, with open, frank eyes, and fair hair and beard. Santa Ana, versed in the thousand wiles of Mexican diplomacy, and rightly appreciating the skilled courage of his guest, would have enlisted his talents in the dictator's personal service. Gaston steadily besought a confirmation of the original contract. Four months were spent with all the tardiness of Spanish negotiation in realizing that object. At last a treaty was prepared, binding the Count to garrison Arizona with five hundred French soldiers, who were to receive a total compensation of 90,000 francs, the Government advancing 250,000 francs for outfit and other expenses. The treaty was solemnly signed, attested, and annulled within a fortnight! Gaston was furious. The dictator blandly repeated his offer of a regiment and personal service at the capital, an offer which the Count spurned as an insult. "You offer me," he said, "a favour that is personal, when I ask for justice to myself and my brave men. Should I accept, what would be your opinion of me? what the opinion of those whom I should command? General, I have the honour to be a Frenchman. When I pledge my word I keep it." So the two adventurers parted in the halls of Montezuma.

Gaston, burning with indignation, easily fell into sympathy with some of the ever-ready malcontents plotting against the new government. The plot was found out, but Gaston received warning in time to put fifty miles of hard riding between him and the fatal anger of Santa Ana.

He returned to San Francisco, his old sense of wrong aggravated by this new grievance. With singular inconsistency we find him writing to a correspondent in France, in bitter complaint of the apathy shown towards his scheme by the "intelligent and rich" Americans, at the same time that he warns his compatriots against the designs of the United States on the territory of Mexico and the world at large. His gloomy forebodings must awaken a smile, in view of the actual results, yet they speak a sen iment which was powerful enough, ten years later, to work out the imperial tragedy of Maximilian.

"Europeans," he says, "are disturbed by the growth of the United States, and rightly so. Unless she be dismembered, unless a powerful rival be built up beside her, America will become, through her commerce, her trade, her population, her geographical position upon two oceans, the inevitable mistress of the world. In ten years Europe dare not fire a shot without her permission. As I write, fifty Americans prepare to sail for Lower California, and go perhaps to victory. *Voila les Etats-Unis!*"

On the 2nd of April, 1854, three hundred French military colonists sailed from San Francisco, upon a formal invitation from the Mexican consul, to perform the duty formerly allotted to De Boulbon; the latter had been declared an outlaw by the Government. Nevertheless he resolved to hazard a descent upon Arizona, counting on the fidelity of those colonists and the moral support of the French Government, still uneasy over the ambitious designs of the United States. On the 24th of May he sailed from San Francisco on the little schooner *Belle*. His departure was hurried, as the United States authorities, warned of his purpose, had taken steps for his arrest and detention. In his haste he was forced to leave behind a small battery which he had bought for the expedition. The captain of the *Belle*, an American, hesitated to put to sea, but Gaston (so says his biographer) promptly put him in irons and took command of the vessel himself. His avowed object was the carrying out of the original contract of 1852, namely, the protection of the mines of Arizona; but Arizona had meanwhile become American territory, under the Gadsden treaty of 1853. Hence the present attempt of Gaston was filibustering, pure and simple, if not something worse.

The voyage was long and tedious, lasting thirty-five days. On the 27th of June they came in sight of Guaymas. Landing at Cape San José, he sent two of his men to the city to prepare the three hundred Frenchmen there for his coming, and to concert a plan of action. The envoys were recognized and thrown into prison by General Yanes, who had succeeded Blanco in the governorship of Sonora. An amicable but fruitless parley followed between the commandant and Gaston. They arranged a sort of armed truce, which lasted until the 8th of July; but it needed only a small spark to explode magazines of such fiery material as formed the two rival garrisons of Guaymas. The French company, overweening, vain, and quick-tempered, met and jostled the dark-browed peons, jealous, revengeful, and proud. Both were armed, both quarrelsome as gamecocks. The French put faith in their national valour, the Mexicans in their national odds of eight to one. At the first outbreak, some petty street brawl, the native soldiers sounded the general alarm. The French rushed to their quarters, whence they sallied, fully armed, and met the irregular attack of the enemy with a resistance as unmethodical as intrepid. For three hours the battle raged on the rocky streets of Guaymas. Gaston, always a gentleman by instinct, refused the proffered leadership, as that honour belonged to Desmarais, the commissioned chief of the three hundred. He commanded a company, however, and fought with splendid courage, until, twice wounded, his men in retreat and everything lost, he broke his sword over his knee, and led the remnant of his force to the French Consulate, where they formally surrendered to their country's representative. An hour later they gave up their arms, upon the pledge of M. Calvo, backed by the promise of General Yanes, that their lives should be spared. Gaston was thrown into prison. Ten days later he was taken before a court-martial, tried, and condemned to death as a traitor and rebel. "Mark that they did not name me once as a filibuster," he wrote home.

The American consul, Major Roman, pleaded earnestly, but vainly, for mercy. M. Calvo would not interfere,

Gaston in the hour of trial bore himself with manly fortitude, begging only, and not in vain, to be spared the indignity of dying with bound hands and bandaged eyes. The faith of his childhood returned to him, and his lifelong unrest shaped itself into perfect peace and resignation. The "old nobility," too, spoke out in his farewell letter to his brother, a curious blending of worldly pride, Christian humility, and philosophic fatalism. "It is my loyalty to my word that has dug my grave. . . . A mysterious chain, beginning at the cradle, leads to the tomb, and life is but a link thereof. . . . M. Calvo will bear witness that I died as became a gentleman. . . . To-morrow morning I shall have burned my last cap and fired my last cartridge. . . . Tell your children that Uncle Gaston died with a priest at his side, and that yet Uncle Gaston was a brave man. . . . If any wonder that I submit to this death, you may say that I look upon a suicide as a deserter. . . . I go to death a gentleman, and I die a Christian." The philosophy of this dying chevalier throws a little light upon his strange character. He died with touching and simple bravery, on August 12, 1854, at the age of thirty-six. Eleven years afterwards another and more imposing filibuster, lured to Mexico, partly by the intrigues of the same commercial house which had held the glittering bait before the eyes of poor Gaston, died with equal firmness at the hands of his executioners. Maximillan of Austria, Prim of Spain, and Napoleon of France, all played with fire like the ill-fated Count Gaston Raoulx de Raousset-Boulbon, and all, like him, suffered.

But another and stranger being had witnessed the bootless expedition to Guaymas in 1852, and drawn his own false moral from the example before him—with what results will be told hereafter.

CHAPTER V.

William Walker — Boyhood and education — Doctor, Lawyer, Journalist — Goes to California — Personal appearance and characteristics — Departure of the Sonora Expedition — A government proclaimed—Stern discipline—Retreat from Sonora —Bad news at San Vincente—The adventurers cross the boundary —Walker resumes the pen.

WHILE De Boulbon, resting upon his fruitless victory of Hermosillo, awaited at San Francisco a chance to profit by the turn of the cards in Mexico, he was offered, and declined, a subordinate command in an expedition planned and conducted by the greatest of modern filibusters.

William Walker was the son of a Scotch banker who emigrated to Tennessee in 1820, marrying there a Kentucky lady named Norvell. William, their eldest son, was born in the city of Nashville, on May 8, 1824. His parents intended to give him a profession, preferably that of the ministry, and though his taste led him otherwise the gravity of the kirk always pervaded his manner, and theological speculations interested him through life. His boyhood was marked by a reserved and studious disposition, yet romantic and venturesome withal. His name appears in the graduating class of 1838 of the University of Nashville. The curriculum of that institution covered a wide course of study, including, besides the branches of common education, mathematics, astronomy, chemistry, navigation, belles-lettres, geology, moral and mental philosophy, logic, political economy, international and constitutional law, oratory, natural theology, the classics, and many other studies. It was not the fault of his *alma mater* if he failed to prove as eminent in statesmanship as he was in arms. Duelling, the carrying of arms, and all wrangling were prohibited by the rules of the college. Cock-fighting was "especially forbidden." The cost of tuition and board was between two hundred and fifty and three hundred dollars a year. Altogether there is no reason to doubt that the University of Nashville, "authorised to grant all the degrees which are or may be granted by any college or university in Europe or America," was quite able to teach a young and ambitious student the elements of a sound education. The moral guidance of youth seems to have been well provided for, and a healthy desire to check extravagance in personal outlay is particularly noted in the regulations.

Having a liking for the medical profession, young Walker was sent to Edinburgh, where he attended a course of lectures. He afterwards visited and studied in France, Germany, and Italy, spending two years in travel, and gaining, together with his medical education, a fair knowledge of the languages and laws of those countries.

Of his professional experience we know little, save that he practised for a time in Philadelphia and Nashville, but, finding the profession unsuited to his health, he went to New Orleans and studied law. He was admitted at the bar in that city, but did not devote himself long to his new pursuit. He obtained a place on the *Crescent* newspaper, and gave himself up to the fascinating business of journalism with all the ardour of a novice. That a man should have tried three professions so different as those of medicine, law, and journalism, before reaching his twenty-fifth year is not remarkable in our country. It was equally in keeping with the character of the man of 1849, that he forsook this latest fancy to join the host of restless spirits bending their steps towards

California. Arriving there in 1850, he became an editor on the *San Francisco Herald* and took sides with the faction of which David C. Broderick was the leader. His literary style was not ill-adapted to the journalism of the day and place, and ere long Walker the advocate found occasion to defend Walker the editor upon a charge for contempt of court. The lawyer failed to save the writer from the penalty of a brief imprisonment and a fine of five hundred dollars. The same pugnacious qualities involved him in a more serious quarrel with a Philadelphian, named William Hix Graham, and appeal was taken to the court of honour. The combatants met on a sandy lot outside of the city limits. Shots were exchanged, apparently without damage to either man, and the seconds were about to give the signal for another fire, when one of them perceived a pool of blood at Walker's feet. The doughty fighter had received a wound in the foot, and, in order to gain another shot, had tried to hide it by throwing sand over the spot with his other foot. The seconds, however, decided that honour was satisfied by the flow of blood, and the duel went no further. After this Walker retired from journalism, and practised law for a time in Marysville, with success enough to satisfy the ambition of anybody who aimed at law-expounding rather than law-making.

Walker was now (in 1852) only twenty-eight years of age. Nature had not dealt lavishly with this man, whose ambition grasped at no less a prize than the conquest of an empire. His figure was slight, though shapely; he stood about five and a half feet high, and never weighed over one hundred and thirty pounds. His closely-cut, sandy hair was thin and almost whitish; his face was freckled and beardless, giving him a boyish appearance. The lower half of his visage was plain, almost commonplace, but his large, rounded forehead and keen gray eyes were strikingly fine. When his usually cold nature gave way to emotions of anger or excitement the eyes dilated and kindled with a greenish light, like those of a bird of prey; the thin, short upper lip became compressed, and the slow, quiet voice rose sharp and short. He never showed other sign of emotion; but, says one who knew him well, "those were sufficient to awe the most truculent desperado into a submission as abject as that of the maniac before his keeper." Add to these a rare frugality of speech, a morality ascetically pure, and a temperance equally patent in speech and action, and we know as much of the outward man as did the thousands of men who feared and loved him and died for his sake.

The Ishmaelite nature urging him to travel again, his "destiny," as he called it, carried him to Sonora, at the moment when De Boulbon's first expedition was nearing its vain catastrophe. No longer a lawyer, a doctor, or an editor, he returned to California with dreams of martial glory, crude as yet, but, to a man of his unyielding courage, full of unlimited promise. People now spoke of "Colonel" Walker. The conferring or the assumption of military titles solely by the grace of popular courtesy, was a curious foible of the Southern gentleman of the old school. Whether this unwritten commission preceded his assumption of a serious military career, or was coeval with it, is uncertain and of little consequence. There was no examination of titles or antecedents among the pioneers of California. The claimant of a military title could best defend it by deeds of daring, and by such William Walker was to prove himself. De Boulbon's short-lived success prompted Walker and a few friends to turn their eyes towards the same field. An agent, named Frederic Emory, was sent to Sonora in 1852 to treat for a contract such as had been granted the French company. Upon the failure of the latter, Walker and a partner, Henry P. Watkins, renewed the negotiations in person. It does not appear that they succeeded or received any encouragement from the jealous natives. Nevertheless, Walker and a few of his friends set themselves to the task of conquering the Western States of Mexico, in the face of difficulties which might have daunted even more daring spirits. The American Government was actively hostile to all filibustering movements. Sonora certainly did not offer a welcome to her unsought liberators. The singular unwillingness (already noticed by De Boulbon) of American capitalists to furnish the sinews of illegal warfare, no doubt continued to mark that unromantic class. On the other hand, Walker had many warm personal friends, chiefly among the natives of the Southern states. He was actually a sincere, even fanatical, believer in slavery. To conquer new territory, and thus to "extend the area" of slavery, was a scheme certain to meet with sympathy throughout the South. The admission of new Northern territories already threatened to overcome the supremacy of the South in the national government. Sectional and party bias, personal interest, and political prejudice moved the citizens of the slave states to withstand this new and growing menace. Like feelings, intensified through years of political minority, stirred the North. So far as the South was concerned in the maintenance of slavery, her interests called for its extension; otherwise, the growing movement for its abolition, aided by the approaching change of political power, would soon compass its overthrow. So, at least, and not without foresight, reasoned the upholders of slavery in that dark and bitter era.

The impending conflict was well styled "irrepressible." Years of angry debate had made compromise impossible, but the wiser and better heads in either party shunned the wager of battle. Disunion was scarcely considered as a theory, among the mass of the people, ere it sprung into being, a fact. Doughty-tongued zealots alone talked of war, and they were those who kept on talking after men of cooler courage had begun to fight.

Walker, then, could confidently invoke the sympathy of the rich and influential slave-holders in a crusade for the extension of their favourite system. He could appeal to the daring and adventurous of every class by the dangerous fascination of his scheme, and to the Californian, especially, through his native hostility and contempt towards his Mexican neighbour. For the rest, he offered as inducements to immigrants in Sonora five hundred acres of land to each man, and four dollars daily pay for military services. Arms and ammunition were procured. Emigrants of strangely unpastoral bearing offered themselves at the rendezvous. A brig was chartered and the day of departure set. At this point the United States marshal seized the vessel. This was in July, 1853. Three months afterwards, the emigrants, learning caution from experience, took their steps so secretly that forty-five of them, including Walker and Emory, sailed in the bark *Caroline*, and arrived at Cape San Lucas, in Lower California, on October 28th. Here they made a brief stay before continuing their voyage to La Paz. They captured that town, together with the governor, Espanosa, on November 3rd. Three days later a vessel arrived with the Mexican colonel, Robollero, appointed to supersede Espanosa; him also they took prisoner. Walker, being now in possession of the government and the archives, called an election, which resulted in his being chosen president. His report does not state whether or not he had any rival for the honour. Ten others of the adventurers were chosen to fill the several offices, civil, military, and "naval." Thirty-four remained mere citizens, as there were not "offices enough to go around." "Our government," wrote the President, "has been formed upon a firm and sure basis." However absurd the proceedings seem to us, in the light of the sequel, to him they appeared the solemn inception of free institutions and a glorious future. A high-sounding proclamation was issued, including a declaration of independence. Two months afterwards Walker annexed, on paper, the neighbouring province of Sonora, and changed the name of the Republic to "Sonora," comprising the State of that name and Lower California. As yet he had not set foot upon the new half of his domain.

His friends in California were active in the meanwhile. Recruiting offices were opened in San Francisco, to which flocked the desperate, the adventurous, the reckless from every land. The Federal Government could not, at least, it did not, take active steps to check them. Between two and three hundred men were enlisted, and their passage engaged on the bark *Anita.* The name of the vessel and the date of her departure were kept secret from all but the leaders of the party.

On the appointed evening, December 7, 1853, they gathered at "head-quarters." Horses and waggons were in readiness, and in a brief time the ammunition and supplies were on the deck of the *Anita.* Before midnight the embarkation was made, and the ship swung into the stream. A tow-boat carried her out of the harbour in safety. Before casting loose the lines several of the *Anita's* sailors secretly stole on board the tow-boat, their desertion not being perceived until the bark was beyond hail and ploughing the waves of the Pacific. The adventurers have been described by a friendly writer as "a hard set." They observed their departure by a merry carouse, the while the good bark tossed on the ocean swell and her captain cursed his recreant crew and his boisterous freight. Then the wind arose. A sea swept the decks, carrying overboard a dozen barrels of pork and making a clean breach through her starboard bulwarks. The adventurers awoke next morning, sobered and sick. A few of them who had been sailors volunteered to aid in working the vessel. The relief came none too soon, as it was found that the ship had been dragging her anchor and several fathom of cable all night, the deserters having failed to make it fast. The filibusters grimly consoled themselves with the reflection that they had not been born to be drowned.

Arrived at San Vincente, the reinforcements went into camp, amusing themselves, while they awaited orders to march, by foraging on the scattered ranches. Horses were procured by forced levies, and paid for in the promissory notes of the "Republic." Here for the first time Walker displayed the traits of stern command which afterwards made his name a word of terror in the ears of men who feared nothing else, human or divine. Half a score of the boldest desperadoes in camp formed a plot to blow up the magazine at night and desert with what plunder they might be able to seize in the confusion of the moment. To carry out their plan involved the risk of killing many of their comrades, as the ammunition was kept in the middle of the camp. Notice of the plot reached Walker, who had two of the ringleaders tried by court-martial and summarily shot. Two others were publicly whipped and drummed out of camp. Walker then ordered a muster of the troops, and after making a stirring appeal to them, called upon all who were willing to abide by his fortunes to hold up their hands. All of the original forty-five, and a few of the *Anita's* passengers, responded; the others shouldered their rifles and prepared to march. Walker confronted the recreants, and quietly ordered them to stack their arms, a command which, after some hesitation, they obeyed. They were then suffered to leave the camp. Less than a hundred men now formed the army of the republic. He gave orders to march to Sonora by the mountain paths, around the head of the Gulf of California. They buried the arms and ammunition of the deserters in *cachés.* Two men deserted on the march and joined the Indians, who harried the little band at every step.

The river Colorado was crossed on rafts. Disease and desertion thinned the ranks. The wounded died for lack of proper treatment, as there was not a case of surgical instruments in the army. They extracted arrows-heads from their wounds with probes improvised from ramrods. Every morning's roll-call showed a dwindling force. Beef was the only food left. Two men quarrelled over a handful of parched corn, and one shot the other dead. They were in rags. The President of Sonora, wearing a boot on one foot, a shoe on the other, fared no better than his followers. Those followers soon numbered less than fifty. A council of war was held, and it was decided to return to San Vincente. The Mexicans hung upon their flanks and rear, cutting off every straggler. Recrossing the mountains, they narrowly escaped annihilation in a gorge which widened out at the middle to a plateau of half a mile across, with a narrow opening at either end. Half way across the plains the Indians appeared on flank and front and opened a galling fire. Walker here showed coolness and generalship. Leaving twelve men hidden in a clump of bushes under command of Lieutenant P. S. Veeder, a cool young soldier, afterwards distinguished in Nicaragua, he retreated with the rest of the command towards the entrance of the valley. That passage had already been closed by the enemy's forces, who met the retreating party with an ill-aimed volley of arrows and bullets. At the same time those guarding the other pass joined their friends on the flanks in charging the Americans. As they passed the thicket where Veeder and his men lay in ambush, they received a deadly volley at short range. Every bullet struck down its man. Walker at the same time turned and delivered an equally well-aimed fire, which put the enemy to full flight. The two detachments then passed unmolested through the further defile before the astonished natives could be rallied to the charge. No bribes of *aguardiente*, with which the Mexicans were wont to ply their Indian allies could thenceforth induce the natives to face the deadly American rifles. They hung upon the line of march like coyotes, prowling about the late scene of each encampment, and robbing each new-made grave of its tenant's blanket, the only shroud of the poor filibuster who fell in the waste places of Sonora.

At San Vincente, where Walker had left in March a party of eighteen men to guard the barracks, he found not one remaining. A dozen had deserted, and the rest, unsuspicious of danger, had been swooped upon by a band of mounted Mexicans, who lassoed and tortured them to death. So many successive reverses sealed the fate of the expedition. To wait for reinforcements, even could they have come, from California was hopeless. Walker had but thirty-five men remaining. They were destitute of everything but ammunition and weapons; of these they had more than enough. At various places they had buried boxes of carbines and pistols. Eight guns were spiked at San Vincente. A hundred kegs of powder were cached on the banks of the Rio Colorado. Years afterwards the peon herdsman or prowling Cucupa Indian stumbled, in the mountain by-paths, over the bleaching skeleton of some nameless one whose resting-place was marked by no cross or cairn, but the Colt's revolver rusting beside his bones bespoke his country and his occupation—the only relic of the would-be Conquistadores of the nineteenth century.

The stolid native who had sworn fealty to the mushroom republic, under pain of imprisonment for refusal, easily forgot his oath when the accursed "Gringo" had turned his back. The *rancherio*, whose sole mementos of vanished horses and cattle were the bonds of the Republic of Sonora, vainly proffered those securities at the cock-pit and the monté-table. The American of the North had come and gone like a pestilence, or like his ante-type of buccaneering days; nought remained save disappointed ambition with the one, and a bitter memory with the other.

The invasion was every way inexcusable. That his interference was unwelcome to the natives Walker soon found out; nor was he slow to learn that nothing less formidable than an army of occupation, backed by a strong power, could push his cherished dream of a new conquest of Mexico beyond the unsubstantial realms of fantasy.

With sinking heart, but bearing the calm front which never failed him, he led his starving, travel-worn band toward the California frontier. The natives made a feeble show of opposing their retreat. A host of ill-trained soldiery, formidable only in numbers, held the mountain heights; their Indian allies were drawn up on the plain to contest the passage. Colonel Melendrez, commanding the Mexican forces, sent four Indians with a flag of truce into the filibuster camp, bearing an offer of protection and free passage across the American border to all except the leader; Walker, with all the arms of the company, must be first given up. Such an offer would have been rejected, in the face of certain death, by men familiar as these were with the Punic faith of the Spaniard. Made as it was to men who had followed their chieftain through hunger and want, battle and defeat, up to this moment, when they could see their country's flag waving over the United States military camp across the border, it was treated with scornful laughter. Melendrez then begged the United States commander to interfere and compel the surrender, a request which, as it could not have been granted without a violation of Mexican territory, was properly refused. Three miles of road lay between the filibusters and the boundary line. Walker, resorting to strategy, left half a dozen men concealed behind some rocks to cover his retreat. The natives, with a wholesome dread of the American rifle, followed him at what seemed a safe distance and rode straight into the ambush. Half a dozen rifles emptied as many saddles, whereupon Melendrez and his Mexicans galloped off at full speed, leaving their Indian allies to follow as best they might. The filibusters lost one man, a victim to his own indiscretion in having borrowed a leaf from the enemy's tactics and fortified his courage with too much *aguardiente*.

So ended the last battle of the Republic of Sonora—if it be not a travesty to call by the name of battle a fruitless fight between a score of men on one side and a hundred ignorant savages on the other. Four and thirty tattered, hungry, gaunt pedestrians, whimsically representing in their persons the president, cabinet, army and navy of Sonora, marched across the line and surrendered as prisoners of war to Major Mckinstry, U.S.A., at San Diego, California. It was the 8th of May, 1854; and so Walker kept his thirtieth birthday.

A parole, pledging the prisoners to present themselves for trial to General Wool, at San Francisco, was signed by all, after which they were allowed to depart.

Of those starving, wounded, battle-scarred survivors of several months' accumulated miseries the names signed to the parole contain at least six of men who had love for their leader, or enough of unconquerable daring, to send them, twelve months later, in search of fresh dangers and glories under the same commander.

Walker came back from Sonora, defeated but not disheartened. He had proved himself a leader of men, even in so small an arena. Thenceforth, until his star of "destiny" was eclipsed in death, his name was worth a thousand men wherever hard fighting and desperate hopes might call him. It must be said in his favour that he sought popularity by none of the tricks of the demagogue. In camp or field he was ever the same cold, self-contained, fearless commander, inflexible in discipline, sparing of speech, prodigal of action. He won the devoted obedience of the wildest spirits by governing himself. His word of command was not "Go," but "Come"—the Napoleonic talisman. Only to the youngest of his followers would he ever unbend his solitary dignity. One of them, whose name, William Pfaff, appears on the San Diego parole, was a youth of fifteen. He was with difficulty restrained from following his leader to Nicaragua. He lived through four years of service in our Civil War, but no dangers or hardships could erase the memory of his experience in Sonora. "The rebellion was a picnic to it," said he, in the fine hyperbole of California.

The trial of the filibuster leader for breaking the neutrality laws of the United States ended in a prompt acquittal. Walker resumed the editorial chair, supporting Broderick in the *San Francisco Commercial*, the personal organ of that ill-fated politician. Let us leave the filibuster in his Elba, and visit the country which was destined to become the scene of his dazzling but brief career of glory, defeat, and death.

CHAPTER VI.

Nicaragua—"Mahomet's Paradise"—Buccaneering visitors—Ringrose and De Lussan—Nelson defeated by a girl—The apocryphal heroine of San Carlos.

NATURE in lavishing her favours on Nicaragua, left little for man to add. It is a tropical country with a temperate climate, one half of its territory having a mean elevation of 5,000 feet above the level of the sea. In that favoured land the primeval curse is stayed; where nature forestalls every necessity, no need for man to toil or want. Fruits grow in the reckless profusion of the tropics, and clothing is a superfluity wisely counted as such. Two hundred and fifty thousand children, young and old, occupy a domain as large as New England. They are poor in accumulated wealth as the poorest peasantry of Europe; they are rich, knowing no want unsatisfied, as a nation of millionaires. But Nicaragua is a country in which to study with doubt the doctrine of the survival of the fittest. The early discoverers called it "Mahomet's Paradise," an apt name for a land of sensuous happiness. The Nicaraguan sees in his country no past, no present, no future. He lives from day to day, secure in the possession of food, raiment, and shelter. He cares not for to-morrow, for he knows that to-morrow will be as to-day, as to-day is the copy of yesterday; that next week, next year, next century, as they come and go, shall find him and his heirs, *frijole*-eating, *tiste*-drinking, hammock-lolling, ignorant, ill-governed, revolutionary, without energy for either large virtues or large vices. To him the earth gives everything, without toil or sweat. When his hour comes to die, his bones enrich a few feet of the good mother's bosom, and the account is balanced. The jaguar and the boa do as much for the world's avail. Man, relieved from the struggle for existence, the fight against nature in her cruel moods of hunger and cold, which were half of the battle in our northern life, might be expected to grow up into the full perfection of body and soul. But, like his own forest trees, the native of the tropics is strangled and warped by the rank growth of a host of parasites, idleness, ignorance, falsehood, and anarchy, the Nessus legacy of despotism.

The awful equity with which nature deals out good and ill alike is rarest seen in Nicaragua. Other tropical lands have fair flowers in whose fragrant cups nestle deadly insects, luscious fruits which poison the lip that tastes them, and soft airs that carry disease upon their wings. In other lands beneath the sun the crystal wave is cut by the shark's fin, the tiger and the cobra lurk in Paphian bowers; but though the wild beast and the noxious serpent are not unknown in Nicaragua, yet they are few and timid and fly the footstep of man. Insects alone abound and annoy—the highest and the lowest forms of life are the plagues of Nicaragua.

There man reaps without sowing, and the harvest never fails. He has but to stretch forth his hand and feast on dainties such as seldom grace the tables of kings; the citron, the lemon, the orange (with often 10,000 on a single tree), the banana, the mango, the papaya, the cocoa, the tamarind, the milk-tree, the butter-tree, and a spontaneous perennial growth of coffee, cacao, sugar, tobacco, and everything that grows or can be grown in any tropical or temperate clime. Half the year he may sling his hammock beneath the shady trees. In the rainy season a few stakes and a thatch of palm leaves afford him ample shelter. Medicinal trees and herbs abound everywhere, for the relief of the few ills to which his flesh is heir. Birds of gayest plumage, flowers of loveliest hue, greet his eyes on every side. In the noble forests, where the pine and the palm grow beside the ceiba, the mimosa, and the stately cactus, the splendours of the rainbow are rivalled in the plumage of parrots, macaws, humming-birds, toucans, and the beautiful winged creature that bears the imperial name of Montezuma. It is the latest and the fairest land of earth, and the heavenly radiance of youth is on its face. So young, that the fires of nature's workshop have not yet died out. The volcano, towering thousands of feet towards heaven, still smoulders or flames, and the earth is shaken ever and anon by the engines of the Titans. Ometepe the glorious lifts his cloud-capped head five thousand feet out of the placid bosom of Lake Nicaragua; Madera, his neighbour, is but eight hundred feet less lofty. Momotombo and Mombacho and El Viejo, and the twin peaks which watch the mouth of Fonseca Bay, are flaming swords guarding the Eden to which the serpent has come, as of old, with a human tongue.

Little note takes the Nicaraguan of the lavish favours of nature, whose grandest mystery but awakens a languid *Quien Sabe?* and whose most winning plea extorts only a more languid *Poco tiempe*—the eternal by and by of indolence. One per cent. of the whole population makes a show of studying the elements of knowledge. Why should they vex their souls in search of education, when all that life needs can be had for the asking? Not, surely, to heap up wealth. Nature takes care even of that, for money grows upon the trees of Nicaragua—that is to say, the fractional currency of the people is nuts, one cacao-nut being equal to a fortieth of a *medio* in value, and passing current as such in all the smaller affairs of trade. Nor is it worth the trouble of mastering letters where illiteracy is no bar to civil or military advancement, and where, especially if the "Serviles" be in power, an unlettered bandit ranks almost as high as a rascally advocate. In the days of President Chamorro the most notorious ruffians held high office, the revenues of the state were farmed out on the system which prevails to-day only in the more barbarous parts of Asia, so that it was a saying in the neighbouring states, where, too, glass-houses are not scarce, that "the calf was not safe in the cow, from the thieves of Nicaragua."

It was not always so in Nicaragua. Years before the mail-clad Spaniard brought the curse of civilization across the western ocean, the simple Aztec built his altars to the sun on every hill-top from sea to sea. Centuries ere the Aztec, there flourished a semi-civilized race whose history is written in hieroglyphics of a language utterly dead and forgotten, and who have left no lineal descendants. Even such fragments of Aztec lore as survived the fanaticism of the Conquistadores in Mexico are wanting to the annals of the earlier Central American civilization. It was a culture of rich growth in its day and place, destined like that of the contemporary Roman Empire, to tempt the cupidity of a hardier race, and after an unavailing struggle, to fall before the might of numbers and superior physique. Howbeit, the Aztec Goths and Vandals overran the isthmus, and when the Spanish invasion came, it met only the late subjects of Montezuma's widespread, ill-governed kingdom.

The religion of Nicaragua before the conquest was a gloomy idolatry. The predecessors of the Aztec are conjectured to have been a gentle race, but no match in prowess for their conquerors. The Spaniards found a people of sun-worshippers degraded by human sacrifice and attendant cannibalism. Between them and distant Anahuac, to which they owed allegiance, lay the dense forests and trackless swamps of Yucatan. The journey by land at this day is long and toilsome. Cortes, nevertheless, projected and carried out an exploration as far as Honduras, until his appalled veterans refused to go further southward.

Don Pedrarias d'Avila, Governor of Panama, undertook its exploration from the south in 1514. Nine years later he was encouraged to send a force for its subjugation, under command of Francisco de Cordova, who secured the submission of its cacique, Nicarao or Nicayá. The conquerors gave that chieftain's name to his country. They founded Leon and Granada, which have remained the leading cities of the country. Nicaragua gave a few recruits to Pizarro. Philip II., with narrow-minded foresight, sent a commission to survey the isthmus and judge of the feasibility of cutting a ship canal. The report was favourable, the route by way of Panama being chosen. It was too favourable, as it pointed out the advantages of such a passage to international commerce. Spain did not want such broad liberality, and Philip decreed the punishment of death to any one who might thereafter propose to wed the two oceans together. But, as high tariffs encourage smuggling, so prohibited commerce takes refuge in privateering. The Buccaneers arose to dispute with Spain the monopoly of her American trade. The isthmus suffered most from their ravages. Panama, then as now, the most important city on the coast, was the depôt for the royal treasure gathered at the adjacent mines of Cana. Drake paid it a predatory visit in 1586. It was afterwards taken and sacked at different times by Morgan, Sharpe, Ringrose, and Dampier. It was burned three times between 1670 and 1680. Finally it was abandoned for the new town, three miles inland.

Perfect discipline, combined with boundless courage, was the key to the buccaneers' success. Strict justice governed their conduct towards one another. All spoil was divided impartially, according to the member's rank or the number of his wounds. They could afford to be generous as well as just. Sir Francis Drake captured one galleon which, if we may believe a buccaneering biographer, was laden with twelve score tons of plate and 720 bowlfulls of coined money.

A strange spirit of morality, and even of piety, finds frequent expression in the narratives of those outlaws. Captain Sawkins, an English buccaneer, had a veritable tender reverence for the Sabbath, and would throw the dice overboard if he found them in use on that day. Sir Francis Drake built and endowed a church at Rio Loa with the proceeds of the sack of Porto Bello. In minor matters they were perhaps less scrupulous, as when "at Chepillo it was deemed convenient," by Captain Ringrose and his comrades, to massacre their Spanish prisoners in cold blood. Roche Brasiliano is honourably mentioned by his biographer, writing two hundred years ago, as one who, while but a private mariner, behaved himself so well that he was beloved and respected by all his fellow pirates—this, too, notwithstanding that his inveterate prejudice towards the Spaniards took the unpleasant form of "roasting them on wooden spits, for not showing him hog-yards where he might steal swine."

Not less edifying and instructive are the memoirs of the Sieur Raveneau de Lussan, a French ensign, who served three years as a freebooter, and carried home a liberal share of what he euphemistically calls his "purchase." An atmosphere of pious moralizing pervades his narrative. He sees the protecting hand of Providence in all their victories, which were usually preceded by prayer and celebrated with thanksgiving, with as much trust in the goodness of their cause as is felt by warriors who have a parliamentary declaration of war and the "God of battles" on their side. Notably does this spirit find expression in his account of their distress at finding so many of their company deficient of weapons while crossing the Isthmus of Panama, until, by the providential capsizing of their canoes on the Rio Grande, "God was pleased to dispose of some of us, who left their arms to those who had lost their own." Further on, the worthy Sieur is forced to marvel at their success against a superior force of Spanish vessels, "which, I must say, without exasperating the matter, was a strange thing and almost a miracle." Perhaps the most ludicrous religious quarrel ever recorded—which is saying much—occurred in the dissensions (purely sectarian) which agitated and ultimately separated the French and English buccaneering fleets. De Lussan and his compatriots went North to Nicaragua, meeting such welcome as they deserved from their Spanish co-religionists.

Nicaragua, though liable to predatory forays, had not wealth enough to tempt the buccaneers from richer prey. Cape Gracias a Dios, on its north-eastern boundary, was a rendezvous of the freebooters; but the Atlantic coast was even less inviting to the plunder-seekers than the Pacific. The narratives of the buccaneers touch lightly on it. Its name of the Mosquito Coast appears to have been well deserved. De Lussan speaks with lively horror of the pestiferous little insect which "is sooner felt than seen."

The buccaneers passed away, but left a legacy. Great Britain in 1742 laid claim to the Bay Islands, which had been captured by English buccaneers just a century before. A war with Spain ensued, without material gain to either party. By the treaty of 1763, England renounced her claim on Central America, and evacuated all the disputed territory, except the Island of Ruatan, on the Atlantic coast of Honduras, a shirking of her obligations which awakened a renewal of hostilities. In 1780 Colonel Polson was sent to invade Nicaragua. Landing a force of two hundred sailors and marines at San Juan del Norte, he ascended the river in boats, carrying with little trouble the half-dozen fortified positions on its banks. At the head of the river, where it receives the waters of Lake Nicaragua, the expedition was confronted by the frowning batteries of Fort San Carlos, then, as now, guarding the mouth of the lake.

At this point in the narrative, history and tradition part company, the former averring, upon historical and biographical English authority, that Horatio Nelson, then a simple unknown captain commanding the naval forces, reduced the fort, inflicted a severe chastisement upon the enemy and returned victorious to his ships. Tradition tells a prettier story.

As the flotilla neared the shore in line of battle, the stillness was unbroken, save by the plash of their oars and the music of the surf. Not a soldier was visible on the ramparts, for the cowardly varlets of the garrison, taking advantage of the Commandante's sickness, had fled to the woods at the first sight of the enemy. The gallant hidalgo in command was left without a single attendant, save his lovely daughter. But she was a true soldier's child, with the spirit of a heroine. The boats drew rapidly near the shore, their oars flashing in the morning sun, the gunners awaiting with lighted matches the order to fire. Nelson stood up to bid his men give way, and at the instant a flash was seen in one of the embrasures of the fort; the next moment the roar of a cannon broke the stillness of lake and forest. Immediately gun after gun echoed the sound, but the first had done the work of an army, by striking down Horatio Nelson. The boats pulled rapidly out of range and down the river, beaten and discouraged. Nor did they escape heavier losses; for the Spaniards so harassed and plagued them on the retreat that, of the two hundred men who had started from San Juan, but ten returned in safety. Nelson's wound cost him the loss of an eye; and he who had never turned his back on a foeman fled from the guns of San Carlos, served by a girl of sixteen. It was the Commandante's daughter, Donna Rafaela Mora, who had fired the battery and saved

Nicaragua. The heroine of Fort San Carlos was decorated by the King of Spain, commissioned a colonel in the royal service, and pensioned for life.

Such is the tradition, accepted as authentic by the natives and supported by the testimony of several trustworthy travellers. None of Nelson's biographers make mention of the heroic maiden. According to those historians, Nelson ascended the river as far as Fort San Juan—probably Castillo Viejo—which he reduced after a somewhat protracted siege and a heavy loss to his forces. They place the scene of the accident by which he lost his eye at the siege of Calvi, in the Island of Corsica. Yet Captain Bedford Pim, of the Royal Navy, in his book of Nicaraguan travel, gives unquestioning credence to the legend of the country; which has also been accepted by other English writers who may be supposed to have a familiar acquaintance with the life of Nelson. So firmly is it believed in Nicaragua that, upon the strength of his inherited glory, General Martinez, a grandson of the heroine, was chosen President of the state in 1857, although there was at the time a regularly-elected President claiming and lawfully entitled to the office—a fact which should suffice to silence the most captious critic. In an iconoclastic age it were needless cruelty to rob the poor Nicaraguan of the only bit of heroic history he possesses. Possibly Nelson's biographers suppressed an incident which did not redound to the glory of their hero; perchance, his Catholic Majesty was imposed upon, or the tradition of the Maid of San Carlos may be but another transplanted solar myth. *Quien sabe?*

CHAPTER VII.

British intrigues on the Isthmus—Morazan and the Confederacy—The Mosquito Dynasty—Bombardment of San Juan—Castellon calls in the foreigner—Doubleday and his free lances—Cole's contract approved by Walker.

SO long as Central America remained a province of Spain, England's policy was one of peaceful words and hostile deeds. Binding herself, by treaty after treaty, to the renunciation of all claims upon the country, she steadily maintained and extended her hold upon various objective points—Ruatan, Belize, and the Bay Islands which command the Gulf of Mexico, being her favourite spoils. Some equivocal clause in a treaty, a frivolous pretence of avenging some imaginary dishonour, a buccaneer's legacy, a negro king's grant, if no better offered, was put forward as the excuse for armed occupation. Spain's ill-gotten possessions were beginning to bear the usual fruit. At length, in 1821, the colonies of the isthmus heard the cry of liberty from the North echoed by a responsive one from the South. Spanish America shook the chain fretted and worn in the friction of centuries, snapped the frail links asunder, and stood up among the nations, free. But the iron had done its work. The cramped limbs refused their offices; the eyes, wont to peer half closed in dungeon light, blinked and were dazed in the sudden noon of liberty. The body was that of a freeman, but the soul was the soul of a slave. When liberty comes to a nation prematurely, she must be born again in pain and travail ere the boon be valued by its receiver.

A disunited union of a few years' duration, a travesty of

power under Iturbide's pasteboard crown, secession, re-union, discord, revolution—the annals of Central America are the Newgate Calendar of history. Yet, among the ignoble or infamous names of Central American rulers, there is one worthy of a brighter page, as its owner was of a better fate. Don Francisco Morazan, first president of the five united states, hardly deserved the title given him of the "Washington of Central America." He was an able, brave, and patriotic man, but cruel and vindictive towards his opponents. He was chosen to the presidency in 1831, and filled the office nine years; at the end of which time the natives had grown heartily tired of the civilized innovations, which were as unfitted to their inferior nature as the stiff garments of fashion to their supple limbs. Morazan had neither the grace nor the wisdom to accept philosophically the people's choice of a reactionary demagogue who catered to their tastes, and so he began to intrigue against the government of his successor, failing in which he was forced to fly to South America. Two years afterwards he landed with only three hundred followers in Costa Rica, and made himself master of the capital. But the President of that state soon rallied a force of five thousand and besieged the invader, who, after a gallant resistance of two days, was compelled to surrender. He was tried and found guilty of conspiring against the confederated states, and was put to death, together with his chief adherents, on the 15th of September, 1842. Guatemala ended the troublesome question of representative government in 1851 by electing Carrera, a half-breed, to the office of president for life.

The states of Central America, torn by internal strife, wasting their scant resources in fruitless wars and sad faction fights, were fast lapsing into a barbarism below that of Nicarao when he bowed to the Spanish yoke. Untainted by foreign blood, the independent native tribes proved themselves superior to the mongrel descendants of Cordova and D'Avila. The Indians of Darien and the Rio Frio region and the mountains of northern Costa Rica to this day preserve their freedom, whilst Nicaragua and Costa Rica have been wrangling, year after year, for the empty honour of being called their sovereign.

To this man-cursed land nature had given a noble heritage, coveted by many a powerful nation, though none dared clutch it single-handed. It is the lake, or inland sea, which covers five thousand square miles of the state, elevated one hundred and seven feet above the mean tide-level of the ocean, a natural reservoir, with an outlet ninety miles long—the San Juan river. By making this outlet navigable for large vessels, a comparatively easy work, and by cutting a canal sixteen and one-third miles in length, across the neck of land lying between the Lake and the Pacific Ocean, a highway could be opened to the commerce of the world, whose benefits it would be hard to over-estimate. It was a noble scheme, appealing to the enterprise of the civilized world and to the enlightened statesmanship of men like Bolivar and Morazan. Humboldt advocated it. Louis Napoleon beguiled his prison hours at Ham by writing a pamphlet showing its feasibility and need. As a commercial undertaking, its value was beyond question: the eye of national aggrandizement saw in it even more alluring features.* The nation that should control that canal might be the dictator of America. Such nation was not, and could not be, that which, like the nerveless Ottoman, holds a point of vantage by the right of geographical position and by that alone. The power which held the key to the Mediterranean, and stood ready to seize the Isthmus of Suez, looked wistfully towards Nicaragua. Many and plausible were the dormant claims of England upon the territory of her weak enemy. For

* An American company at the present writing is engaged in the work, with every prospect of success in fully completing it.

years she had exercised a nominal protectorate over the eastern coast known as the Mosquito kingdom.

The monarchs of Mosquito were ignorant negroes, ruling a scattered tribe, the savage descendants of a slave cargo wrecked upon the coast in the seventeenth century. They were appointed at various times by British man-of-war captains, being installed or dethroned at the will of their masters. Nicaragua, while never acknowledging this authority, lacked power to assert her own over the comparatively worthless tracts of her eastern coast, holding possession only of the river and town of San Juan. In 1839, the reigning king of Mosquito, His Majesty Robert Charles Frederick the First, cancelled a debt contracted for sundry liquors and other royal supplies, by making a grant of territory amounting to twenty-two and a half million acres or more. The grantees, Peter and Samuel Shepard, transferred the grant to the Central American Colonization Company, an American Association. This was the foundation of what became afterwards known as the Kinney Expedition.

The royal line of Mosquito may be classed among the unfortunate dynasties of the world. The first monarch, whose name is lost to history, was killed in a drunken brawl; his half-brother and successor was dethroned by a British captain, who placed a distant scion, George Frederick by name, on the vacant throne. The reign the latter was short. His son, Robert Charles Frederick the First, was a merry monarch, "scandalous and poor," who sold his birthright to the Shepards for a mess of Jamaica rum and sundry pairs of cotton breeches. His son, George William Clarence, was reigning in 1850.

The superior swiftness of American ships had enabled the United States to forestall their English rivals in seizing California; whereupon the latter took the bold step, in 1848, of occupying at the same time Tigre Island, on the Pacific coast of the isthmus, and San Juan del

Norte, on the Atlantic, which latter place they christened Greytown, in honour of a governor of Jamaica. England thus had the keys of the isthmus in her hands; the canal, worthless without a safe entrance and exit might fall to the lot of him who chose the barren glory of building it. But, strange to say, the United States possessed at that time a useful diplomatic servant in their minister to Central America, the Honourable E. G. Squier, one, moreover, whose claim to honour rests upon a broader basis than the thankless triumphs of public service. He promptly seconded the protest of Honduras against the utterly indefensible robbery of her territory, Tigre Island. His government took up the question, and the island was reluctantly given up.

At the same time, the United States formally protested against the seizure of San Juan. Long and wordy negotiations ensued, ending in the so-called Clayton-Bulwer Treaty. It was a practical victory for Great Britain, as it entrapped the American Government into an obligation to refrain from "ever holding any exclusive control over the said ship canal, erecting or maintaining any fortifications commanding the same, or in the vicinity thereof, occupying, fortifying, colonizing or assuming or exercising any dominion over Nicaragua, Costa Rica, the Mosquito Coast, or any part of Central America." Great Britain, with apparent fairness, bound herself to equal neutrality. The difference was that the United States promised to abstain from ever taking any steps to control the only avenue then available between the Eastern and the Western States of the Union, thus being placed upon the same footing with distant European nations which could have no such vital interests in the isthmus. Great Britain agreed to refrain from acts which were not only dangerous and inexcusable, but of very doubtful feasibility. Another difference: the United States kept the pledge; Great Britain broke it within fourteen months. The treaty was signed by both parties, and proclaimed on the 5th of July, 1850. In August of the following year, Captain Jolly, of the Royal Navy, solemnly annexed the island of Ruatan to the colony of Belize, which, notwithstanding the treaty, had remained a nominal dependency of England. In July, 1852, Augustus Frederick Gore, Colonial Secretary of Belize, proclaimed that "Her Gracious Majesty, our Queen, has been pleased to constitute and make the islands of Ruatan, Bonacca, Utilla, Barbarat, Helene, and Morat to be a colony to be known and designated as the Colony of the Bay Islands." It was the buccaneer's legacy *re livivus*.

Now, if ever, was a favourable time for the application of a theory set forth by a President of the United States nearly thirty years before: "That the American Continents, by the free and independent position which they have assumed and maintain, are henceforth not to be considered as subjects for future colonization by any European power." So reads the extract from President Monroe's seventh annual message, dated the 2nd December, 1823, and known as the "Monroe Doctrine." This bold assumption of a protectorate over two continents was nothing more than the expression of its author's private opinion, unsupported by official action, either at home or abroad. But it fell like a bombshell into the diplomatic circles of the world. It was criticized, derided, repudiated by every nation of Europe; but it was secretly feared and not openly disobeyed by any, even in the much-vexed discussion of the Central American question. England carefully based her claim to the coveted territory upon the alleged facts of long possession and colonization. It is needless to say that the "Monroe Doctrine," even had it been incorporated in the American constitution, could not have been entertained for a moment in the high court of nations, save after the manner that such doubtful claims are always conceded to the right of might.

The British no longer claimed for themselves or their royal puppets of Mosquito authority over the port of San Juan. Nevertheless, the traditional British man-of-war within a day's sail of anywhere continued to haunt the Carribean Sea. The Transit Company's steamers sailed regularly between New York and San Juan. In May, 1854, a captain of one of them shot a negro in the streets of San Juan, and fled from arrest to the United States Consulate. The American minister, Borland, refused to surrender the fugitive to the officers of justice. A mob surrounded the consulate, and during the fray which ensued the minister was hit on the cheek by a bottle thrown by some rioter. Consul Fabens, then on board the steamer *Northern Light*, sent a boat ashore to take off the minister and his criminal guest, Captain Smith. Before the steamer sailed with the minister on board, a guard of fifty Americans was armed and left behind to protect the Transit Company's property at Puntas Arenas, a point of land opposite the town of San Juan. The boat which carried Minister Borland to the steamer was fired upon by the natives, but, as it appears, not with fatal results. Still the indignity offered to the representative of a great nation must be atoned for. The United States sloop-of-war *Cyane* was sent out as soon as the matter was reported at Washington. Her commander, Captain Hollins, on arriving off the town, found the inevitable British man-of-war lying between him and the shore. He promptly notified the Nicaraguan authorities of his intention to bombard the town, which was thereupon hastily evacuated. The captain of H.B.M. ship *Express* refused to move out of range, until the guns of the *Cyane* had been trained to rake his decks, when he reluctantly dropped astern, after protesting that the American superiority of armament alone saved the dispute from being settled by the last argument of kings and captains. The disparity is to be regretted, in view of the wearisome and vain diplomacy afterwards spent upon a question which force alone, or the show of it, could finally settle.

While the guns of the *Cyane* were squandering powder on the frail huts of San Juan in lieu of a worthier target, Nicaragua was too deeply engrossed in her usual internecine strife to resent the outrage from abroad. Don Frutó Chamorro, who succeeded Pineda as president in 1851, found himself towards the close of his term, ambitious of another lease of power. Chamorro was the leader of the Legitimist, or Servile party, as it was called; Don Francisco Castellon was the choice of the Liberal or Democratic party. At the biennial election in 1853, both parties claimed the victory, and, as is usual in such disputes, possession was the strongest point of law. Chamorro proclaimed himself duly elected, and was installed in office at Granada, the chief city of the Servile faction. Leon, the larger and more prosperous city, favoured the cause of Castellon, whereupon Chamorro promptly arrested his rival with several of his adherents, and banished them from the country. They took refuge in Honduras, whose president, Cabanas, received them hospitably. Chamorro, to make his position more secure, had himself, on April 30, 1854, proclaimed president for two terms or four years. A usurpation so bold was calculated to defeat its own object.

Castellon landed at Realejo within a week after its declaration, with only thirty-six followers. The Leonese rallied to his support, and drove Chamorro out of the department and into the Servile stronghold, the city of Granada. Soon after they obtained control of the lake and river and laid siege to Granada. The siege lasted nine months without material advantage on either side. Castellon was proclaimed Provisional Director by his party. Chamorro dying on the 12th of March, 1855, was succeeded by Senator Don Jose Maria Estrada, a weak substitute for his brave, popular, and ambitious predecessor. Each party had now a *de facto* president. General Jose Trinidad Munoz, a veteran of Santa Ana's, and like that luckless hero, fully impressed with the delusion that he was a physical and mental counterpart of the great Napoleon, commanded the army of Castellon. The Serviles were headed by Don Ponciano Corral, a clever, unscrupulous man, who relied upon the military assistance of adjacent states to strengthen the arms of his party.

Such was the state of affairs in Nicaragua in August, 1854, when an American, named Byron Cole, presented himself before Castellon with a novel offer. Cole, who had been formerly a Boston editor, was proprietor of the newspaper which we left under the editorial management of the late President of Sonora. His faith in the military genius of his editor was in nowise abated by the disastrous end of the Sonora expedition. Arriving in the camp of the Democrats when their earlier conquests were gradually slipping from their hands, and the long siege of Granada had been raised in despair, Cole's offer of aid was eagerly embraced by Castellon and his party.

They had already known and rated the value of the American rifleman as an auxiliary. At an early period of the civil war, an adventurous Californian pioneer, named C. W. Doubleday, found himself at the port of San Juan del Sur, the Pacific terminus of the Transit. He was homeward-bound after years of absence, but being thrown into the society of some Democratic leaders, he did not require much persuasion before deciding to abandon his cabin passage already paid to New York, and become an apostle of Democratic principles among his fellow passengers. He worked with such good effect that thirty of them volunteered under his lead and marched to the aid of the army investing Granada. They were reckless fighters, who looked upon Central American warfare as holiday pastime. Nevertheless, although reinforced from time to time by occasional American recruits, who had drifted into the country on their way to or from California, ere the siege was raised they had been reduced by war and disease to the number of four. Doubleday then organized from the flower of the native army a corps of sharpshooters with whom he covered the retreat to Leon, losing nearly all his company, but impressing the native soldiery with a favourable opinion of the Americans as bold and reckless fighters.

Cole's plan to bring in a formidable American contingent to aid the Democratic cause, came at a time when foreign help was doubly welcome. Castellon's Honduran allies had been abruptly recalled to meet an invasion of their own country by Guatemala. The Serviles, now in possession of lake and river, were slowly but surely advancing on Leon. The strength which the Leonese might have received from the Democratic states adjoining was needed by these at home to protect themselves against their aristocratic enemies, and against the alert, wily intrigues of European agents.

Therefore, in October, 1854, Byron Cole made a contract with the government of Castellon to supply to the Democratic army three hundred American "colonists liable to military duty." The settlers should be entitled to a grant of 52,000 acres of land, and should have the privilege of becoming citizens upon a formal declaration of that intention. Cole took his contract and sailed for California to receive his chief's ratification.

CHAPTER VIII.

Purchase of the *Vesta*—May 4th, 1855, sailing of the " Immortal Fifty-six " — The American Phalanx—First battle of Rivas—Punishing a desperado—Trouble in Castellon's Cabinet—Battle at Virgin Bay—Death of Castellon.

WALKER submitted the contract, worded with legal precision, to the civil and military authorities at San Francisco, and was gratified to learn that it in nowise threatened to violate the neutrality laws of the country. General Wool, to whom Walker had surrendered on his return from Sonora, professed himself satisfied; the district attorney of the United States found no flaw; but everybody in San Francisco knew that Walker was about to colonize Nicaragua with filibusters, and smiled at the peaceful fiction. The legal difficulties overcome, there remained the graver question of funds. To add to his embarrassments, Walker fell sick. It was late in April before he had succeeded in getting the few thousand dollars needed to charter and fit out a vessel. Meanwhile General Jerez, commanding the Democratic army at Leon, had made one or two contracts with other Americans, unknown to his superiors. The Granadinos, too, not to be behind their Democratic rivals, had sent Don Guadalupe Saenz to California to drum up recruits for their side. But nothing came of either venture, and the Leonese, now hemmed in their own department by the victorious Legitimists, looked wistfully for the coming of Walker. He at last succeeded in collecting the barely necessary amount of money, and cast about him for a suitable vessel to carry the new Argonauts.

In the shipping intelligence of the day is chronicled amongst the clearances at the San Francisco Custom House, on April 21st, the brig *Vesta*, Captain Briggs, for Realejo, forty-seven passengers. She did not sail, however, though some fifty or sixty passengers had taken their quarters on board. For at the last moment a new obstacle arose. Walker had bought her outright, though she was a slow, unseaworthy craft, some thirty years old, as nothing better offered, and found out, when too late, that she was liable for several debts incurred by the former owners. The sheriff seized her and, for security, had her sails stripped off and stored on shore. New creditors with old claims also appeared, ready to serve other attachments as soon as the first should be dissolved. Everybody who held a claim, real or fictitious, against the luckless craft, hastened to present it, knowing that Walker must pay their demands or incur a delay of tedious litigation, and delay meant death to his hopes. A revenue cutter drew up alongside the brig, ready to prevent a possible attempt at departure. The expeditionists grew restive, but Walker quieted them with the promise of a speedy departure. Seeking out the creditor who had attached the vessel, Walker persuaded him to grant a release on easy terms, but it took his last dollar to defray the sheriff's extravagant fees of three hundred dollars. The last charge was paid on the 3rd of May, and Walker was authorized to ask the revenue cutter's aid in having the brig's sails bent on, which was rapidly and noiselessly done at night. But though out of the hands of the Government officers, the *Vesta* was still liable to detention by civil process, and a sheriff's keeper remained on board. The captain fearing to risk illegal steps, a new commander, M. D. Eyre, was hastily engaged. He went on board about midnight, having hired a tugboat to carry the brig out to sea, and about the hour of one on the morning of May 4, 1855, the legal functionary was put on board the tow-boat, the lines cast off, and fifty-six filibusters embarked on a voyage of 2,700 miles in a crazy brig bound for a hostile port. A story is told that just before putting to sea, Walker invited the sheriff's officer into the cabin and addressed him briefly as follows: "Here, sir, are wine and cigars; also handcuffs and irons. Please make choice of which you will have. This vessel is going to sea." The officer, according to this rather apocryphal story, was a man of the world, and the *Vesta* put to sea.

Walker breathed more freely as the Golden Gate closed behind him, and the tug-boat *Resolute*, fading to a smoky speck on the water, loosened the last tenacious tentacle of the polypus—law. Harassed like Cortez by petty trials, he was, like him, sailing with a few chosen followers to a new destiny. He confided in the superiority of civilization over barbarism, and the certainty that he would receive his country's support the moment that success should first crown his arms: success which condones even greater faults than illegal warfare. The cost of failure he did not count. The stout-hearted hunter who enters a lion's den does not ask what will happen if nerve or steel fail him confronting his angry foe. Despite the result, there is something thrilling in the story of the fifty-six men who stole out of a harbour by night to conquer an empire—and all but succeeded! For not by numbers nor resources should such enterprises be judged, but by the deeds of the adventurers. As Prescott says, "It is not numbers that give importance to a conflict, but the consequences that depend upon it; the magnitude of the stake, and the skill and courage of the players—the more limited the means, even, the greater may be the science shown in the use of them."

They sailed down the Pacific coast—a long and stormy voyage—and, after touching at Tigre Island for a pilot, cast anchor in the port of Realejo, Nicaragua, on the 16th day of June. Old Realejo, at which the *Vesta's* voyage ended, was the site of a once prosperous Spanish town with a good harbour and deep tide-water; but so often had the buccaneers ravaged it, that the inhabitants had abandoned it and built a new town of the same name five miles further up the river, accessible only to boats of light draught. The strangers re-embarked in several canoes, or *bongoes*, hollowed from the ceiba tree, and by four o'clock that day arrived at New Realejo. Castellon and his cabinet were at Leon, the Democratic capital, whither Walker and Major Crocker set out the next day escorted by Colonel Ramirez and Captain Doubleday of the native army. The Provisional Director warmly received his new ally, and promptly and formally accepted the immigrants into the military service of Nicaragua. They were organized as a separate corps, under the name of "La Falange Americana," or American Phalanx, and placed under the immediate command of their own officers. Commissions were issued on the 20th of June to Walker as colonel, Achilles Kewen as lieutenant-colonel, and Timothy Crocker as major. Orders were given them at once to proceed by water to Rivas, a city of 11,000 inhabitants, in the Meridional department, which was held by the enemy. Colonel Ramirez, with two hundred natives, was detailed to help the Falange, but only half that number answered the roll-call, when the *Vesta* weighed anchor at Realejo, on the 23rd of June.

Walker had seen enough of his new friends to convince him that his ambition had nothing to fear from such rivals. Castellon was an amiable and irresolute gentleman; Munoz was ambitious and vain, but incapable. The native soldiery were ill-trained and fickle-minded. Faction had stifled any faint sparks of patriotism in their breasts. A few hundred of them who bore the proud title of *veteranos*, had smelt powder and could face an enemy after a march of forty miles under a tropical sun. They wore a tasteful uniform and carried muskets and knapsacks.

But the hundred recruits of Ramirez were a Falstaffian corps of indolent, good-natured rascals, who devoted all the intervals between skirmishing to gambling and gossip. As their country's proverb hath it, "they would gamble away the sun before sunrise." In striking contrast with those children of nature were the men of California, with iron nerves and dauntless courage, in whose characters vice lost half its evil by losing, if not its grossness, all its meanness; men who "deemed no crime, or curse, or vice as dark as that of cowardice." Their manliness was incapable of treachery, falsehood, or the meaner passions, born of a society in which law, the only remedy for wrong, too easily becomes the strongest shield of the wrong-doer. Having summed up their virtues in the comprehensive ones of courage and loyalty, there is little else to be said in their favour. For themselves they would have asked no higher praise, and strict justice can accord them little beyond.

It was a bold move to attack the enemy in his stronghold. Rivas and the adjoining country are the most densely populated parts of Nicaragua. The city of Rivas contains eleven thousand inhabitants, while the department of that name and the adjacent Oriental department number respectively twenty thousand and ninety-five thousand. Four days after leaving Realejo, the party, to the number of one hundred and sixty-five, landed at a point on the coast near the town of Brito, and immediately began a forced march to Rivas. Midnight and a severe rain storm overtook them in the midst of a strange country, but they trudged patiently along, ankle-deep in mud, shielding their precious ammunition from the falling torrents. On the second night of their march the weather proved a useful ally, enabling them to surprise and overpower a picket of the enemy at the village of Tola. Next morning they were rewarded by a first sight of Lake Nicaragua in all its matchless beauty. Walker, who had beheld the glories of Switzerland, Italy, and California, pauses in the recital of his dangerous adventures to note the charms of the earthly paradise upon which he had come to launch the horrors of war. Between him and the lake six hundred Legitimists troops lay at Rivas, awaiting the attack.

No time was lost in forming the plan of assault. To the Falange was awarded the post of honour, the native command of Ramirez being reserved to support them. Kewen and Crocker led the Americans, who, at the word of command, advanced steadily, receiving the enemy's fire with the coolness of veterans, and reserving their own until it could tell most effectively. Then after pouring in a volley they charged with a yell, and drove the advance guard of the Serviles down the narrow streets to the plaza. A stubborn resistance was made at this point. Crocker was dangerously wounded in two places, his right arm was broken by a musket shot, but he carried his pistol in his left hand and continued to fire it into the faces of the enemy, until a third shot laid him dead. Walker, who had joined his countrymen in the charge, now called for the native reserves to decide the issue; but they were nowhere to be seen. The poltroons had fled at the first shot. The enemy perceived the defection and pressed the abandoned Falange so hard that they were driven for shelter to some adobe huts, behind whose walls they held their own for three hours. It was a losing game with so small a force, for every man lost was equal to thrice the number of enemies added. Achilles Kewen was the next officer to fall. The hardy pioneer, Doubleday, was shot in the head, though not fatally. Seeing six of his men dead, and twice as many wounded, Walker ordered a sortie. The enemy had lost a hundred and fifty in killed and wounded, and General Boscha, their commander, deemed it wiser to offer no opposition to the departure of the Americans.

The Serviles, with cowardly ferocity, killed the wounded men who had been left on the plaza, and celebrated their victory by burning the bodies. The ghastly bonfire lit up the city as the weary filibusters halted on their retreat near the Transit road to San Juan del Sur. The following morning they resumed the march to that city, where they arrived about sunset, on June 30th, in a most deplorable plight. Some were hatless, some shoeless, and all exhausted with battle and travel, as they marched into the town. There is a whole epitome of filibustering in the fact that at such a time two recruits were found to join the ranks of the Falange. "The Texan, Harry McLeod, and the Irishman, Peter Burns," deserve mention for this characteristic piece of hardihood.

The *Vesta* was cruising off the coast, awaiting orders from Walker, who therefore impressed a Costa Rican schooner, the *San Jose*, for the purpose of carrying his command to Realejo, defending his action upon the ground that the same vessel had already been used to carry General Guardiola from Honduras to Nicaragua upon a hostile mission, thus forfeiting her neutral rights. The schooner was confiscated a year afterwards, by Walker, for sailing under a false register, and, being converted into a man-of-war and renamed the *Granada*, played quite an important part in the climax of this tragedy.

In this critical hour of his fortunes, Walker's firmness was put to a severe test. A couple of dissolute Americans, who had been living for some time at San Juan, either through drunken folly or private spite, or for the purpose of plunder, set fire to the barracks on shore, for a time placing the whole town in danger of destruction. Walker, foreseeing that the act would be at once attributed to his men, took measures to punish the offenders. One of them escaped from the party detailed to execute him. The other, a gambler named Dewey, took refuge in the hold of a small boat attached to the stern of the *San Jose*. The desperado was well armed, and any attempt to capture him would have proved fatal to one or more of his assailants. So all the night Walker and a guard of men kept watch over the boat, ready to shoot or seize the villain if he tried to escape. At daybreak the schooner put to sea, towing astern the boat in which Dewey lay sheltered behind a poor native woman, his wretched mistress. The gambler, as everybody on board knew, was a dead shot, while his guard lay under the disadvantage of fearing to injure the woman if they fired. At last he rose to cut the boat's painter, and at that moment a rifle ball ended his career. The poor woman was wounded also, but not mortally. Walker takes pains to recount minutely the details of this incident, in order to vindicate the character of his followers. So severe a punishment was not lost upon those of his men who might be inclined to take a baser view of filibusterism than their leader did.

On the same day they met the *Vesta* at sea, and embarking on board the old brig, arrived at Realejo on July 1st. Walker was justly incensed at the defection of his native allies at Rivas, and positively refused to continue in the Democratic service without better guarantees of support on emergency than the jealousy of the native commanders seemed likely to allow. The Falange remained several days at Leon, where the firmness of their leader alone averted a collision between them and the troops of Munoz, who had set the example of hostility and distrust towards the new-comers. At last, finding the Cabinet unable to agree upon a fixed policy (though a modified contract had been drawn up, by the terms of which the Falange were to be enlisted in the army of Nicaragua to the number of three hundred, and receive one hundred dollars a month per man, and five hundred acres of land each at the close of the war), Walker withdrew his men from Leon to Realejo. There he embarked them on the *Vesta*, with the pretended purpose of departing for Honduras, and entering the service of President Cabañas. Nothing, however, was farther from his intention. The Meridional department, commanding the Transit route, was the point at whose acquisition he steadily aimed. To maintain his foothold in Nicaragua he well knew he must keep open his communication with the United States and the recruits who were sure to flock thence to his standard.

Castellon was perplexed, fearing equally to part with his valuable allies and to displease Munoz by retaining them. The fortune of war decided the question. The Legitimists under Corral and his Hondureño ally, Guardiola, were drawing close to Leon. Santos Guardiola (his name is still muttered with a curse throughout the length and breadth of the isthmus) was a native of Honduras, who joined the Guatemalan enemies of his country, and, by his unparalleled cruelties to young and old, men and women alike, acquired the dread name of "The Tiger of Honduras." He was sprung from the stock which produces nine-tenths of the murderers and thieves of Central America, the offspring of Indo-African amalgamation known as "Sambos."

A deadlier foe, the cholera, was also beginning to ravage the Democratic department. To meet Corral and his forces, Munoz went forth with six hundred men, and a sharp engagement occurred at Sauce, in which the enemy was repulsed, but Munoz was slain. The loss of that commander influenced Castellon more than the temporary victory, and he continued to beg Walker to return. But Walker had already secured the co-operation of an influential partisan, Don Jose Maria Valle, who readily enlisted a hundred and sixty men for the enterprise against the Meridional department, and, with the easy loyalty of his nation, proposed that Walker should pronounce against Castellon and set up an independent government. Walker was honourable enough to reject the ungrateful suggestion, although he did not hesitate to disobey the Provisional Director's commands when they crossed his own policy. Accordingly, on the 23rd of August the *Vesta* sailed once more for the Meridional department, and arrived at San Juan del Sur on the 29th. The Legitimists fled at his approach. While the Americans were there the steamer from San Francisco arrived and departed, carrying back with her, as a recruiting agent, the afterwards notorious Parker H. French.

After a stay of four days Walker set out for Rivas, where Guardiola and six hundred Serviles lay waiting to regain the laurels lost at Sauce. The Americans, after a few hours' march, halted for breakfast at Virgin Bay, on the lake, and were at once attacked by Guardiola's whole force, who had made a forced march towards San Juan, and then, doubling, followed the Americans to Virgin Bay. Attacked on front and flank, Walker made a good disposition of his little force. Previous experience had taught him that no superiority of discipline, skill, and courage sufficed to counterbalance the numerical odds of eight to one on an open field. He was now to try the effect of pitting the same against a proportion of only five to one, with the ground in his favour. The Falange, as usual, bore the brunt of battle; but the natives, being better officered than before, fought well. Guardiola was driven back at every point, notwithstanding that his men showed desperate courage, as sixty of their dead bodies attested. But no courage could withstand the deadly marksmanship of the Americans, who, with rifle or revolver, always engaged at close quarters and never wasted a shot. The combat, which hardly deserves the name of a battle, lasted only two hours; sufficiently long to inflict on the enemy a loss of sixty killed and a hundred wounded. At its conclusion Guardiola withdrew his demoralized forces and fled to Rivas. Walker, Doubleday, and a few others were wounded, but none of the Americans, and but three of their native allies, were killed.

Walker now returned to San Juan, where he picked up a few recruits from among the ranks of homeward-bound Americans on the steamer from California. Here also he learned of the death of Castellon, who had fallen a victim to the cholera. His successor, Don Nasario Escoto, warmly congratulated Walker on his success at Virgin Bay, and promised further aid. Learning from intercepted letters of the authorities at Granada that the city was in an almost defenceless condition, he determined to attack the Legitimist stronghold without awaiting the advance of Corral, who had replaced Guardiola in the command of the enemy. To show his contempt of the latter, he sent the intercepted correspondence to the Legitimist headquarters, and was not a little surprised at receiving a polite acknowledgment of the courtesy, and a hieroglyphic document from Corral, which proved to consist of Masonic signs. A freemason in the Falange, De Brissot, interpreted them to mean an overture for confidential negotiations. No reply was made to the proposition.

Recruits continued to flock to the Democratic standard. Colonel Charles Gilman, a one-legged veteran of Sonora, came down with thirty-five men from California. The native allies now numbered about two hundred and fifty. Two small cannon were procured and mounted. By the 11th of October Walker had everything in readiness for his most audacious stroke, the capture of Granada, a city as dear to the Legitimist cause, and especially to its proud inhabitants, as was its namesake to the Moors of old Spain.

Corral was massing his forces at Rivas, hoping, yet fearing, to meet his enemy on the Transit road. No suspicion of an attack on the capital seems to have entered his mind. Dissension was rife in the Legitimist camp

Guardiola and Corral quarrelling for the supreme command. The native Democrats on the other side, whatever of jealousy they may have felt towards their foreign allies, carefully veiled their feelings and made a show of the utmost cordiality. Walker enforced absolute discipline without distinction of nationality, a spice of grim humour sometimes seasoning his decisions. Two native officers, having quarrelled all night over some old or new feud, were ordered to settle the affair by going out and fighting a duel next morning, but their courage had oozed away by daybreak, and the trouble was heard of no more.

At last, on the morning of October 11th, the Democratic army, about four hundred strong, took the line of march over the white Transit road to Virgin Bay. The Falange were in good spirits as they marched gaily along the dusty highway. They were nearly all in the prime of life—tall, robust, and spirited. Their only distinctive uniform, if it might be called such, was the red ribbon which they wore tied around their black "slouch" hats. They wore blue or red woollen shirts, coarse trousers tucked into heavy boots, with a revolver and a bowie knife in each belt, and a precious rifle on every man's shoulder. Many new faces were in the ranks, and some old ones were missing which could ill be spared from a service of trust and danger. Ten of the original fifty-six had fallen in battle—Kewen, a brave veteran of Mexico and Cuba, Crocker, McIndoe, Cotham, Bailey, Hews, Wilson, William and Frank Cole, and Estabrook. Some were absent on leave, amongst them the pioneer, Doubleday, who had returned home piqued by an untimely rebuke from his commander. The estrangement did not last long. Doubleday soon wearied of a peaceful life, and was welcomed back by Walker on his return to active service.

CHAPTER IX.

A Servile victory in the North—Walker in the enemy's stronghold—Negotiations for peace—Execution of Mayorga—Rivas chosen Provisional Director—Corral's treason and punishment—Newspaper history.

CORRAL lay with the main body of the Legitimist army at Rivas, keeping, through his scouts and spies, a close watch on the movements of his enemy. One of those spies, having been caught within the Democratic lines, was tried by court-martial and summarily shot. Corral fancied that he had his foes in a trap, and he accordingly devoted all his efforts to prevent their retreat to San Juan, as well as to cut off reinforcements from California. Matters, indeed, looked desperate with the Democrats. On the North the Leonese had just been routed in battle by General Martinez at Pueblo Nuevo, and the victor had only halted for a time at Granada to receive a triumphal ovation before coming down to Rivas to join in the extermination of the filibusters.

It had been a gala day in the city of Granada. From early dawn to midnight her ten thousand citizens filled the streets and plazas with revelry and congratulations. Salvos of artillery thundered a welcome to the victors, joy bells rang all day, and *bombas* and rockets wasted precious powder in their honour. *Aguardiente* flowed freely as water, until the valiant soldiers prayed that Walker might be spared destruction long enough to meet the heroes of Pueblo Nuevo. Far into the night lasted the grand fiesta, till the last drunken reveller had hied him home or lain down in the street to dream of renewed happiness on the morrow. The tardiest lover had tinkled his farewell on the guitar. In the grand plaza the guard nodded around the watch fire, while from distant pickets came at intervals the long-drawn nasal "Alerte!" of the sentinels. It was a melodious cry, equally unlike the sharp challenge of the Frenchman or the stern English monosyllables.

Granada slept, the while a little steamer, with lights cloaked and furnaces hidden, steamed slowly along the shore. Not a sound broke the stillness of the lake, save the lap of surf or the plash of the startled saurian. The jaguar prowling among the orange trees on the shore challenged the unfamiliar noise, and the night birds passed along the cry of warning which was lost upon the ears of the sleepy sentinels. They drowsed over their waning fires until the gray of morning broke on the mountains, and from convent and church tower the joy-bells renewed the merry peals. Here and there a straggling sentry discharged his piece in response. Another and another shot were heard; then, suddenly, a short, sharp volley such as never came from the mouth of smooth-bore musket. The joy-bells changed to a loud alarm as a terrified sentinel rushed in from the South suburb, crying, "The enemy are on us! the Filibusteros!" Close upon his heels came the broken and demoralized picket, with the advanced guard of Americans under Walker and Valle galloping on their track.

The surprised garrison, after the first panic, rallied and made a short stand on the plaza, until an impetuous charge of the invaders swept them away. In less time than has been taken to tell it one hundred and ten filibusters had taken by assault the city of Granada, without losing a man—literally, for a drummer-boy was the only victim on their side.

The surprise was complete, and the consequence of supreme importance to Walker, who, from the chief city of the Servile party, might dictate terms to Central America. Corral had been completely outgeneralled, nobody but Walker himself and his trusted aids, Valle and Hornsby, having been acquainted with the object of the expedition when it set out from Virgin Bay.

Walker, as soon as he had organized a provisional government and convinced his native allies by vigorous measures that the conquered city was not to be subjected to the usual treatment of plunder and violence, sent a delegation to negotiate with Corral. The envoys were met with a polite negative, while the United States minister, Mr. Wheeler, who had accompanied them in the character of a peacemaker, was thrown into prison and threatened with other punishments, whence ensued much diplomatic correspondence and official shedding of ink.

Meanwhile the hope of a peaceable understanding was seriously jeopardized by the folly of one of Walker's new recruits, Parker H. French. He had come to San Juan with a body of new men from California, and after crossing the Transit had seized one of the lake steamers, with the intention of capturing Fort San Carlos, at the head of the San Juan River, the same stronghold which in its days of power had been the key to the Transit route and to lake navigation. French was easily repulsed, and made his way to Granada to report his misadventures. Tidings of his deeds reaching Rivas in the meantime, some Legitimist soldiers, by way of reprisal, attacked and killed six or seven Californian passengers who were awaiting at Virgin Bay a chance of passage to the Atlantic coast. Shortly afterwards the commandant of Fort San Carlos fired into a westward-bound steamer, killing some passengers who were as innocent of complicity with French or the filibusters as had been the other victims at Virgin Bay. The protest of the American minister being treated with contempt, Walker, with questionable justice, retaliated by ordering a court-martial on the Legitimist Secretary of State, Don

Mateo Mayorga, who had been captured at the taking of Granada. Such a method of holding a cabinet minister responsible for the acts of his government was enforcing the principles of constitutional rule with a vengeance. The court was composed of the secretary's countrymen, who brought in a verdict of guilty, and Mayorga was promptly executed. Although personally refraining from interfering in the case, and only reluctantly sanctioning the sentence of death, it is evident that Walker had begun to learn the Central American method of conducting warfare. But the execution, if morally unjustified, proved to be a wise act politically. Corral at once agreed to treat for peace, and a meeting between him and Walker was arranged to take place at Granada on the 23rd of October.

Again the bells of Granada rang out in joy, and the light-hearted populace welcomed the festival whether of peace or of war. The Falange, now some tenscore strong, joined with the native soldiery in a military welcome to their late enemies.

At the approach of Corral, Walker, attended by his staff, rode out of the suburbs to meet him. The commanders saluted one another with grave cordiality, and re-entered the city side by side, proceeding to the grand cathedral, where Padre Vijil, the curate of Granada, offered up a High Mass, and *Te Deums* of thanksgiving were sung. Nor did the good father fail in his sermon to show the advantages to his beloved country attending the presence of the strange American of the North. Unlike many of his cloth, the father was a fervent Democrat, and remained through life a warm friend of the Americans. He was a man of singularly broad and far-seeing mind, who placed country before party, and human brotherhood above the differences of birth or creed—a type of character sufficiently rare even among colder and less impulsive nations.

Handsome Corral was the darling of the Granadinos. He had the superficial traits which draw popularity—

dash, openhandedness, physical beauty, and a sunny disposition; but he was weak, vain, and untrustworthy, for all that. We have seen how he coquetted with Walker, while in command of the Legitimist forces, treating for peace and imprisoning its envoys. Having come to Granada to complete the negotiations, he now betrayed the rights of his principal, the President, so called, Estrada, and entered into a sacred compact with the Leonese, whose acts were sanctioned by their nominal President.

By the terms of the agreement Don Patricio Rivas was appointed President *pro tempore*, with the following cabinet: Mazimo Jerez, Minister of Relations; Firmin Ferrer, Minister of Public Credit; Parker H. French, Minister of Hacienda, Ponciano Corral, Minister of War. Walker was appointed generalissimo of the army, which consisted of twelve hundred men, distributed throughout the country in small garrisons. Five hundred men were stationed at Leon, and the remainder at Virgin Bay, Granada, Rivas, and other fortified positions. The general in chief received a salary of five hundred dollars a month, and his subordinates were awarded correspondingly liberal pay, or promises to pay. There were seven surgeons and two chaplains attached to the forces; the former held no sinecure.

During the progress of the negotiations Corral, with the small subtlety of miniature politics, had sought to entrap Walker in various ways, such as requiring him to take the oath upon the Crucifix, and similar ceremonial punctilioes, to which Walker, as a Protestant, might have been expected to object, but, like a man of sense, did not. He rightly judged that the keeping of an oath was of more importance than the form of taking it; and therein he differed from Corral, who was detected, a few days after the formation of the government, in treasonable correspondence with the neighbouring states. A native courier deceived the traitor, and placed in Walker's hands the fatal letters containing indisputable proofs of the writer's guilt.

To Xatruch, a Legitimist refugee, he had written, nine days after the signing of the treaty, begging him to foment hostility against the new administration. In a similar strain he wrote to Guardiola, the Honduran Servile leader, conjuring him to arouse the Legitimist element everywhere against the American intruders: "Nicaragua is lost, lost are Honduras, San Salvador, and Guatemala if they let this thing prevail. Let them come quickly, if they would meet auxiliaries." General Martinez, commanding at Managua, was also implicated in the treason, but received warning in time to fly the country.

Walker at once requested the President and Cabinet to meet him, and laid before them the evidence of Corral's guilt. A court-martial was convened, the members of which were all Americans, such, it is said, being the wish of the accused, who knew that he could expect no mercy from his countrymen. From the same motive, he did not deny his guilt, but threw himself on the mercy of his judges, relying, as it proved, overmuch on the magnanimity which the Americans had heretofore displayed. He was sentenced to die by the fusillade at noon of the next day, November the 7th. The time of execution was subsequently postponed two hours. The friends of the condemned made earnest appeals for mercy in his behalf, being seconded by the leading public citizens, and particularly by Padre Vijil, the gentle apostle of peace; but Walker, though much moved and fully aware of the odious construction which his enemies would put upon the act, firmly refused the petition. The treason was too flagrant, the example unfortunately too necessary, and mercy to such a traitor would have been injustice to every loyal man in the state.

Corral died at the appointed hour, and the lesson was

not wholly lost upon his accomplices. Walker has been bitterly censured for this piece of stern justice, especially at home in the United States, where the act was misrepresented as that of a suspicious tyrant who thus rid himself of a dangerous rival. But there is not the slightest reason for regarding Corral's death as aught but the well-merited punishment of an utterly unscrupulous villain. His whole conduct in connection with the late war was consistent with his last and fatal treachery. Even the morality of Nicaragua, loose as it was in matters of public faith, while lamenting the fate of Handsome Ponciano, confessed that he was well-named "Corral," the beautiful but deadly serpent of the country.

That impartial justice governed the action of Walker is evident from an incident which occurred on the very day on which Corral was indicting his treason to Xatruch and Guardiola. Patrick Jordan, a soldier of the Falange, while intoxicated, shot and mortally wounded a native boy. Jordan was tried by court-martial and sentenced to death. Padre Vijil and many others, including the mother of the murdered boy, begged in vain for leniency to the culprit. On the 3rd of November, two days after the commission of his crime, Jordan was shot at sunrise. Walker's detractors commented characteristically upon this execution, picturing the impartial judge as another Mokanna, delighting in the suffering of friend as of foe. The historian, groping in the darkness of contemporaneous journalism for facts of current history, wherever those facts bear upon the so-called political issues of the time, finds himself floundering at every step in sloughs of falsehoods or quicksands of misrepresentation. The evil, unhappily, is confined to no party or epoch. Walker being a champion, and a bigoted one, of a certain party, paid the inevitable penalty, that of being equally overpraised and underrated, according to the political prejudices of his critics.

To Don Buonaventura Selva was given to the vacant portfolio of war. The representative of the United States recognized the new administration. The neighbouring states of Liberal tendencies sent assurances of hearty friendship; those in which the Servile party was supreme maintained a diplomatic silence. Peace reigned throughout the length and breadth of Nicaragua, the peace of her own slumbering volcanoes.

CHAPTER X.

Filibusterism abroad—Kinney's Expedition—The filibusters and their allies—An aristocracy of leather—Pierce and Marcy—A rupture with the United States—Costa Rica declares war—Schlessinger's fiasco—Cosmopolitan adventurers—Steamers withdrawn—History of the Transit Company—Vanderbilt plans vengeance—The printing-press on the field.

IN the United States, particularly in California, Walker's amazing success gave an impulse to filibustering of a different, because more sanguine, nature from that produced by the first expeditions of Lopez to Cuba. France and England also awoke to behold with dismay this solution of the Central American problem. Not less alarmed was the Conservative element in Spanish America, the more reactionary part of which talked wildly of calling in a European protectorate and of breaking off commercial intercourse with the North Americans. Mexico, Cuba, Ecuador, and Central America were threatened by invading expeditions, while Nicaragua was made the objective point of an actual invasion from the Atlantic coast. It will be remembered that the Mosquito king's grant to the Shepards had been transferred to a colonization company in the United States; upon the strength of which Henry L. Kinney, of Philadelphia, proceeded to occupy his property. But there were many difficulties in the way. The grant had been revoked by his Majesty in a lucid interval. Great Britain, as guardian of the kingdom, repudiated the contract. Nicaragua steadily declined to recognize the rights of either party to her territory; and, to complete the adventurer's misfortune, the Federal authorities arrested him when about to lead his first detachment of colonists to his tropical possessions. Not to rehearse the tedious litigation which followed, it suffices to say that the Kinney Expedition, having succeeded in embarking, was shortly afterwards wrecked on Turk's Island, finally reaching San Juan del Norte in a most forlorn plight. There new misfortunes overtook them. Most of the military colonists sailed up the river to share the more promising fortunes of Walker, to whom Kinney himself, despairing of success unaided, at last made overtures for an alliance offensive and defensive. But the messenger found Walker firmly entrenched in power and, as a member of the government, bound to consider all foreign claims on the Mosquito coast as mere usurpations. Had it been otherwise, he might perhaps have returned a less peremptory answer than the brief threat: "Tell Mr. Kinney, or Colonel Kinney, or whatever he calls himself, that if I find him on Nicaraguan soil, I will most assuredly hang him." The new element in Nicaragua did not fail to uphold the sovereign independence of the country with zeal, even if it may have sometimes lacked discretion. Walker was a stickler for dignity, and never failed to exact the respect due to himself, his office, and his flag. An English merchant, of Realejo, who had resisted a Government levy, and, with the sublime assurance of his race, had hoisted the Union Jack over his house, was caustically invited by Walker to lower the emblem or produce his Government's license to display the flag of a representative. "If he refuses," said Walker, "tear it down, trample it under foot, and put the fellow in irons." The Englishman knew enough of law to see that he had no authority for the display of bunting, which he accordingly furled, paid the requisition, and cursed the Yankee lawyer who had taught him a lesson. Walker was versed in the law of nations, but he unfortunately overlooked the fact that those wise statutes are framed for the control of strong nations dealing with their peers. It is not enough to be right, or to know one's rights, unless the power to maintain them accompany the knowledge. A touch of the lawyer's weakness for technical rights always marked this curious outlaw.

In the dazzling success of the Falange, the disasters of Kinney were forgotten, and many a band of hardy adventurers was tempted to rival their deeds. For a time it seemed as though the spirit of the Vikings had been revived in the land discovered by Eric the Red. On the Pacific coast those incursions sometimes assumed, as we have seen, formidable proportions. Sonora, Arizona, Lower California, and even the Sandwich Islands, were the various goals of ambitious adventurers, some of whom never carried their schemes into effect; others, like Colonel Crabbe, made a really imposing campaign for a brief space, only to die fruitless deaths, the victims of Spanish cruelty.

The filibusters were by no means impelled to risk life and liberty through an abstract love of freedom or disinterested affection for their oppressed allies. They were, on the contrary, rather prone to turn to their own advantage the fruits of hard-won victory. Their extenuation lies in the worthless character of their allies, who invariably deserted them in extremity, and left the foreigner to save himself. It was so in Cuba, in Sonora, in Nicaragua, though there were honourable exceptions everywhere. A contempt and mistrust of the native character, often but ill-concealed, did not serve to make the alliance any more sincere. In Nicaragua, for the present at least, gratitude was stronger than prejudice, and the party favouring the Americans was powerful and enthusiastic. The common people remained faithful throughout; it was the *calzados*, the middle and upper classes composing the Conservative party, who hated the foreigner because they felt his superiority, and his still more galling consciousness thereof. The *calzados* were those who wore shoes, as distinguished from the barefoot rabble. Aristocracy, based on such inherent merit, is naturally jealous of its prerogatives.

Almost every steamer from California brought down a squad, greater or less, of recruits. Amongst the earliest was a brother of the Achilles Kewen killed at the first battle of Rivas. E. J. C. Kewen was one of the most valuable of Walker's staff, on which he served throughout the war. Quite characteristic of the time and place is the matter-of-fact way in which the San Francisco papers state that Colonel Kewen participated as second in a duel at that place on the day preceding his departure for Nicaragua. Business before pleasure.

During the four months which followed the formation of the new government, Walker gathered about him a force of Americans and other foreigners numbering twelve hundred. They came from all parts of the Union, but chiefly from the Southern and Pacific states. Recruiting offices were opened in San Francisco, whose agents penetrated the mining camps and interior towns, unnoticed or unhindered by the Government authorities. Whenever any opposition was offered, the volunteers frequently bought through tickets to New York, and stopped at Nicaragua to enjoy a little filibustering. In the east more stringent precautions were taken by the authorities, though without much effect, as the colonists were responding to the invitation of the Nicaraguan Government, and could not be legally hindered.

Among the adventurers were many idle and desperate characters attracted by visions of beauty and booty, with the broad license of a freebooter's camp. To such the reality proved a terrible revelation; they found, instead of a free lance's easy discipline, a system of military government emulating in its stringent laws that of the great Frederick. Walker's abstemiousness was supplemented by the virtue, much rarer in men of his class, of absolute personal chastity in thought, word, and deed. Drunkenness, debauchery, and profanity were vices which he abhorred. The man who was detected selling liquor to a soldier was punished by a fine of 250 dols.; the drunkard was sent to the guard-house for ten days. With whisky of a vile quality selling at 2½ dols. a bottle, and the terrors of punishment before the eyes of both buyer and seller, drunkenness was rare in Granada. On the outposts discipline was more lax, officers and men availing themselves of secrecy to evade their general's stern commands. The well-behaved, on the other hand, were treated with the greatest favour, receiving their regular pay of a hundred dollars a month, according to some—a quarter of that sum, according to others—and a contingent title to five hundred acres of land.

The assurance of peace alone was needed to make Nicaragua, the veritable "Mahomet's Paradise" which its discoverers had named it. But there was no such assurance or prospect in view. Even had Walker been willing to rest content with his present wonderful success, he would not have been permitted so to curb his ambition. His enemies were too many and too powerful and implacable. Great Britain, which had been trespassing, secretly or openly, for half a century, on the rights of the weak Spanish-American republics, could not allow so rich a prize to pass into the hands of the hated "Yankee." Money, men, and arms were furnished to the neighbouring states, and every pretext was made use of to stir up a crusade against the Americans.

Enemies as bitter, though less powerful to injure openly, influenced the administration at Washington. The Secretary of State, William L. Marcy, was a politician who is best remembered by his enunciation of the notorious political maxim, "To the victors belong the spoils." Marcy had no personal ill-will towards Walker or his political friends, he was not the man to indulge a wanton grudge, but he carried into the great office which he filled the aims, sympathies, prejudices, and alliances of a thorough politician. To him the traditions of his country, the dignity of his high position, the honour of the republic were secondary ideas. What his party would say, how his acts would be criticized at Albany or on Wall Street, these were the thoughts which swayed his mind and governed his conduct. Like master, like man, Franklin Pierce was mentally as small as his secretary. So when a minister plenipotentiary from Nicaragua presented his credentials at Washington, and the other resident ministers protested against his being received, a terrible consternation fell upon the minds of President and Secretary. Mr. Marcolletta, the former minister, though recalled by the Government of Nicaragua, stoutly refused to resign. The other foreign ministers espoused his cause, and the secretary had the amazing stupidity to argue the case gravely with those officious gentlemen. Colonel Wheeler, the minister to Nicaragua, being appealed to, confirmed the *de facto* and *de jure* claims of the Rivas Government, adding, as a proof of the country's tranquility, the striking fact, that "not a single prisoner, for any offence, is now confined in the Republic—a circumstance unknown before in the country."

Mr. Marcy had now no choice but to acknowledge the credentials of the new representative, when the discovery of a grave blunder of Walker's saved him the humiliation. No official objection could be urged against the minister, but unfortunately for him, there were pronounced personal objections strong enough to warrant the district attorney in New York in ordering his arrest on a criminal process. The individual, Parker H. French, was the same one-armed hero whose fiasco before Fort San Carlos had brought the Falange into disrepute and provoked the Virgin Bay massacre. Walker discovered when too late the unworthy antecedents of his envoy, whose conduct in Nicaragua should have been enough to disqualify him; but regarding his arrest as a violation of diplomatic privilege, he had him recalled, dismissed the American minister to Nicaragua, and suspended diplomatic intercourse with the United States. Some months later, and after the United States had declined to receive a second minister, Don Firmin Ferrer, Walker sent a third representative, in the person of the good Padre Vijil, who proved acceptable at Washington, as much on account of his high character as for the news which he brought with him, that Walker had routed his Costa Rica enemies, and frightened back the Serviles of the North. Franklin Pierce was not the man to turn his back upon a friend in prosperity, though his good will was not shared by Mr. Marcy. The Nicaraguan minister was received in form, but met with such studied discourtesy from the Secretary of State and his underlings that the cultured and amiable gentleman was glad to return, after a brief sojourn, to the better-mannered society of Nicaragua.

But the fickle conduct of President Pierce and his cabinet had exposed the weak joint in Walker's armour to his quick-eyed enemies in Central America and in Europe. The filibuster, so far from having the support of his native country, was apparently without a friend there. English consuls and men-of-war captains saw that they might crush out with impunity this adventurer and restore the supremacy of European influence on the isthmus. All the Servile partisans in the neighbouring states and the disaffected Legitimists of Nicaragua united to expel the foreign element. The Costa Rican consul-general in London wrote to his President, Don Juan Rafael Mora, in a letter which fell into Walker's hands, that the British Government would sell to Costa Rica two thousand army muskets, at a nominal price, for the purpose of "kicking Walker and his associates out of Nicaragua." British friendship was not purely disinterested nor did it proceed solely from hatred of Americans. Seventeen million dollars invested by English capitalists in Costa Rican bonds were the substantial basis of that interest. It is painful to reflect upon the fact that those bonds were afterwards defaulted to the last dollar.

A deputation sent from Nicaragua to negotiate a treaty of peace with Costa Rica was ignominiously expelled the latter country. Guatemala, San Salvador, and Honduras also declined to recognize the new administration.

On the 26th of February, 1856, Costa Rica declared war against Nicaragua, for the expressed purpose of driving the foreign invaders from the soil of Central America. Distant Peru sympathized with the crusaders by advancing a loan of $150,000 to aid the righteous campaign. President Mora at once collected a force of nine thousand men, and prepared to march on Guanacaste. A counter declaration of war was immediately issued by President Rivas. Walker, as general-in-chief, summoned his men to meet him on the plaza of Granada, and, having had the proclamation of hostilities read to them, made a stirring address, concluding with a peroration well suited to his hearers: "We have sent them the olive branch; they have sent us back the knife. Be it so. We shall give them war to the knife, and the knife to the hilt."

Unfortunately the officer chosen to lead the advance on Costa Rica proved to be a knife more dangerous to the hand which held than to the breast before it. Colonel Louis Schlessinger was given the command, partly by way of compensation for the ill-treatment which he had received from the Costa Ricans when he went thither as one of the peace commissioners. Another of the commissioners named Arguello had deserted to the enemy. The third, Captain W. A. Sutter, son of the famous discoverer of gold in California, alone showed himself possessed of ability and honesty. Walker was not happy in his choice of civil officers, but it must be remembered that the supply of such material was limited. Heaven-inspired statesmen do not flock to the support of a cause so dangerous and and unpromising as his.

If Schlessinger was a poor diplomat, he was a worse soldier. Starting with a force of two hundred men, he crossed the border of Guanacaste on the 19th of March. Five companies, of forty men each, had been divided, according to their nationalities or origin, into a French company, under Captain Legaye, a German under Prange, a New Orleans under Thorpe, a New York under Creighton, and a Californian under Rudler. The American companies comprised men of every English-speaking nation, "blown from the four parts of the earth." This division, which a skilful commander might have turned to account by exciting a generous rivalry, was but a source of weakness in the hands of the incapable Schlessinger, himself a foreigner and little popular with his men.

Their first and only engagement occurred at the Hacienda of Santa Rosa, twelve miles within the boundary of Guanacaste. Schlessinger allowed himself to be surprised, the enemy under a skilful officer, the Prussian Baron von Bulow, attacking him with a force of five hundred regulars, and winning an easy victory. Schlessinger did not even make a show of resistance, but ran away at the first shot, followed by the German and French companies. Captain Rudler and Major O'Neill made a brave stand with the New York and California companies, until some fifty of their command were killed, when the survivors made the best of their way off the field and across the border. Only a poor drummer-boy remained beating his drum with childish glee until shot down at his post. The wounded and the prisoners were all put to death by order of President Mora, who had proclaimed no quarter to every filibuster taken in arms. So ended the battle of Santa Rosa, on the 20th of March.

Schlessinger was court-marshalled on his return, found guilty of cowardice, and sentenced to death, but he escaped punishment by breaking his parole during the trial and fleeing to Costa Rica. More than twenty years afterwards he reappears in the courts of that country, claiming reward for the service rendered the state on the occasion just narrated.

The heterogeneous character of the filibusters, even at this early date, may be seen from a list of the prisoners butchered after the battle of Santa Rosa, of whom six were natives of the United States, three of Ireland, three of Germany, one of Italy, one of Corfu, one of Samos, one of France, two of Prussia, and one of Panama.

So unexpected was the rout that the victors, fearing a ruse, did not pursue their advantage. The demoralized fugitives returned in straggling parties, some without arms, some in rags, and all crest-fallen and disgraced. To cover their shame they exaggerated the numbers and prowess of the enemy, who, indeed, had behaved with great skill and courage, proving a formidable foe when well led.

For some days a panic prevailed in the Democratic headquarters. Matters were in a critical condition. The Legitimists in the State, always secretly disaffected, hastened to spread the news of the defeat among their friends in the North. Honduras and the neighbouring republics grew firmer in their refusal to recognize the Rivas Government, and Guardiola began to mass his savage troops on the border of Leon. The demoralization spread among the Americans themselves. Faint-hearted officers, erstwhile thirsting for glory, suddenly began to long for a return home, and to send in applications for furlough. Walker lay tossing on a bed of fever, the while his enemies conspired against him and fair-weather friends deserted him. But he had many a stout heart among his trusty veterans, men who welcomed danger as a gambler courts his risks, and who bade good-bye to their shrinking comrades with a fine scorn worthy of Pizarro's old lieutenant, Carvajal, who sang:

> "The wind blows the hairs off my head, mother—
> Two by two it blows them away."

Another misfortune at this moment overtook the adventurers. The steamers of the Transit Company were suddenly withdrawn, and all communication with California was suspended. Though it stopped desertion, this isolation also cut off the coming of recruits. This action of the company was the result of a misunderstanding of long date. By the terms of its charter it was bound to pay to the Government of Nicaragua ten thousand dollars annually, and 10 per cent. of its net profits. The company claimed, and the Government denied, that the ten thousand dollars had been paid with some regularity; but by a process of bookkeeping, well known to financiers, the accounts never showed a balance of net profit upon which to levy the additional tithe. Against this deception the weak and ephemeral administrations of Nicaragua had at times feebly protested. The agents of the company bullied, deceived, or bribed them into silence, and went on reaping a golden harvest, until the installation of the Rivas administration. Cornelius Vanderbilt was then managing the company's affairs in New York, while its Western business was conducted by Morgan and Garrison at San Francisco. Vanderbilt, a man of boundless ambition and no weak scruples, soon made himself master of the company's resources. Nicaragua had never challenged the Wall Street autocrat until Walker took the country's affairs in hand. One of his first steps was the appointment of a commission to examine the Transit Company's books. The commission reported that the Government had been defrauded flagrantly and systematically for years, and that a balance, amounting to over $250,000 was lawfully due to it. Vanderbilt peremptorily declined either to acknowledge or liquidate the debt, repeating the vague threats with which he had been used to awe the little officials of former days.

Thereupon the ex-lawyer of California simply directed the authorities to seize the company's property as security, revoking at the same time the old charter and granting a new one to Messrs. Randolph and Crittenden. This occurred on the 18th of February. The last act of the old company had been the transportation of two hundred and fifty recruits from San Francisco, the draft for whose passage money was paid by Vanderbilt, some days afterwards, while he was yet ignorant of the sequestration of his property. The Wall Street dictator was very angry, but bided his time and quietly despatched a draft for a much larger sum, payable to the order of Juan Rafael Mora, President of Costa Rica. He then made a formal protest and appeal to Secretary Marcy, invoking the help of the United States. Marcy, however, was too old a politician to identify himself openly with the unsavoury interests of the Transit Company, a corporation whose history is summed up by Minister Squier, as "an infamous career of deception and fraud." He quieted his friend Vanderbilt with promises which were only too well kept. The vengeance of the money king was not contented with abetting Walker's enemies. Nothing short of the filibuster's ruin would suffice to soothe the wounded pride of Vanderbilt. The man of millions was no mean power in affairs commercial and political at home. When he undertook to use his resources against an almost penniless adventurer abroad, the might of money proved to be all but omnipotent.

In December Kewen was sent to California to dispose of a million dollars' worth of the bonds of the State of Nicaragua. He was instructed to sell no bonds below a minimum of 90 per cent. of the face value, and it does not appear that he did dispose of any below that price—few, indeed—at or above it.

Another feature of a stable government appeared about this time. In the early Spanish invasions the outward adjuncts of religion always followed in the wake of the army. It was in keeping with the changed condition of affairs that the printing-press should accompany the filibuster. Two newspapers were already in full play in Nicaragua. *El Nicaraguense*, of Granada, and the *Herald*, of Masaya. Like the occasionally militant churchmen of Ferdinand, the editors and printers of Nicaragua were not strictly men of peace, but were wont, when occasion served, to exchange the pen for the sword. On this account their war despatches ought to have been most authentic, being commonly written and published on the field. John Tabor, the editor and proprietor of *El Nicaraguense*, was twice wounded in the pursuit of his novel duties, but lived to accompany Walker on his second invasion, in 1857, when, alas! his ready press was not called upon to chronicle any glorious victories.

CHAPTER XI.

The Costa Ricans invade Nicaragua—Second battle of Rivas—The enemy meet a new foe—Rivas orders an election—Walker a candidate—Treason of Rivas—Murder of Estrada—Coalition of the Northern States against Nicaragua—Walker chosen President—Inauguration and recognition by the United States minister—Tradition of the "Gray-eyed Man."

WALKER was less concerned about his enemies in the United States than those nearer home, though he never committed the mistake of undervaluing a dangerous foe or the weakness of forgiving him. Three thousand Costa Ricans had crossed the border and overrun the southern part of Rivas. It was no time for fever of body or mind. Walker arose from his bed and summoned his forces to strike a vigorous blow for his rights. Rivas, the President, was at Leon, watching and waiting; he had placed the southern departments under martial law, and given absolute power to the commander-in-chief. Walker no longer opposed the enemy's march on Rivas, as his object in holding the Transit had been lost with the withdrawal of the steamers. All the American troops at Rivas and Virgin Bay were accordingly removed to Granada, with the ostensible purpose of retreating at once to Leon. When the enemy entered Virgin Bay they found there only the native inhabitants and a few foreign *employés* of the Transit Company. Without a word of warning, they opened fire on the latter, killing some nine or ten unarmed servants of Mr. Vanderbilt, and with a zeal for which that gentleman would have been far from grateful, burned all of the company's property in wharves and warehouses which they could find. After completing the work of destruction, they marched to Rivas, where President Mora took up his abode and cautiously awaited the movements of Walker. The latter kept his counsel so well that no one knew whether he intended retreating to Leon or abandoning the country entirely. The latter course seemed the more probable, as the lake steamer, *San Carlos*, had been for some days engaged in carrying men and munition across the lake and down the river to Forts San Carlos and Castillo Viejo. A sidelight was thrown on these movements, when Lieutenant Green, with only fifteen men, surprised a Costa Rica force of two hundred at the mouth of the Serapiqui, killing twenty-seven of them and putting the rest to flight.

At last, on the morning of April 9th, Walker rode out of Granada at the head of five hundred men, four-fifths of them Americans, and pressed rapidly southward towards Rivas, where Mora lay encamped, with Prussian von Bulow and three thousand regulars. There were several English, French, and Germans acting with the Costa Ricans, some as volunteers and many as mercenaries. At eight o'clock, on the morning of the 11th, Walker's forces entered Rivas in four detachments by as many different routes. The order of battle was that of a simultaneous assault, the several detachments to unite at the centre of the town. It was faithfully carried out, although the Costa Ricans, soon recovering from their surprise, behaved gallantly, using their firearms with precision and coolness, and picking off the American leaders with fatal accuracy. The combat lasted through four hours. At its termination Walker had gained possession of the plaza and cathedral, but at a cost of fifty killed and wounded. About two hundred of the enemy were killed and twice as many wounded. They were receiving reinforcements, but did not venture from behind their adobe walls to renew the contest. Setting fire to the houses near the plaza, they kept up a desultory sharp-shooting from the adjacent buildings. The Americans improvised a temporary hospital within the cathedral, whence at daybreak the wounded were deported, well guarded by their comrades. Mora did not oppose their departure, being well content to be rid of his troublesome visitors.

Walker's loss in officers was severe. Early in the fight Colonel Machado, commanding the native soldiers, fell mortally wounded. Five captains and six lieutenants also perished, and there were twelve other officers among the wounded. Of Walker's staff Captain Sutter alone survived. This mortality was due not more to the marksmanship of the enemy than to the reckless courage of the victims, who made it a point of honour to volunteer for every desperate adventure. Ten of them at one time had charged, armed only with revolvers, on a barricade, whence they dislodged over a hundred of the enemy's riflemen.

By this time the aspect of affairs had changed materially, and the situation of the invading army had become extremely perilous. The Legitimists, whom Mora had expected to unite with him in expelling the American usurpers, he found to be few and faint of heart, while the wanton insolence of his own men had tended to alienate whatever of sympathy they might have found among the poorer classes. In a word, the repulse of Walker at Rivas, if that can be called a repulse which was an unhindered withdrawal, was to Mora the signal of defeat. Unable to conquer an enemy of one-sixth his strength, and not daring to lessen his odds in the hazard of a pitched battle—much less in a siege of Granada—he lay at Rivas exhausted and impotent. It needed but one other enemy to complete his overthrow. That enemy, always a potent one beneath the tropic sun, appeared.

The bodies of two hundred Costa Ricans had been thrust heedlessly into the vaults and wells of Rivas, along with some fifty dead filibusters. Hundreds more lay in the wretched hospitals, with festering wounds and scant nursing. Cleanliness and good living did not distinguish the Costa Rican soldier. A strict discipline was maintained, but one day an Enemy passed the outpost, unchallenged of the watchful sentinel. The patrol crying "Alerté!" was stricken dead by a silent hand. The soldier at the *monte* table, the officer in his hammock, the camp follower in the slums, and the staff-officer in the palace—all ages, all ranks, all valour succumbed before the dread foe. The Cholera was in Rivas, that malady more terrible than a legion of filibusters. With the cholera, desertion. President Mora set the example, news of trouble at home hastening his flight southward. General Cañas remained in command until he heard of the arrival at Granada of some hundreds of recruits, whom the veteran Hornsby had gathered in the United States and brought to the country by way of the river San Juan.

Anticipating justly that Walker would soon resume an offensive attitude, Cañas hastily abandoned his wounded and fled to Guanacaste. The march thither was long and painful; the fugitives could be traced for leagues by the bones of their dead comrades. Whom the cholera struck down no brotherly hand stayed to lift up. About five hundred worn stragglers entered Costa Rica, the remnant of the gallant host that had marched forth to drive the filibusters into the sea. With them they carried the seeds of the pestilence, which being sown broadcast in the country, swept off ten thousand of its inhabitants.

Nor was Walker exempt from trouble during this period. Many of his most cherished friends were carried off by the plague, among others his young brother, James, whom he loved, in his undemonstrative way, very tenderly. The condition of political affairs was unsatisfactory. President Rivas, who had remained with his cabinet at Leon, seems to have dreaded an invasion from the North more than he did that of the Costa Ricans. He was a weak man, easily played upon by designing persons who had succeeded in imbuing him with a jealousy of Walker, which, so far at least, was entirely groundless. The north-eastern districts of the State had been for some time harassed by roving bands of freebooters, pretended and real Legitimists, whose depredations become a serious annoyance. Against these guerillas Walker sent a body of cavalry, under Domingo Goicouria, who speedily restored order in the district.*

An election for President held in May had been conducted with such irregularity that it was decided by President Rivas to order one to be held anew in June. In this decision the opposing candidates, Salazar and Jerez, acquiesced. Both of them were, like Rivas, of the Leonese, or Liberal party; so the Granadinos, or Legitimists, dreading the influence of their rivals, cast about them for a strong candidate to represent their interests. No Legitimist of sufficient popularity being available, they chose Walker, preferring a neutral foreigner to a hostile countryman. It was therefore understood, in political parlance, that Walker was the "first choice" of the still powerful Legitimist party. The effect was at once to unite the opposing Leonese leaders. Rivas, supported by Salazar and Jerez, delayed issuing the call for a new election, and entertained with favour the suggestion that the American auxiliaries be reduced to the number of two hundred, at the very time when that number of new recruits were disembarking from the California steamer. The steamers had resumed their trips under the management of a company favourable to "immigration."

Walker proceeded to Leon to confer with Rivas, receiving on the way a popular ovation which encouraged him to maintain his rights with firmness. To the proposition of

* Goicouria was a devoted Cuban patriot, who was executed many years afterwards by the Spaniards at Havana.

disbanding his forces he replied that the men were ready to leave the country as soon as they should receive their stipulated pay, a claim which he knew that the Government exchequer was in no condition to defray. Not to embarrass the resources of the republic, however, he arrested Don Salazar on a charge of having defrauded the Government of the duties upon some valuable Brazil wood, and of having sold the same wood to the Government, with a profit to himself seldom overlooked by contractors. The act was an offence against an old and seldom enforced law of the country. The arrest was doubtless meant to warn Salazar that he could not conspire with impunity against his vigilant ally, as he was not immediately brought to trial. Rivas, Jerez, and Salazar now decided to pronounce against their formidable rival, but with native duplicity they concealed their design, the President, on the 10th of June, issuing a decree for a general election to take place on the fourth Sunday of the month. Next day Walker departed for Granada, and Rivas and Salazar immediately fled from Leon, proclaiming that Walker was a traitor. They took refuge in Guatemala, where General Carrera was preparing a force with which to invade Nicaragua.

Walker, as general in chief of a state disturbed by a revolution within and threatened with invasion from without, was, of course, the head of the government in the absence of the civil ruler. At least, there was nobody to dispute that proposition. He accordingly appointed a provisional director, Don Firmin Ferrer, pending the election which was to occur in a few weeks.

In the election, when it was held, all the districts took part except the north-eastern, which was disturbed by the presence of an invading army on its border and two pretenders to the presidency within its precincts. One of them was Rivas; the other the almost forgotten Legitimist puppet of Corral, Don Jose Estrada. Estrada did little of an official character save issue proclamations which nobody heeded; still, as a pretender is always a potential element in monarchy or republic, whom a cunning invader might use to his own advantage, the partisans of Rivas feared to leave to Carrera that poor excuse for betraying their interests. Estrada was murdered in cold blood by a band of ruffians from Leon. With him perished the last of the strictly Legitimist claimants. To further insure their personal interests, Rivas and his friends appointed General Ramon Belloso commander-in-chief of the army of invasion. The allied forces were from Guatemala, Honduras, and San Salvador, and it was from the last and smallest state that it was deemed wise to choose the commander, as the one least likely or able to usurp power after victory.

The lack of representation in the election of the north-eastern district was of little consequence, as it was the least populous part of the state, and its vote would have had no influence to change the result. The voting was entirely free and unaccompanied by disturbance. In Nicaragua every male inhabitant over eighteen years old, criminals excepted, is entitled to the suffrage. Representatives, senators, and president, are all chosen by a college of electors who are themselves elected by popular vote. Such, at least, was the law at this period.

When the votes were counted it was found that 23,236 ballots had been cast, of which Walker had received more than twice as many as all his rivals, viz., 15,835, Rivas having 867, Salazar 2,087, and Ferrer 4,447. Walker was accordingly declared elected, and, on the 12th of July, 1856, he was formally inaugurated President of Nicaragua. It is worth noting that he was chosen by the largest vote ever polled in the country, and that his actual tenure of office was longer than that of any of his predecessors in the presidency with the exception of two, Pineda and Chamorro. The former held office for four months—the latter for one month—longer than did Walker. In six years there had been no less than fifteen presidents inaugurated. Reform, even through filibusterism, was sadly needed in Nicaragua.

So far as legality was concerned, Walker's title was as sound as that of any prince or president in the world. It only remained for the world to acknowledge it. The first recognition came, unwittingly enough, from his enemy, Secretary Marcy. That statesman, after much consideration of the case, had sent instructions to the United States minister, Colonel Wheeler, whose suspension had been but temporary, to recognize the existing government of Nicaragua, under the supposition that the Rivas administration still held office. Thus much had been conceded to the reasonable demands of Padre Vijil. Mr. Wheeler, with a possible appreciation of the humour of the situation, yet with a strict obedience to the letter of his instructions, thereupon tendered to President Walker the good wishes and felicitations of the United States Government. But Mr. Marcy never forgave the instrument of his blunder, and one of his last official acts was to beg of President Pierce, as a personal favour, the dismissal of Minister Wheeler, a request which the dying administration was contemptible enough to grant.

We now behold Walker at the zenith of his fame, the lawful ruler of a country whose position and resources made it a prize worth the ambition of all Europe and America to possess. Besides a powerful native party, he had an army of his countrymen at his back numbering over a thousand men, a line of steamers under his control —for the California agents of the Transit Company were his friends as long as their interests and his were the same—and a strong party in the United States in sympathy with his cherished project for the extension of slavery. The tradition vouched for by Crowe in his "Gospel in Central America," as current among the Indians of Nicaragua—"that a grey-eyed man would come from the far North to overturn the Spanish domination and regenerate the native race"—seemed likely to be confirmed, in part, at least.

The ceremony of inaugurating the new President was performed with great pomp at the capital on the 12th of July. The acting provisional director, Don Firmin Ferrer, administered the oath of office, Walker kneeling to make the solemn affirmation. The President-elect was dressed in his customary civilian costume of decorous black, in manner and attire a striking contrast to the gaily decked natives who flocked to the ceremony. The inauguration was celebrated on a large staging erected in the plaza, which was festooned with the flags of Nicaragua, the United States, France, and the unborn republic of Cuba. The text of the oath which Ferrer administered, with a highly eulogistic address, was as follows:

"You solemnly promise and swear to govern the free Republic of Nicaragua, and sustain its independent and territorial integrity with all your power, and to execute justice according to the principles of republicanism and religion."

"I promise and swear."

"You promise and swear, whenever it may be in your power, to maintain the law of God, the true profession of the Evangelists, and the religion of the Crucifixion."

"I promise and swear."

"In the name of God and the sainted Evangelists, you swear to comply with these obligations and to make it your constant guard to fulfil all that is herein promised."

"I swear."

"And for this the succession is committed to you firmly, by these presents, by authority of the Secretary of the Government charged with the general despatches."

At the end of this ceremony Walker delivered an inaugural address of the usual character pertaining to such prosaic compositions. The President was not without hopes of establishing friendly relations with the Great Powers, and among his first acts was the sending of ministers to England and France. The envoys either never reached the fields of their missions or failed to receive official recognition, as the Blue-books of those governments make no mention of diplomatic intercourse between the filibuster cabinet and their own. The nations of Europe, in their blind jealousy of American influence, would, or could not, understand that the aims of Walker were, if successful, likely to prove an unsurmountable obstacle to the very American expansion which they feared. To build up a strong confederacy of slave states, which should antagonize the powerful free states of the North, was the prime, if not the sole, object which won for Walker the sympathy and aid of the Southern States. By opposing and frustrating this scheme, Great Britain unwittingly lent herself to the service of the party of union in the United States, thereby weakening the cause which she afterwards favoured, of Southern secession.

The shrewd English observer, Laurence Oliphant, writing, in 1860, his personal recollections of "Patriots and Filibusters," shows the mistake into which his Government fell, as he frankly says, through "no mere considerations of morality," but through a mistaken notion of self-interest. Walker never intended that Central America should become a part of the Union. Like Aaron Burr, he wished to keep all the fruits of conquest for his personal glory and aggrandisement; but he was sincere in representing to his countrymen that the effects of establishing a powerful slave empire south of the United States would be of incalculable advantage to the pro-slavery party at home.

CHAPTER XII.

Administration of President Walker—The Allies advance towards Granada—Naval victory—Review of the filibuster army—Filibusters and their allies—Assault on Masaya—Civil government—The slavery decree—Antiquated logic.

WALKER wisely gave the most important places in his cabinet to his native adherents. His faithful friends, Don Firmin Ferrer and Mateo Pineda, were appointed respectively Ministers of Foreign Affairs and of War. Don Mannel Carascossa received the Treasury portfolio, and that of Hacienda was given to the Cuban, Don Domingo Goicouria. Hundreds of recruits continued to pour in from California and the Atlantic states. In the Northern departments the Allies also received strong reinforcements, and by the 1st of July they had undisturbed possession of Leon, whence they soon spread over the country, annoying the foraging parties sent out of Granada to collect cattle in the district of Chontales. A detachment of cavalry which Walker sent against them was repulsed near the river Tipitapa, and one of the leaders, Byron Cole, was slain. Cole was the early friend of Walker, and the negotiator of the contract under which the filibusters had come to Nicaragua. Belloso, reinforced by a strong body under command of General Martinez, was now emboldened to advance to Masaya, which he fortified and made the base of operation against Granada, fifteen miles distant.

Xatruch, Jerez, and Zavala were acting with the enemies of their country. Rivas was of little importance among his dubious friends. Salazar, who had been so prominent in inciting the invasion, was captured on the coast of Nicaragua by Lieutenant Fayssoux, and carried a prisoner to Granada, where he was tried for treason, found guilty, and executed.

Fayssoux, the only commander in the navy of the ephemeral republic, was a splendid specimen of the sailor-filibuster. A native of Louisiana, he had seen service in Cuba with Lopez and Pickett. Walker, having confiscated the schooner *San Jose* for carrying a false register, had her fitted out with some guns and placed her under the command of Fayssoux. Her first exploit was an engagement with the Costa Rican brig, *Once de Abril*, carrying thrice the armament and six times the crew of the *Granada*, as the *San Jose* was now christened. The Costa Rican was blown out of the water after a two-hours' fight, and the *Granada* remained mistress of the Pacific waters until a heavier antagonist came upon the scene.

The position of the Allies at Masaya was well chosen. It is an eagle's nest, hung high a thousand feet, on the crest of a volcanic upheaval. Half-way down its sides lies the Lake of Masaya, imprisoned within its walls of adamant. To the south lies the lava desert, well named "the Hell of Masaya," barring the road from Granada.

Belloso from his eyrie was wont to swoop down on detached parties of foraging filibusters, or to strike with quick and deadly blow the solitary hamlets whose people might be suspected of a leaning towards the liberal cause. Walker did not need control of the northern districts, and would have been content to leave Masaya and its barren crags in undisturbed possession of Belloso's rough riders, but for the daily waspish annoyance to his foragers and the loss of prestige in the eyes of the conquered Leonese. Characteristically he chose the bold plan of attacking the enemy in his stronghold,

FILIBUSTER'S FLAG, SEPT. 27, 1856.

regardless of the enormous odds against him. At the head of only eight hundred men he rode out of Granada, on the morning of October 11th, and took the high road for Masaya.

There was a gallant review of the little army, proud in the bravery of new uniforms and waving banners, and under the eyes of wives, sisters, and sweethearts, of whom not a few had followed the flag down to the seat of war. For the filibusters had "come to stay," they boasted. What further ambition they dreamed may not be known; but something was hinted in the device upon the flag of the First Rifle battalion, the corps of one-legged Colonel Sanders, a grim and hard-fighting old colonel withal. It bore, in place of the old-time five volcanoes and pious legend, the filibuster's five-pointed red star, and the motto, in sword-cut Saxon, "Five or None"—a hint to the allied states of new and stronger alliance yet to be.

The march was leisurely and uninterrupted. By ten o'clock at night they halted near the suburbs of Masaya, threw out pickets, and went into camp. It was a glorious tropical night. The early evening had been misty, but night fell without the laggard twilight of temperate zones, and the full moon shone in all her splendour upon a scene worthy the pencil of Salvator Rosa. Before the filibusters' bivouac lay the Lake of Masaya, reflecting the watch-fires of the town. In the distance rose the towering cone of Mount Masaya, clouded in dense volumes of smoke, and grandly indifferent to the puny preparations of the insects about to bring their mimic thunders into play on the morrow. The filibusters lay in groups around their fires, the very flower and perfection of that lost race called the "49-ers." They smoked their pipes tranquilly; they took an occasional sip of *aguardiente*—but it was a temperate potation, for the General was at hand, and woebetide the luckless wretch who unfitted himself for duty in that dread presence on the eve of battle.

They talked of the past much, of the present little, and of the future not at all, save in connection with mining prospects. For it was a religious belief with those queer adventurers that in coming to Nicaragua they had been governed by a marvellous inspiration of good sense. It was to them a question of practical business, they believed; and if its pursuit involved a little incidental fighting, why, that was to be reckoned among the taxes to fortune. Hence they had not wasted their hours in Nicaragua, but had diligently, as their duties would allow, visited every rivulet and hill, and talked knowingly of "indications," and "colour," and other technical lore. Regarding themselves as industrious, if rather enterprising, men of business, they would have resented any intimation of romance or recklessness in their present occupation.

They spoke in a short, terse way which it was the despair of their allies to understand. Ollendorf had furnished the Spanish student with no equivalent for the wondrous vocabulary of California. The Nicaraguan, who uses not over one-fifth of the words in his glorious Castilian inheritance, was at the verbal mercy of the man who possessed a whole mine of phrases unknown to the lexicographers, and who pitied with a fine scorn the ignorant wretch, native or foreign, who knew not the *patois* of the mining camp. He even improved upon the language of the country, when he condescended to use it, changing such household words as "nigua" or "jigua," into the more expressive "jigger," nor omitting to prefix it with the Anglo-Saxon shibboleth known to all mankind—the watchword which, hundreds of years ago, gave to English soldiers in foreign towns the charming sobriquet of the "Goddams." The prefix was not inapt, for the "jigger" is the most pestiferous parasite of all his race, and a living thorn in the flesh of his victim. Spanish verbs, like "buscar," "pasear," &c., masqueraded with English terminals and marvellous compound tenses, a wonder of philology. Nor did the sonorous native names come forth unrefined from the furnace of California speech. "Don Jose de Machuca y Mendoza" was a style of nomenclature altogether too lofty for democratic tongues, which found it easier and much more sociable to pronounce "Greaser Joe." Whatever was to come of the incongruous alliance, for the present there was a touch of nature, a community of courage, which made the parties kin in thought and action. The native, whether friend or foe, was no coward. In endurance he was the peer of his northern rival, though he lacked the physical strength and wild hardihood of the pioneer. The bivouac before Masaya was but one of a score of such.

The enemy, who had kept up a desultory firing through the night, appeared in force at daybreak a few hundred yards away. Walker began the engagement by a general advance on the town under cover of a well-directed fire from his battery of howitzers. In a short time the First Rifles had driven the enemy out of the main plaza, which was immediately occupied by the whole force of the assailants. The position was excellent as far as it went, but the enemy still held two other plazas and the intervening houses, and to dislodge them would have entailed a heavier loss of life than could be afforded. The artillery was accordingly brought up, and sappers were detailed to cut passages through the adobe house walls. Slowly but steadily the work proceeded, the besieging lines converging towards the enemy's stronghold. The day was thus consumed in engineering, with an occasional skirmish in the narrow streets.

While the combatants lay on their arms that night awaiting the morrow which was to see the city in the possession of the invaders, what was happening in Granada? Zavala and eight hundred swarthy Serviles, making a forced march from Diriomio, had entered the Jalteva at noon of the 12th. A scant garrison of a hundred and fifty men, mostly invalids, was all that remained to oppose them; and Zavala, feeling sure of an easy victory, divided his forces so as to surround the little band. The latter were distributed in the church, armoury, and hospital, whither also repaired all the civilians who could, having little confidence in the security of their neutral position. General Fry, commanding the garrison, hastily prepared for a desperate resistance. He had two or three field pieces, which were placed to best advantage and managed by Captain Siringle, an ingenious experimenter, with an enterprising eye to church bells and such raw material.

Zavala found himself, to his great astonishment, repulsed at every point after several hours' hard fighting. In his rage, he wreaked vengeance on the neutral residents who had trusted to the peacefulness of their character or the protection of their government rather than to the rifles of the filibuster garrison. The American minister's house was assaulted, though unsuccessfully. Three of his countrymen, a merchant and a couple of missionaries, were murdered in cold blood. Padre Rossiter, the army chaplain, knew his countrymen, and boldly took up a musket in defence of his life, as did also Judge Basye of the Supreme Court. Honest Padre Vijil took a middle course by discreetly flying to the swamp until the storm was over. Nor did the civilizing mission of the worthy editor of *El Nicaraguense* prevent him from seeking liberty under the sword. He went back to his desk, the wiser for a broken thigh.

So for twenty-one long hours the siege lasted, while recruits flocked to the side of the assailants, and the little garrison struggled bravely against the fearful odds. To the threats and the promises alike of the enemy they returned but defiances and the cry, "Americans never surrender!" Renegade Harper, acting as interpreter, assured them that Walker had been annihilated at Masaya, and that Belloso, with four thousand men, was on the road to Granada. No quarter was the penalty if they delayed longer to surrender. But they did delay. The hospital patients limped to the windows and rested their rifles there. The women and children stood by to supply them with cartridges. At night a courier was despatched in hot haste to Masaya. Eluding the enemy's pickets, he made his way along the road, only to meet the advance guard of Walker's returning forces. The news of Zavala's movement had already reached Masaya, putting the loyalty of an ambitious soldier to as severe a test as well might be. To abandon his assured victory for the safety of a hundred or two non-combatants was something of a sacrifice, but Walker did not hesitate a moment. The sacred ties of comradeship were strong in the hearts of those wild men, who, almost without awaiting the word of command, took up the march for Granada.

In a few hours they arrived in the Jalteva, where they were confronted and for a time repulsed by a strong battery placed to bar the way, and well handled by the enemy. The advance guard fell back, as well they might, for the position was skilfully chosen for the defence of a narrow roadway. In the moment of confusion Walker rode up, and pointing to the Lone Star flag which still floated over the church, called for volunteers to succour their beleaguered comrades. The response was a cheer and a fierce charge, led by the commander in person, before which the enemy was scattered like chaff. Following up this advantage, the Americans moved upon the plaza before the church, where stood Zavala and his forces, now themselves on the defensive. But the intrepid resistance of the garrison, followed by the capture of the battery, had utterly demoralized the Serviles, who scarcely struck a blow in their own defence. In mad panic they fled through the city, only to be met in the suburbs by a detachment placed to intercept them.

Barely half of Zavala's army escaped capture or death. Masaya had not been taken, but Walker had achieved a greater victory and inflicted a heavy loss upon the allies. Four hundred of them had fallen in the battle of Masaya, and an equally large number was supposed to have perished before Granada. Walker's loss was less than a hundred killed and wounded in both engagements. Lieutenant-colonel Lainé, a young Cuban aid of the general, was made prisoner at Masaya and shot by his captors, who refused an exchange. Walker was so incensed at this, that, in reprisal, he had two of his prisoners, a colonel and a captain, shot next day, and sent word to Belloso that a heavier reckoning would follow any future acts of atrocity.

With those engagements active hostilities ended for a time. The enemy grew more wary in his movements.

Civil government had not been neglected during the prosecution of military enterprises. An elaborate revision of the constitution and laws of the country was perfected; changes of a most serious nature being introduced. Walker reviews with complacency the laws of his government, especially those affecting the rights of property and the more vital right of liberty. Whether we look with approval or blame upon his course up to this point, it is impossible to excuse acts which in his eyes were not only just but even praiseworthy. A law was passed making "all documents connected with public affairs equally valuable, whether written in Spanish or in English." The American residents who knew both languages could here find an opportunity of outwitting the natives with the purpose, which Walker commends, of having the "ownership of the lands of the state fall into the hands of those speaking English." To further the same end, the military scrip of the republic was made receivable for Government lands sold under forfeit. Still further to aid the same purpose, he passed a law requiring a registry of all deeds; a thing heretofore unknown in the country, as "it gave an advantage to those familiar with the habit of registry." The Spaniards of California have had reason to regret that familiarity in their American neighbours. There is no pretence in all these acts of any higher or worthier purpose than that avowed by their author, viz., the practical confiscation of the lands of the Government for the benefit of his adherents. Finally, on the 22nd of September, "the President of the Republic of Nicaragua, in virtue of the power in him vested," decreed that "Inasmuch as the act of the Constituent Assembly, decreed on the 30th of April, 1838, provides that the Federal decrees given previous to that date shall remain in force, unless contrary to the provisions of that Act; and inasmuch as many of the decrees heretofore given are unsuited to the present condition of the country, and are repugnant to its welfare and prosperity as well as to its territorial integrity; therefore:—

"Article I. All acts and decrees of the Federal Constituent Assembly, as well as of the Federal Congress are declared null and void.

"Article 2. Nothing herein contained shall affect rights heretofore vested under the acts and decrees hereby repealed."

The principal decree which this was intended to repeal was an Act of the Federal Constituent Assembly of the 17th of April, 1824, abolishing slavery and indemnifying the slave-owners in the then confederated states of Central America.

Thus the institution of slavery, without any restriction, was reimposed on Nicaragua. Walker, so far from denying that this was the object of the decree, expressly avows it, saying, "By this Act must the Walker administration be judged. If the slavery decree, as it has been called, was unwise, Cabañas and Jerez were right when they sought to use the Americans for the mere purpose of raising one native faction and depressing another. Without such labour as the new decree gave, the Americans could have played no other part in Central America than that of the Pretorian guard at Rome or of the Janizaries in the East, and for such degrading service as this they were ill suited by the habits and traditions of their race." He admits that annexation to the United States was no part of the programme of the American adventurers in Nicaragua, knowing that it could not be constitutionally effected after the passage of a slavery law.

To-day it seems strange to read such arguments as Walker used to defend the institution of slavery. But by the lurid light of his sentences we can see something of the bitter conflict which then raged between the friends and the enemies of slavery. His contempt for the Abolitionist party speaks in every line, whilst his defence of the now obsolete system of unspeakable wrong seems as puerile as the solemnly sincere essays of a Mather on the evils of witchcraft. He admires the "wisdom and excellence of the Divine economy in the creation of the black race," and the providence of letting Africa lie idle until the discovery of America gave a chance of utilizing the raw material of slavery. No self-appointed theological dragoman to the court of Heaven ever showed more readiness in interpreting the sentiments of Providence than he does when he piously asks, "And is it not thus that one race secures for itself liberty with order, while it bestows on the other comfort and Christianity?"

Did the author of such views look at his subject through a moral single-convex lens which presented every object inverted? Was he colour-blind to right and wrong, or did he wilfully and deliberately present the side which he knew to be ignoble and the opposite of true? He was perfectly sincere. Walker was no worse, and no better, than nine-tenths of his fellow citizens in the Southern States, who honestly believed in the divine right of slave-holding, and testified to their conviction by the willing sacrifice of their blood and treasure. A wrong defeated, dead and buried, is a wrong which becomes visible to the blindest eyes. Whether we, who pass prompt sentence on it, might perceive its enormity so plainly, had the "leaded dice of war" turned up differently, is a speculation as idle as any other on the might-have-beens of history.

The severe punishment inflicted on the allies at Masaya and Granada had the effect of keeping them for a time in check. A few days after those engagements, Walker received a most valuable ally in the person of General Charles Frederic Henningsen, an able officer, who had seen service and achieved distinction in many lands.

CHAPTER XIII.

Henningsen—Early service with Zumalacarregui—Campaigning with the Prophet of the Caucasus—Joins Kossuth—Arrival in America —Omotepe—A gallant defence—Watters carries the barricades.

HENNINGSEN was an Englishman, of Scandinavian descent, with all of the old Norse daring and fire. At the age of nineteen he left his home to take service under Don Carlos, in 1834. He was assigned to duty on the staff of the sturdy old partisan, Zumalacarregui, from whose rough school of war he graduated with the rank of colonel and an honour of nobility, the only rewards left in the power of the Bourbon to bestow. Not so generously did his rival reward the devotion of poor Narciso Lopez, whose valour and wisdom had contributed so much to the defeat of the Carlists; upon him a grateful sovereign seventeen years afterwards conferred the order of the iron collar of the garrote, in the market-place of Havana. Henningsen, on his return to England, published a couple of volumes of personal recollections, which still hold a place in literature. His story was told in a simple and direct style, which showed marked literary ability. But the world was then too full of doing for an active mind to content itself with thinking or saying. Schamyl the Prophet had unfurled his sacred banner, lit the fires of revolution on the Caucasus, and thrown the gauge of battle to the mighty Czar himself. His cause was just enough, his case was desperate enough, to enlist the sympathies of the young English knight-errant, who soon found himself battling beside wild mountaineers in Caucasian snows, and completing the education begun on the vine-clad hills of Spain. That campaign over, he improved his leisure in writing two or three books on Russian life, which increased his literary reputation without inducing him to take up a life of letters. The restraints of civilization were two irksome, and he fled to the wilds of Asia Minor, where the news of Hungary's revolt against Austrian and Russian despotism found him. He arrived on the scene of action too late to take part in anything but the sorrowful ending. Gorgey's treason, if such indeed it were, had turned the scale against the patriots. Henningsen submitted a plan of operations to Kossuth, who decided that it was now too late for offensive action. All that remained was to offer his sword to the forlorn hope. The offer was gladly accepted. He joined Bem in the last ditch at Komorn, aiding not a little in the stout defence of that place.

When the pitiful collapse came, Henningsen was one of the chieftains who were outlawed and had a price set upon their heads. He narrowly escaped capture and its inevitable consequence, death. Once he was saved by the tact of a lady, a relative of Kossuth, who, when the police were searching for a likeness of the fugitive, allowed them to find a portrait of some stranger, upon which she had hastily written the words, "From your friend, C. F. Henningsen." Being questioned, she averred that the likeness was not Henningsen's, but with so much apparent confusion as to make them disbelieve her. Copies of it were accordingly printed and distributed with the hue and cry, to the manifest benefit of the fugitive. Again, upon the very border of Turkey, he was chased so closely by a party of Haynau's bloodhound troop that capture seemed inevitable, and he had prepared a dose of poison, which he always carried with him, to be swallowed at the moment of arrest. His Caucasian experience had taught him that mercy was not to be expected of Cossack victors.

More fortunate than many of his comrades, he managed to elude his foes and escape across the boundary, to join Kossuth. With him he crossed the Atlantic, never to return. In the United States he shared the social and political distinction of his leader.

Henningsen at this period was thirty years old, tall and strikingly handsome, with the polish and breeding of a man of the world and a scholar. In Washington he met and loved a Southern belle, at the time when Southern society ruled in the national capital. The lady, who was a widow, was a niece of Senator Berrien, of Georgia. She returned his affection, and they were married after a brief courtship.

It was a critical period in American politics. It was the reign of King Pierce the Irresolute, to be followed shortly by that of King Buchanan the Unready. Henningsen by his matrimonial alliance was thrown into the society of those who favoured slavery, wherein he imbibed opinions in harmony with the upholders of that institution. The adherents of slavery felt that in the political field they were fighting a losing battle. The more farsighted saw that the success of their cause could be promoted only by "extending the area of freedom," as they phrased it. Thus the filibusters acquired new importance in the eyes of friend and of foe at home.

Henningsen's wife, with the spirit of a Roman matron, acquiesced heroically when her knight volunteered to go forth and do battle for a cause which would have won his sympathy for its very danger alone. His reputation as a soldier was well established. He had introduced the Minié rifle into the United States service, and was an authority upon his speciality, the use of artillery. Nor did he come empty-handed to Nicaragua; but brought with him military stores, arms, and ammunition, to the value of thirty thousand dollars, the contribution of himself and his wife, besides an equally liberal offering from

VOLCANO OF OMOTEPE, VIRGIN BAY.

(After a Pen-and-Ink Sketch.)

George Law and other sympathisers with the cause. Walker immediately placed him on active service, with the rank of brigadier-general.

Henningsen had scarcely assumed his command before he was sent to clear the Transit road of marauding bands of Costa Ricans, a large body of whom had landed at San Juan del Sur, under General Cañas. Henningsen scattered them promptly, and admitted a force of recruits from California, who had arrived on the steamer *Cortes*. The reappearance of the Costa Ricans on the Transit was too dangerous a menace to the communication with the United States, however; and Walker saw that to preserve his case of supplies, and at the same time to garrison the large city of Granada, was a task too serious for his slender forces. But as he did not wish to let the latter important stronghold fall into hostile hands, with the moral and material benefits accruing from the possession of the seat of government, he resolved to destroy the city. Previous to evacuating Granada he made another attack on Masaya, in order that the enemy might remain on the defensive and not suspect his intended movement of retreat southward. A trifling engagement took place, in which the artillery was well handled. On the 19th of November the sick and wounded were transported in the lake steamer to the island of Omotepe, where they were placed in charge of Colonel Fry and a corps of medical attendants.

This island is one of the healthiest places in the country, being a volcanic upheaval, with a mountain towering from its centre to a height of five thousand feet. A few families of native Indian fishermen, rude and savage, are its only inhabitants, and their frail huts dot the margin of the lake. In the interior a dense jungle bars the road to the mountain top. The rank growth of the tropics hides the ruined monuments of a civilization which preceded Conquistador and Aztec. The traveller who cuts his way through the rank vegetation finds himself, here and there, in the presence of quaintly sculptured, hideous idols overturned. In remoter nooks, whither his Indian guide cares not to lead him, he would see the gods whom the Christians threw down, reinstated on their pedestals; and the good folk of Granada say in whispers, that thither, at stated times, flock silent, dusky worshippers, to offer up unholy rites and pray for the return of the gods of their fathers, who fed on human victims, and spoke to their people in the awful accents of the volcano. Little knew or recked the bold filibusters, quarantined beneath the frowning peak of Omotepe, of the alleged idolatrous practices or the evil repute in which the islanders were held by their mainland neighbours. They nursed their wounds with scant patience, recovered, and sought a chance to get new ones, or died and were forgotten, as though their passports to the realm of Death had been viséd by the most legitimate of all lawful war-makers.

Walker, having entrusted to Henningsen the duty of destroying Granada, set out for Rivas. Upon his departure, many of the men and some of the officers, feeling that the severe restraints of discipline were withdrawn, plunged into a wild debauch. Henningsen, with the aid of such as were in decent condition, began the work of firing the town. As the smoke of the burning houses arose in the air the enemy's pickets saw and reported it to General Belloso, who rightly surmised the cause and ordered an immediate attack. The miserable debauchees awoke from their stupor to find that they had aroused a formidable foe. Five thousand furious Serviles were pouring into the city, and had already secured a strong strategic point in church of the Guadaloupe, whence their sharpshooters were keeping in play the useful men whom Henningsen could gather about him.

Under a fierce fire Henningsen continued the work of destruction until almost the entire town was reduced to ashes. His position, encumbered as he was with sick and wounded, was so perilous that he determined to capture the Guadaloupe church at any cost, as that important position commanded the passage to the lake. That end was not attained without the loss of many valuable lives and two days of hard fighting. Finally, on the 27th of November, the church was carried by assault, and all the American force, with their supplies, ammunition, and non-combatants, were safely transferred to the new quarters. A guard of thirty men, detailed to protect the wharf on the lake, three miles away, had been betrayed and captured two days before. Henningsen, in order to secure communication with the lake, began throwing up a line of earthworks along the whole distance, the enemy contesting every inch of the road. To keep the latter in check, Captain Swingle and his howitzers were employed night and day. When ammunition ran short the ingenious gunner made balls from scraps of iron piled in a mould of clay and soldered together with lead.

As soon as they had effected communication with some adobe huts halfway to the lake, Henningsen removed the sick and wounded to the more healthful land near the water. It was none too soon, for over a hundred men had perished from the ravages of cholera and typhus in the crowded quarters of the Guadaloupe. Lieutenant Sumpter with seventy men was left to garrison the church. Meanwhile the enemy had not been idle; they had thrown up earthworks between the lake and Henningsen's defences, and gathered a strong force to prevent the advance of relief from that direction.

For three weeks the unequal fight lasted, until of the four hundred men who had remained to burn Granada, less than one hundred and fifty answered to the roll-call on the 13th of December. To Zavala's demand for their surrender Henningsen sent back word that he would parley only at the cannon's mouth. Their position, nevertheless, was so critical that many of the men talked openly of forsaking their helpless comrades and cutting their way to the lake. Finding that the first sign of such a proceeding would be greeted with a volley of grape, for Henningsen had learned from his chief the way to deal with insubordination, a few of the malcontents deserted to the enemy. The rest imitated the heroic fortitude of their officers, and all shared together their sorry rations of mule and horse meat as long as they lasted. That was not long; they had reached the limit of their supplies on the 12th of December, and Henningsen sent a message to Walker begging immediate relief. A native boy of the Sandwich Islands, who had come to Nicaragua on the *Vesta*, and who was known in the army as "Kanaka John," volunteered to carry the note. It was given to him sealed and enclosed in a bottle. The boy made his way unperceived through the enemy's lines, and reached the water in time to see the lake steamer, *La Virgen*, lying beyond the line of surf, with lights shrouded and not a sign of life on board. The amphibious Kanaka swam out and boarded the steamer, where he found Walker and three or four hundred new recruits from the States.

Colonel John Watters, with a hundred and sixty men, was at once ordered to relieve the beleaguered force under Henningsen. Watters on landing was met by a stout resistance from a large body of Allies guarding the wharf and adjacent earthworks; but the Californians rushed upon the barricade with a yell and carried it by storm. Henningsen heard the distant firing, and, recognizing the sharp note of the American rifle, made a sortie against the nearest post of the enemy. The firing lasted all night, for Belloso was frantic at the thought that the prey for which he had hungered so long was about slipping from his paws. Watters, finding the enemy so strong, made a detour so as to enter Granada by the north-eastern road, and sent a courier to notify Henningsen of his approach. It was daybreak ere the relief reached the city, having carried four strong lines of barricades on the march, and routed thrice their number of Allies. The enemy, as soon as the junction was effected, abandoned further opposition to the retreat of the filibusters and withdrew from the lake road. The evacuation of the Guadaloupe was completed in peace on the morning of December 14, 1856.

When the Allies entered the place they found only a wilderness of smouldering ruins to mark the site of the city beloved by the Serviles and hated by the Leonese. The latter rejoiced secretly, the former mourned aloud, over the loss of the proudest city of the isthmus. In the Plaza they found a scornful souvenir of the destroyer, a lance stuck in the earth and bearing a raw hide, upon which was inscribed the legend, "Aqui fué Granada"—"Here was Granada!"

Three hundred men, including Watters' command, embarked on the lake steamer and sailed to Virgin Bay. Three-fourths of the garrison of Granada had died in the three weeks' siege. The Allies had suffered more severely. Of the six thousand who joined their standard at Masaya only two thousand now remained; but they received new strength in the arrival of General Cañas with the Costa Ricans who, on the appearance of Walker and Henningsen at Virgin Bay, had evacuated Rivas and marched northward. Belloso and Zavala were constrained to turn the command of the Allied forces over to Cañas, as the success of the Costa Ricans in another quarter had given them a moral superiority over their less fortunate friends. The importance of that success can be estimated only by narrating its effect on the fortunes of Walker.

CHAPTER XIV.

Vanderbilt joins issue—Titus outwitted—Siege of Rivas—Death in the Falange—Desertion—Captain Fayssoux and Sir Robert McClure—Battle of San Jorge—Allies assault Rivas—Famine and devotion—Commander Davis as a peacemaker.

PRESIDENT PIERCE had recognized the government of Rivas and Walker, as a cheap concession to the friends of the filibusters in the United States, for president Pierce was looking to a re-nomination in the forthcoming convention. No party so weak but the average Presidential candidate will scatter his bait before it. The nomination was not given him, but it was too late to recall the friendly act. The recognition of Walker's administration was, as we have seen, an accidental courtesy which Mr. Marcy would not hesitate to retract if occasion offered. The friends of Walker saw that to establish his power firmly he must be aided liberally and without delay. The bonds of the republic were accordingly offered for sale, and freely disposed of in many places. Thousands of dollars were collected in the Southern cities and expended in the purchase of munitions of war, and for the transportation of recruits. Every steamer carried out large numbers of enlisted men and consignments of war material. For the former, California could always be relied on, but the latter had to be procured in "the States." Vanderbilt saw a chance to revenge himself by cutting off the base of supplies, and cast about him for an able tool.

He found willing instruments in the persons of Webster

and Spencer, two adventurers of daring character and questionable antecedents. Webster drew up a plan of operations which met the approval of Vanderbilt, and Spencer was entrusted with its execution. This Spencer was a man of good family. His father had been Secretary of War. His brother was hanged for mutiny at the yard-arm of the frigate *Somers* in 1842, the only American officer who ever achieved that infamy. Spencer went to San Jose, the capital of Costa Rica, whence he set out, with one hundred and twenty picked men, for the head waters of the River San Carlos, which flows into the San Juan. Arrived there, they constructed rafts and floated down to the mouth of the Serapiqui. There they surprised a force of Americans, and continuing the descent to San Juan del Norte, soon made themselves masters of the Transit Company's steamers. With them and a reinforcement of eight hundred Costa Ricans, commanded by a brother of President Mora, they speedily captured all the fortified positions on the river and both of the lake steamers. Lake and river being thus secured, it only remained for Mora to cross the district of Chontales and effect a junction with the Allies at Granada.

The enemy had effectually cut off Walker's communication with the Atlantic states. California remained open to him just so long as the agents of the line in San Francisco, whose friendship for him was, of course, secondary to their self-interest, should consider it profitable to continue running their steamers.

Vanderbilt had triumphed. We may anticipate events so far as to say that President Mora's indebtedness to the Wall Street magnate taught him respect for the absolute power of money. But ere many years his confidence in another rich friend was repaid by treachery, which drove him from power into exile, disgrace, and death. Eighteen days after the execution of Walker at Trujillo, Juan Rafael

Mora and General Cañas perished by the fusillade, after an abortive attempt to regain their lost power. It is recorded of the wealthy ingrate who had betrayed Mora that he died not long after his victim, and of a strange disease—ossification of the heart.

Many attempts to recover control of the lost river route were made during the months of January, February, March, and April, 1857. Various expeditions from New Orleans and New York landed at San Juan del Norte, where eight British men-of-war were concentrated to watch the operations. The interference of the latter, though annoying, was not openly hostile, yet it was marked enough to affect seriously the fortunes of the expeditions. The English commander incited desertion by spreading among the men rumours of the terrible dangers they must risk in attempting the passage of the river. Many Europeans were thereby induced to claim British protection, which was gladly granted, though the loss of such deserters may have been a questionable calamity. A strong force, under the command of a certain Colonel Titus, a windy "Border ruffian" from Kansas, succeeded in ascending the river as far as Castillo Viejo, and were on the point of capturing that key to the situation, when their leader weakly allowed himself to be hoodwinked and befooled by its commandant. The latter, finding himself sore pressed, begged for a twenty-four hours' truce before surrendering; which being granted, he sent for reinforcements, and by the time the truce had expired was prepared to laugh at the simplicity of his antagonists.

The mistake was irreparable. Through the incompetence of Titus and Lockridge, the key to Nicaragua was lost, perhaps for ever. With the Transit route in his power, Walker could have brought a host of recruits into the country and bidden defiance to all Spanish America. Without it, the labour of years was wasted and the conqueror thrown on the defensive. Knowing naught of the disasters which had befallen his arms on the river, Walker waited and watched through the long weeks for the relief which was never to come.

Towards the end of January the Allies had advanced to Obraje, nine miles from Rivas, and soon occupied San Jorge, within a league of the American outworks. Rivas, embowered in her orange groves and cocoa palms, was slowly being encircled by the entrenchments of the Allies, now numbering some seven thousand. They held those points, in spite of repeated attempts to dislodge them. Walker, not desiring to waste his men's lives in useless attacks, contented himself with occasional forays, while Henningsen prudently strengthened the fortifications and was careful of his scanty ammunition. Aided by the ingenious Captain Swingle, he cast round-shot from all sorts of old iron, and gathered together the bronze and silver bells of the churches to melt into cannon balls.

The Transit road between San Juan del Sur and Virgin Bay still was theirs, and nearly every steamer from San Francisco brought down a little band of recruits whose arrival was hailed with joy. But the advantages resulting from such additions to the garrisons were more than offset by the losses from desertion and death. The latter had made sad havoc in the ranks of the tried veterans. In February, Major Calvin O'Neill died in a skirmish with the Allies. He was a favourite soldier of the commander, having distinguished himself in almost every engagement during the campaign. His brother was slain in the evacuation of Granada, and the survivor had grown reckless of life thereafter. He was only twenty-one years old at the time of his death, but the Irishman's instinctive military bias and courage made up for the inexperience of youth. Other brave officers fell during the next few months, Conway, Higby, Dusenberry, and a score of veterans who were the flower of the army. The surviving members of the Falange found themselves surrounded by strange faces. The brave men died, and the cravens deserted. Unfortunately the evil did not end with the loss of worthless deserters; their example had a baneful effect upon good but reckless men, who otherwise would have remained faithful. It was not in weak human nature to content itself with scant rations of mule meat and plantains, while snug treason flaunted itself across the picket lines, boasting of rich fare and no duty. The hungry sentry was tempted by the sight of his late comrades and taunted by the sound of a brass band, which had deserted *en masse* one night, and now drew from the instruments bought with the money of the republic, seductive dancing tunes and Servile melodies, instead of the loyal strains of the "Blue, White, and Blue," which they had been hired to play. On his confused mind, perchance, dawned the suspicion that the Nicaragua which he had come thousands of miles to see and enjoy was to be found rather in the fleshpots of the Allied army than in the hungry camp of the filibusters. Small wonder if the poor fellow forgot his duty and elected to follow the example before him.

Early in February the monotony of the siege was broken by the arrival at San Juan del Sur of the American man-of-war *St. Mary's*, Commander C. H. Davis. Promptly in her wake came the British steamer *Esk*, Captain Sir Robert McClure. The two formidable ships lay not many cable lengths apart in the harbour. The day after his arrival Sir Robert sent a boat's crew aboard a small schooner lying near the shore to ask the meaning of the ensign which she was flying at the masthead. It was a handsome flag, composed of three horizontal stripes, blue, white, and blue; in the middle stripe, which was twice the width of either of the outer ones, was a five-pointed red star. The ensign was that of the new republic of Nagaragua, and the vessel, as her commander, Fayssoux, politely replied, was the Nicaraguan schooner-of-war *Granada*.

Sir Robert then ordered him to come on board the *Esk*, and bring his commission with him; to which the plucky Louisianian, with the blood of revolutionary ancestors boiling at the impertinence, replied that he would do nothing of the kind; and when the English captain threatened a broadside, the Nicaraguan commander beat to quarters—he had a score of men—loaded his two six-pound carronades, and awaited destruction as calmly as if he had the deck of a seventy-four under his feet. But Sir Robert, either fearing to exceed his authority, or labouring under the delusion that the *St. Mary's* captain might not relish the idea of seeing his fellow-countrymen annihilated before his eyes, softened the demand into a request for a friendly visit, which Captain Fayssoux thereupon paid him. A nobler motive may have actuated Sir Robert, for he was a sailor, and had traditions of his country's honour, which it were worth an American officer's commission to entertain. The latter has never forgotten the awful example handed down from the early days of Commodore Porter, who was court-martialled and forced out of the service because he exacted an apology from some Spanish vagabonds who had imprisoned an American officer visiting Porto Rico under a flag of truce.

When Sir Robert went to Rivas, some days afterwards, to demand an explanation of Fayssoux's conduct, he was met by Walker, at the outset of the interview, with the stern inquiry: "I presume, sir, you have come to apologize for the outrage offered to my flag and the commander of the Nicaraguan schooner-of-war *Granada*." And the gallant sailor actually forgot his wrath in his wonder, and made a suitable apology to the wounded dignity of the chief of a thousand men and one schooner. "If they had another schooner," said he, "I believe they would have declared war on Great Britain." Had he known the mission of the *St. Mary's* at San Juan, he might have come to a different conclusion; for the instructions of Commander Davis, which he faithfully obeyed, directed him to aid the Allies in forcing Walker and his men to capitulate. Why? Walker says, because Commodore Mervin, who had given the orders, was a bosom friend of Secretary Marcy—a possibly sufficient reason, since Marcy's power was absolute in the conduct of the minor foreign relations. Davis says, because the interests of humanity prompted him to save Walker in spite of himself—a reason perhaps as good as the other. The reader must guess at the true motive, as Blue-books do but fulfil their mission in confusing the truth.

The enemy receiving large reinforcements, was enabled to mass about two thousand men at San Jorge, where they were a constant danger and annoyance. Walker determined to dislodge them. On the 16th of March he took personal command of four hundred men, and marched out to meet the enemy, two thousand five hundred strong. Henningsen, with two six-pounders, one twelve-pounder, and four mortars, went ahead to clear the way. Swingle and the rest of the battery remained to guard Rivas; and it was well that they did so, for a large force of Costa Ricans made a determined assault as soon as Walker was out of sight, and were not repulsed until after a fight of some hours' duration. They fell back on the road to San Jorge, a couple of hundred of them taking up a position behind the adobe walls of a planter's house, and there lying in wait for the return of Walker and his command.

The latter arrived before daybreak at the suburbs of San Jorge and at once opened a brisk fire on the town; but the enemy were on the alert, and swarmed like angry bees out of their streets and lanes, pressing on the battery and throwing out lines of skirmishers on either side, who opened a galling fire on the American cavalry. Henningsen thereupon threw a shower of grape and canister among the plantain fields on the right and left, driving in the skirmishers, while Walker led the main body of his men towards the centre of the town. The enemy contested every inch of the ground, until driven to within three hundred yards of the plaza, where their immense superiority of numbers and the shelter afforded by the adobe walls and church towers gave them a position of impregnable strength. Walker, nevertheless, called for forty volunteers to storm the place. But fifteen responded, and with that handful he charged boldly into the plaza, fighting with desperate but vain courage against the tremendous odds. Two horses were killed under him, and a spent ball struck him in the throat. His men were brave to madness, but they were worn out with the long day's service, their ammunition was running short, and Walker at last gave order to retire to Rivas. They left the field on which they had fought from daybreak almost to sunset in good order, Walker riding at the head of the column, and Henningsen covering the rear with his guns. No opposition was made to their departure, and not until the head of the column came abreast of the planter's house at Cuatros Esquinas did they learn of the presence there of the 200 Costa Ricans who had been repulsed by Swingle in the morning.

As Walker and his staff rode by the dark and silent house, a blaze of musketry lit up its front, not thirty yards away. Fortunately the marksman's aim was bad, and not over half a dozen saddles were emptied; but the column was thrown into temporary confusion, and some of the men fell back, while others stood panic-stricken, until another volley sent them galloping in dismay. Walker, with the invincible calmness which never deserted him, reined in his horse, drew his revolver and fired its six shots into the house; then putting spurs to his steed, he rode by, erect as if on parade, while the musket balls fell like hail around him. A long-haired Californian, Major Dolan, who was riding behind him, deliberately imitated his commander, emptying his pistol to the last shot, then hurling the empty weapon at the house, with an imprecation, as he dropped from his saddle, riddled with bullets. His clothing caught in the trappings of his horse, and he was thus dragged out of the *melée*, to survive and fight another day. The rest of the force ran the gauntlet as best they could. Many were killed in a vain attempt to carry the house by storm. The rear guard with the artillery made a detour, and losing their way, did not arrive at Rivas until the next morning. To the poor marksmanship alone of the enemy can be charged the small loss of the filibusters before San Jorge and in the ambuscade at Cuatros Esquinas, the total number in killed and wounded being only some sixty or seventy.

A week afterwards, the whole Allied force, led in by a deserter, made a concerted attack on Rivas, at daybreak, from four different directions. They were beaten off with dreadful slaughter, leaving six hundred dead on the field. The attack was most serious on the north side of the city, where a small battery was placed in a position to rake the American lines. It was handled well and bravely by an Italian gunner who, though exposed to a galling fire from the American sharpshooters, continued to load and fire with the utmost deliberation, advancing his piece a little nigher after each discharge. Henningsen, an adept in the same branch of warfare, stood upon the parapet of the low wall, rolling and smoking cigarettes, as he watched with admiration the actions of his cool adversary, and directing the management of a small gun which the American artillerymen were serving with less than their usual skill. At last, losing patience with his men, he leaped into the embrasure, and sighting the gun himself, threw a six-pound ball straight into the enemy's piece, which it dismounted, killing four of the gunners and wounding the Italian captain. The latter being made prisoner, the hostile batteries ceased to annoy the besieged for some time, until the gallant gunner, escaping from his captors, was enabled to resume his duties.

In this assault the besieged suffered but a trifling loss, as the shelter of the adobe walls ensured them safety against any force which it was in the power of the enemy to bring against them. When the latter pushed their barricades too close to the walls of Rivas, the besieged fired hot shot into them and burned the swarming hordes out of their nests. Mora cared nothing for the lives of his wretched conscripts, whom he could afford to lose by hundreds, as long as the Americans fell by dozens and were not reinforced, and while the Allies could cut off supplies of food and ammunition from the beleaguered city. Unfortunately for Walker, a more dangerous enemy than death or hunger assailed Rivas. Desertion, which had begun with the weak-hearted new men, gradually spread like a pestilence, until he hardly knew in whom to trust. Whole companies deserted at a time; pickets abandoned their posts; foraging parties sent out to collect food for the hungry garrison never came back. As early as October, a company of rangers sent into the Chontales district had deserted with their equipments, on a wild attempt to reach the Atlantic by way of the Blewfields river. They never reached the coast, for some French settlers whom they had attempted to plunder fell upon them and slew them to a man.

Famine threatened Rivas. There was not an ounce of bread in the city; the men were living on scanty rations of horse and mule meat, seasoned with sugar in lieu of salt; the hospital was filled with wounded and fever patients. Henningsen said jestingly that, rather than surrender, they would devour the prisoners. Once it was whispered in the ranks that Walker and Henningsen, in anticipation of a successful assault on the town, had prepared a magazine with which to blow up the citadel in the moment of defeat, and with it friend and foe together.

The rumour was a silly falsehood, but so much impression did it make upon some of the hardier spirits that, as General Henningsen told the author, seven of them came to him, each begging for the privilege of firing the train. Walker was not reduced to any such straits; he had yet three forlorn hopes; the arrival, by the San Juan river of Lockridge with reinforcements; assistance from California, and, as a last resource, flight to the north on board his schooner *Granada*. The first never came, because Lockridge, defeated before Castillo Viejo, had given up the hopeless task. The second failed when Morgan refused to co-operate with his partner, Garrison, in continuing to run the steamers from San Francisco. On the *Granada*, then, depended the only hope of retreat with honour. Walker, however, did not as yet know that the first and second hopes had failed him.

On the 10th of April, the Allies made another attack on the town, and were again repulsed with even greater loss than on the previous occasion. Commander Davis, who had been negotiating with the Allies, sent word to Walker, on the 23rd of April, offering a safe convoy to the women and children from Rivas to San Juan del Sur, an offer which was thankfully accepted.

On being relieved of his non-combatants, Walker felt that no obstacle now stood in the way of his evacuation of the city, whenever he deemed it proper, and a safe withdrawal on board of the schooner. Fayssoux had continued to keep a close watch of the enemy's movements in San Juan, preventing them throwing up fortifications or doing anything which should embarrass the occupation of the town by Walker. Commander Davis, acting as a peace-maker between the belligerents, but finding his office one of perilous delicacy for a raw diplomat, and being governed apparently by secret instructions, which new orders from Washington might nullify at any moment if he delayed too long, now brought matters to an unexpected crisis, by demanding Walker's surrender to the United States authorities. Such an astonishing demand had never before been made by a subordinate naval officer upon the President of a friendly government. It was indignantly and promptly rejected. Davis then assured Walker of the truth of two rumours which had reached Rivas; the first, that Lockridge had given up his attempt to retake the Transit route; the second, that no more steamers were to come from San Francisco. Accepting both statements, which were true, Walker replied that he purposed holding the city as long as his supplies lasted, after which he intended carrying his command on board the Nicaragua schooner-of-war *Granada*, and removing whithersoever he pleased. To which Davis responded, that it was his "unalterable and deliberate intention" to take possession of the schooner before he sailed from San Juan; that his instructions on that point were clear and imperative; and nothing but a countermand of his orders should induce him to depart from that intention. The enemy had previously made Fayssoux an offer of five thousand dollars to surrender the schooner; but what could not be won by force or bribe was more cheaply gained through the extraordinary action of an officer holding the commission and authority of the United States. Walker has been accused of ingratitude because he protested against the interference of Commander Davis. It was said that the United States had saved the filibusters from extermination; but there was not a man in Rivas who did not spurn the spurious claim. Ungrateful step-children, they had cherished a different ideal of a mother country!

CHAPTER XV.

Ultimatum of Captain Davis—Evacuation of Rivas—Statistics of the campaign — Henningsen's opinion of his men — Characteristic anecdotes—Frederick Ward—A filibuster's apeothosis.

THE ultimatum of Davis, backed by the power at his command, destroyed Walker's last hope of retaining his hold in Nicaragua; this, too, at a time when the tide of fortune had begun to show signs of turning. In despair of ever taking the city by assault, the Allies had sat down to besiege it with scant patience. The formidable army of seven thousand which had invested Rivas in January had decreased within two months, through death and defection, to a comparatively small force of less than two thousand, two-thirds of them Costa Ricans and other foreigners. These were, moreover, short of powder, threatened with cholera and the rainy season; and so reduced as to be unable to man effectively the investing works, through which the American scouts penetrated freely when they pleased. With the garrison, desertion had done its worst. Walker had still with him 260 of his best fighting men, with plenty of arms and ammunition and two or three days' provisions. To cut his way through the hostile lines and reach his schooner would have been a much less difficult feat than Henningson's evacuation of Granada. Capitulation had never been discussed or thought of by Walker, nor had Commander Davis hinted at his intention of seizing the *Granada*, until her possession had become of vital importance to the besieged.

The Leonese in the North had begun to murmur at the

cost and misery of this prolonged, fruitless war, whose advantages, should it end favourably to the Allies, would most likely be reaped by those whom they loved no better than they did the Americans of the North. Walker, had he been allowed to embark his fighting men in safety, might expect to awaken in those old friends a new and stronger friendship, and resume the fight against the Serviles from the original point at Realejo. The possession of over a hundred prisoners, whom he could have carried with him as hostages, was a sufficient guarantee for the safety of the sick and wounded whom he would have been compelled to leave behind. Such, at least, are the arguments embodied in Henningsen's protest, and the facts conceded by all authorities justify his conclusions. But half of Walker's ammunition was on board the schooner, without which it would have been madness to attempt a change of base in presence of the enemy.

Walker, finding that Davis was firm in his determination, sent General Henningsen and Colonel Watters to meet the naval autocrat at the headquarters of the Allies and arrange terms of capitulation. An agreement was drawn up and submitted to Walker, on the 13th of April, but he declined to sign it, as it contained no provisions guaranteeing the safety in person and property of his native adherents who should have to remain in Nicaragua. Among the latter were many devoted men who had kept faithful to his fortunes throughout all, and on whom the wrath of the enemy would fall as soon as the dread filibusters should leave the country. On the next day an agreement was submitted and accepted by both parties, the provisions of which were as follows:—

"RIVAS, *May* 1, 1857.

"An agreement is hereby entered into between General William Walker, on the one part, and Commander C. H.

Davis, of the United States Navy, on the other part, and of which the stipulations are as follows:—Firstly. General William Walker, with sixteen officers of his staff, shall march out of Rivas, with their side-arms, pistols, horses, and personal baggage, under the guarantee of the said Captain Davis, of the United States Navy, that they shall not be molested by the enemy, and shall be allowed to embark on board the United States vessel of war, the *St. Mary's*, in the harbour of San Juan del Sur, the said Captain Davis undertaking to transport them safely, on the *St. Mary's*, to Panama.

"Secondly. The officers of General Walker's army shall march out of Rivas with their side-arms, under the guarantee and protection of Captain Davis, who undertakes to see them safely transported to Panama in charge of a United States officer.

"Thirdly. The privates and non-commissioned officers, citizens, and *employés* of departments, wounded or unwounded, shall be surrendered, with their arms, to Captain Davis, or one of his officers, and placed under his protection and control, he pledging himself to have them transported safely to Panama, in charge of a United States officer, in separate vessels from the deserters from the ranks, and without being brought into contact with them.

"Fourthly. Captain Davis undertakes to obtain guarantees, and hereby does guarantee that all natives of Nicaragua, or of Central America, now in Rivas, and surrendered to the protection of Captain Davis, shall be allowed to reside in Nicaragua, and be protected in life and property.

"Fifthly. It is agreed that all such officers as have wives and families in San Juan del Sur shall be allowed to remain there under the protection of the United States consul, till an opportunity offers of embarking for Panama or San Francisco.

"General Walker and Captain Davis mutually pledge themselves to each other that this agreement shall be executed in good faith."

Such is the text of the treaty between the representative of the United States and his captive. The lenity, unheard of before in Central American warfare, which the Allies thus offered to the men whom they had vowed to exterminate, shows how highly they valued the services of Captain Davis. That they did not keep their merciful promise to the native prisoners, but harried them in the good old-fashioned way as soon as the gallant captain had sailed away, does not detract from the merit of their promise. They would have promised anything to be rid of the troublesome filibustero.

No stipulation had been made for the surrender of the ammunition and weapons of the besieged. Henningsen, therefore, before the evacuation began, set his gunners to work destroying all the artillery and ammunition, consisting of one four-pound brass gun, three five-pounders, two twelves, and three sixes, and four light iron twelve-pound mortars, also 55,000 cartridges, 300,000 caps, and 1,500 pounds of powder; no contemptible supply of saltpetre for a garrison lacking in bread.

The total number of men surrendering was 463, including 170 sick and wounded. One hundred and two prisoners taken from the Allies were set free and sent within the enemy's lines. Forty natives who had abided with him to the last, bade their grey-eyed chieftain a sorrowful adieu on the bright May morning that was his last in Rivas.

Bravely and deliberately the filibusters marched out of the town, Walker riding at the head, with blade on thigh and pistol in belt, and the same impassive visage that he would have worn in mounting a throne or a gallows. After him, Henningsen, tall, martial, frank of face, then bearded like a whiskered Pandour, and not without traces of powder from his morning's work. Gaunt Hornsby, a Northern Quixote in face and figure, rode beside phlegmatic Bruno Von Natzmer, erst Prussian cornet of hussars and friend of Baron Bulow, until differences of national adoption set them lustily to fighting each other; more fortunate than the Costa Rican baron, he lived to fight another day; Henry and Swingle, doughty gunners, rejoicing that the beloved cannon for whose dainty throats they had oft compounded precious balls of church-bell metal, should at least be saved from the hated Greaser's clutch; Watters—Colonel Jack—he of the relief of Granada; Williamson, West, and a dozen others, brave men and true, accompanied their leader. Other brave men and true, scores and hundreds, lay beneath the orange trees of Rivas and Granada and San Jorge, and a score of hard-fought fields, who never again might follow a filibuster's flag or awake to martial trump until that of Gabriel sounds their *reveileé*.

Walker and sixteen of his officers were to go on board the *St Mary's*, thence to Panama, and home. It is a striking, and in its way, an heroic picture, that of the filibuster chief parting from his wild, wayward, but devoted comrades. First, he must say not adieu but *au revoir* to 250 privates and non-commissioned officers, escorted by a United States lieutenant, who curses his job, to Virgin Bay, thence homeward as circuitously as may be; also to the sad contingent of sick and wounded, homeward bound by another course; finally, he gives a look of pitying scorn upon a battalion of recreant deserters whom, for their own safety, Captain Davis must despatch to the home which yearns not for them, by yet another route.

So fared they forth from Rivas and on to their several fates; Walker to gaze from the decks of the *St Mary's* at his beloved schooner *Granada*, now captured by Davis, as promised and turned over, as also (privately) promised

GENERAL CHARLES FREDERIC HENNINGSEN.

to the Costa Ricans, and commanded, not without much pomp and glory, by a Jamaico negro—horribly satirical sequel to that slavery decree which was to have regenerated Central America. Commander Davis, most respectable of naval magnates, passed from Rivàs unto well-earned promotion, chiefly by dint of meritorious longevity, and died, in the fulness of time, an admiral, having achieved nothing more important in his long life than the forcible overthrow of the filibuster chief.

The "Blue, White, and Blue" has floated over Nicaraguan soil for the last time, save that one brief moment when it shall flutter and fall before the "Stars and Stripes" in the port of San Juan del Norte. So many and such varying stories have been told of the number of men who fought and died under its folds, that a summary of the actual force which during twenty months held possession of a country may not be uninteresting.

It has been estimated by those who estimate by guess, that 5,000 Americans perished in Nicaragua—that is to say, five-sevenths as many Americans as were killed and wounded in the Revolutionary War. It has also been guessed that Walker had from 10,000 to 20,000 men at his command. These guesses have been gravely crystallized into history, where history has condescended to notice the subject at all. The actual records of the adjutant-general, P. R. Thompson, show that exactly 2,843 men were enlisted in all the campaigns. In addition to these, however, must be reckoned native volunteers, civilians who volunteered, and others who were impressed for temporary service—whose combined strength may have swelled the total to about 3,500.

Against them was arrayed a force, in all, of 21,000 Servile Nicaraguans, Costa Ricans, Hondurans, Guatemalans and San Salvadorians, with at least 10,000 Indian auxiliaries. The Allies admitted a loss of 15,000 in all the campaigns. One-third, perhaps, of the Americans died in Nicaragua. I take the assertions of General Henningsen, in the absence of any official figures. Some estimate of their deeds may be gathered from the surgical report, which showed that the proportion of wounds treated was 137 to every hundred men. Those who did not shirk their duty must have carried away many a scar, when they were fortunate enough to carry away their lives, to average the immunity of the cowardly and the false. It is not placing the proportion too high to say that about one thousand five hundred was the number of those who were steadfast and true.

These were mostly Californians, when to be Californian meant to belong to that race of giants who had come from all parts of the earth in search of gold, and then journeyed two thousand miles further in search of adventure. Nine-tenths of them were Americans, of every rank in life, from college to prison graduates, who boasted that "California was the pick of the world, and they were the pick of California"; nor quarrelled with him who chose to put it, "California is the sink of the world, and we are the sewer of California." Young Southerners drifted to Nicaragua, as naturally as young Northerners ran away to sea. A son and a nephew of Senator Bayard ran away from school to join the filibusters, and might have added some military glory to the family name, but that the filibusters sent them home at the request of the American State department. Henningsen's first aid was a youth of nineteen, named Burbank, who had run away from the Virginia military institute, and would have been entitled, had he lived, to a fortune of 100,000 dollars, which in those days was esteemed wealth. A rather worthless sergeant did actually fall heir to a fortune of that amount, which he was summoned home to enjoy, but purposely missed the steamer and remained to die in Nicaragua.

All the strange, wild natures for whom even California

had grown too tame, drifted naturally into the filibuster's camp. "I have heard," says Henningsen, "two greasy privates disputing over the correct reading and comparative merits of Æschylus and Euripides. I have seen a soldier on guard incessantly scribbling strips of paper, which turned out to be a finely versified translation of his dog's-eared copy of the 'Divina Commedia.'"

The same appreciative commander testifies to the invincible heroism and fortitude of those men: "I have often seen them marching with a broken or compound-fractured arm in splints, and using the other to fire the rifle or revolver. Those with a fractured thigh, or wounds which rendered them incapable of removal, often (or, rather, in early times, always) shot themselves, sooner than fall into the hands of the enemy. Such men," he adds, "do not turn up in the average of every-day life, nor do I ever expect to see their like again. I was on the Confederate side in many of the bloodiest battles of the late war; but I aver that if, at the end of that war, I had been allowed to pick five thousand of the bravest Confederate or Federal soldiers I ever saw, and could resurrect and pit against them one thousand of such men as lie beneath the orange trees of Nicaragua, I feel certain that the thousand would have scattered and utterly routed the five thousand within an hour. All military science failed, on a suddenly given field, before assailants who came on at a run, to close with their revolvers, and who thought little of charging a battery, pistol in hand." Ten men, all officers, did in the first battle of Rivas actually charge and capture a battery manned by over a hundred Costa Ricans, half of the little band being slain in the heroic feat.

Their enemies testify to the splendid courage of the filibusters and their indomitable *sang-froid* when called upon to face the fusillade which almost always awaited them if captured. Chevalier Belly tells of a filibuster captured, with a broken leg, and condemned to be shot, who curtly replied to the questions of an officious person, as to why he had come to Nicaragua, whether he believed in a future state, and so forth; until losing patience at what he deemed such idle speech, he burst out: "Here, we've had enough of this fooling! If you mean to have this funeral come off bring on your mourners and let us get through with it."

Men who possessed the military genius, which upon a broader field had earned them fame and fortune, lie in unhonoured graves; because on their field bravery and skill meant only increased chances of death. Men of highest education, family, and wealth, lie beside felons and outcasts. Some survived to pursue their adventurous career in other lands, many to die in the American Civil War. One of them, Frederick Townsend Ward, descendant of straitest Puritan ancestry, a native of Salem, Massachusetts, graduated from the filibuster's school to wander over to distant China, where, the Taiping rebellion occurring in the nick of time, he entered the Imperial service, in which he presently attained to the chief command. So well did the doughty filibuster practise the lessons learned in his old school, that he soon became one of the greatest men in the Celestial kingdom, and was loaded with wealth and honours (two million dollars, it is said, of the former, but the native executors produced no assets), and might have risen to any position in that most conservative kingdom, perhaps even to the very throne and office of heaven's vice-gerent, had not an unlucky ball cut short his career at the siege of Ning-Po, and sent him to enjoy the most remarkable honours ever paid to a Yankee living or dead. For the grateful Pagans have erected two temples in his honour, and have solemnly enrolled his name among those of their country's gods. Even to this day there is kept perennially blooming over his tomb a spotless lily, emblematic of I know not what, which is constantly tended and nursed by loving hands, and shall perchance be so tended centuries to come, when Taiping and Filibuster shall have grown dim and hoary traditions in the busy, forgetful world outside the Middle Kingdom. China remembers the services of Ward. With us *alter tulit honores,* and an Englishman wears the glory of having suppressed the Taiping rebellion. Of a different type was the young Californian, Joaquin Miller, who has lived to embalm in heroic verse the memory of his chief—albeit, Walker, simple and severe, masquerades in a garb which he would have little yearned for or admired.

To the more ignorant of his followers Walker's ulterior designs were naturally inexplicable. They thought that his purpose was merely that of a freebooter. Hence there arose a legend that he had amassed a mighty treasure which, like that of Captain Kidd, still lies hidden, awaiting discovery by some lucky seeker. Long years after his death the following story was told by a relative of one of the surviving filibusters, named Samuel Lyons :

"By his bravery and strategy Samuel became one of Walker's most trusted men, and he was one of the four officers who helped Walker bury his treasure. There were five mule loads of it—gold and silver, money and bullion, including a great deal which had been plundered from the churches, the chapels, and private mansions. At eleven o'clock one moonlight night Walker and four officers buried the treasure under a big tree near the brow of a hill. I have heard Samuel tell how they scraped away the leaves on the ground before they dug the pit. I have a pretty good idea of the locality myself, but he knows just where it is, and can find it even if the tree is removed. The treasure was buried just before the two final engagements which crushed the hopes of Walker. The next morning after that little moonlight excursion the first of these engagements occurred, and in it two of the officers who had seen the treasure buried were killed.

After that engagement the army—if it could be called one—lived on bananas alone for two weeks in a big banana plantation, and had a hard time of it. Then came the last engagement, in which Walker, Samuel, and the rest were captured. There is only one of the four accompanying officers who is not accounted for; but as nothing was heard of him after that engagement Samuel has always believed that he was killed then or executed with the captives who met death in that way. He certainly was not with the party that so wonderfully escaped with Samuel, and who, I think, were the sole survivors of that engagement. If he be dead, or rather, if he died then, Samuel alone has the secret."

Most lovers of the marvellous would be satisfied with this delectable dish of treasure and gore, but another "survivor," with a still more able-bodied imagination, gravely corrects the first narrator, by saying:

"The writer hereof knows something of that treasure, and personally examined it, and in lieu of five mule loads, there were *five tons of it*. It is well known that the most horrible chapter in that most horrible of wars was the burning and pillaging of Granada by General Henningsen, under Walker's orders, in November, 1856. The churches—some twenty or more, immensely rich in plate and jewels—were secretly and systematically despoiled, and their great booty was safely stowed away on board a Lake Nicaragua steamer before the doomed city was given up to pillage. What became of that immense spoil has been a mysterious secret, and was so regarded by the filibusters at the time. *It was worth millions.* To allay suspicion as to its true disposition Walker gave out that it was shipped to New Orleans to be disposed of on account of his government, and that the proceeds thereof would be used in purchasing military supplies. That spoil was buried, and, to my own personal knowledge, the officer who had it in charge and commanded the squad who guarded it now lives in San Bernardino. He informs me (and we have frequently discussed the matter) that, under the immediate supervision of Walker, he and five other officers and about twenty men buried that treasure in the village of St. George, on Lake Nicaragua, under a room in the house wherein the booty was so sacredly guarded. Walker exacted the most solemn oath of secrecy, giving substantial gratuities and promising future rewards to the whole party if they would faithfully guard the secret of the hidden church-spoil of the burned city. Inside of a month the whole party who were in the secret, save my friend and informant and two or three of the officers therein engaged, were sent away on a feigned expedition; were given out as deserters; were pursued by a large party of cavalry, and, by Walker's order, shot to a man when overhauled by the pursuing party. Soon thereafter, at a desperate battle fought at St. George on January 16, 1857, the last man of the party who assisted in burying the church spoil, save my friend of San Bernardino, was killed, and in such a way as to confirm in the mind of my informant the opinion that all had been killed by Walker's order, and that the General intended to be the only custodian of the secret of the hidden treasure. Although my informant was a faithful and trusted officer, high in Walker's favour, still the prompt and tragic ending of his comrades and sharers in the dread mystery produced such an impression on his mind that he at once deserted. He carried the secret with him and yet has it, and he is the only man living who knows where the Granada booty lies hidden, *and he don't know*. And why not? Well, the spoil was buried in December; in January the enemy, by a forced march, possessed themselves of St. George; Walker took position at Rivas, three miles distant, and, within the next three months, utterly exhausted his army in his vain endeavours to repossess himself of the insignificant village that contained this immense wealth. In the terrific conflicts that ensued the village was razed to the ground. This the writer hereof knows, because he fought through all of those engagements."

Nothing (save truth) is lacking to make this circumstantial narrative all that it should be. Like most of the improbable charges made against Walker, it emanated from his deserters, who have done more than any others to blacken his memory.

CHAPTER XVI.

Walker returns to the United States—Crabbe's expedition—Renewed attempts of Walker—The expedition to San Juan del Norte.

WALKER'S reception in New York, on his return to the United States, was like that of a conqueror. The city wore a holiday appearance; tens of thousands of citizens flocked to see the hero; Broadway was decked with banners as on a national festival. Public meetings were called to give him welcome and sympathy. Walker received the homage with dignified modesty, and resolutely avowed his determination to recover his lost power at the first opportunity. As the lawful President of Nicaragua, he protested against the action of the United States, to him a foreign power, in driving him from his country. He went to Washington, to lay before the State Department his complaint against Commander Davis, and was received with diplomatic politeness; but the case was referred to the consideration of Congress, where it was effectually buried under a mountain of verbiage. Thence he made a journey through the South, being welcomed and fêted with even more enthusiasm than he had received in the North. Arriving at New Orleans, he made his first appearance publicly in a box at one of the theatres. When the audience became aware of his presence they turned with one impulse from the mimic romance of the stage to gaze at the living hero whose exploits made tame the wildest flights of imagination, and cheer upon cheer went up from pit and gallery. Walker was hailed as a hero and a martyr, and his bitterest enemies were silenced for the time, when Henningsen, whom they had expected, from some unknown reason, to villify his commander, not only disappointed that hope, but lauded everywhere the character and principles of the great filibuster. He also laid before Secretary Cass an indignant protest against the outrage inflicted upon a friendly nation, whose only offence towards the United States lay in the fact that its president had the misfortune to be by birth an American. Technically the filibusters had serious reason for complaint. But the demand for reparation fell upon deaf ears. The President of the United States cared nothing for the fact that the title of the President of Nicaragua to his office was in law as good as that of James Buchanan to his. Buchanan, as Walker soon saw, was not the man to add another bramble to his already too painful bed of thorns; and the bold filibuster decided to seek outside the pale of law that redress which was denied him within it.

While Walker and his men were battling for their lives in Rivas, during the months of March and April, 1857, another and a bloody scene in the tragedy of filibusterism was being enacted on the stage which had witnessed the failures of De Boulbon and Walker. Towards the end of March one hundred and fifty men from California were led across the boundary line into the northern part of Sonora by Henry A. Crabbe, a former friend of Walker, and like him, a man of bold and ambitious character. He had been one of the most useful agents in organizing the latter's expedition to Nicaragua, and through him Walker had secured some of his most efficient officers, Hornsby, Fisher, and De Brissot, all of whom had been concerned in a contract between Crabbe and Jerez similar in its terms to that afterwards made between Castellon and Walker.

Crabbe was an ex-Senator of the State of California; in his party were seven former members of the legislature and one present senator, together with the former State treasurer and State comptroller; men who had outlived their popularity, perhaps, or who had become tired of humdrum life and sought a new career in Sonora, the graveyard of adventurers. Nor was the military element lacking. Colonel Watkins, who had been with Walker in his expedition to the same country, and a former lieutenant in the regular army, Colonel T. D. Johns, superintended the military department as the expedition crossed the line. They marched through the country without hindrance until they passed Sonoyta and approached Caborca, on the Gulf of California, near Point Lobos. There for the first time the Mexicans showed a hostile front. Crabbe had issued an address to the inhabitants, in which he claimed that his business in the country was peaceable, his object being the prosecution of a mining scheme in Sonora; and maintained that, while his party were armed, they had come so only for self-defence against the Apache Indians. The truth of the matter was that Crabbe had been invited to Sonora by the partisans of a political minority, whose leader, Don Ignacio Pesqueira, had meanwhile gained his political ends without the aid of foreign allies, and was much disturbed lest the inopportune arrival of the latter should reflect upon his present loyalty. Crabbe, who had at much cost and labour organized his immigrants and arranged for the future immigration of nine hundred more men, was not disposed to abandon his project. He was allied by marriage with some of the leading families in the State, and may have cherished hopes of exchanging places with Pesqueira in Sonorian affairs. If he counted upon the assistance of the native population he was doomed to a cruel disappointment.

On the 1st of April, when the expeditionists were within six miles of Caborca, they were fired upon by an ambushed party of natives; at the same time a strong force appeared in front, drawn up to contest the road. The filibusters opened fire upon them, killing at the first volley Colonel Rodriguez, the commander, and driving the Mexicans before them into the town. The fugitives rallied in the plaza and fortified themselves in the main church. The assailants occupied the houses opposite, whereupon the natives, seeing that the church was not attacked, plucked up courage to occupy the adjacent buildings and harass the invaders. Crabbe soon perceived his error in allowing the enemy to assume the offensive, and made one or two futile attempts to carry the church by assault. The fighting lasted through eight days. On the last, Crabbe with fifteen men tried to blow up the church by means of gunpowder, but the enemy kept up such a sharp fire that he was compelled to desist, with four of his men shot down and himself badly wounded. He now sent a flag of truce, offering to withdraw his forces, if they should be allowed to leave the country. The Mexicans had themselves made such a proposition to him on the second day of the fight, which he had then rejected, as they now did, their relative positions having so much changed in the meanwhile. Gabilondo, the Mexican commander, disposed his force of five hundred men so as to completely hem in the unfortunate adventurers, until the Mexicans, having cut through the walls of the intervening houses, fought hand to hand in the passages and slowly drove the Americans into the last house on the street.

Night fell upon the scene where fifty-eight surviving filibusters stood at bay, overcome with hunger, thirst, and hard fighting. They placed sentries and sought to snatch a few moments' rest, which was rudely broken by the crackling sound of fire above their heads. An Indian archer had lodged a flaming arrow in the thatched roof, and soon the fiery flakes were dropping upon the heads of the men within. In this desperate strait Crabbe sent word to the enemy that he was willing to surrender as a prisoner of war, on condition that he and his men should be given a fair trial. Gabilondo replied, accepting the terms of capitulation and promising to send the prisoners to El

Altar for trial. They were ordered to leave the house one by one, and without their arms, and then, their hands being bound, they were marched to the barracks. Crabbe was separated from the rest and brought before the Mexican commander, who offered to give him his life if he would point out where he had buried his treasure, some ten thousand dollars. Crabbe, remembering the bad faith of Pesqueira, and rightly judging that the possession of the money by Gabilondo would be anything but a guaranty of the owner's safety, refused, and was sent to his cell. The surrender had taken place at eleven o'clock in the evening. One hour after midnight a sergeant entered the barracks and read to the assembled prisoners their sentence of death by the fusillade at daybreak.

At the appointed hour they were led out on the plaza, where, after their executioners, with an eye to thrift, had first stripped them of their valuable articles of clothing, they were shot in cold blood, without the form of a trial. A boy of twelve was spared to witness the brutal scene. The bodies were rifled of their rings, and in some cases even of the gold fillings in their teeth, after which they were thrown into a burial ground where the wild hog and the coyote fattened on them. To Crabbe was accorded the honour of dying last and alone. He was tied to a post and riddled with bullets. His head was cut off and exhibited in a jar of vinegar for several days, a sight which so stimulated the heroism of the natives that they fell upon a party of sixteen peaceful travellers a few days afterwards and cut them off to a man, while another bold band crossed into the American territory and murdered four sick men, presumed to have been adherents of Crabbe. Of the nine hundred men who were to have joined Crabbe from California, only some fifty appeared in the vicinity of Caborca, where being set upon by the natives they succeeded only with great difficulty in making their way back across the boundary line.

Mr. Forsyth, the American minister to Mexico, took pains to investigate the matter, and laid before his own Government and that of Mexico the results of his inquiry. He pronounced the execution of the prisoners "legal murder," a conclusion which apparently satisfied both parties, the Americans because it was "legal," and the Mexicans because it was "murder," and so the matter was allowed to drop. It ended filibusterism in that country. The American apostle of liberty no longer heeds the cry of the oppressed of any faction. Nor is it likely, since the world was shocked by the execution of the Austrian archduke, that many Europeans will be found treading the wine-press for the "regeneration" of Mexico.

With the expulsion of the filibusters terminated for a time the war in Nicaragua. The Allied states formed a kind of protectorate over the republic, having first rewarded themselves, after the fashion of greater powers, by gathering a goodly share of the fruits of victory. Costa Rica was rewarded by the possession of Guanacaste and a strip of land bordering along the lake and the southern side of the San Juan river, a sufficiently small return for her outlay in the war, which had entailed a loss of four thousand men, women, and children slain by cholera. The "Tiger of Honduras" was given material aid in driving from power at home the partisans of Cabañas. General Martinez, a descendant of the apocryphal heroine of San Carlos, was appointed President of Nicaragua, and at once sent a minister to Washington, who was received without question. Mr. Buchanan thus gave himself a plausible excuse for declining to recognize the claims of Walker. Señor Yrissari, the new minister, negotiated a new treaty for the construction of a canal, the terms of which not being considered favourable to Costa Rica, that state and Nicaragua were soon again preparing to grapple each other's throats.

In spite of the vigilance of the United States authorities

Walker continued planning schemes to resume the offensive on Nicaraguan soil. Being arrested on charge of organizing an unlawful expedition, he was acquitted, only to renew his preparations. Thirteen days after his discharge at New Orleans he appeared off the harbour of San Juan del Norte on board the steamer *Fashion*, but did not stop at that port until after he had landed Colonel Anderson and fifty men at the mouth of the river Colorado, a southerly branch of the San Juan. Returning to the harbour of San Juan, the *Fashion* boldly came to anchor under the guns of the United States frigate *Saratoga*, and landed her cargo of war material and passengers to the number of a hundred and fifty men. The officers and most of the men were old veterans of Nicaragua, including the tried soldiers, Hornsby, Von Natzmer, Swingle, Tucker, Henry, Hoof, Fayssoux, Cook, McMullen, Haskins, Buttrick, and others. Captain Chatard, of the *Saratoga*, sent a boat on board the *Fashion*, but the passengers had landed before the lieutenant in command could prevent them. The only steps which the American officer felt himself authorized to take were to order the filibusters to respect American property on the Transit Company's ground, an injunction which Walker obeyed, after protesting that it was infringement of his rights as President of Nicaragua, from and through whom the company held its privileges.

Walker immediately formed his camp and awaited the reinforcements which he was daily expecting from the United States. Colonel Anderson, having ascended the Colorado and San Juan, suddenly appeared before Castillo Viejo and captured it without difficulty, a feat which the incompetent Titus and Lockridge had been unable to achieve with eight times his force. He also captured three or four of the river steamers, and was in a fair way to obtain supreme control of the Transit route, when the arrival at San Juan, on December 6th, of Commodore

Hiram Paulding and the U.S. frigate *Wabash* gave a new turn to affairs.

Captain Chatard, not content with exercising a kind of police superintendence over the port of San Juan, began a series of petty annoyances, which, had they been intended to provoke Walker into a collision with the United States forces, could not have been better contrived. While the American captain professed to maintain a strict neutrality, he nevertheless issued orders to the expeditionists, and sent his boats out to practise firing where the filibusters on duty were exposed to injury unless they abandoned their posts. His officers insisted upon landing and entering Walker's camp without a pass; and when Walker, with more dignity than discretion, threatened to shoot anybody found trespassing within his lines, Captain Chatard retorted in a note (which Walker sent to Commodore Paulding), assuring him that he would retaliate. "The childish follies," as Walker characterized them, of Captain Chatard failing to provoke a collision, Commodore Paulding, on the 7th of December, sent an imperative summons to surrender. Resistance to such a demand, backed as it was by two frigates and a complaisant British captain, who volunteered to aid Paulding in annihilating the American filibusters, would have been madness. On the next day Commodore Paulding landed a force of three hundred and fifty men in howitzer barges and formed them in order of battle, while the broadsides of the *Saratoga* were sprung to bear on the camp. Captain Engle proceeded to the tent of General Walker and presented the demand for surrender, adding, "General, I am sorry to see you here. A man like you is worthy to command better men." Walker replied briefly that the virtue of his men would be apparent if their number and equipments were one half those of his captors.

The flag of the filibusters was then hauled down, and the prisoners were sent on board the *Saratoga* for transportation to the United States. Walker, being offered the choice of returning by way of Aspinwall, availed himself of the favour and went home at his own expense. Colonel Anderson, on learning of the capture, surrendered his command on the river and returned to New Orleans. Arriving at New York, Walker gave himself up to a United States marshal, in fulfilment of his parole to Commodore Paulding, and was sent a prisoner of war to Washington. But President Buchanan was by no means ready to support the act of his naval subordinate, and absolutely refused to accept the surrender or to recognize Walker as in the custody of the Government. In a message to Congress he reviewed at length the action of Commodore Paulding, which he pronounced unlawful, but cited the approbation of the *de facto* government of Nicaragua as justifying the proceedings. In short, Paulding had infringed the rights of that country by an act of hostility towards its president and upon its soil; but, reasoned Mr. Buchanan, inasmuch as the enemies of Walker now in possession of the government of Nicaragua do not complain, therefore Commodore Paulding's action was not reprehensible. Nevertheless, it was a grave error and a dangerous precedent, should it be allowed to go unrebuked. Acting upon the logical sequence of that opinion, Walker demanded that the Government of the United States should indemnify him for his losses and, by granting free transportation to a new expedition, restore the *status quo ante*. Needless to say, the petition was not granted. He then instituted civil suits against Paulding, claiming damages for illegal arrest and detention, suits which lingered in the courts and never arrived at a decision.

The *Fashion* was condemned for having sailed from Mobile under a false clearance, and sold by the United States marshal for two hundred dollars. Her cargo, which was brought back by the frigates *Saratoga* and *Wabash*, showed that the filibusters had made ample preparations for the equipment of a force sufficient to have easily reconquered the country had they been able to secure a foothold. That their failure should be caused by the action of their fellow countrymen they had never dreamed. Walker, before his departure, had satisfied himself that he should suffer no harm if only he could get away in quiet. Least of all did he dream of being molested on foreign soil. Proof came readily, when it was too late to be of any service, that Paulding had transgressed his powers in breaking up the expedition. The cause of his enmity was not difficult to fathom. Fate seems to rejoice in a certain kind of ironical cruelty, whereby she sends to a Napoleon the gad-fly, Hudson Lowe, and thwarts the ambition of a Walker by the pipe-clay petulance of a naval martinet. It is as though Cæsar had caught a cold, and died of it, in crossing the Rubicon. Paulding and other petty potentates chose to take offence at the disrespectful manner in which Walker, a mere uncommissioned adventurer, had dared speak of Commander Davis. They resented it as an insult to "the service," and when the subsequent correspondence with Commander Chatard was laid before the Commodore, his indignation knew no bounds. The man who would threaten to shoot a naval officer for penetrating his military lines without a pass could be only a pirate and outlaw. As such, Paulding had the filibuster arrested, although permitting him, with charming inconsistency, to go to New York on parole.

But the irreparable mischief was done, and Walker found slight consolation in having his persecutor suspended from active service, or in the prosecution of endless civil suits for damages, a species of vengeance which carries its own punishment.

CHAPTER XVII.

Walker's "History of the War"—Lands at Ruatan and takes Trujillo—Retreats before the English forces—Surrender—Trial and execution of the last of the Filibusters.

DURING the following two years Walker continued his efforts to regain power in Nicaragua, his friends maintaining their unshaken confidence in his ability to succeed and in the "destiny" which had lately played him such sorry tricks. On the 30th of October, 1858, President Buchanan found it necessary to issue a proclamation calling attention to certain plans of emigration companies intending to colonise Nicaragua, the leading promoter of which was William Walker. "This person," it said, "who has severed the ties of loyalty which bind him to the United States, and who aspires to the presidency of Nicaragua, has notified the Collector of the port of Mobile that two or three hundred of those emigrants will be ready to embark and sail for that port towards the middle of November;" and the president warned the intending emigrants that they would not be allowed to carry out their project.

In spite, however, of this proclamation a party of one hundred and fifty filibusters, commanded by Colonel Anderson, embarked about the 1st of December on the schooner *Susan* at the port of Mobile. The voyage terminated abruptly by shipwreck off the coast of Honduras, whence the expeditionists were rescued by a British vessel of war and carried back to their home. Doubleday thus describes the ruse by which the adventurers deceived the Federal authorities in escaping from Mobile :—

"No customs official had molested us while fast to the dock, but when we had reached the open bay a shadowy vessel ran athwart our bow in the semi-obscurity of the night, hailing us as she passed by announcing herself a United States revenue cutter, commanded by Captain Morris. He had orders if we should persist in sailing with our present cargo, to sink us as soon as we were a marine league from the shore, that distance constituting in their parlance the open sea. This we agreed among ourselves was unpleasant. She carried heavy guns while we carried none, and besides not even Walker was quite prepared as yet to make war with the United States.

"Captain Harry Maury, who commanded our schooner, was a thorough sailor, intimately acquainted with the varying depths of the bay of his native Mobile, and a true type of the oft-quoted chivalry of the South. He furthermore had a rather intimate convivial acquaintance with Captain Morris of the cutter.

"We therefore readily agreed that he should try his diplomatic talent, to extricate us from our unpleasant situation, for he assured us that Morris was a man to carry out his instructions.

"As the cutter again came around within hailing distance, Maury hailed, asking permission to go aboard with a friend or two, for discussion of the situation. Receiving a cordial invitation to bring as many of his friends as he pleased, Colonel Anderson and I accompanied him.

"The wind being very light the two vessels kept almost side by side while we were in the cabin of the cutter. Maury remarked that to men who were prospectively so near Davy Jones' locker, a glass of grog would not be unacceptable.

"Morris, hospitably inclined, set forth champagne, drinking fraternally with those whom a hard duty compelled him to immolate, and, as bottle succeeded bottle, I saw that it was to become a question of endurance.

"Perfect courtesy was sustained and still further tested when Maury invited Morris to come aboard the schooner and try our wine, pledging himself that he should be returned in safety to his own vessel. Whatever Morris might have decided an hour before, he now promptly accepted the invitation, following us in his own boat.

"Drinking was resumed on the schooner, and, as Morris was helped into his boat, Maury told him that he would not keep so good a fellow chasing us through the darkness of the night, but would anchor and wait for daylight, cautioning him not to run into us when our anchor went down.

"The night had become exceedingly dark, and as the captain of the cutter reached his deck, Captain Maury called out, cautioning Morris not to run into us when we should bring up.

"At the same time the order was given in a loud voice to 'let go,' and by a preconcerted arrangement the anchor chain rattling through one hawse-hole was pulled in at the other.

"Morris, supposing he heard the chain carrying our anchor down, let go his own. As he brought up we shot ahead, and then came the delicate part of the business.

"Maury had reckoned on the difference in draught between our vessel and the cutter—about six inches—together with his superior knowledge of the depths in the bay, to carry us over by a short cut into the sea. He had arranged his manœuvre to coincide with our arrival at the spot on which he wished to make the test.

"We therefore headed directly across the channel, and Morris, quickly perceiving the trick we had played him, followed as soon as he could pull in his anchor. Even this delay gave us a start which in the thick darkness deprived him of the advantage of our pilotage. We afterward learned that he did not go far before he was fast on the bottom, and of course had to wait for high tide to get off." *

Shortly after the sailing of the *Susan*, the Collector of the port of New Orleans detained a steamship with a party of three hundred "emigrants" who were compelled to give up their design of colonizing in Central America. No further attempt was made by Walker until September, 1859, when the guns of a United States frigate were brought to bear upon the steamer *Philadelphia* at New Orleans, forcibly compelling her passengers to disembark. About the same time Lord Lyons, the British minister, notified the American executive that his Government had resolved to interfere in repelling forcibly any future attempts of Walker against Nicaragua. A fleet of English vessels of war was permanently stationed at San Juan del Norte, while a similarly strong force guarded the Pacific gate. The United States also kept a strong force in the Carribean Sea to watch the movements of the exiled president. Napoleon was hardly more of a nightmare to the Holy Alliance than was Walker to the two powerful countries which did him the honour of this surveillance.

Meanwhile he was employing his enforced leisure in writing a history of his Nicaraguan career, which he published in the spring of 1860. The book, which was written in the third person, after the style of "Cæsar's Commentaries," is valuable chiefly as a reflection of the author's character. His modesty in alluding to his own exploits is extreme; but he makes no hesitation of avowing his principles as an ardent champion of slavery, devoting many pages to an exposition of arguments which were never logical and are now mournful and ridiculous. That

* "The Filibuster War in Nicaragua."

he was sincere is unquestionable. He was a man who would live or die in support of his convictions, and who had too much sincerity of purpose ever to succeed in any undertaking which required duplicity. A proof of his impolitic honesty is found in the fact that at this period of his career he embraced the Catholic religion, a step not calculated to win him favour among either his political friends or enemies. It has been incorrectly stated that he joined the faith on becoming President of Nicaragua; it would have been a wise stroke of worldly policy for him to have done so. But the fact is, that he stoutly maintained his independence of thought until his reason was convinced, even though it might injure him with the clerical party in that country. In Napoleon's place Walker would never have donned the turban nor sought to conciliate the Pontiff, though the empire of a world rewarded the stroke. Empires are neither won nor held by men of such obstinate conscience.

The evident impossibility of running the gauntlet of the British and American cruisers in the Carribean Sea determined him to seek a new pathway to his cherished goal; and that way, he decided, lay through the exposed part of the enemy's territory, the eastern coast of Honduras. It would seem that at that time the Island of Ruatan, a fertile land with a population of about 1,700 souls, was not under the usual British man-of-war captain's sovereignty, but owed a nominal allegiance to the Republic of Honduras. Upon the always ready invitation of some of its inhabitants, Walker prepared to use it as a base of operations against his former enemy, President Alvarez, and as a stepping-stone to the real point of attack. Accordingly, in the early part of August, 1860, having made arrangements for a strong body of reinforcements to follow and join him at Trujillo, he sailed in the schooner *Clifton* from Mobile with a force of about a hundred men, including the veterans Rudler, Henry, Dolan, and Anderson, and landed at Ruatan on the 15th of the month. There he issued a proclamation to the people of Honduras, which was an explicit avowal of his objects and desires :

"More than five years ago, I, with others, was invited to the Republic of Nicaragua and was promised certain rights and privileges on the condition of certain services rendered the state. We performed the services required of us, but the existing authorities of Honduras joined a combination to drive us from Central America. In the course of events the people of the Bay Islands find themselves in nearly the same position as the Americans held in Nicaragua in November, 1855. The same policy which led Guardiola to make war on us will induce him to drive the people of the Islands from Honduras. A knowledge of this fact has led certain residents of the Islands to call upon the adopted citizens of Nicaragua to aid in the maintenance of their rights of person and property; but no sooner had a few adopted citizens of Nicaragua answered this call of the residents of the Islands by repairing to Ruatan than the acting authorities of Honduras, alarmed for their safety, put obstacles in the way of carrying out the treaty of November 28, 1859. Guardiola delays to receive the Islands because of the presence of a few men whom he has injured; and thus, for party purposes, not only defeats the territorial interests of Honduras, but thwarts, for the moment, a cardinal object of Central American policy. The people of the Bay Islands can be ingrafted on your Republic only by wise concessions properly made. The existing authorities of Honduras have, by their past acts, given proof that they would not make the requisite concessions. The same policy which Guardiola pursued toward the naturalized Nicaraguans prevents him from pursuing the only course by which Honduras can expect to hold the Islands. It becomes, therefore, a common object with the naturalized Nacaraguans, and with the people of the Bay Islands, to place in the government of Honduras those who will yield the rights lawfully required in the two states. Thus, the Nicaraguans will secure a return to their adopted country, and the Bay Islanders will obtain full guarantees from the sovereignty under which they are to be placed by the treaty of November 28, 1859. To obtain, however, the object at which we aim, we do not make war against the people of Honduras, but only against a government which stands in the way of the interests, not only of Honduras, but of all Central America. The people of Honduras may therefore rely on all the protection they may require for their rights, both of person and property.

"WILLIAM WALKER."

To capture the town of Trujillo, on the mainland, was but the work of half an hour, only a few of the assailants being wounded. Walker received a slight wound in the face. Scarcely had the town been occupied when a British war-steamer, the *Icarus*, appeared on the scene. Captain Salmon, her commander, immediately notified Walker that the British Government held a mortgage against the revenues of the port, as security for certain claims, and that he intended to protect the interests of his Government by taking possession of the town. Walker replied that he had made Trujillo a free port, and consequently could not entertain any claims for revenues which no longer existed. The captain refused to recognize any change in the government of Honduras, and sent a peremptory demand for surrender, promising, in case of compliance, to carry the prisoners back to the United States, and threatening to open fire on the town if it were not surrendered. Meanwhile General Alvarez, with 700 soldiers, was preparing to make an assault by land. Thus hemmed in, Walker determined to evacuate Trujillo, which he did the following night, retreating down the coast with only seventy men. In their haste they were compelled to leave behind all their heavy baggage and accoutrements, carrying only thirty rounds of ammunition each; the rest they destroyed at Trujillo. When the British landed next morning they were only in time to protect the sick and wounded in the hospital from the ferocious Hondurians. The *Icarus* immediately took Alvarez and a strong force on board and steamed down the coast in pursuit.

At the mouth of the Rio Negro they learned that Walker lay encamped at the Indian village of Lemas, whither the boats of the *Icarus* were sent. They found the adventurers in no condition to oppose such overwhelming odds. They had carried with them from Trujillo only two barrels of bread, and being without blankets or overcoats, many had been attacked with fever from sleeping on the damp unhealthy ground. To reach Nicaragua in such miserable plight would have been impossible, even had they any hope of meeting a hospitable reception there. The Indians through whose territory they should have to pass were fierce and hostile to all intruders, and Olancho ("Olancho, ancho para intrar, angosto para salir": "Easy to enter, hard to leave") lay in the way. To Captain Salmon's demand for unconditional surrender, Walker replied with the inquiry, whether he was surrendering to the British or to the Hondurenos? Captain Salmon twice assured him, distinctly and specifically, that it was to her Majesty's forces; whereupon the filibusters laid down their arms and were carried on board the *Icarus*. On arriving at Trujillo, Captain Salmon turned his prisoners over to the Honduran authorities, despite their protest and demand for trial before a British tribunal. But Captain Salmon was only a young and rather pompous commander who disdained to argue the case, although he so far interested himself as to secure the pardon of all except the leader and one faithful follower, Colonel Rudler. West, Dolan, and other veterans who had joined this last forlorn hope were either unknown to the Hondurenos, or not deemed of sufficient importance to merit severe punishment.

Captain Salmon offered to plead for Walker, if the latter would ask his intercession as an American citizen. But Walker, with the bitter remembrance of all the injuries which his nativity had brought upon him, thanked his captor, and refused to demean himself by denying the country which had adopted and honoured him.

He was arraigned before a court-martial on the 11th of September, and, after a brief examination, he was condemned to die by the fusillade next morning. He heard his sentence with calmness, and was remanded to prison to pass the night in preparing for death. At half-past seven o'clock on the morning of September 12th he was led out to the place of execution. He walked unfettered, with calm and firm tread. He carried a crucifix in his left hand, a hat in his right. A priest walked by his side, reciting the prayers for the dying. Two soldiers marched before him carrying drawn sabres ; three more followed him with bayonets at the charge. Upon entering the hollow square of soldiery on the plaza he begged the priest to ask pardon in his name of any one whom he had wronged in his last expedition. Then, mounting the fatal stool, he addressed his executioners in Spanish, for none of his comrades had been allowed to witness the execution, and said:

"I am a Roman Catholic. The war which I made, in accordance with the suggestion of some of the people of Ruatan, was unjust. I ask pardon of the people. I receive death with resignation. Would that it might be for the good of society!"

Then, calm as he had ever been, whether in peace or in war, he awaited the fatal signal. The captain of the firing party gave a sharp order, dropped the point of his sabre, and, at the sign, three soldiers stepped forward to within twenty feet of the condemned, and fired their muskets. All of the balls took effect, but still the victim was not dead; whereupon a fourth soldier advanced, and placing the muzzle of his piece at the forehead of the victim, blew out his brains. And so died the last of the filibusters!

CHAPTER XVIII.

Character of Walker—A private's devotion—Anecdote—After-fate of the filibusters—Henningsen's epitaph—Last Cuban expedition—The *Virginius* tragedy—An Englishman to the rescue—Finis.

AS Walker was the last, so he was the greatest of American filibusters. He was not a great man, nor by any means a good one; but he was the greatest and the best of his class. His fault was ambition. It was a fault with him because it was a failure. From such a verdict there is no appeal. No apology can be offered for ambition ungratified; and successful ambition needs none. But the world's estimate of his personal character and actions has been needlessly severe. He was not the insatiable monster of cruelty that his enemies have painted. He was a man of deep, if narrow, learning, fertile resources, and grand audacity. He was calm and temperate in words and actions, and mercilessly just in exacting obedience from the turbulent spirits who linked their fortunes with his. He lacked worldly wisdom; nothing could induce him to forego the least of his rights to gain a greater ultimate advantage. He would maintain the dignity of his office, though it cost him the office itself. The lawyer belittled the lawgiver in his attempt virtually to confiscate the lands of Nicaragua by the help of an unworthy legal device; while his design for the restoration of slavery was as impolitic as it was futile, unjust, and barbarous. The action was, doubtless, the result of an honest belief in that "divine institution," as well as of a desire to show his sympathy with his devoted friends in the United States; but the effect was only to put another weapon into the hands of his foreign enemies, without materially strengthening him at home. It was a defiance to his powerful British opponents, and a wanton outrage upon the free states of Central America, alienating the sympathies of all who hoped from the evil of conquest to extract the good of civilization. Judged, as he wished to be judged, by his public policy, Walker was unequal to the office of a Liberator. It would be unfair to criticize the domestic administration of one who held his office by the sword, yet it is true that he preserved order and enforced justice with more success than any ruler of Nicaragua who has filled the position since the independence of the country. Doctor Scherzer, the intelligent German traveller, writing at a time when Walker's success seemed assured, heartily rejoices in the new and grand career opening before Central America. He warmly commends Walker's administration of justice, without palliating his errors, and sees "the morning star of civilization rising in the Tropic sky."

Walker was humane in war, and allowed retaliatory measures to be taken against the Costa Ricans only after the latter had shamelessly abused his lenity by repeated massacres of defenceless prisoners and non-combatants. The tales of his cruelty to his men have uniformly proceeded from the lips of worthless and disgraced adventurers, who were mainly deserters. Had he been the cold and haughty tyrant painted by his enemies, the infatuated devotion of his followers is unaccountable by any human rule. Neither ambition nor recklessness can explain the conduct of men who followed him through life, with unswerving loyalty. "Private Charles Brogan" s recorded among the surrendering men at the end of the Sonora campaign. As "Private Brogan" his name figures among the *Vesta's* passengers. So again, it appears on the army register and in the lists of wounded, all through the

Nicaraguan campaign. Yet again, in 1857, when the second descent on Nicaragua ended ingloriously at San Juan del Norte, "Private Charles Brogan" heads the list of captured rank and file. Did he see his chief perish bravely at Trujillo? or had he himself gone before and escaped the tragic sight? This chronicler knows not, and history, alas! has forgotten greater men than the poor follower of the half-forgotten filibuster. All honour here to thee, Private Charles Brogan, whom no vision of fame or fortune tempted to serve so loyally and long the ill-starred chieftain of a contraband cause!

The truth is, Walker's attitude towards his officers of high rank was one of studied formality, which the necessities of his position made imperative. Familiarity in his intercourse with such volunteers would have been death to discipline. But towards his humbler followers he showed the kindness and consideration of a friend, and won their respect by sharing their dangers. "I have known him," says Henningsen, "to get up from a sick bed, ride forty miles to fight the Costa Ricans, whipping soundly a force of thrice his numbers, and then, after giving his horse to a wounded soldier, tramp back his forty miles, without, as the boys used to say, 'taking the starch out of his shirt collar.'" The men who did their duty spoke well of him always; but it was, of necessity, the knaves and cowards, mainly, who survived such bloody campaigns, and returned to defame their comrades. Few even of these accused him of selfishness, save in his ambition. For money he cared nothing; and the soldiers of fortune complained of hard fighting and no pillage.

He had a certain grim sense of humour, which finds occasional expression in the pages of his book. Of Guardiola's attempt to fire the hearts of his men by plying them with *aguardiente* before an engagement, in which they were ignominously routed, he says: "The empty demijohns which were picked up on the road after the action looked like huge cannon-balls that had missed their mark." There is wisdom as well as humour in his remark, that "the best manner of treating a revolutionary movement in Central America is to treat it as a boil: let it come to a head, and then lance it, letting all the bad matter out at once." The pompous pretence of his native friends and enemies amused the shrewd judge of men, who possessed a happy knack of epitomizing a character in a single phrase, as when he calls the native custom of indiscriminate conscription, "an inveterate habit of catching a man and tying him up with a musket in his hand, to make a soldier of him." Kinney "had acquired that sort of knowledge and experience of human nature to be derived from the exercise of the mule trade." He mentions his enemy Marcy only with a contemptuous allusion to the blunder of that statesman in referring to Nicaragua as a country of South America, and dismisses Mora from his notice with the qualified clemency: "Let us pass Mora in exile, as Ugolino in hell, afar off and with silence."

His sense of the ridiculous was too keen to allow him ever to depart from the rigid simplicity of manner and dress which was in such striking contrast with the gaudy attire and pompous demeanour of his native friends. His uniform consisted of a blue coat, dark pantaloons, and black felt hat with the red ribbon of the Democratic army; his weapons were a sword and pistols buckled in his belt, and these he carried only in battle, where they were rather for use than ornament.

His character is in many respects like that of Cortes. Both were unlicensed conquerors; both were served by volunteers; served well by the faithful and brave, and obeyed through fear by the knavish and cowardly. Bodily fatigue or danger had no terrors for either, nor were they chary of demanding equal courage and endurance from their followers. Cortes triumphed over his enemies in the field; but barely succeeded in defeating the machinations of his foes in the Spanish Cabinet. Had Walker been a Conquistador he would have conquered Mexico as Cortes did. Had Cortes been a Californian filibuster he might have conquered Nicaragua, but he would assuredly have succumbed to Marcy and Vanderbilt.

Unquestionably Walker was carried away by his firm belief in his destiny. He never doubted, until he felt the manacles on his wrists at Trujillo, that he was destined to play the part of a Cortes in Central America. He had risked death a hundred times in battle and skirmish without fear or doubt. Possibly he welcomed it, when at last it came, and was sincere in hoping that it might be for the good of society.

So died, in his thirty-seventh year, the man whose fame had filled two continents, who had more than once imperilled the peace of the world which remembers him only in the distorted and false character of a monster and an outlaw. The country which gave him birth, and little besides, save injustice, forgot amid the bloody conflict into which it was soon plunged, the fame and fate of the filibusters. Into the vortex of civil war were swept many of the restless spirits who had survived the sanguinary fields of Central America, and in it perished many of the bravest and ablest who had learned their first lesson in that stern school.

As most of them were of Southern birth, so they generally joined the ranks of the Confederacy. At the first call to arms, Henningsen offered his services to the seceding states, and was given a regiment in Wise's Legion of Northern Virginia. Frank Anderson went with him as lieutenant-colonel, and did good service for the lost cause. He was one of Walker's oldest veterans, having served in both the expeditions to Nicaragua. At the first battle of Rivas he was wounded three times, and left on the field for dead, but managed to drag himself into hiding before his comrades were all massacred, and so escaped to rejoin his command.

Henningsen served throughout the war; but, in spite of his experience on many fields, and the marked ability with which he filled his subordinate position, he never rose to distinction in the Confederacy. He was a natural leader in irregular warfare, as might have been expected of a pupil in the schools of Zumalacarregui, Schamyl, and Walker; and the scientific campaigning of the Peninsula gave no scope for his talents. But he had espoused the cause with honest convictions of its justice, and he supported it faithfully to the end. When that end and ruin came he returned to private life, a man without a career, and lived quietly and unobtrusively until his death in June, 1877. In his later years he was a devoted adherent of the patriots who were waging a fruitless war for freedom in Cuba. Once he visited the island in connection with a projected uprising, but saw no promise of success in the attempt. His death was sudden. He had been ill but a few days; a faithful friend, Colonel Gregg, a soldier who had fought against him in the Civil War, watched by his bedside; the sick man slept, while the tireless brain dreamed, what dreams who can say? of the chequered career about to close forever. Suddenly his eyes opened, and in them was something of the old fire, as he half sat up in his bed, and pointing to a print on the wall of the arms of "Cuba Libre," said, "Colonel, we'll free Cuba yet!" The ruling passion found voice in his last words—the next instant he fell back dead.

Henningsen was considered to have been the military genius of the Nicaraguan campaign by the detractors of Walker, who could not deny the wonderful success of the latter. But Henningsen himself always repudiated the undeserved fame, and was foremost in awarding to his chieftain whatever of glory was won in that profitless field. He died as he had lived, a true, simple-hearted gentleman, a knight-errant born centuries too late. Colonel John T. Pickett, a kindly philosopher, and one who in his heyday followed a filibuster's luckless banner, has engraved upon the tomb of Henningsen the apt motto from Gil Blas: "*Inveni portum. Spes et fortuna valete! Sat me lusistis. . . . Ludite nunc alios.*"

The filibusters whom the winds had blown from every quarter of the earth to the sunny vales of Nicaragua were drifted back, when the storm had broken and spent its fury, to the world of peace and prose. A few only of the worthier survive to recall that strange page in life's romance. Rudler, who was with his leader in all his campaigns, and who was sentenced to four years' imprisonment after the surrender in Honduras, returned to share the fortunes of the seceding South, as did also Wheat, Hicks, Fayssoux, Hornsby, and many others. In the vicissitudes of American life a few, like Doubleday and Kewen, even achieved wealth, which is perhaps as strange a climax to the career of a filibuster as any that could be conceived. The two O'Neils were men of invincible courage. Both died in battle, Calvin, the younger, at the age of twenty-one, after making a reputation for heroism that was marked even among that valiant group. Reluctantly we part with the wild band, Homeric heroes in more features than one; with Henry and Swingle, the ingenious gunners, Von Natzmer, the Prussian hussar, Pineda, the great-hearted native of an unworthy country, Hornsby, Rawle, Watters, and the Fifty-six who were "Immortal" for a day.

That most entertaining cosmopolitan, Laurence Oliphant, came very near adding the distinction of being a filibuster to his other experiences. He did, in fact, join an expedition which set out from New Orleans in December, 1856, for San Juan del Norte, with the intention of reinforcing Walker at Rivas. But the good steamer *Texas* reached her destination too late, Spencer and his Costa Ricans having closed the Transit. Among the adventurous spirits in the company was one who had taken part in the last ill-fated expedition of Lopez to Cuba, and spent a year and a half in a Spanish dungeon. "The story of his escape from a more serious fate," says Oliphant, "was characteristic of many other stirring narratives of a similar description, with which on moonlight nights we used to beguile the evening hours. He had served as an officer on General Lopez's staff during one of the expeditions to Cuba. When that officer, together with many of the more prominent members of the expedition, after a desperate resistance, was captured by the Spanish troops, my friend, who was one of the number, found himself with many of his countrymen thrown into the Havanna jail, and informed that he was to prepare for his execution on the following day. As an act of grace, however, permission was given to all the captives to indite a farewell letter to their friends, informing them of their approaching execution. Most of his fellow-victims could think of some one belonging to them to whom such a piece of information might prove interesting; but the poor captain racked in vain the chambers of his memory for a solitary individual to whom he could impart the melancholy tidings without feeling that his communication would be what in polite society would be called an 'unwarrantable intrusion of his personal affairs upon a comparative stranger.' He could think of nobody that cared about him; revolving this forlorn state of matters in his mind, ashamed to form the only exception to the general scribbling that was taking place, he determined to choose a friend, and then it flashed upon him, that as all the letters would probably be opened, he had better choose a good one. Under his present circumstances, who more appropriate than the Secretary of State for Foreign Affairs at Washington, then Daniel Webster? Not only should he make a friend of him, but an intimate friend, and then the Spanish Governor might shoot him if he chose, and take the risk. He accordingly commenced: 'Dan, my dear old boy, how little you thought when we parted at the close of that last agreeable visit of a week, which I paid you the other day, that within a month I should be "cribbed, cabined, and confined" in the infernal hole of a dungeon from which I indite this. I wish you would send the Spanish minister a case of that very old Madeira of yours, which he professes to prefer to the wines of his own country, and tell him the silly scrape I have got myself into, if indeed it be not too late, for they talk of sending me to "the bourne" to-morrow. However, one never can believe a word these rascals say, so I write this in the hope that they are lying as usual,—and am, my dear old schoolmate, your affectionate friend,——.' For once the absence of friends proved a real blessing. Had the captain been occupied by domestic considerations, he never would have invented so valuable an ally as was thus extemporised, and he was rewarded for his shrewd device on the following morning, by finding himself the only solitary individual of all the party allowed to 'stand over.' In a couple of hours Lopez and his companions had gone to the bourne, to which our captain so feelingly alluded; and when, at last, the trick was discovered, the crisis was past, and the Spanish Government finally condemned him to two years' confinement in chains in the dungeon at Ceuta, which was afterwards commuted to eighteen months. He had just returned from this dismal abode in time once more to gratify the adventurous propensities which had already so nearly cost him his life; and it is due to him to say, that even the daring and reckless spirits by whom he was surrounded, agreed in saying that he placed an unusually low estimate on that valuable possession."

There is little to add to the history of filibusterism, which may be ranked among the dead industries or the lost arts, just as one chooses to regard it. Contrary to the predictions of the prophets, the disbandment of a million of men at the end of the Americal Civil War was effected without trouble. The European Powers breathed more freely when it was accomplished, satisfied that the aggressive "Yankee" was not so grasping as he had been painted. Maximilian of Mexico slept peacefully, and his late unruly subjects renewed their fraternal quarrels, undisturbed by interference from abroad, and finally settled into uninteresting peace and prosperity. Filibusterism died because, in sooth, it had no longer a reason for being. To "extend the area" of an abolished slavery were as paradoxical as Quixotic. Nevertheless, the peculiar institution chanced to prove the cause of yet one final, fallacious, and ghastly episode.

Cuba, once coveted as an ally by the slaveholders of the United States, was now the only spot on the civilized globe afflicted with the barbarous stain. The "ever-faithful isle" was trebly cursed with slavery, foreign rule, and martial law. Like a spendthrift come to his last penny, Spain, having squandered a continent, clung with tenacity to its remaining possession in the Western world. Thrones were set up and knocked down at home, republics were born and strangled, but no change for the better was ever felt in the wretched colony. Rather, it suffered from every change, since each involved a change of masters. Hungry, avaricious masters they were, spurred on by the uncertain tenure of their office, to reap as rich plunder as might be got out of the hapless colony, ere a new turn of the cards at home should force them to make room for other needy patriots. The power of the Captain-General is almost absolute at the best of times. In such times as those it is well-nigh omnipotent. The colony was denied representation in the Cortes, while taxed beyond endurance to support the government, and robbed by an army of officials appointed to rule over her without her consent or choice.

LA REPUBLICA
DE
CUBA,
Pagara al portador
CINCO PESOS
SERIE
F
5
Nº
9691
de 1869.

Cuba at last rebelled. The planters who found themselves robbed of the fruits of their industry as fast as they were gathered, and who saw the system of slavery develop into the most intolerable of all wrongs, the wrong unprofitable, at last determined to strike for their liberty. They freed and armed their slaves. They burned their plantations, and in September, 1868, hoisted the lone star flag in the mountains and bade defiance to the Spaniard. The leading insurgents were all men of wealth and influence, while their followers were necessarily ignorant and undisciplined. But success meant freedom to both classes; and they threw themselves into the unequal struggle with sublime desperation. All, or mostly all, of the leaders perished during the long and bloody contest, which ended only after it had lasted eight years, at a cost to Spain of two hundred thousand lives and over seven hundred million dollars. The figures are those of Governor-General Don Joaquin Javellar. Even yet the embers smoulder, awaiting only a favorable moment to be fanned into another terrible flame.

The Junta of Cuban patriots in New York sent out several cargoes of war material, and enlisted many American adventurers; but no regular expedition was at any time organized. Among those who participated in the guerilla conflict were Domingo de Goicouria, once Minister of Hacienda in Nicaragua, and Colonel Jack Allen, also not unknown to filibuster fame. Poor Goicouria paid the penalty at the fatal garrote, as did also the aged Santa Rosa, comrade of Lopez and Crittenden.

The culminating tragedy came to pass in October, 1873. On the 23rd of that month, the steamer *Virginius*, a former blockade-runner, cleared from Kingston, Jamaica, for Port Limon, Costa Rica, with passengers to the number of a hundred or more. Her true destination was the island of Cuba, her mission the transportation of arms and filibusters. Among the passengers were the patriot leaders, Cespedes, Ryan, Varona, and Del Sol. The steamer touched at Port Au Prince, received her cargo of arms, ammunition, medicines, and equipments, and made sail for Cuba. She was seen and chased by the Spanish gunboat *Tornado*, which, by a curious coincidence, was also a former blockade-runner and a sister ship of the *Virginius*—a favoured sister, since she speedily overhauled and captured her prey.

The *Virginius*, though flying the American flag on the high seas, was made a prize and carried into the port of Santiago de Cuba. Captain Fry, her commander, an American citizen and former officer in the United States and Confederate navies, protested in vain against the outrage. He was denied communication with his consul, and thrown into prison, with all his passengers and crew. The four insurgent leaders were first tried by summary court martial and sentenced to death. The sentence was promptly executed, at sunrise on the 6th of November, five days after the capture. Ryan and Varona refused to kneel, and were shot as they stood. The heads of the four were cut off and carried on pikes through the city and before the windows of the prison, where their comrades lay awaiting a similar fate. The news of the tragedy had been carried to the United States, and the American and English consuls interested themselves to protect the remaining prisoners; but the sham trials went on in spite of their protests. On the 7th of November, Captain Fry and fifty-one companions were brutally butchered in the presence of a ferocious mob, who mangled the senseless remains.

There still survived ninety-three unfortunates. By this time the telegraph had spread the terrible news throughout the world, and awakened a tempest of indignation everywhere save in Havanna and Madrid. Even in Spain, at the time enjoying a government nominally republican, there was some surprise at the horrible tragedy, and Señor

Castelar, his humanity spurred up by a peremptory despatch from the English Foreign Office, was moved to beseech of his lieutenant to be a little less hasty in his action. The appeal was unheeded, and all of the hapless victims were condemned to immediate execution. But General Burriel had made an epicure's mistake in prolonging his feast.

There was no American vessel of war in the neighbourhood of Santiago de Cuba, but, what was more to the purpose, as far as the fate of the prisoners was concerned, there was the inevitable British man-of-war within a day's sail. The sloop *Niobe* lay in the harbour of Kingston, with half of her crew on shore liberty, when the news of the massacre reached her commander, Sir Lambton Lorraine. He sailed at once for Santiago. An English captain does not need instructions in such an emergency. He has standing orders and can trust to his nation for support of his acts. "I am an English subject," said Thompson, a sailor of the *Virginius*, "and they won't dare lay hands on me." He knew his countrymen, but he mistook the Spaniard. He and fifteen compatriots were among the murdered fifty-three.

Then did the hearts of other British subjects and American citizens fail them as they awaited their doom. The Americans had long abandoned hope. The English were giving way to despair, when a glad sight met their eyes. It was the *Niobe* entering the harbour, with the cross of St. George flying at her peak. She did not stop to salute the fort, but gracefully rounded to, a few cables' lengths from the *Tornado* and her prize, with port-holes open and her crew at quarters. Ere her anchor fell, the captain's gig was in the water, and soon its oars were flashing spray as it sped shoreward. In the stern sheets sat the young commander.

His veto of the massacres was delivered not a moment too soon. Burriel demurred, questioning the Englishman's right to interfere. Lorraine insisted on the right, claiming that there were British subjects among the prisoners. To the Spaniard's denial of that fact, he answered that he would take upon himself, then, the responsibility of protecting American citizens, in the absence of their own defenders. The delicate points of this officious interference Señor Burriel might have debated, long and ingeniously, with a different kind of adversary. But the English sailor was no casuist. His arguments were brutally direct. "Stop the murders, or I bombard your town," they said in so many words. Indeed, he was a very rash and impulsive young man. Under a free government he would have been cashiered, without benefit of clergy. Only a few months before, so the rumour went, he had fired hot shot and shell into the town of Omoa, Honduras; and there was no guessing what he might not be tempted to do with Santiago, upon such very strong provocation. Extreme measures were averted, however, by Burriel's consenting to reprieve his prisoners.

Then arose the question of reparation. Minister Sickles at Madrid took high and dignified ground, insisting upon the fullest apology for the insult offered to his country's flag, and indemnity to the families of the murdered men. Castelar assented to a treaty covering every demand of Mr. Sickles, and was about to sign it formally, when he received advices from Washington which made him retract his concession, and made General Sickles telegraph his resignation. It appeared that the Spanish minister at Washington had proved himself a skilful diplomat by negotiating with the American Secretary of State a protocol, the terms of which were as extraordinary as the secret manner in which they were drawn up.

By this arrangement, which settled the question for ever, the United States waived its demands for a salute to the insulted flag, accepting a formal apology instead, waived the question of indemnity, and did not press for the punishment of the guilty officials of Santiago. What the Government did demand and obtain, it would be hard to say. The only visible reparation was the conditional surrender of the captured vessel, for trial before an American court of admiralty. Should it transpire that she had been in lawful possession of her American register, then she was to be given to her owners; if otherwise, she was to be restored to her captors. Strangely enough, there was no provision made in the latter contingency for the rendition and punishment of the survivors. All possible dispute on that point was happily averted by the inscrutable catastrophe which befell the luckless craft. She foundered, opportunely, in a gale off Cape Fear on her voyage to the United States, to the great relief of two governments.

There was much indignation in the United States over the awful tragedy and accompanying insult to the national flag. A vast amount of money was expended on the navy, and certain commanders were ordered to review their forces and manœuvre their squadrons almost in sight of the Cuban shores. Warlike talk was in the air; but the sober second thought of the people was averse to a war in defence of the insulted banner, when it had been used to shelter adventurers in an illegal undertaking. The American is slow to be angered, and has none of the Englishman's sentimental reverence for bunting, unless it covers a clearly just cause. Sir Lambton was speedily promoted by his Government. Somebody in the American Congress proposed a resolution of thanks to him also, but it was promptly tabled, with a perception of the fitness of things hardly to have been expected in that sagacious body. More fitting and spontaneous was the gift sent to him by the miners of far Nevada, a fourteen-pound silver brick, emblematic of the highest expression of eulogy.

The *Virginius* tragedy, and the indifference with which

it was beheld by the American Government, were sufficient warnings, had any been needed, to the Filibuster, that his day was past. In unmistakable language he was told that his country's flag should not and would not shield him in the violation of international law. Theoretically the execution of the *Virginius* adventurers was as much of an outrage on the dignity of the United States as if it had occurred on American soil. Practically, the delicate points of flag and register and high-seas neutrality were dismissed from consideration, and the evidently hostile mission of the vessel was held to excuse the severe punishment meted out to her passengers. Whether or not the lesson may be heeded when the example shall have grown old, it is plain that for the present at least, the race of filibusters is extinct.

They were a virile race, with virtues and vices of generous growth. They played no mean part on the world's stage, albeit a part often wayward and mistaken. They were American dreamers. Had they been Greeks or Norsemen, or free to roam the world in the days of Cortes, Balboa, and Pizarro, victors like them, History would have dealt more kindly by them. As it is, spite of faults and failures, they do not deserve the harshest of all fates, oblivion.

THE END.

THE LIFE OF

COLONEL DAVID CROCKETT.

(Abridged.)

INTRODUCTION.

THE brief reference in the foregoing pages to David Crockett, as an intrepid soldier, does but scant justice to the memory of one who, taken altogether, was perhaps the most picturesque figure in American border life. He is entitled to remembrance, not only for his heroic qualities, but also because he was the first of the school of extravagant humorists to whom has been given the distinctive name of American.

Borrowing nothing, save his inherited Celtic sense of fun, from the old world, the garb of his humour is wholly native. With a naïve affectation of simplicity, and even of ignorance, he is in his wildest flights of humour always shrewdly conscious of his own extravagance. There is much in Crockett that suggests a later, and more illustrious backswoodsman, the wise, kindly, story-loving Abraham Lincoln.

The tragic death of Crockett is told in the story of the Alamo. In the following pages will be found the narrative of his life, written by himself in the year before his death. A spurious "life" of him had been published by an anonymous scribbler, and it was in order to correct its misrepresentations that he wrote his autobiography.

In this abridged narrative I have omitted many passages of merely local or ephemeral nature, chiefly containing political allusions of no interest to the readers of to-day. The few which are retained on account of the context refer to Andrew Jackson and his quarrel over the United States Bank, Crockett being a bitter political opponent of the grim President who, too, could fight as stoutly as any backswoodsman of them all, and who did not deserve the censures of his quondam comrade in arms.

With this preliminary explanation the reader is introduced to Colonel David Crockett, who writes his own unique preface.

PREFACE.

FASHION is a thing I care mighty little about, except when it happens to run just exactly according to my own notion; and I was mighty nigh sending out my book without any preface at all, until a notion struck me, that perhaps it was necessary to explain a little the reason why and wherefore I had written it.

Most of authors seek fame, but I seek for justice—a holier impulse than ever entered into the ambitious struggles of the votaries of that *fickle, flirting* goddess.

A publication has been made to the world, which has done me much injustice; and the catchpenny errors which it contains, have been already too long sanctioned by my silence. I don't know the author of the book—and indeed I don't want to know him; for after he has taken such a liberty with my name, and made such an effort to hold me up to public ridicule, he cannot calculate on anything but my displeasure. If he had been content to have written his opinions about me, however contemptuous they might have been, I should have less reason to complain. But when he professes to give my narrative (as he often does) in my own language, and then puts into my mouth such language as would disgrace even an outlandish African, he must himself be sensible of the injustice he has done me, and the trick he has played off on the public. I have met with hundreds, if not with thousands of people, who have formed their opinions of my appearance, habits, language, and everything else from that deceptive work.

They have almost in every instance expressed the most profound astonishment at finding me in human shape, and with the *countenance, appearance*, and *common feelings* of a human being. It is to correct all these false notions, and to do justice to myself, that I have written.

In the following pages I have endeavoured to give the reader a plain, honest, homespun account of my state in life, and some few of the difficulties which have attended me along its journey, down to this time. I am perfectly aware that I have related many small and, as I fear, uninteresting circumstances; but if so, my apology is, that it was rendered necessary by a desire to link the different periods of my life together, as they have passed, from my childhood onward, and thereby to enable the reader to select such parts of it as he may relish most, if, indeed, there is anything in it which may suit his palate.

I have also been operated on by another consideration. It is this: —I know, that obscure as I am, my name is making a considerable deal of fuss in the world. I can't tell why it is, nor in what it is to end. Go where I will, everybody seems anxious to get a peep at me; and it would be hard to tell which would have the advantage, if I, and the "Government," and "Black Hawk," and a great eternal big caravan of *wild varments* were all to be showed at the same time in four different parts of any of the big cities in the nation. I am not so sure that I shouldn't get the most custom of any of the crew. There must therefore be something in me, or about me, that attracts attention, which is even mysterious to myself. I can't understand it, and I therefore put all the facts down, leaving the reader free to take his choice of them.

On the subject of my style, it is bad enough, in all conscience, to please critics, if that is what they are after. They are a sort of vermin, though, that I sha'n't even so much as stop to brush off. If they want to work on my book, just let them go ahead; and after they are done, they had better blot out all their criticisms, than to know what opinion I would express of *them*, and by what sort of a curious name I would call *them*, if I was standing near them, and looking over their shoulders. They will, at most, have only their trouble for their pay. But I rather expect I shall have them on my side.

But I don't know anything in my book to be criticised on by honourable men. Is it on my spelling?—that's not my trade. Is it on my grammar?—I hadn't time to learn it, and make no pretensions to it. Is it on the order and arrangement of my book?—I never wrote one before, and never read very many; and, of course, know mighty little about that. Will it be on the authorship of the book?—this I claim, and I'll hang on to it, like a wax plaster. The whole book is my own, and every sentiment and sentence in it. I would not be such a fool, or knave either, as to deny that I have had it hastily run over by a friend or so, and that some little alterations have been made in the spelling and grammar; and I am not so sure that it is not the worse of even that, for I despise this way of spelling contrary to nature. And as for grammar, it's pretty much a thing of nothing at last, after all the fuss that's made about it. In some places I wouldn't suffer either the spelling, or grammar, or anything else to be touched and therefore it will be found in my own way.

But if anybody complains that I have had it looked over, I can only say to him, her, or them—as the case may be—that while critics were learning grammar, and learning to spell, I and "Doctor Jackson, LL.D.," were fighting in the wars; and if our books, and messages, and proclamations, and cabinet writings, and so forth, and so on, should need a little looking over, and a little correcting of the spelling and the grammar to make them fit for use, it's just nobody's business. Big men have more important matters to attend to than crossing their *t*'s—, and dotting their *i*'s—, and such like small things. But the "Government's" name is to the proclamation, and my name's to the book; and if I didn't write the book, the "Government" didn't write the proclamation, which no man *dares to deny!*

But just read for yourself, and my ears for a heel tap, if before you get through you don't say, with many a good-natured smile and hearty laugh, "This is truly the very thing itself—the exact image of its Author,

"DAVID CROCKETT."

CHAPTER I.

AS the public seem to feel some interest in the history of an individual so humble as I am, and as that history can be so well known to no person living as to myself, I have, after so long a time, and under many pressing solicitations from my friends and acquaintances, at last determined to put my own hand to it, and lay before the world a narrative on which they may at least rely as being true. And seeking no ornament or colouring for a plain, simple tale of truth, I throw aside all hypocritical and fawning apologies, and according to my own maxim, just "*go ahead.*" Where I am not known, I might, perhaps, gain some little credit by having thrown around this volume some of the flowers of learning; but where I am known, the vile cheatery would soon be detected, and like the foolish jackdaw, that with *borrowed* tail attempted to play the peacock, I should be justly robbed of my pilfered ornaments, and sent forth to strut without a tail for the balance of my time. I shall commence my book with what little I have learned of the history of my father, as all *great men* rest many, if not most, of their hopes on their noble ancestry. Mine was poor, but I hope honest, and even that is as much as many a man can say. But to my subject.

My father's name was John Crockett, and he was of Irish descent. He was either born in Ireland or on a passage from that country to America across the Atlantic. He was by profession a farmer, and spent the early part of his life in the state of Pennsylvania. The name of my mother was Rebecca Hawkins. She was an American woman, born in the state of Maryland, between York and Baltimore. It is likely I may have heard where they were married, but if so, I have forgotten. It is, however, certain that they were, or else the public would never have been troubled with the history of David Crockett, their son.

I have an imperfect recollection of the part which I have understood my father took in the revolutionary war. I personally know nothing about it, for it happened to be a little before my day; but from himself, and many others who were well acquainted with its troubles and afflictions, I have learned that he was a soldier in the revolutionary war, and took part in that bloody struggle. He fought, according to my information, in the battle of King's Mountain against the British and Tories, and in some other engagements of which my remembrance is too imperfect to enable me to speak with any certainty. At some time, though I cannot say certainly when, my father, as I have understood, lived in Lincoln county, in the state of North Carolina. How long, I don't know. But when he removed from there, he settled in that district of country which is now embraced in the east division of Tennessee, though it was not then erected into a state.

He settled there under dangerous circumstances, both to himself and his family, as the country was full of Indians, who were at that time very troublesome. By the Creeks my grandfather and grandmother Crockett were both murdered in their own house, and on the very spot of ground where Rogersville, in Hawkins county, now stands. At the same time the Indians wounded Joseph Crockett, a brother to my father, by a ball, which broke his arm; and took James a prisoner, who was still a younger brother than Joseph, and who, from natural defects, was less able to make his escape, as he was both deaf and dumb. He remained with them for seventeen years and nine months, when he was discovered and recollected by my father and his eldest brother, William Crockett; and was purchased by them from an Indian trader, at a price which I do not now remember; but so it was, that he was delivered up to them, and they returned him to his relatives. He now lives in Cumberland county, in the state of Kentucky, though I have not seen him for many years.

My father and mother had six sons and three daughters. I was the fifth son. What a pity I hadn't been the seventh! For then I might have been, by *common consent*, called *doctor*, as a heap of people get to be great men. But, like many of them, I stood no chance to become great in any other way than by accident. As my father was very poor, and living as he did, *far back in the back woods*, he had neither the means nor the opportunity to give me, or any of the rest of his children, any learning.

But before I get on the subject of my own troubles, and a great many very funny things that have happened to me, like all other historians and biographers I should not only inform the public that I was born myself, as well as other folks, and that this important event took place, according to the best information I have received on the subject, on the 17th of August, in the year 1786; whether by day or night, I believe I never heard, but if I did, I have forgotten. I suppose, however, it is not very material to my present purpose, nor to the world, as the more important fact is well attested, that I was born; and, indeed, it might be inferred, from my present size and appearance, that I was pretty *well born*, though I have never yet attached myself to that numerous and worthy society.

At the time my father lived at the mouth of Lime Stone, on the Nolachucky river; and for the purpose not only of showing what sort of a man I now am, but also to show how soon I began to be a *sort of a little man*, I have endeavoured to take the *back track* of life, in order to fix on the first thing that I can remember. But even then, as now, so many things were happening, that as Major Jack

Downing would say, they are all in "a pretty considerable of a snarl," and I find it "kinder hard" to fix on that thing, among them all, which really happened first. But I think it likely, I have hit on the outside line of my recollection; as one thing happened at which I was so badly scared, that it seems to me I could not have forgotten it, if it had happened a little time only after I was born. Therefore it furnishes me with no certain evidence of my age at the time; but I know one thing very well, and that is, that when it happened, I had no knowledge of the use of breeches, for I had never had any nor worn any.

But the circumstance was this: My four elder brothers, and a well-grown boy of about fifteen years old, by the name of Campbell, and myself, were all playing on the river's side; when all the rest of them got into my father's canoe, and put out to amuse themselves on the water, leaving me on the shore alone.

Just a little distance below them, there was a fall in the river, which went slap-right straight down. My brothers, though they were little fellows, had been used to paddling the canoe, and could have carried it safely anywhere about there; but this fellow Campbell wouldn't let them have the paddle, but fool like, undertook to manage it himself. I reckon he had never seen a water craft before; and it went just any way but the way he wanted it. There he paddled, and paddled, and paddled—all the while going wrong—until, in a short time, here they were all going, straight forward, stern foremost, right plump to the falls; and if they had only a fair shake, they would have gone over as slick as a whistle. It was'ent this, though, that scared me; for I was so infernal mad that they had left me on the shore, that I had as soon have seen them all go over the falls a bit, as any other way. But their danger was seen by a man by the name of Kendall, but I'll be shot if it was Amos; for I believe I would know him yet if I was to see him. This man Kendall was working in a field on the bank, and knowing there was no time to lose, he started full tilt, and here he come like a cane brake afire; and as he ran, he threw off his coat, and then his jacket, and then his shirt, for I know when he got to the water he had nothing on but his breeches. But seeing him in such a hurry, and tearing off his clothes as he went, I had no doubt but that the devil or something else was after him—and close on him, too—as he was running within an inch of his life. This alarmed me, and I screamed out like a young painter.* But Kendall didn't stop for this. He went ahead with all might, and as full bent on saving the boys, as Amos was on moving the deposites. When he came to the water he plunged in, and where it was too deep to wade he would swim, and where it was shallow enough he went bolting on; and by such exertions as I never saw at any other time in my life, he reached the canoe, when it was within twenty or thirty feet of the falls; and so great was the suck, and so swift the current, that poor Kendall had a hard time of it to stop them at last, as Amos will to stop the mouths of the people about his stockjobbing. But

* "Painter"—South-western dialect for *panther*.

he hung on to the canoe, till he got it stop'd, and then draw'd it out of danger. When they got out, I found the boys were more scared than I had been, and the only thing that comforted me was, the belief that it was a punishment on them for leaving me on shore.

Shortly after this, my father removed, and settled in the same county, about ten miles above Greenville.

There another circumstance happened, which made a lasting impression on my memory, though I was but a small child. Joseph Hawkins, who was a brother to my mother, was in the woods hunting for deer. He was passing near a thicket of brush, in which one of our neighbours was gathering some grapes, as it was in the fall of the year, and the grape season. The body of the man was hid by the brush, and it was only as he would raise his hand to pull the bunches that any part of him could be seen. It was a likely place for deer; and my uncle, having no suspicion that it was any human being, but supposing the raising of the hand to be an occasional twitch of a deer's ear, fired at the lump, and as the devil would have it, unfortunately shot the man through the body. I saw my father draw a silk handkerchief through the bullet hole, and entirely through his body; yet after a while he got well, as little as any one would have thought it. What become of him, or whether he is dead or alive, I don't know; but I reckon he didn't fancy the business of gathering grapes in an out-of-the-way thicket soon again.

The next move my father made was to the mouth of Cove creek, where he and a man by the name of Thomas Galbreath undertook to build a mill in partnership. They went on very well with their work until it was nigh done, when there came the second epistle to Noah's fresh, and away went their mill, shot, lock, and barrel. I remember the water rose so high, that it got up into the house we lived in, and my father moved us out of it, to keep us from being drowned. I was now about seven or eight years old, and have a pretty distinct recollection of everything that was going on. From his bad luck in that business, and being ready to wash out from mill building, my father again removed, and this time settled in Jefferson county, now in the State of Tennessee; where he opened a tavern on the road from Abbingdon to Knoxville.

His tavern was on a small scale, as he was poor; and the principal accommodations which he kept, were for the waggoners who travelled the road. Here I remained with him until I was twelve years old; and about that time, you may guess, if you belong to Yankee land, or, reckon, if like me you belong to the back-woods, that I began to make up my acquaintance with hard times, and a plenty of them.

An old Dutchman, by the name of Jacob Siler, who was moving from Knox county to Rockbridge, in the state of Virginia, in passing, made a stop at my father's house. He had a large stock of cattle that he was carrying on with him; and I suppose made some proposition to my father to hire some one to assist him.

Being hard run every way, and having no thought, as I believe, that I was cut out for a Congressman or the like, young as I was, and as little as I knew about travelling, or being from home, he hired me to the old Dutchman, to go four hundred miles on foot, with a perfect stranger that I never had seen until the evening before. I set out with a heavy heart, it is true, but I went ahead, until we arrived at the place, which was three miles from what is called the Natural Bridge, and made a stop at the house of a Mr. Hartley, who was father-in-law to Mr. Siler, who had hired me. My Dutch master was very kind to me, and gave me five or six dollars, being pleased, as he said, with my services.

This, however, I think was a bait for me, as he persuaded me to stay with him, and not return any more to my father. I had been taught so many lessons of obedience by my father, that I at first supposed I was bound to obey this man, or at least I was afraid openly to disobey him; and I therefore staid with him, and tried to put on a look of perfect contentment until I got the family all to believe I was fully satisfied. I had been there about four or five weeks, when one day myself and two other boys were playing on the road-side, some distance from the house. There came along three waggons. One belonged to an old man by the name of Dunn, and the others to two of his sons. They had each of them a good team, and were all bound for Knoxville. They had been in the habit of stopping at my father's as they passed the road, and I knew them. I made myself known to the old gentleman, and informed him of my situation; I expressed a wish to get back to my father and mother, if they could fix any plan for me to do so. They told me that they would stay that night at a tavern seven miles from there, and that if I could get to them before day the next morning, they would take me home; and if I was pursued, they would protect me. This was a Sunday evening; I went back to the good old Dutchman's house, and as good fortune would have it, he and the family were out on a visit. I gathered my clothes, and what little money I had, and put them all together under the head of my bed. I went to bed early that night, but sleep seemed to be a stranger to me. For though I was a wild boy, yet I dearly loved my father and mother, and their images appeared to be so deeply fixed in my mind, that I could not sleep for thinking of them. And then the fear that when I should attempt to go out, I should be discovered and called to a halt, filled me with anxiety; and between my childish love of home, on the one hand, and the fears of which I have spoken, on the other, I felt mighty queer.

But so it was, about three hours before day in the morning I got up to make my start. When I got out, I found it was snowing fast, and that the snow was then on the ground about eight inches deep. I had not even the advantage of moonlight, and the whole sky was hid by the falling snow, so that I had to guess at my way to the big road, which was about a half mile from the house. I however pushed ahead and soon got to it, and then pursued it, in the direction to the waggons

I could not have pursued the road if I had not guided myself by the opening it made between the timber, as the snow was too deep to leave any part of it to be known by either seeing or feeling.

Before I overtook the waggons, the earth was covered about as deep as my knees; and my tracks filled so briskly after me, that by daylight my Dutch master would have seen no trace which I left.

I got to the place about an hour before day. I found the waggoners already stirring, and engaged in feeding and preparing their horses for a start. Mr. Dunn took me in and treated me with great kindness. My heart was more deeply impressed by meeting with such a friend, and "at such a time," than by wading the snow-storm by night, or all the other sufferings which my mind had endured. I warmed myself by the fire, for I was very cold, and after an early breakfast, we set out on our journey. The thoughts of home now began to take the entire possession of my mind, and I almost numbered the sluggish turns of the wheels, and much more certainly the miles of our travel, which appeared to me to count mighty slow. I continued with my kind protectors, until we got to the house of a Mr. John Cole, on Roanoke, when my impatience became so great, that I determined to set out on foot and go ahead by myself, as I could travel twice as fast in that way as the waggons could.

Mr. Dunn seemed very sorry to part with me, and used many arguments to prevent me from leaving him. But home, poor as it was, again rushed on my memory, and it seemed ten times as dear to me as it ever had before. The reason was, that my parents were there, and all that I had been accustomed to in the hours of childhood and infancy was there; and there my anxious little heart panted also to be. We remained at Mr. Cole's that night, and early in the morning I felt that I could not stay; so, taking leave of my friends, the waggoners, I went forward on foot, until I was fortunately overtaken by a gentleman, who was returning from market, to which he had been with a drove of horses. He had a led horse, with a bridle and saddle on him, and he kindly offered to let me get on his horse and ride him. I did so, and was glad of the chance, for I was tired, and was, moreover, near the first crossing of Roanoke, which I would have been compelled to wade, cold as the water was, if I had not fortunately met this good man. I travelled with him in this way, without any thing turning up worth recording until we got within fifteen miles of my father's house. There we parted, and he went on to Kentucky, and I trudged on homeward, which place I reached that evening. The name of this kind gentleman I have entirely forgotten, and I am sorry for it; for it deserves a high place in my little book. A remembrance of his kindness to a little straggling boy, and a stranger to him, has however a resting place in my heart, and there it will remain as long as I live.

CHAPTER II.

HAVING gotten home, as I have just related, I remained with my father until the next fall, at which time he took it into his head to send me to a little country school, which was kept in the neighbourhood by a man whose name was Benjamin Kitchen; though I believe he was no way connected with the cabinet.* I went four days, and had just began to learn my letters a little, when I had an unfortunate falling out with one of the scholars—a boy much larger and older than myself. I knew well enough that though the school-house might do for a still hunt, it wouldn't do for *a drive*, and so I concluded to wait until I could get him out, and then I was determined to give him salt and vinegar. I waited till in the evening, and when the larger scholars were spelling, I slip'd out, and going some distance along his road, I lay by the way-side in the bushes, waiting for him to come along. After awhile, he and his company came on sure enough, and I pitched out from the bushes and set on him like a wild cat. I scratched his face all to a flitter jig, and soon made him cry out for quarters in good earnest. The fight being over, I went on home, and the next morning was started again to school; but do you think I went? No, indeed. I was very clear of it; for I expected the master would lick me up as bad as I had the boy. So, instead of going to the school-house, I laid out in the woods all day until in the evening the scholars were dismissed, and my brothers, who were also going to school, came along, returning home. I wanted to conceal this whole business from my father, and I persuaded them not to tell on me, which they agreed to.

Things went on in this way for several days; I starting with them to school in the morning, and returning with them in the evening, but lying out in the woods all day. At last, however, the master wrote a note to my father, inquiring why I was not sent to school. When he read this note, he called me up, and I knew very well that I was in a devil of a hobble, for my father had been taking a few *horns*, and was in a good condition to make the fur fly. He called on me to know why I had not been at school? I told him I was afraid to go, and that the master would whip me, for I knew quite well if I was turned over to this old Kitchen, I should be cooked up to a cracklin, in little or no time. But I soon found that I was not to effect a much better fate at home; for my father told me, in a very angry manner, that he

* President Jackson's intimate friends and unofficial advisers, W. B. Lewis, Amos Kendall, Duff Green, and Isaac Hill, were called by his enemies "the kitchen cabinet."

would whip me an eternal sight worse than the master, if I didn't start immediately to the school. I tried again to beg off, but nothing would do but to go to the school. Finding me rather too slow about starting, he gathered about a two-year-old hickory, and broke after me. I put out with all my might, and soon we were both up to the top of our speed. We had a tolerable tough race for about a mile; but mind me, not on the school-house road, for I was trying to get as far t'other way as possible. And I yet believe, if my father and the schoolmaster could both have levied on me about that time, I should never have been called on to sit in the councils of the nation, for I think they would have used me up. But fortunately for me, about this time, I saw just before me a hill, over which I made headway, like a young steamboat. As soon as I had passed over it, I turned to one side, and hid myself in the bushes. Here I waited until the old gentleman passed by, puffing and blowing, as tho' his steam was high enough to burst his boilers. I waited until he gave up the hunt, and passed back again: I then cut out, and went to the house of an acquaintance a few miles off, who was just about to start with a drove. His name was Jesse Cheek, and I hired myself to go with him, determining not to return home, as home and the school-house had both become too hot for me. I had an elder brother, who also hired to go with the same drove. We set out and went on through Abbingdon, and the county seat of the Withe county, in the state of Virginia; and then through Lynchburgh, by Orange court-house, and Charlottesville, passing through what was called Chester Gap, on to a town called Front Royal, where my employer sold out his drove to a man by the name of Vanmetre: and I was started homeward again, in company with a brother of the first owner of the drove, with one horse between us; having left my brother to come on with the balance of the company.

I travelled on with my new comrade about three days' journey; but much to his discredit, as I then thought, and still think, he took care all the time to ride, but never to tie; at last I told him to go ahead, and I would come when I got ready. He gave me four dollars to bear my expenses upwards of four hundred miles, and then cut out and left me.

I purchased some provisions, and went on slowly, until at length I el in with a waggoner, with whom I was disposed to scrape up a hasty acquaintance. I inquired where he lived, and where he was going, and all about his affairs. He informed me that he lived in Greenville, Tennessee, and was on his way to a place called Gerardstown, fifteen miles below Winchester. He also said, that after he should make his journey to that place, he would immediately return to Tennessee. His name was Adam Myers, and a jolly good fellow he seemed to be. On a little reflection, I determined to turn back and go with him, which I did; and we journeyed on slowly as waggons commonly do, but merrily enough. I often thought of home, and, indeed, wished bad enough to be there; but, when I thought of the schoolhouse, and Kitchen, my master, and the race with my father, and the big hickory he carried, and of the fierceness of the storm of wrath that I had left him in, I was afraid to venture back; for I knew my father's nature so well, that I was certain his anger would hang on to him like a turkle does to a fisherman's toe, and that, if I went back in a hurry, he would give me the devil in three or four ways. But I and the waggoner had travelled two days, when we met my brother, who, I before stated, I had left behind when the drove was sold out. He persuaded me to go home, but I refused. He pressed me hard, and brought up a great many mighty strong arguments to induce me to turn back again. He pictured the pleasure of meeting my mother, and my sisters, who all loved me dearly, and told me what uneasiness they had already suffered about me. I could not help shedding tears, which I did not often do, and my affections all pointed back to those dearest friends, and as I thought, nearly the only ones I had in the world; but then the promised whipping—that was the thing. It came right slap down on every thought of home; and I finally determined that make or break, hit or miss, I would just hang on to my journey, and go ahead with the waggoner. My brother was much grieved at our parting, but he went his way, and so did I. We went on until at last we got to Gerardstown, where the waggoner tried to get a back load, but he could not without going to Alexandria. He engaged to go there, and I concluded that I would wait until he returned. I set in to work for a man by the name of John Gray, at twenty-five cents per day. My labour, however, was light, such as ploughing in some small grain, in which I succeeded in pleasing the old man very well. I continued working for him until the waggoner got back, and for a good long time afterwards, as he continued to run his team back and forward, hauling to and from Baltimore. In the next spring, from the proceeds of my daily labour, small as it was, I was able to get me some decent clothes, and concluded I would make a trip with the waggoner to Baltimore, and see what sort of a place that was, and what sort of folks lived there. I gave him the balance of what money I had for safe keeping, which, as well as I recollect, was about seven dollars. We got on well enough until we came near Ellicott's Mills. Our load consisted of flour in barrels. Here I got into the waggon for the purpose of changing my clothing, not thinking that I was in any danger; but, while I was in there, we were met by some wheelbarrow men, who were working on the road, and the horses took a scare and away they went, like they had seen a ghost. They made a sudden wheel around, and broke the waggon tongue slap, short off, as a pipe-stem; and snap went both of the axletrees at the same time, and of all devilish flouncing about of flour barrels that ever was seen, I reckon this took the beat. Even *a rat* would have stood a bad chance in a *straight* race among them, and not much better in a crooked one; for he would have been in a good way to be ground up as fine as ginger by their rolling over him. But this proved to me, that if a fellow is born to be hung, he will never be drowned; and, further, that if he is born for a seat in Congress, even flour barrels can't make a mash of him. All these dangers I escaped unhurt, though, like most of the office-holders of these times, for a while I was afraid to say my soul was my own; for I didn't know how soon I should be knocked into a cocked hat, and get my walking papers for another country.

We put our load into another waggon, and hauled ours to a workman's shop in Baltimore, having delivered the flour, and there we intended to remain two or three days, which time was necessary to repair the runaway waggon. While I was there, I went, one day, down to the wharf, and was much delighted to see the big ships, and their sails all flying; for I had never seen any such things before, and, indeed, I didn't believe there were any such things in all nature. After a short time my curiosity induced me to step aboard of one, where I was met by the captain, who asked me if I didn't wish to take a voyage to London? I told him I did, for by this time I had become pretty well weaned from home, and I cared but little where I was, or where I went, or what become of me. He said he wanted just such a boy as I was, which I was glad to hear. I told him I would go and get my clothes, and go with him. He enquired about my parents, where they lived, and all about them. I let him know that they lived in Tennessee, many hundred miles off. We soon agreed about my intended voyage, and I went back to my friend the waggoner, and informed him that I was going to London, and wanted my money and my clothes. He refused to let me have either, and swore that he would confine me, and take me back to Tennessee. I took it to heart very much, but he kept so close and constant a watch over me, that I found it impossible to escape from him, until he had started homeward, and made several days journey on the road. He was, during this time, very ill to me, and threatened me with his waggon whip on several occasions. At length I resolved to leave him at all hazards; and so, before day, one morning, I got my clothes out of his waggon, and cut out, on foot, without a farthing of money to bear my expenses. For all other friends having failed, I determined then to throw myself on Providence, and see how that would use me. I had gone, however, only a few miles when I came up with another waggoner, and such was my situation, that I felt more than ever the necessity of endeavouring to find a friend. I therefore concluded I would seek for one in him. He was going westwardly, and very kindly enquired of me where I was travelling? My youthful resolution which had brooked almost every thing else, rather gave way at this enquiry; for it brought the loneliness of my situation, and every thing else that was calculated to oppress me, directly to view. My first answer to his question was in a sprinkle of tears, for if the world had been given to me, I could not, at that moment, have helped crying. As soon as the storm of feeling was over, I told him how I had been treated by the waggoner but a little before, who kept what little money I had, and left me without a copper to buy even a morsel of food.

He became exceedingly angry, and swore that he would make the other waggoner give up my money, pronouncing him a scoundrel, and many other hard names. I told him I was afraid to see him, for he had threatened me with his waggon whip, and I believed he would injure me. But my new friend was a very large, stout-looking man, and as resolute as a tiger. He bid me not to be afraid, still swearing he would have my money, or whip it out of the wretch who had it.

We turned and went back about two miles, when we reached the place where he was. I went reluctantly; but I depended on my friend for protection. When we got there, I had but little to say; but approaching the waggoner, my friend said to him, "You damn'd rascal, you have treated this boy badly." To which he replied, it was my fault. He was then asked, if he did not get seven dollars of my money, which he confessed. It was then demanded of him; but he declared most solemnly, that he had not that amount in the world; that he had spent my money, and intended paying it back to me when we got to Tennessee. I then felt reconciled, and persuaded my friend to let him alone, and we returned to his waggon, geared up, and started. His name I shall never forget while my memory lasts; it was Henry Myers. He lived in Pennsylvania, and I found him what he professed to be, a faithful friend and a clever fellow.

We travelled together for several days, but at length I concluded to endeavour to make my way homeward; and for that purpose set out again on foot, and alone. But one thing I must not omit. The last night I stayed with Mr. Myers, was at a place where several waggoners also stayed. He told them, before we parted, that I was a poor little straggling boy, and how I had been treated; and that I was without money, though I had a long journey before me, through a land of strangers, where it was not even a wilderness.

They were good enough to contribute a sort of money-purse, and presented me with three dollars. On this amount I travelled as far as Montgomery court-house, in the state of Virginia, where it gave out. I set in to work for a man by the name of James Caldwell, a month, for five dollars, which was about a shilling a day. When this time was out, I bound myself to a man by the name of Elijah Griffith, by trade a hatter, agreeing to work for him four years. I remained with him about eighteen months, when he found himself so involved in debt, that he broke up, and left the country. For this time I had received nothing, and was, of course, left without money, and with but very few clothes, and them very indifferent ones. I, however, set in again, and worked about as I could catch employment, until I got a little money, and some clothing; and once more cut out for home. When I reached New River, at the mouth of a small stream, called Little River, the white caps were flying, so that I couldn't get any body to attempt to put me across. I argued the case as well as I could, but they told me there was great danger of being capsized, and drowned, if I attempted to cross. I told them if I could get a canoe I would venture, caps or no caps. They tried to persuade me out of it; but finding they could not, they agreed I might take a canoe, and so I did, and put off. I tied my clothes to the rope of the canoe, to have them safe, whatever might happen. But I found it a mighty ticklish business, I tell you. When I got out fairly on the river, I would have given the world, if it had belonged to me, to have been back on shore.

But there was no time to lose now, so I just determined to do the best I could, and the devil take the hindmost. I turned the canoe across the waves, to do which, I had to turn it nearly up the river, as the wind came from that way; and I went about two miles before I could land. When I struck land, my canoe was about half full of water, and I was as wet as a drowned rat. But I was so much rejoiced, that I scarcely felt the cold, though my clothes were frozen on me; and, in this situation, I had to go above three miles, before I could find any house, or fire to warm at. I, however, made out to get to one at last, and then I thought I would warm the inside a little, as well as the outside, that there might be no grumbling.

So I took "a leetle of the creater"—that warmer of the cold, and cooler of the hot—and it made me feel so good that I concluded it was like the negro's rabbit, "good any way." I passed on until I arrived in Sullivan county, in the state of Tennessee, and there I met with my brother, who had gone with me when I started from home with the cattle drove.

I stayed with him a few weeks, and then went on to my father's, which place I reached late in the evening. Several waggons were there for the night, and considerable company about the house. I enquired if I could stay all night, for I did not intend to make myself known, until I saw whether any of the family would find me out. I was told that I could stay, and went in, but had mighty little to say to any body. I had been gone so long, and had grown so much, that the family did not at first know me. And another, and perhaps a stronger reason was, they had no thought or expectation of me, for they all had long given me up for finally lost.

After a while, we were all called to supper. I went with the rest. We had sat down to the table and begun to eat, when my eldest sister recollected me: she sprung up, ran and seized me around the neck, and exclaimed, "Here is my lost brother."

My feelings at this time it would be vain and foolish for me to attempt to describe. I had often thought I felt before, and I suppose I had, but sure I am, I never had felt as I then did. The joy of my sisters and my mother, and, indeed, of all the family, was such that it humbled me, and made me sorry that I hadn't submitted to a hundred whippings, sooner than cause so much affliction as they had suffered on my account. I found the family had never heard a word of me from the time my brother left me. I was now almost fifteen years old; and my increased age and size, together with the joy of my father, occasioned by my unexpected return, I was sure would secure me against my long dreaded whipping; and so they did. But it will be a source of astonishment to many, who reflect that I am now a member of the American Congress—the most enlightened body of men in the world—that at so advanced an age, the age of fifteen, I did not know the first letter in the book.

CHAPTER III.

I HAD remained for some short time at home with my father, when he informed me that he owed a man, whose name was Abraham Wilson, the sum of thirty-six dollars, and that if I would set in and work out the note, so as to lift it for him, he would discharge me from his service, and I might go free. I agreed to do this, and went immediately to the man who held my father's note, and contracted with him to work six months for it. I set in, and worked with all my might, not losing a single day in the six months. When my time was out, I got my father's note, and then declined working with the man any longer, though he wanted to hire me mighty bad. The reason was, it was a place where a heap of bad company met to drink and gamble, and I wanted to get away from them, for I know'd very well if I stayed there, I should get a bad name, as nobody could be respectable that would live there. I therefore returned to my father, and gave him up his paper, which seemed to please him mightily, for though he was poor, he was an honest man, and always tried mighty hard to pay off his debts.

I next went to the house of an honest old Quaker, by the name of John Kennedy, who had removed from North Carolina, and proposed to hire myself to him, at two shillings a day. He agreed to take me a week on trial; at the end of which he appeared pleased with my work, and informed me that he held a note on my father for forty dollars, and that he would give me that note if I would work for him six months. I was certain enough that I should never get any part of the note; but then I remembered it was my father that owed it, and I concluded it was my duty as a child to help him along, and ease his lot as much as I could. I told the Quaker I would take him up at his offer, and immediately went to work. I never visited my father's house during the whole time of this engagement, though he lived only fifteen miles off. But when it was finished, and I had got the note I borrowed one of my employer's horses, and, on a Sunday evening, went to pay my parents a visit. Some time after I got there, I pulled out the note and handed it to my father, who supposed Mr. Kennedy had sent it for collection. The old man looked mighty sorry, and said to me he had not the money to pay it, and didn't know what he should do. I then told him I had paid it for him, and it was then his own; that it was not presented for collection, but as a present from me. At this, he shed a heap of tears; and as soon as he got a little over it, he said he was sorry he could not give me any thing, but he was not able, he was too poor.

The next day, I went back to my old friend, the Quaker, and set in to work for him for some clothes; for I had now worked a year without getting any money at all, and my clothes were nearly all worn out, and what few I had left were mighty indifferent. I worked in this way for about two months; and in that time a young woman from North Carolina, who was the Quaker's niece, came on a visit to his house. And now I am just getting on a part of my history that I know I never can forget. For though I have heard people talk about hard loving, yet I reckon no poor devil in this world was ever cursed with such hard love as mine has always been, when it came on me. I soon found myself head over heels in love with this girl, whose name the public could make no use of; and I thought that if all the hills about there were pure chink, and all belonged to me, I would give them if I could just talk to her as I wanted to; but I was afraid to begin, for when I would think of saying any thing to her, my heart would begin to flutter like a duck in a puddle; and if I tried to outdo it and speak, it would get right smack up in my throat, and choke me like a cold potatoe. It bore on my mind in this way, till at last I concluded I must die if I didn't broach the subject; and so I determined to begin and hang on a trying to speak, till my heart would get out of my throat one way or t'other. And so one day at it I went, and after several trials I could say a little. I told her how well I loved her; that she was the darling object of my soul and body; and I must have her, or else I should pine down to nothing, and just die away with the consumption.

I found my talk was not disagreeable to her; but she was an honest girl, and didn't want to deceive nobody. She told me she was engaged to her cousin, a son of the old Quaker. This news was worse to me than war, pestilence, or famine; but still I knowed I could not help myself. I saw quick enough my cake was dough, and I tried to cool off as fast as possible; but I had hardly safety pipes enough, as my love was so hot as mighty nigh to burst my boilers. But I didn't press my claims any more, seeing there was no chance to do any thing.

I began now to think, that all my misfortunes growed out of my want of learning. I had never been to school but four days, as the reader has already seen, and did not yet know a letter.

I thought I would try to go to school some; and as the Quaker had a married son, who was living about a mile and a half from him, and keeping a school, I proposed to him that I would go to school four days in the week, and work for him the other two, to pay my board and schooling. He agreed I might come on those terms; and so at it I went, learning and working backwards and forwards, until I had been with him nigh on to six months. In this time I learned to read a little in my primer, to write my own name, and to cypher some in the three first rules in figures. And this was all the schooling I ever had in my life, up to this day. I should have continued longer, if it hadn't been that I concluded I couldn't do any longer without a wife; and so I cut out to hunt me one.

I found a family of very pretty little girls that I had known when very young. They had lived in the same neighbourhood with me, and I had thought very well of them. I made an offer to one of them, whose name is nobody's business, no more than the Quaker girl's was, and I found she took it very well. I still continued paying my respects to her, until I got to love her as bad as I had the Quaker's niece; and I would have agreed to fight a whole regiment of wild cats if she would only have said she would have me. Several months passed in this way, during all of which time she continued very kind and friendly. At last the son of the old Quaker and my first girl had concluded to bring their matter to a close, and my little queen and myself were called on to wait on them. We went on the day, and performed our duty as attendants. This made me worse than ever; and after it was over, I pressed my claim very hard on her, but she would still give me a sort of evasive answer. However, I gave her mighty little peace, till she told me at last she would have me. I thought this was glorification enough, even without spectacles. I was then about eighteen years old. We fixed the time to be married; and I thought if that day come, I should be the happiest man in the created world, or in the moon, or any where else.

I had by this time got to be mighty fond of the rifle, and had bought a capital one. I most generally carried her with me wherever I went, and though I had got back to the old Quaker's to live, who was a very particular man, I would sometimes slip out and attend the shooting matches, where they shot for beef; I always tried, though, to keep it a secret from him. He had at the same time a bound boy living with him, who I had gotten into almost as great a notion of the girls as myself. He was about my own age, and was deeply smitten with the sister to my intended wife. I know'd it was in vain to try to get the leave of the old man for my young associate to go with me on any of my courting frolics; but I thought I could fix a plan to have him along, which would not injure the Quaker, as we had no notion that he should ever know it. We commonly slept upstairs, and at the gable end of the house there was a window. So one Sunday, when the old man and his family were all gone to meeting, we went out and cut a long pole, and, taking it to the house, we set it up on end in the corner, reaching up the chimney as high as the window. After this we would go up stairs to bed, and then putting on our Sunday clothes, would go out at the window, and climb down the pole, take a horse apiece, and ride about ten miles to where his sweetheart lived, and the girl I claimed as my wife. I was always mighty careful to be back before day, so as to escape being found out; and in this way I continued my attentions very closely until a few days before I was to be married, or at least thought I was, for I had no fear that any thing was about to go wrong.

Just now I heard of a shooting match in the neighbourhood, right between where I lived and my girl's house; and I determined to kill two birds with one stone—to go to the shooting match first, and then to see her. I therefore made the Quaker believe I was going to hunt for deer, as they were pretty plenty about in those parts; but, instead of hunting them, I went straight on to the shooting-march, where I joined in with a partner, and we put in several shots for the beef. I was mighty lucky, and when the match was over I had won the whole beef. This was on a Saturday, and my success had put me in the finest humour in the world. So I sold my part of the beef for five dollars in the real grit, for I believe that was before bank-notes was invented; at least, I had never heard of any. I now started on to ask for my wife; for, though the next Thursday was our wedding-day, I had never said a word to her parents about it. I had always dreaded the undertaking so bad, that I had put the evil hour off as long as possible; and, indeed, I calculated they knowed me so well, they wouldn't raise any objection to having me for their son-in-law. I had a great deal better opinion of myself, I found, than other people had of me; but I moved on with a light heart, and my five dollars jingling in my pocket, thinking all the time there was but few greater men in the world than myself.

In this flow of good humour I went ahead till I got within about two miles of the place, when I concluded I would stop awhile at the house of the girl's uncle; where I might enquire about the family, and so forth, and so on. I was indeed just about ready to consider her uncle my uncle; and her affairs, my affairs. When I went in, tho', I found her sister there. I asked how all was at home? In a minute I found from her countenance something was wrong. She looked mortified, and didn't answer as quick as I thought she ought, being it was her *brother-in-law* talking to her. However, I asked her again. She then burst into tears, and told me her sister was going to deceive me; and that she was to be married to another man the next day. This was as sudden to me as a clap of thunder of a bright sunshiny day. It was the capstone of all the afflictions I had ever met with; and it seemed to me that it was more than any human creature could endure. It struck me perfectly speechless for some time, and made me feel so weak, that I thought I should sink down. I however recovered from my shock after a little, and rose and started without any ceremony, or even bidding any body good-bye. The young woman followed me out to the gate, and entreated me to go on to her father's, and said she would go with me. She said the young man who was going to marry her sister, had got his license, and asked for her; but she assured me her father and mother both preferred me to him; and that she had no doubt but that, if I would go on I could break off the match. But I found I could go no further. My heart was bruised, and my spirits were broken down; so I bid her farewell, and turned my lonesome and miserable steps back again homeward, concluding that I was only born for hardships, misery, and disappointment. I now began to think, that in making me, it was entirely forgotten to make my mate; that I was born odd, and should always remain so, and that nobody would have me.

But all these reflections did not satisfy my mind, for I had no peace day nor night for several weeks. My appetite failed me, and I grew daily worse and worse. They all thought I was sick; and so I was. And it was the worst kind of sickness—a sickness of the heart, and all the tender parts, produced by disappointed love.

CHAPTER IV.

I CONTINUED in this down-spirited situation for a good long time, until one day I took my rifle and started a hunting. While out I made a call at the house of a Dutch widow, who had a daughter that was well enough as to smartness, but she was as ugly as a stone fence. She was, however, quite talkative, and soon began to laugh at me about my disappointment.

She seemed disposed, though, to comfort me as much as she could; and, for that purpose, told me to keep in good heart, that "there was as good fish in the sea as had ever been caught out of it." I doubted this very much; but whether or not, I was certain that she was not one of them, for she was so homely that it almost gave me a pain in the eyes to look at her.

But I couldn't help thinking, that she had intended what she had said as a banter for me to court her! ! !—the last thing in creation I could have thought of doing. I felt little inclined to talk on the subject, it is true; but, to pass off the time, I told her I thought I was born odd, and that no fellow to me could be found. She protested against this, and said if I would come to their reaping, which was not far off, she would show me one of the prettiest little girls there I had ever seen. She added that the one who had deceived me was nothing to be compared with her. I didn't believe a word of all this, for I had thought that such a piece of flesh and blood as she was had never been manufactured, and never would again. I agreed with her, though, that the little varment had treated me so bad, that I ought to forget her, and yet I couldn't do it. I concluded the best way to accomplish it was to cut out again, and see if I could find any other that would answer me; and so I told the Dutch girl that I would be at the reaping, and would bring as many as I could with me.

I employed my time pretty generally in giving information of it, as far as I could, until the day came; and I then offered to work for my old friend, the Quaker, two days, if he would let his bound boy go with me one to the reaping. He refused, and reproved me pretty considerable roughly for my proposition; and said, if he was in my place he wouldn't go; that there would be a great deal of bad company there; and that I had been so good a boy, he would be sorry for me to get a bad name. But I knowed my promise to the Dutch girl, and I was resolved to fulfil it; so I shouldered my rifle, and started by myself. When I got to the place, I found a large company of men and women, and among them an old Irish woman, who had a great deal to say. I soon found out from my Dutch girl, that this old lady was the mother of the little girl she had promised me, though I had not yet seen her. She was in an out-house with some other youngsters, and had not yet made her appearance. Her mamma, however, was no way bashful. She came up to me, and began to praise my red cheeks, and said she had a sweetheart for me. I had no doubt she had been told what I come for, and all about it. In the evening I was introduced to her daughter, and I must confess, I was plaguy well pleased with her from the word go. She had a good countenance, and was very pretty, and I was full bent on making up an acquaintance with her.

It was not long before the dancing commenced, and I asked her to join me in a reel. She very readily consented to do so; and after we had finished our dance, I took a seat alongside of her, and entered into a talk. I found her very interesting; while I was sitting by her, making as good a use of my time as I could, her mother came to us, and very jocularly called me her son-in-law. This rather confused me, but I looked on it as a joke of the old lady, and tried to turn it off as well as I could; but I took care to pay as much attention to her through the evening as I could. I went on the old saying, of salting the cow to catch the calf. I soon become so much pleased with this little girl, that I began to think the Dutch girl had told me the truth, when she said there was still good fish in the sea.

We continued our frolic till near day, when we joined in some plays, calculated to amuse youngsters. I had not often spent a more agreeable night. In the morning, however, we all had to part; and I found my mind had become much better reconciled than it had been for a long time. I went home to the Quaker's, and made a bargain to work with his son for a low-priced horse. He was the first one I had ever owned, and I was to work six months for him. I had been engaged very closely five or six weeks, when this little girl run in my mind so, that I concluded I must go and see her, and find out what sort of people they were at home. I mounted my horse and away I went to where she lived, and when I got there I found her father a very clever old man, and the old woman as talkative as ever. She wanted badly to find out all about me, and as I thought to see how I would do for her girl. I had not yet seen her about, and I began to feel some anxiety to know where she was.

In a short time, however, my impatience was relieved, as she arrived at home from a meeting to which she had been. There was a young man with her, who I soon found was disposed to set up claim to her, as he was so attentive to her that I could hardly get to slip in a word edgeways. I began to think I was barking up the wrong tree again; but I was determined to stand up to my rack, fodder or no fodder. And so, to know her mind a little on the subject, I began to talk about starting, as I knowed she would then show some sign, from which I could understand which way the wind blowed. It was then near night, and my distance was fifteen miles home. At this my little girl soon began to indicate to the other gentleman that his room would be the better part of his company. At length she left him, and came to me, and insisted mighty hard that I should not go that evening ; and, indeed, from all her actions and the attempts she made to get rid of him, I saw that she preferred me all holler. But it wasn't long before I found trouble enough in another quarter. Her mother was deeply enlisted for my rival, and I had to fight against her influence as well as his. But the girl herself was the prize I was fighting for; and as she welcomed me, I was determined to lay siege to her, let what would happen. I commenced a close courtship, having cornered her from her old beau; while he set off, looking on, like a poor man at a country frolic, and all the time almost gritting his teeth with pure disappointment. But he didn't dare to attempt anything more, for now I had gotten a start, and I looked at him every once in a while as fierce as a wild-cat. I staid with her until Monday morning, and then I put out for home.

It was about two weeks after this that I was sent for to engage in a wolf hunt, where a great number of men were to meet, with their dogs and guns, and where the best sort of sport was expected. I went as large as life, but I had to hunt in strange woods, and in a part of the country which was very thinly inhabited. While I was out it clouded up, and I began to get scared : and in a little while I was so much so, that I didn't know which way home was, nor any thing about it. I set out the way I thought it was, but it turned out with me, as it always does with a lost man, I was wrong, and took exactly the contrary direction from the right one. And for the information of young hunters, I will just say, in this place, that whenever a fellow gets bad lost, the way home is just the way he don't think it is. This rule will hit nine times out of ten. I went ahead, though, about six or seven miles, when I found night was coming on fast ; but at this distressing time I saw a little woman streaking it along through the woods like all wrath, and so I cut on too, for I was determined I wouldn't lose sight of her that night any more. I run on till she saw me, and she stopped ; for she was as glad to see me as I was to see her, as she was lost as well as me. When I came up to her, who should she be but my little girl, that I had been paying my respects to. She had been out hunting her father's horses, and had missed her way, and had no knowledge where she was, or how far it was to any house, or what way would take us there. She had been travelling all day, and was mighty tired; and I would have taken her up, and toated her, if it hadn't been that I wanted her just where I could see her all the time, for I thought she looked sweeter than sugar ; and by this time I loved her almost well enough to eat her.

At last I came to a path, that I know'd must go somewhere, and so we followed it, till we came to a house, at about dark. Here we staid all night. I set up all night courting ; and in the morning we parted. She went to her home, from which we were distant about seven miles, and I to mine, which was ten miles off.

I now turned into work again ; and it was about four weeks before I went back to see her. I continued to go occasionally, until I had worked long enough to pay for my horse, by putting in my gun with my work, to the man I had purchased from; and then I began to count whether I was to be deceived again or not. At our next meeting we set the day for our wedding; and I went to my father's, and made arrangements for an infair, and returned to ask her parents for her. When I got there, the old lady appeared to be mighty wrathy; and when I broached the subject, she looked at me as savage as a meat axe. The old man appeared quite willing, and treated me very clever. But I hadn't been there long, before the old woman as good as ordered me out of her house. I thought I would put her in mind of old times, and see how that would go with her. I told her she had called me her son-in-law before I had attempted to call her my mother-in-law, and I thought she ought to cool off. But her Irish was up too high to do anything with her, and so I quit trying. All I cared for was to have her daughter on my side, which I knowed was the case then; but how soon some other fellow might knock my nose out of joint again I couldn't tell. I, however, felt rather insulted at the old lady, and I thought I wouldn't get married in her house. And so I told her girl, that I would come the next Thursday, and bring a horse, bridle, and saddle for her, and she must be ready to go. Her mother declared I shouldn't have her; but I know'd I should, if somebody else didn't get her before Thursday. I then started, bidding them good day, and went by the house of a justice of the peace, who lived on the way to my father's, and made a bargain with him to marry me.

When Thursday came, all necessary were made at my father's to receive my wife; and so I took my eldest brother and his wife, and another brother, and a single sister that I had, and two other young men with me, and cut out to her father's house to get her. We went on until we got within two miles of the place, where we met a large company that had heard of the wedding, and were waiting. Some of that company went on with my brother and sister, and the young man I had picked out to wait on me. When they got there, they found the old lady as wrathy as ever. However, the old man filled their bottle, and the young men returned in a hurry. I then went on with my company, and when I arrived I never pretended to dismount from my horse, but rode up to the door, and asked the girl if she was ready; and she said she was. I then told her to light on the horse I was leading; and she did so. Her father, though, had gone out to the gate, and when I started, he commenced persuading me to stay and marry there; that he was entirely willing to the match, and that his wife, like most women, had entirely too much tongue; but that I oughtn't to mind her. I told him if she would ask me to stay and marry at her house, I would do so. With that he sent for her, and after they had talked for some time out by themselves, she came to me and looked at me mighty good, and asked my pardon for what she had said, and invited me to stay. She said it was the first child she ever had to marry; and she couldn't bear to see her go off in that way; that if I would light she would do the best she could for us. I couldn't stand every thing, and so I agreed, and we got down, and went in. I sent off then for my parson, and got married in a short time; for I was afraid to wait long, for fear of another defeat. We had as good treatment as could be expected; and that night all went on well. The next day we cut out for my father's, where we met a large company of people, that had been waiting a day and a night for our arrival. We passed the time quite merrily, until the company broke up; and having gotten my wife, I thought I was completely made up, and needed nothing more in the whole world. But I soon found this was all a mistake—for now having a wife, I wanted every thing else; and, worse than all, I had nothing to give for it.

I remained a few days at my father's, and then went back to my new father-in-law's; where, to my surprise, I found my old Irish mother in the finest humour in the world.

She gave us two likely cows and calves, which, though it was a small marriage portion, was still better than I had expected, and, indeed, it was about all I ever got. I rented a small farm and cabin, and went to work; but I had much trouble to find out a plan to get anything to put in my house. At this time, my good old friend the Quaker came forward to my assistance, and gave me an order to a store for fifteen dollars' worth of such things as my little wife might choose. With this, we fixed up pretty grand, as we thought, and allowed to get on very well. My wife had a good wheel, and knowed exactly how to use it. She was also a good weaver, as most of the Irish are, whether men or women; and being very industrious with her wheel, she had, in little or no time, a fine web of cloth, ready to make up; and she was good at that too, and at almost any thing else that a woman could do.

We worked on for some years, renting ground, and paying high rent, until I found it wan't the thing it was cracked up to be; and that I couldn't make a fortune at it just at all. So I concluded to quit it, and cut out for some new country. In this time we had two sons, and I found I was better at increasing my family than my fortune. It was therefore the more necessary that I should hunt some better place to get along; and as I knowed I would have to move at some time, I thought it was better to do it before my family got too large, that I might have less to carry.

The Duck and Elk river country was just beginning to settle, and I determined to try that. I had now one old horse, and a couple of two-year-old colts. They were both broke to the halter, and my father-in-law proposed that, if I went, he would go with me, and take one horse to help me move. So we all fixed up, and I packed my two colts with as many of my things as they could bear; and away we went across the mountains. We got on well enough, and arrived safely in Lincoln county, on the head of the Mulberry fork of Elk river. I found this a very rich country, and so new, that game, of different sorts, was very plenty. It was here that I began to distinguish myself as a hunter, and to lay the foundation for all my future greatness; but mighty little did I know of what sort it was going to be. Of deer and smaller game I killed abundance; but the bear had been much hunted in those parts before, and were not so plenty as I could have wished. I lived here in the years 1809 and 1810, to the best of my recollection, and then I moved to Franklin County, and settled on Beans Creek, where I remained till after the close of the last war.

CHAPTER V.

I WAS living ten miles below Winchester when the Creek war commenced; and as military men are making so much fuss in the world at this time, I must give an account of the part I took in the defence of the country. If it should make me president, why I can't help it; such things will sometimes happen; and my pluck is, never "to seek, nor decline office."

It is true, I had a little rather not; but yet, if the government can't get on without taking another president from Tennessee to finish the work of "retrenchment and reform," why, then, I reckon I must go in for it. But I must begin about the war, and leave the other matter for the people to begin on.

The Creek Indians had commenced their open hostilities by a most bloody butchery at Fort Mimms. There had been no war among us for so long, that but few, who were not too old to bear arms, knew any thing about the business. I, for one, had often thought about war, and had often heard it described; and I did verily believe in my own mind that I couldn't fight in that way at all; but my after experience convinced me that this was all a notion. For when I heard of the mischief which was done at the fort, I instantly felt like going, and I had none of the dread of dying that I expected to feel. In a few days a general meeting of the militia was called for the purpose of raising volunteers; and when the day arrived for that meeting, my wife, who had heard me say I meant to go to the war, began to beg me not to turn out. She said she was a stranger in the parts where we lived, had no connections living near her, and that she and our little children would be left in a lonesome and unhappy situation if I went away. It was mighty hard to go against such arguments as these; but my countrymen had been murdered, and I knew that the next thing would be, that the Indians would be scalping the women and children all about there if we didn't put a stop to it. I reasoned the case with her as well as I could, and told her that if every man would wait till his wife got willing for him to go to war, there would be no fighting done until we would all be killed in our own houses; that I was as able to go as any man in the world; and that I believed it was a duty I owed to my country. Whether she was satisfied with this reasoning or not she did not tell me; but seeing I was bent on it, all she did was to cry a little and turn about to her work. The truth is, my dander was up, and nothing but war could bring it right again.

I went to Winchester, where the muster was to be, and a great many people had collected, for there was as much fuss among the people about the war as there is now about moving the deposites. When the men were paraded, a lawyer by the name of Jones addressed us, and closed by turning out himself, and enquiring, at the same time, who among us felt like we could fight Indians? This was the same Mr. Jones who afterwards served in Congress from the State of Tennessee. He informed us he wished to raise a company, and that then the men should meet and elect their own officers. I believe I was about the second or third man that step'd out; but on marching up and down the regiment a few times, we found we had a large company. We volunteered for sixty days, as it was supposed our services would not be longer wanted. A day or two after this we met and elected Mr. Jones our captain, and also elected our other officers. We then received orders to start on the next Monday week; before which time, I had fixed as well as I could to go, and my wife had equip'd me as well as she was able for the camp. The time arrived; I took a parting farewell of my wife and my two little boys, mounted my horse, and set sail, to join my company. Expecting to be gone only a short time, I took no more clothing with me than I supposed would be necessary, so that if I got into an Indian battle, I might not be pestered with any unnecessary plunder, to prevent my having a fair shake with them. We all met and went ahead, till we passed Huntsville, and camped at a large spring called Beaty's spring. Here we stayed for several days, in which time the troops began to collect from all quarters. At last we mustered about thirteen hundred strong, all mounted volunteers, and all determined to fight, judging from myself, for I felt wolfish all over. I verily believe the whole army was of the real grit. Our captain didn't want any other sort; and to try them he several times told his men, that if any of them wanted to go back home, they might do so at any time, before they were regularly mustered into the service. But he had the honour to command all his men from first to last, as not one of them left him.

Gen'l Jackson had not yet left Nashville with his old foot volunteers, that had gone with him to Natchez in 1812, the year before. While we remained at the spring, a Major Gibson came, and wanted some volunteers to go with him across the Tennessee river and into the Creek nation, to find out the movements of the Indians. He came to my captain, and asked for two of his best woodsmen, and such as were best with a rifle. The captain pointed me out to him, and said he would be security that I would go as far as the major would himself, or any other man. I willingly engaged to go with him, and asked him to let me choose my own mate to go with me, which he said I might do. I chose a young man by the name of George Russell, a son of old Major Russell, of Tennessee. I called him up, but Major Gibson said he thought he hadn't beard enough to please him—he wanted men, not boys. I must confess I was a little nettled at this; for I know'd George Russell, and I know'd there was no mistake in him; and I didn't think that courage ought to be measured by the beard, for fear a goat would have the preference over a man. I told the major he was on the wrong scent; that Russell could go as far as he could, and I must have him along. He saw I was a little wrathy, and said I had the best chance of knowing, and agreed that it should be as I wanted it. He told us to be ready early in the morning for a start; and so we were. We took our camp equipage, mounted our horses, and thirteen in number, including the major, we cut out. We went on, and crossed the Tennessee river at a place called Ditto's Landing; and then travelled about seven miles further, and took up camp for the night. Here a man by the name of John Haynes overtook us. He had been an Indian trader in that part of the nation, and was well acquainted with it. He went with us as a pilot. The next morning, however, Major Gibson and myself concluded we should separate and take different directions to see what discoveries we could make; so he took seven of the men, and I five, making thirteen in all, including myself. He was to go by the house of a Cherokee Indian, named Dick Brown, and I was to go by Dick's father's; and getting all the information we could, we were to meet that evening where the roads came together, fifteen miles the other side of Brown's. At old Mr. Brown's I got a half-blood Cherokee to agree to go with me, whose name was Jack Thompson. He was not then ready to start, but was to fix that evening, and overtake us at the fork road where I was to meet Major Gibson. I know'd it wouldn't be safe to camp right at the road; and so I told Jack, that when he got to the fork he must holler like an owl, and I would answer him in the same way; for I know'd it would be night before he got there. I and my men then started, and went on to the place of meeting, but Major Gibson was not there. We waited till almost dark, but still he didn't come. We then left the Indian trace a little distance, and turning into the head of a hollow, we struck up camp. It was about ten o'clock at night, when I heard my owl, and I answered him. Jack soon found us, and we determined to rest there during the night. We stayed also next morning till after breakfast: but in vain, for the major didn't still come.

I told the men we had set out to hunt a fight, and I wouldn't go back in that way; that we must go ahead, and see what the red men were at. We started, and went to a Cherokee town about twenty miles off; and after a short stay there, we pushed on to the house of a man by the name of Radcliff. He was a white man, but had married a Creek woman, and lived just in the edge of the Creek nation. He had two sons, large likely fellows, and a great deal of potatoes and corn, and, indeed, almost everything else to go on: so we fed our horses and got dinner with him, and seemed to be doing mighty well. But he was bad scared all the time. He told us that there had been ten painted warriors at his house only an hour before, and if we were discovered there, they would kill us, and his family with us. I replied to him, that my business was to hunt for just such fellows as he had described, and I was determined not to go back until I had done it. Our dinner being over, we saddled up our horses, and made ready to start. But some of my small company I found were disposed to return. I told them, if we were to go back then, we should never hear the last of it; and I was determined to go ahead. I knowed some of them would go with me, and that the rest were afraid to go back by themselves; and so we pushed on to the camp of some of the friendly Creeks, which was distant about eight miles. The moon was about the full, and the night was clear; we therefore had the benefit of her light from night to morning, and I knew if we were placed in such danger as to make a retreat necessary, we could travel by night as well as in the day time.

We had not gone very far, when we met two negroes, well mounted on Indian ponies, and each with a good rifle. They had been taken from their owners by the Indians, and were running away from them, and trying to get back to their masters again. They were brothers, both very large and likely; and could talk Indian as well as English. One of them I sent on to Ditto's Landing, the other I took back with me. It was after dark when we got to the camp, where we found about forty men, women, and children.

They had bows and arrows, and I turned in to shooting with their boys by a pine light. In this way we amused ourselves very well for a while, but at last the negro, who had been talking to the Indians, came to me and told me they were very much alarmed, for the "red sticks," as they called the war party of the Creeks, would come and find us there; and, if so, we should all be killed. I directed him to tell them that I would watch, and if one would come that night, I would carry the skin of his head home to make me a moccasin. When he made this communication, the Indians laughed aloud. At about ten o'clock at night we all concluded to try to sleep a little; but that our horses might be ready for use, as the treasurer said of the drafts on the United States' bank, on "certain contingencies," we tied them up with our saddles on them, and every thing to our hand, if in the night our quarters should get uncomfortable. We lay down with our guns in our arms, and I had just gotten into a doze of sleep, when I heard the sharpest scream that ever escaped the throat of a human creature. It was more like a wrathy painter than any thing else. The negro understood it, and he sprang to me; for tho' I heard the noise well enough, yet I wasn't wide awake enough to get up. So the negro caught me, and said the red sticks was coming. I rose quicker then, and asked what was the matter? Our negro had gone and talked with the Indian who had just fetched the scream, as he come into camp, and learned from him, that the war party had been crossing the Coosa river all day at the Ten islands; and were going on to meet Jackson, and this Indian had come as a runner. This news very much alarmed the friendly Indians in camp, and they were all off in a few minutes. I felt bound to make this intelligence known as soon as possible to the army we had left at the landing; and so we all mounted our horses, and put out in a long lope to make our way back to that place. We were about sixty-five miles off. We went on to the same Cherokee town we had visited on our way out, having first called at Radcliff's, who was off with his family; and at the town we found large fires burning, but not a single Indian was to be seen. They were all gone. These circumstances were calculated to lay our dander a little, as it appeared we must be in great danger; though we could easily have licked any force of not more than five to one. But we expected the whole nation would be on us, and against such fearful odds we were not so rampant for a fight.

We therefore stayed only a short time in the light of the fires about the town, preferring the light of the moon and the shade of the woods. We pushed on till we got again to old Mr. Brown's, which was still about thirty miles from where we had left the main army. When we got there, the chickens were just at the first crowing for day. We fed our horses, got a morsel to eat ourselves, and again cut out. About ten o'clock in the morning we reached the camp, and I reported to Colonel Coffee the news. He didn't seem to mind my report a bit, and this raised my dander higher than ever; but I knowed I had to be on my best behaviour, and so I kept it all to myself; though I was so mad that I was burning inside like a tar-kiln, and I wonder that the smoke hadn't been pouring out of me at all points.

Major Gibson hadn't yet returned, and we all began to think he was killed; and that night they put out a double guard. The next day the Major got in, and brought a worse tale than I had, though he stated the same facts so far as I went. This seemed to put our colonel all in a fidget; and it convinced me, clearly, of one of the hateful ways of the world. When I made my report, it wasn't believed, because I was no officer; I was no great man, but just a poor soldier. But when the same thing was reported by Major Gibson!! why, then it was all as true as preaching, and the Colonel believed it every word.

He, therefore, ordered breastworks to be thrown up near a quarter of a mile long, and sent an express to Fayetteville, where General Jackson and his troops was, requesting them to push on like the very mischief, for fear we should all be cooked up to a cracklin before they could get there. Old Hickory-face made a forced march on getting the news; and on the next day, he and his men got into camp, with their feet all blistered from the effects of their swift journey. The volunteers therefore, stood guard altogether, to let them rest.

CHAPTER VI.

ABOUT eight hundred of the volunteers, and of that number I was one, were now sent back, crossing the Tennessee river, and on through Huntsville, so as to cross the river again at another place, and to get on the Indians in another direction.—After we passed Huntsville, we struck on the river at the Muscle Shoals, and at a place on them called Melton's Bluff. This river is here about two miles wide, and a rough bottom; so much so, indeed, in many places, as to be dangerous; and in fording it this time, we left several of the horses belonging to our men, with their feet fast in the crevices of the rocks. The men, whose horses were thus left, went ahead on foot. We pushed on till we got to what was called the Black Warriors' town, which stood near the very spot where Tuscaloosa now stands, which is the seat of government for the State of Alabama.

This Indian town was a large one; but when we arrived we found the Indians had all left it. There was a large field of corn standing out, and a pretty good supply in some cribs. There was also a fine quantity of dried beans, which were very acceptable to us; and without delay we secured them as well as the corn, and then burned the town to ashes; after which we left the place.

In the field where we gathered the corn we saw plenty of fresh Indian tracks, and we had no doubt they had been scared off by our arrival.

We then went on to meet the main army at the fork road, where I was first to have met Major Gibson. We got that evening as far back as the encampment we had made the night before we reached the Black Warriors' town, which we had just destroyed. The next day we were entirely out of meat. I went to Colonel Coffee, who was then in command of us, and asked his leave to hunt as we marched. He gave me leave, but told me to take mighty good care of myself. I turned aside to hunt, and had not gone far when I found a deer that had just been killed and skinned, and his flesh was still warm and smoking. From this I was sure that the Indian who had killed it had been gone only a few very minutes; and though I was never much in favour of one hunter stealing from another, yet meat was so scarce in camp, that I thought I must go in for it. So I just took up the deer on my horse before me, and carried it on till night. I could have sold it for almost any price I would have asked; but this wasn't my rule, neither in peace nor war. Whenever I had any thing, and saw a fellow-being suffering, I was more anxious to relieve him than to benefit myself. And this is one of the true secrets of my being a poor man to this day. But it is my way; and while it has often left me with an empty purse, which is as near the devil as anything else I have seen, yet it has never left my heart empty of consolations which money couldn't buy; the consolations of having sometimes fed the hungry and covered the naked.

I gave all my deer away, except a small part I kept for myself, and just sufficient to make a good supper for my mess; for meat was getting to be a rarity to us all. We had to live mostly on parched corn. The next day we marched on, and at night took up camp near a large cane brake. While here, I told my mess I would again try for some meat; so I took my rifle and cut out, but hadn't gone far, when I discovered a large gang of hogs. I shot one of them down in his tracks, and the rest broke directly towards the camp. In a few minutes the guns began to roar, as bad as if the whole army had been in an Indian battle, and the hogs to squeal as bad as the pig did, when the devil turned barber. I shouldered my hog, and went on to the camp; and when I got there I found they had killed a good many of the hogs, and a fine fat cow into the bargain, that had broke out of the cane brake. We did very well that night, and the next morning marched on to a Cherokee town, where our officers stop'd, and gave the inhabitants an order on Uncle Sam for their cow, and the hogs we had killed. The next day we met the main army having had, as we thought, hard times, and a plenty of them, though we had yet seen hardly the beginning of trouble.

After our meeting we went on to Radcliff's where I had been before while out as a spy; and when we got there we found he had hid all his provisions. We also got into the secret that he was the very rascal who had sent the runner to the Indian camp, with the news that the "red sticks" were crossing at the Ten Islands; and that his object was to scare me and my men away, and send us back with a false alarm.

To make some atonement for this we took the old scoundrel's two big sons with us and made them serve in the war.

We then marched to a place which we called Camp Wills, and here it was that Captain Cannon was promoted to a colonel, and Colonel Coffee to a general. We then marched to the Ten Islands, on the Coosa river, where we established a fort; and our spy companies were sent out. They soon made prisoners of Bob Catala and his warriors, and, in a few days afterwards, we heard of some Indians in a town about eight miles off. So we mounted our horses, and put out for that town, under the direction of two friendly Creeks we had taken for pilots. We had also a Cherokee colonel, Dick Brown, and some of his men with us. When we got near the town we divided, one of our pilots going with each division. And so we passed on each side of the town, keeping near to it, until our lines met on the far side. We then closed up at both ends, so as to surround it completely; and then we sent Captain Hammond's company of rangers to bring on the affray. He had advanced near the town when the Indians saw him, and they raised the yell, and came running at him like so many red devils. The main army was now formed in a hollow square around the town, and they pursued Hammond till they came in reach of us. We then gave them a fire, and they returned it, and then ran back into their town. We began to close on the town by making our files closer and closer, and the Indians soon saw they were our property. So most of them wanted us to take them prisoners; and their squaws and all would run and take hold of any of us they could, and give themselves up. I saw seven squaws have hold of one man, which made me think of the Scriptures. So I hollered out the Scriptures was fulfilling; that there was seven women holding to one man's coat tail. But I believe it was a hunting-shirt all the time. We took them all prisoners that came out to us in this way; but I saw some warriors run into a house, until I counted forty-six of them. We pursued them until we got near the house, when we saw a squaw sitting in the door, and she placed her feet against the bow she had in her hand, and then took an arrow, and, raising her feet she drew with all her might, and let fly at us, and she killed a man, whose name, I believe, was Moore. He was a lieutenant, and his death so enraged us all, that she was fired on, and had at least twenty balls blown through her. This was the first man I ever saw killed with a bow and arrow. We now shot them like dogs; and then set the house on fire, and burned it up with the forty-six warriors in it. I recollect seeing a boy who was shot down near the house; his arm and thigh was broken, and he was so near the burning house that the grease was stewing out of him. In this situation he was still trying to crawl along; but not a murmur escaped him, though he was only about twelve years old. So sullen is the Indian, when his dander is up, that he had sooner die than make a noise, or ask for quarters.

The number that we took prisoners, being added to the number we killed, amounted to one hundred and eighty-six; though I don't remember the exact number of either. We had five of our men killed. We then returned to our camp, at which our fort was erected, and known by the name of Fort Strother. No provisions had yet reached us, and we had now been for several days on half rations. However we went back to our Indian town on the next day, when many of the carcases of the Indians were still to be seen. They looked very awful, for the burning had not entirely consumed them, but given them a very terrible appearance, at least what remained of them. It was, somehow or other, found out that the house had a potato cellar under it, and an immediate examination was made, for we were all as hungry as wolves. We found a fine chance of potatoes in it, and hunger compelled us to eat them, though I had a little rather not if I could have helped it, for the oil of the Indians we had burned up on the day before had run down on them, and they looked like they had been stewed with fat meat. We then again returned to the army, and remained there for several days almost starving, as all our beef was gone. We commenced eating the beef-hides, and continued to eat every scrap we could lay our hands on. At length an Indian came to our guard one night and hollered, and said he wanted to see "Captain Jackson." He was conducted to the general's markee, into which he entered, and in a few minutes we received orders to prepare for marching.

In an hour we were all ready, and took up the line of march. We crossed the Coosa river, and went on in the direction to Fort Taladega. When we arrived near the place we met eleven hundred painted warriors, the very choice of the Creek nation. They then encamped near the fort, and had informed the friendly Indians who were in it, that if they didn't come out and fight with them against the whites, they would take their fort and all their ammunition and provisions. The friendly party asked three days to consider of it, and agreed that if on the third day they didn't come out ready to fight with them, they might take their fort. Thus they put them off. Then they immediately started their runner to General Jackson, and he and the army pushed over, as I have just before stated.

The camp of warriors had their spies out, and discovered us coming sometime before we got to the fort. They then went to the friendly Indians, and told them Captain Jackson was coming, and had a great many fine horses and blankets, and guns, and everything else; and if they would come out and help to whip him, and to take his plunder, it should all be divided with those in the fort. They promised that when Jackson came they would then come out and help to whip him. It was about an hour by the sun in the morning when we got near the fort. We were piloted by friendly Indians, and divided as we had done on a former occasion, so as to go to the right and left of the fort, and, consequently, of the warriors who were camped near it. Our lines marched on, as before, till they met in front, and then closed in the rear, forming again into a hollow square. We then sent on old Major Russell, with his spy company, to bring on the battle; Captain Evans' company went also. When they got near the fort, the top of it was lined with friendly Indians, crying out as loud as they could roar, "How-dy-do, brother, how-dy-do?" They kept this up till Major Russell had passed by the fort, and was moving on towards the warriors. They were all painted as red as scarlet, and were just as naked as they were born. They had concealed themselves under the bank of a branch, that ran partly around the fort, in the manner of a half moon. Russell was going right into their circle, for he couldn't see them, while the Indians on the top of the fort were trying every plan to show him his danger. But he couldn't understand them. At last two of them jumped from it, and ran and took his horse by the bridle, and pointing to where they were, told him there were thousands of them lying under the bank. This brought them to a halt, and about this moment the Indians fired on them, and came rushing forth like a cloud of Egyptian locusts, and screaming like all the young devils had been turned loose, with the old devil of all at their head. Russell's company quit their horses, and took into the fort, and their horses ran up to our line, which was then in full view. The warriors then came yelling on, meeting us, and continued till they were within shot of us, when we fired and killed a considerable number of them. They then broke like a gang of steers, and ran across to the other line, where they were again fired on; and so we kept them running from one line to the other, constantly under a heavy fire, until we had killed upwards of four hundred of them. They fought with guns, and also with their bows and arrows; but at length they made their escape through a part of our line which was made up of drafted militia, which broke ranks, and they passed. We lost fifteen of our men, as brave fellows as ever lived or died. We buried them, all in one grave, and started back to our fort; but before we got there two more of our men died of wounds they had received; making our total loss seventeen good fellows in that battle.

We now remained at the fort a few days, but no provision came yet, and we were all likely to perish. The weather also began to get very cold; and our clothes were nearly worn out, and horses getting very feeble and poor. Our officers proposed to General Jackson to let us return home and get fresh horses, and fresh clothing, so as to be better prepared for another campaign; for our sixty days had long been out, and that was the time we had entered for.

But the general took "the responsibility" on himself, and refused. We were, however, determined to go, as I am to put back the deposites, *if I can.* With this, the general issued his orders against it, as he has against the bank. But we began to fix for a start, as provisions were too scarce; just as Clay, and Webster, and myself are preparing to fix bank matters, on account of the scarcity of money. The general went and placed his cannon on a bridge we had to cross, and ordered out his regulars, and drafted men to keep us from crossing; just as he has planted his Globe and K. C. to alarm the bank men, while his regulars and militia in Congress are to act as artillery men. But when the militia started to guard the bridge, they would holler back to us to bring their knapsacks along when we come, for they wanted to go as bad as we did; just as many a good fellow now wants his political knapsack brought along, that if, when we come to vote, he sees he has a *fair shake to go*, he may join in and help us to take back the deposites.

We got ready and moved on till we came near the bridge, where the general's men were all strung along on both sides, just like the office-holders are now, to keep us from getting along to the help of the country and the people. But we all had our flints ready picked, and our guns ready primed, that if we were fired on we might fight our way through, or all die together; just as we are now determined to save the country from ready ruin, or to sink down with it. When we came still nearer the bridge we heard the guards cocking their guns, and we did the same; just as we have had it in Congress, while the "government" regulars and the people's volunteers have all been setting their political triggers. But, after all, we marched boldly on, and not a gun was fired, nor a life lost; just as I hope it will be again, that we shall not be afraid of the general's Globe, nor his K. C., nor his regulars, nor their trigger snapping; but just march boldly over the executive bridge, and take the deposites back where the law placed them, and where they ought to be. When we had passed no further attempt was made to stop us; but the general said, we were "the damned'st volunteers he had ever seen in his life; that we would volunteer and go out and fight, and then at our pleasure would *volunteer* and go home again, in spite of the devil." But we went on; and near Huntsville we met a reinforcement who were going on to join the army. It consisted of a regiment of volunteers, and was under the command of some one whose name I can't remember. They were sixty-day volunteers.

We got home pretty safely, and in a short time we had procured fresh horses, and a supply of clothing better suited for the season; and then we returned to Fort Deposite, where our officer held a sort of a "*national convention*" on the subject of a message they had received from General Jackson—demanding that on our return we should serve out *six months*. We had already served three months instead of two, which was the time we had volunteered for. On the next morning the officers reported to us the conclusions they had come to; and told us, if any of us felt bound to go on and serve out the six months, we could do so; but that they intended to go back home. I knowed if I went back home I wouldn't rest, for I felt it my duty to be out; and when out I was, somehow or other, always delighted to be in the very thickest of the danger. A few of us, therefore, determined to push on and join the army. The number I do not recollect, but it was very small.

When we got out there I joined Major Russell's company of spies. Before we reached the place General Jackson had started. We went on likewise, and overtook him at a place where we established a fort, called Fort Williams, and, leaving men to guard it, we went ahead; intending to go to a place called the Horseshoe bend of the Talapoosa river.—When we came near that place we began to find Indian sign plenty, and we struck up camp for the night. About two hours before day we heard our guard firing, and we were all up in little or no time. We mended up our camp fires, and then fell back in the dark, expecting to see the Indians pouring in; and intending, when they should do so, to shoot them by the light of our own fires. But it happened that they did not rush in as we had expected, but commenced a fire on us as we were. We were encamped in a hollow square, and we not only returned the fire, but continued to shoot, as well as we could in the dark, till day broke, when the Indians disappeared. The only guide we had in shooting was to notice the flash of their guns, and then shoot as directly at the place as we could guess.

In this scrape we had four men killed and several wounded, but whether we killed any of the Indians or not we never could tell, for it is their custom always to carry off their dead, if they can possibly do so. We buried ours, and then made a large log heap over them and set it on fire, so that the place of their deposite might not be known to the savages, who we knew would seek for them, that they might scalp them. We made some horse litters for our wounded, and took up a retreat. We moved on till we came to a large creek which we had to cross; and about half our men had crossed, when the Indians commenced firing on our left wing, and they kept it up very warmly. We had left Major Russell and his brother at the camp we had moved from that morning, to see what discovery they could make as to the movements of the Indians; and about this time, while a warm fire was kept up on our left, as I have just stated, the major came up in our rear, and was closely pursued by a large number of Indians, who immediately commenced a fire on our artillery men. They hid themselves behind a large log, and could kill one of our men almost every shot, they being in open ground and exposed. The worst of all was, two of our colonels just at this trying moment left their men, and, by a *forced march*, crossed the creek out of the reach of the fire. Their names, at this late day, would do the world no good, and my object is history alone, and not the slightest interference with character. An opportunity was now afforded for Governor Carroll to distinguish himself, and on this occasion he did so, by greater bravery than I ever saw any other man display. In truth, I believe, as firmly as I do that General Jackson is president, that if it hadn't been for Carroll, we should all have been genteely licked that time, for we were in a devil of a fix; part of our men on one side of the creek, and part on the other, and the Indians all the time pouring it on us, as hot as fresh mustard to a sore shin. I will not say exactly that the old general was whipped; but I will say, that if we escaped it at all, it was like old Henry Snider going to heaven, "mit a tam tite squeeze." I think he would confess himself, that he was nearer whip'd this time than he was at any other, for I know that all the world couldn't make him acknowledge that he was *pointedly* whip'd. I know I was mighty glad when it was over, and the savages quit us, for I begun to think there was one behind every tree in the woods.

CHAPTER VII.

SOON after this an army was to be raised to go to Pensacola, and I determined to go again with them, for I wanted a small taste of British fighting, and I supposed they would be there.

Here again the entreaties of my wife were thrown in the way of my going, but all in vain; for I always had a way of just going ahead at whatever I had a mind to. One of my neighbours, hearing I had determined to go, came to me, and offered me a hundred dollars to go in his place as a substitute, as he had been drafted. I told him I was better raised than to hire myself out to be shot at; but that I would go, and he should go too, and in that way the government would have the services of us both. But we didn't call General Jackson "the government" in those days, though we used to go and fight under him in the war.

I fixed up, and joined old Major Russell again; but we couldn't start with the main army, but followed on, in a little time, after them. In a day or two we had a hundred and thirty men in our company; and we went over and crossed the Muscle Shoals at the same place where I had crossed when first out, and when we burned the Black Warriors' town. We passed through the Choctaw and Chickesaw nations on to Fort Stephens, and from thence to what is called the Cut-off, at the junction of the Tom-Bigby with the Alabama river. This place is near the old Fort Mimms, where the Indians committed the great butchery at the commencement of the war.

We were here about two days behind the main army, who had left their horses at the Cut-off, and taken it on foot; and they did this because there was no chance for forage between there and Pensacola. We did the same, leaving men enough to take care of our horses, and cut out on foot for that place. It was about eighty miles off; but in good heart we shouldered our guns, blankets, and provisions, and trudged merrily on. About twelve o'clock the second day we reached the encampment of the main army, which was situated on a hill, overlooking the city of Pensacola.—My commander, Major Russell, was a great favourite with Gen'l Jackson, and our arrival was hailed with great applause, though we were a little after the feast; for they had taken the town and fort before we got there.—That evening we went down into the town, and could see the British fleet lying in sight of the place. We got some liquor, and took a "horn" or so, and went back to the camp. We remained there that night, and in the morning we marched back towards the Cut-off. We pursued this direction till we reached old Fort Mimms, where we remained two or three days. It was here that Major Russell was promoted from his command, which was only that of a captain of spies, to the command of a major in the line. He had been known long before at home as old Major Russell, and so we continued to call him in the army. A Major Childs, from East Tennessee, also commanded a battalion, and he, and the one Russell was appointed to command, composed a regiment, which, by agreement with General Jackson, was to quit his army and go to the south, to kill up the Indians on the Scamby river.

General Jackson and the main army set out the next morning for New Orleans, and a Colonel Blue took command of the regiment which I have before described. We remained, however, a few days after the general's departure, and then started also on our route.

As it gave rise to so much war and bloodshed, it may not be improper here to give a little description of Fort Mimms, and the manner in which the Indian war commenced. The fort was built right in the middle of a large old field, and in it the people had been forted so long and so quietly, that they didn't apprehend any danger at all, and had, therefore, become quite careless. A small negro boy, whose business it was to bring up the calves at milking time, had been out for that purpose, and on coming back he said he saw a great many Indians. At this the inhabitants took the alarm, and closed their gates and placed out their guards, which they continued for a few days. But finding that no attack was made, they concluded the little negro had lied; and again threw their gates open, and set all their hands out to work their fields. The same boy was out again on the same errand, when, returning in great haste and alarm, he informed them that he had seen the Indians as thick as trees in the woods. He was not believed, but was tucked up to receive a flogging for the supposed lie; and was actually getting badly licked at the very moment when the Indians came in a troop, loaded with rails, with which they stop'd all the port-holes of the fort one side except the bastion, and then they fell in to cutting down the picketing. Those inside the fort had only the bastion to shoot from, as all the other holes were spiked up; and they shot several of the Indians while engaged in cutting. But as fast as one would fall, another would seize up the axe and chop away, until they succeeded in cutting down enough of the picketing to admit them to enter. They then began to rush through, and continued until they were all in. They immediately commenced scalping, without regard to age or sex; having forced the inhabitants up to one side of the fort, where they carried on the work of death as a butcher would in a slaughter pen.

The scene was particularly described to me by a young man who was in the fort when it happened, and subsequently went on with us to Pensacola. He said that he saw his father, and mother, his four sisters, and the same number of brothers, all butchered in the most shocking manner, and that he made his escape by running over the heads of the crowd, who were against the fort wall, to the top of the fort, and then jumping off, and taking to the woods. He was closely pursued by several Indians, until he came to a small byo, across which there was a log. He knew the log was hollow on the under side, so he slip'd under the log and hid himself. He said he heard the Indians walk over him several times back and forward. He remained, nevertheless, still till night, when he came out and finished his escape. The name of this young man has entirely escaped my recollection, though his tale greatly excited my feelings. But to return to my subject. The regiment marched from where Gen'l Jackson had left us to Fort Montgomery, which was distant from Fort Mimms about a mile and a half, and there wer emained for some days.

Here we supplied ourselves pretty well with beef, by killing wild cattle which had formerly belonged to the people who had perished in the fort, but had gone wild after their massacre.

When we marched from Fort Montgomery, we went some distance back towards Pensacola; then we turned to the left, and passed through a poor piny country, till we reached the Scamby river, near which we encamped. We had about one thousand men, and as a part of that number, one hundred and eighty-six Chickesaw and Choctaw Indians with us. That evening a boat landed from Pensacola, bringing many articles that were both good and necessary; such as sugar and coffee, and liquors of all kinds. The same evening, the Indians we had along proposed to cross the river, and the officers thinking it might be well for them to do so, consented; and Maj. Russell went with them, taking sixteen white men, of which number I was one. We camped on the opposite bank that night, and early in the morning we set out. We had not gone far before we came to a place where the whole country was covered with water, and looked like a sea. We didn't stop for this, tho', but just put in like so many spaniels, and waded on, sometimes up to our arm-pits, until we reached the pine hills, which made our distance through the water about a mile and a half. Here we struck up a fire to warm ourselves, for it was cold, and we were chilled through by being so long in the water. We again moved on, keeping our spies out; two to our left near the bank of the river, two straight before us, and five others on our right. We had gone in this way about six miles up the river, when our spies on the left came to us leaping the brush like so many old bucks, and informed us that they had discovered a camp of Creek Indians, and that we must kill them. Here we paused for a few minutes, and the prophets pow-wowed over their men awhile, and then got out their paint, and painted them, all according to their custom when going into battle. They then brought their paint to old Major Russell, and said to him, that as he was an officer, he must be painted too. He agreed, and they painted him just as they had done themselves. We let the Indians understand that we white men would first fire on the camp, and then fall back, so as to give the Indians a chance to rush in and scalp them. The Chickesaws marched on our left hand, and the Choctaws on our right, and we moved on till we got in hearing of the camp, where the Indians were employed in beating up what they called chainy briar root. On this they mostly subsisted. On a nearer approach we found they were on an island, and that we could not get to them. While we were chatting about this matter, we heard some guns fired, and in a very short time after a keen whoop, which satisfied us, that wherever it was, there was war on a small scale. With that we all broke, like quarter horses, for the firing; and when we got there we found it was our two front spies, who related to us the following story:—As they were moving on, they had met with two Creeks who were out hunting their horses; as they approached each other, there was a large cluster of green bay bushes exactly between them, so that they were within a few feet of meeting before either was discovered. Our spies walked up to them, and speaking in the Shawnee tongue, informed them that General Jackson was at Pensacola, and they were making their escape, and wanted to know where they could get something to eat. The Creeks told them that nine miles up the Conaker, the river they were then on, there was a large camp of Creeks, and they had cattle and plenty to eat: and further, that their own camp was on an island about a mile off, and just below the mouth of the Conaker. They held their conversation and struck up a fire, and smoked together, and shook hands, and parted. One of the Creeks had a gun, the other had none; and as soon as they had parted, our Choctaws turned round and shot down the one that had the gun, and the other attempted to run off. They snapped several times at him, but the gun still missing fire, they took after him, and overtaking him, one of them struck him over the head with his gun, and followed up his blows till he killed him.

The gun was broken in the combat, and they then fired off the gun of the Creek they had killed, and raised the war-whoop. When we reached them, they had cut off the heads of both the Indians; and each of those Indians with us would walk up to one of the heads, and taking his war club would strike on it. This was done by every one of them; and when they had got done, I took one of their clubs, and walked up as they had done, and struck it on the head also. At this they all gathered round me, and patting me on the shoulder, would call me "Warrior—warrior."

They scalped the heads, and then we moved on a short distance to where we found a trace leading in towards the river. We took this trace and pursued it, till we came to where a Spaniard had been killed and scalped, together with a woman, who we supposed to be his wife, and also four children. I began to feel mighty ticklish along about this time, for I knowed if there was no danger then, there had been; and I felt exactly like there still was. We, however, went on till we struck the river, and then continued down it till we came opposite to the Indian camp, where we found they were still beating their roots.

It was now late in the evening, and they were in a thick cane brake. We had some few friendly Creeks with us, who said they could decoy them. So we all hid behind trees and logs, while the attempt was made. The Indians would not agree that we should fire, but pick'd out some of their best gunners, and placed them near the river. Our Creeks went down to the river's side, and hailed the camp in the Creek language.—We heard the answer, and an Indian man started down towards the river, but didn't come in sight. He went back and again commenced beating his roots, and sent a squaw. She came down, and talked to our Creeks until dark came on. They told her they wanted her to bring them a canoe. To which she replied, that their canoe was on our side; that two of their men had gone out to hunt their horses and hadn't yet returned. They were the same two we had killed.—The canoe was found, and forty of our picked Indian warriors were crossed over to take the camp. There was at last only one man in it, and he escaped; and they took two squaws, and ten children, but killed none of them, of course.

We had run nearly out of provisions, and Major Russell had determined to go up the Conaker to the camp we had heard of from the Indians we had killed. I was one that he selected to go down the river that night for provisions, with the canoe, to where we had left our regiment. I took with me a man by the name of John Guess, and one of the friendly Creeks, and cut out. It was very dark, and the river was so full that it overflowed the banks and the adjacent low bottoms. This rendered it very difficult to keep the channel, and particularly as the river was very crooked. At about ten o'clock at night we reached the camp, and were to return by morning to Major Russell, with provisions for his trip up the river; but on informing Colonel Blue of this arrangement, he vetoed it as quick as General Jackson did the bank bill; and said, if Maj. Russell didn't come back the next day, it would be bad times for him. I found we were not to go up the Conaker to the Indian camp, and a man of my company offered to go up in my place to inform Major Russell.—I let him go; and they reached the Major, as I was told, about sunrise in the morning, who immediately returned with those who were with him, to the regiment, and joined us where we crossed tho river, as hereafter stated.

The next morning we all fixed up, and marched down the Scamby to a place called Miller's Landing, where we swam our horses across, and sent on two companies down on the side of the bay, opposite to Pensacola, where the Indians had fled when the main army first marched to that place. One was the company of Captain William Russell, a son of the old Major, and the other was commanded by a Captain Trimble. They went on, and had a little skirmish with the Indians. They killed some, and took all the balance prisoners, though I don't remember the numbers.

CHAPTER VIII.

WHEN we made a move from the point where we met the companies, we set out for Chatahachy, the place for which we had started when we left Fort Montgomery. At the start we had taken only twenty days' rations of flour, and eight days' rations of beef; and it was now thirty-four days before we reached that place. We were, therefore, in extreme suffering for want of something to eat, and exhausted with our exposure and the fatigues of our journey. I remember well, that I had not myself tasted bread but twice in nineteen days. I had brought a pretty good supply of coffee from the boat that had reached us from Pensacola, on the Scamby, and on that we chiefly subsisted. At length, one night our spies came in, and informed us they had found Holm's village on the Chatahachy river; and we made an immediate push for that place. We travelled all night, expecting to get something to eat when we got there. We arrived about sunrise, and near the place prepared for battle. We were all so furious, that even the certainty of a pretty hard fight could not have restrained us. We made a furious charge on the town, but to our great mortification and surprise, there was not a human being in it. The Indians had all run off and left it. We burned the town, however; but, melancholy to tell, we found no provision whatever. We then turned about, and went back to the camp we had left the night before, as nearly starved as any set of poor fellows ever were in the world.

We staid there only a little while, when we divided our regiment; and Major Childs, with his men, went back the way we had come for a considerable distance, and then turned to Baton-Rouge, where they joined General Jackson and the main army on their return from Orleans. Major Russell and his men struck for Fort Decatur, on the Talapoosa river. Some of our friendly Indians, who knew the country, went on ahead of us, as we had no trail except the one they made to follow. With them we sent some of our ablest horses and men, to get us some provisions, to prevent us from absolutely starving to death. As the army marched, I hunted every day, and would kill every hawk, bird, and squirrel that I could find. Others did the same; and it was a rule with us, that when we stop'd at night, the hunters would throw all they killed in a pile, and then we would make a general division among all the men. One evening I came in, having killed nothing that day. I had a very sick man in my mess, and I wanted something for him to eat, even if I starved myself. So I went to the fire of a Captain Cowen, who commanded my company after the promotion of Major Russell, and informed him that I was on the hunt of something for a sick man to eat. I knowed the captain was as bad off as the rest of us, but I found him broiling a turkey's gizzard. He said he had divided the turkey out among the sick, that Major Smiley had killed it, and that nothing else had been killed that day. I immediately went to Smiley's fire, where I found him broiling another gizzard. I told him, that it was the first turkey I had ever seen have two gizzards. But so it was, I got nothing for my sick man. And now, seeing that every fellow must shift for himself, I determined that in the morning, I would come up missing; so I took my mess and cut out to go ahead of the army. We know'd that nothing more could happen to us if we went than if we staid, for it looked like it was to be starvation any way; we therefore determined to go on the old saying root hog or die. We passed two camps, at which our men, that had gone on before us, had killed Indians. At one they had killed nine, and at the other three. About daylight we came to a small river, which I thought was the Scamby; but we continued on for three days, killing little or nothing to eat; till, at last, we all began to get nearly ready to give up the ghost, and lie down and die; for we had no prospect of provision, and we knew we couldn't go much further without it.

We came to a large prairie, that was about six miles across it, and in this I saw a trail which I knowed was made by bear, deer, and turkeys. We went on through it till we came to a large creek, and the low grounds were all set over with wild rye, looking as green as a wheat field. We here made a halt, unsaddled our horses, and turned them loose to graze.

One of my companions, a Mr. Vanzant, and myself, then went up the low grounds to hunt. We had gone some distance, finding nothing; when, at last, I found a squirrel; which I shot, but he got into a hole in the tree. The game was small, but necessity is not very particular; so I thought I must have him, and I climbed that tree thirty feet high, without a limb, and pulled him out of his hole. I shouldn't relate such small matters, only to show what lengths a hungry man will go to, to get something to eat. I soon killed two other squirrels, and fired at a large hawk. At this a large gang of turkeys rose from the cane brake, and flew across the creek to where my friend was, who had just before crossed it. He soon fired on a large gobler, and I heard it fall. By this time my gun was loaded again, and I saw one sitting on my side of the creek, which had flew over when he fired; so I blazed away, and down I brought him. I gathered him up, and a fine turkey he was. I now began to think we had struck a breeze of luck, and almost forgot our past sufferings, in the prospect of once more having something to eat. I raised the shout, and my comrade came to me, and we went on to our camp with the game we had killed. While we were gone, two of our mess had been out, and each of them had found a bee tree. We turned into cooking some of our game, but we had neither salt nor bread. Just at this moment, on looking down the creek, we saw our men, who had gone on before us for provisions, coming to us. They came up, and measured out to each man a cupfull of flour. With this, we thickened our soup, when our turkey was cooked, and our friends took dinner with us, and then went on.

We now took our tomahawks, and went out and cut our bee-trees, out of which we got a fine chance of honey; though we had been starving so long that we feared to eat much at a time, till, like the Irish by hanging, we got used to it again. We rested that night without moving our camp; and the next morning myself and Vanzant again turned out to hunt. We had not gone far, before I wounded a fine buck very badly; and while pursuing him, I was walking on a large tree that had fallen down, when from the top of it a large bear broke out and ran off. I had no dogs, and I was sorry enough for it; for of all the hunting I ever did, I have always delighted most in bear hunting. Soon after this, I killed a large buck; and we had just gotten him to camp, when our poor starved army came up.—They told us, that to lessen their sufferings as much as possible, Captain William Russell had had his horse led up to be shot for them to eat, just at the moment that they saw our men returning, who had carried on the flour.

We were now about fourteen miles from Fort Decatur, and we gave away all our meat, and honey, and went on with the rest of the army. When we got there, they could give us only one ration of meat, but not a mouthful of bread. I immediately got a canoe, and taking my gun, crossed over the river, and went to the Big Warriors' town. I had a large hat, and I offered an Indian a silver dollar for my hat full of corn. He told me that his corn was all "*shuestea*," which in English means, it was all gone. But he showed me where an Indian lived, who, he said, had corn. I went to him and made the same offer. He could talk a little broken English, and said to me, "You got any powder? You got bullet?" I told him I had. He then said, "Me swap my corn, for powder and bullet." I took out about ten bullets, and showed him; and he proposed to give me a hat full of corn for them. I took him up, mighty quick. I then offered to give him ten charges of powder for another hat full of corn. To this he agreed very willingly.—So I took off my hunting shirt, and tied up my corn; and though it had cost me very little of my powder and lead, yet I wouldn't have taken fifty silver dollars for it. I returned to the camp, and the next morning we started for the Hickory Ground, which was thirty miles off. It was here that General Jackson met the Indians, and made peace with the body of the nation.

We got nothing to eat at this place, and we had yet to go forty-nine miles, over a rough and wilderness country, to Fort Williams. Parched corn, and but little even of that, was our daily subsistence. When we reached Fort Williams, we got one ration of pork and one of flour, which was our only hope until we could reach Fort Strother.

The horses were now giving out, and I remember to have seen

thirteen good horses left in one day, the saddles and bridles being thrown away. It was thirty-nine miles to Fort Strother, and we had to pass directly by Fort Talladego, where we first had the big Indian battle with the eleven hundred painted warriors. We went through the old battle ground, and it looked like a great gourd patch; the sculls of the Indians who were killed still lay scattered all about, and many of their frames were still perfect, as the bones had not separated. But about five miles before we got to this battle ground, I struck a trail, which I followed until it led me to one of their towns. Here I swap'd some more of my powder and bullets for a little corn.

I pursued on, by myself, till some time after night, when I came up to the rest of the army. That night my company and myself did pretty well, as I divided out my corn among them. The next morning we met the East Tennessee troops, who were on the road to Mobile, and my youngest brother was with them. They had plenty of corn and provisions, and they gave me what I wanted for myself and my horse. I remained with them that night, though my company went across the Coosa river to the fort, where they also had the good fortune to find plenty of provisions. Next morning, I took leave of my brother and all my old neighbours, for there were a good many of them with him, and crossed over to my men at the fort. Here I had enough to go on, and after remaining a few days, cut out for home. Nothing more, worthy of the reader's attention, transpired till I was safely landed at home once more with my wife and children. I found them all well and doing well; and though I was only a rough sort of a backwoodsman, they seemed mighty glad to see me, however little the quality folks might suppose it. For I do reckon we love as hard in the backwood country, as any people in the whole creation.

But I had been home only a few days, when we received orders to start again, and go on to the Black Warrior and Cahawba rivers, to see if there was no Indians there. I know'd well enough there was none, and I wasn't willing to trust my craw any more where there was neither any fighting to do, nor any thing to go on; and so I agreed to give a young man, who wanted to go, the balance of my wages if he would serve out my time, which was about a month. He did so, and when they returned, sure enough they hadn't seen an Indian any more than if they had been all the time chopping wood in my clearing. This closed my career as a warrior, and I am glad of it, for I like life now a heap better than I did then; and I am glad all over that I lived to see these times, which I should not have done if I had kept fooling along in war, and got used up at it. When I say I am glad, I just mean I am glad I am alive, for there is a confounded heap of things I an't glad of at all. I an't glad, for example, that the "government" moved the deposites, and if my military glory should take such a turn as to make me president after the general's time, I'll move them back; yes, I, the "government," will "take the responsibility," and move them back again. If I don't, I wish I may be shot.

But I am glad that I am now through war matters, and I reckon the reader is too, for they have no fun in them at all; and less if he had to pass through them first, and then write them afterwards. But for the dulness of their narrative, I must try to make amends by relating some of the curious things that happened to me in private life, and when *forced* to become a public man, as I shall have to be again, if ever I consent to take the presidential chair.

CHAPTER IX.

I CONTINUED at home now, working my farm for two years, as the war finally closed soon after I quit the service. The battle at New Orleans had already been fought, and treaties were made with the Indians which put a stop to their hostilities.

But in this time, I met with the hardest trial which ever falls to the lot of man. Death, that cruel leveller of all distinctions,—to whom the prayers and tears of husbands, and of even helpless infancy, are addressed in vain,—entered my humble cottage, and tore from my children an affectionate good mother, and from me a tender and loving wife.

It is a scene long gone by, and one which it would be supposed I had almost forgotten; yet when I turn my memory back on it, it seems as but the work of yesterday. It was the doing of the Almighty, whose ways are always right, though we sometimes think they fall heavily on us; and as painful as is even yet the remembrance of her sufferings, and the loss sustained by my little children and myself, yet I have no wish to lift up the voice of complaint. I was left with three children; the two eldest were sons, the youngest a daughter, and, at the time, a mere infant. It appeared to me, at that moment, that my situation was the worst in the world. I couldn't bear the thought of scattering my children, and so I got my youngest brother, who was also married, and his family to live with me. They took as good care of my children as they well could, but yet it wasn't all like the care of a mother. And though their company was to me in every respect like that of a brother and sister, yet it fell far short of being like that of a wife. So I came to the conclusion it wouldn't do, but that I must have another wife.

There lived in the neighbourhood, a widow lady whose husband had been killed in the war. She had two children, a son and daughter, and both quite small like my own. I began to think, that as we were both in the same situation, it might be that we could do something for each other; and I therefore began to hint a little around the matter, as we were once and a while together. She was a good industrious woman, and owned a snug little farm, and lived quite comfortable. I soon began to pay my respects to her in real good earnest; but I was as shy about it as a fox when he is going to rob a henroost. I found that my company wasn't at all disagreeable to her; and I thought I could treat her children with so much friendship as to make her a good stepmother to mine, and in this I wasn't mistaken, as we soon bargained, and got married, and then went ahead. In a great deal of peace we raised our first crop of children, and they are all married and doing well. But we had a second crop together; and I shall notice them as I go along, as my wife and myself both had a hand in them, and they therefore belong to the history of my second marriage.

The next fall after this marriage, three of my neighbours and myself determined to explore a new country. Their names were Robinson, Frazier, and Rich. We set out for the Creek country, crossing the Tennessee river; and after having made a day's travel, we stop'd at the house of one of my old acquaintances, who had settled there after the war. Resting here a day, Frazier turned out to hunt, being a great hunter; but he got badly bit by a very poisonous snake, and so we left him and went on. We passed through a large rich valley, called Jones's valley, where several other families had settled, and continued our course till we came near to the place where Tuscaloosa now stands. Here we camped, as there were no inhabitants, and hobbled out our horses for the night. About two hours before day, we heard the bells on our horses going back the way we had come, as they had started to leave us. As soon as it was daylight, I started in pursuit of them on foot, and carrying my rifle, which was a very heavy one. I went ahead the whole day, wading creeks and swamps, and climbing mountains; but I couldn't overtake our horses, though I could hear of them at every house they passed. I at last found I couldn't catch up with them, and so I gave up the hunt, and turned back to the last house I had passed, and staid there till morning. From the best calculation we could make, I had walked over fifty miles that day; and the next morning I was so sore, and fatigued, that I felt like I couldn't walk any more. But I was anxious to get back to where I had left my company, and so I started and went on, but mighty slowly, till after the middle of the day. I now began to feel mighty sick, and had a dreadful head-ache. My rifle was so heavy, and I felt so weak, that I lay down by the side of the trace, in a perfect wilderness too, to see if I wouldn't get better. In a short time some Indians came along. They had some ripe melons, and wanted me to eat some, but I was so sick I couldn't. They then signed to me, that I would die, and be buried; a thing I was confoundedly afraid of myself. But I asked them how near it was to any house? By their signs, again, they made me understand it was a mile and a half. I got up to go; but when I rose, I reeled about like a cow with the blind staggers, or a fellow who had taken too many "horns." One of the Indians proposed to go with me, and carry my gun. I gave him half a dollar, and accepted his offer. We got to the house, by which time I was pretty far gone, but was kindly received, and got on to a bed. The woman did all she could for me with her warm teas, but I still continued bad enough, with a high fever, and generally out of my senses. The next day two of my neighbours were passing the road, and heard of my situation, and came to where I was. They were going nearly the route I had intended to go, to look at the country; and so they took me first on one of their horses, and then on the other, till they got me back to where I left my company. I expected I would get better, and be able to go on with them, but, instead, of this, I got worse and worse; and when we got there, I wan't able to sit up at all. I thought now the jig was mighty nigh up with me, but I determined to keep a stiff upper lip. They carried me to a house, and each of my comrades bought him a horse, and they all set off together, leaving me behind. I knew but little that was going for about two weeks; but the family treated me with every possible kindness in their power, and I shall always feel thankful to them. The man's name was Jesse Jones. At the end of two weeks I began to mend without the help of a doctor, or of any doctor's means. In this time, however, as they told me, I was speechless for five days, and they had no thought that I would ever speak again,—in Congress or any where else. And so the woman, who had a bottle of Batesman's draps, thought if they killed me, I would only die any how, and so she would try it with me. She gave me the whole bottle, which throwed me into a sweat that continued on me all night; when at last I seemed to wake up, and spoke, and asked her for a drink of water. This almost alarmed her, for she was looking every minute for me to die. She gave me the water, and, from that time, I began slowly to mend, and so kept on till I was able at last to walk about a little. I might easily have been mistake for one of the Kitchen Cabinet, I looked so much like a ghost. I have been particular in giving a history of this sickness, not because I believe it will interest any body much now, nor, indeed, do I *certainly* know that it ever will. But if I should be forced to take the "white house," then it will be a good history; and every one will look on it as important. And I can't, for my life, help laughing now, to think, that when my folks get around me, wanting good fat offices, how so many of them will say, "What a good thing it was that that kind woman had a bottle of draps that saved PRESIDENT CROCKETT's life,—the second greatest and best"!!!! Good, says I, my noble fellow! You take the post office; or the navy; or the war office; or maybe the treasury. But if I give him the treasury, there's no devil if I don't make him agree first to fetch back them deposites. And if it's even the post-office, I'll make him promise to keep his money 'counts without any figuring, as that throws the whole concern heels over head in debt, in little or no time.

But when I got so I could travel a little, I got a waggoner who was passing along to hawl me to where he lived, which was about twenty miles from my house. I still mended as we went along, and when we got to his stopping-place, I hired one of his horses, and went on home. I was so pale, and so much reduced, that my face looked like it had been half soled with brown paper.

When I got there, it was to the utter astonishment of my wife; for she supposed I was dead. My neighbours who had started with me had returned and took my horse home, which they had found with theirs; and they reported that they had seen men who had helped to bury me: and who saw me draw my last breath. I know'd this was a whopper of a lie, as soon as I heard it. My wife had hired a man, and sent him out to see what had become of my money and other things; but I had missed the man as I went in, and he didn't return until some time after I got home, as he went all the way to where I lay sick, before he heard that I was still in the land of the living and a-kicking.

The place on which I lived was sickly, and I was determined to leave it. I therefore set out the next fall to look at the country which had been purchased of the Chickesaw tribe of Indians. I went on to a place called Shoal Creek, about eighty miles from where I lived, and here again I got sick. I took the ague and fever, which I supposed was brought on by my camping out. I remained here for some time, as I was unable to go farther; and in that time I became so well pleased with the country about there, that I resolved to settle in it. It was just only a little distance in the purchase, and no order had been established there; but I thought I could get along without order as well as any body else. And so I moved and settled myself down on the head of Shoal Creek. We remained here some two or three years, without any law at all; and so many bad characters began to flock in upon us, that we found it necessary to set up a sort of temporary government of our own. I don't mean that we made any president, and called him the "government," but we met and made what we called a corporation; and I reckon we called *it* wrong, for it wan't a bank, and hadn't any deposites; and now they call the bank a corporation. But be this as it may, we lived in the backwoods, and didn't profess to know much, and no doubt used many wrong words. But we met, and appointed magistrates and constables to keep order. We didn't fix any laws for them, tho'; for we supposed they would know law enough, whoever they might be; and so we left it to themselves to fix the laws.

I was appointed one of the magistrates; and when a man owed a debt, and wouldn't pay it, I and my constable ordered our warrant, and then he would take the man, and bring him before me for trial. I would give judgment against him, and then an order for an execution would easily scare the debt out of him. If any one was charged with marking his neighbour's hogs, or with stealing any thing, which happened pretty often in those days,- I would have him taken, and if there was tolerable grounds for the charge, I would have him well whip'd and cleared. We kept this up till our Legislature added us to the white settlements in Giles county; and appointed magistrates by law, to organize matters in the parts where I lived. They appointed nearly every man a magistrate who had belonged to our corporation. I was then, of course, made a squire according to law; though now the honour rested more heavily on me than before. For, at first, whenever I told my constable, says I—"Catch that fellow, and bring him up for trial"—away he went, and the fellow must come, dead or alive; for we considered this a good warrant, though it was only in verbal writing. But after I was appointed by the assembly, they told me, my warrants must be in real writing, and signed; and that I must keep a book, and write my proceedings in it. This was a hard business on me, for I could just barely write my own name ; but to do this, and write the warrants too, was at least a huckleberry over my persimmon. I had a pretty well informed constable, however, and he aided me very much in this business. Indeed I had so much confidence in him, that I told him, when we should happen to be out any where, and see that a warrant was necessary, and would have a good effect, he needn't take the trouble to come all the way to me to get one, but he could just fill out one ; and then on the trial I could correct the whole business if he had committed any error. In this way I got on pretty well, till by care and attention I improved my handwriting in such manner as to be able to prepare my warrants, and keep my record book, without much difficulty. My judgments were never appealed from, and if they had been they would have stuck like wax, as I gave my decisions on the principles of common justice and honesty between man and man, and relied on natural born sense, and not on law-learning to guide me; for I had never read a page in a law book in all my life.

CHAPTER X.

ABOUT the time we were getting under good headway in our new government, a Capt. Matthews came to me and told me he was a candidate for the office of colonel of a regiment, and that I must run for first major in the same regiment. I objected to this, telling him that I thought I had done my share of fighting, and that I wanted nothing to do with military appointments.

He still insisted, until at last I agreed, and of course had every reason to calculate on his support in my election. He was an early settler in that country, and made rather more corn than the rest of us; and knowing it would afford him a good opportunity to electioneer a little, he made a great corn husking, and a great frolic, and gave a general treat, asking every body over the whole country. Myself and my family were, of course, invited. When I got there, I found a very large collection of people, and some friend of mine soon informed me that the captain's son was going to offer against me for the office of major, which he had seemed so anxious for me to get. I cared nothing about the office, but it put my dander up high enough to see, that after he had pressed me so hard to offer, he was countenancing, if not encouraging a secret plan to beat me. I took the old gentleman out, and asked him about it. He told me it was true his son was going to run as a candidate, and that he hated worse to run against me than any man in the county. I told him his son need give himself no uneasiness about that; that I shouldn't run against him for major, but against his daddy for colonel. He took me by the hand, and we went into the company. He then made a speech, and informed the people that I was his opponent. I mounted up for a speech too. I told the people the cause of my opposition, remarking that as I had the whole family to run against any way, I was determined to levy on the head of the mess. When the time for the election came, his son was opposed by another man for major; and he and his daddy were both badly beaten. I just now began to take a rise, as in a little time I was asked to offer for the Legislature in the counties of Lawrence and Heckman.

I offered my name in the month of February, and started about the first of March with a drove of horses to the lower part of the State of North Carolina. This was in the year 1821, and I was gone upwards of three months. I returned, and set out electioneering, which was a bran-fire new business to me. It now became necessary that I should tell the people something about the government, and an eternal sight of other things that I knowed nothing more about than I did about Latin and law, and such things as that. I have said before that in those days none of us called Gen'l Jackson the government, nor did he seem in as fair a way to become so as I do now; but I knowed so little about it, that if any one had told me he was "the government," I should have believed it, for I had never read even a newspaper in my life, or any thing else, on the subject. But over all my difficulties, it seems to me I was born for luck, though it would be hard for any one to guess what sort. I will, however, explain that hereafter.

I went first into Heckman county, to see what I could do among the people as a candidate. Here they told me that they wanted to move their town nearer to the centre of the county, and I must come out in favour of it. There's no devil if I knowed what this meant, or how the town was to be moved; and so I kept dark, going on the identical same plan that I now find is called "*non-committal.*" About this time there was a great squirrel hunt on Duck river, which was among my people. They were to hunt two days, then to meet and count the scalps, and have a big barbecue, and what might be called a tip-top country frolic. The dinner, and a general treat, was all to be paid for by the party having taken the fewest scalps. I joined one side, taking the place of one of the hunters, and got a gun ready for the hunt. I killed a great many squirrels, and when we counted scalps, my party was victorious.

The company had every thing to eat and drink that could be furnished in so new a country, and much fun and good humour prevailed. But before the regular frolic commenced, I mean the dancing, I was called on to make a speech as a candidate; which was a business I was as ignorant of as an outlandish negro.

A public document I had never seen, nor did I know there were such things; and how to begin I couldn't tell. I made many apologies, and tried to get off, for I know'd I had a man to run against who could speak prime, and I know'd, too, that I wa'n't able to shuffle and cut with him. He was there, and knowing my ignorance as well as I did myself, he also urged me to make a speech. The truth is, he thought my being a candidate was a mere matter of sport; and didn't think for a moment that he was in any danger from an ignorant backwoods bear hunter. But I found I couldn't get off, and so I determined just to go ahead, and leave it to chance what I should say. I got up and told the people, I reckoned they know'd what I had come for, but if not, I could tell them. I had come for their votes, and if they didn't watch mighty close, I'd get them too. But the worst of all was, that I could not tell them any thing about government. I tried to speak about something, and I cared very little what, until I choaked up as bad as if my mouth had been jamm'd and cram'd chock full of dry mush.—There the people stood, listening all the while, with their eyes, mouths, and ears all open, to catch every word I would speak.

At last I told them I was like a fellow I had heard of not long before. He was beating on the head of an empty barrel near the road-side, when a traveller, who was passing along, asked him what he was doing that for? The fellow replied that there was some cider in that barrel a few days before, and he was trying to see if there was any then, but if there was he couldn't get at it. I told them that there had been a little bit of a speech in me a while ago, but I believed I couldn't get it out. They all roared out in a mighty laugh, and I told some other anecdotes, equally amusing to them, and believing I had them in a first-rate way, I quit and got down, thanking the people for their attention. But I took care to remark that I was as dry as a powder horn, and that I thought it was time for us all to wet our whistles a little; and so I put off to the liquor stand, and was followed by the greater part of the crowd.

I felt certain this was necessary, for I knowed my competitor could talk government matters to them as easy as he pleased. He had, however, mighty few left to hear him, as I continued with the crowd, now and then taking a horn, and telling good-humoured stories, till he was done speaking. I found I was good for the votes at the hunt, and when we broke up, I went on to the town of Vernon, which was the same they wanted me to move. Here they pressed me again on the subject, and I found I could get either party by agreeing with them. But I told them I didn't know whether it would be right or not, and so couldn't promise either way.

Their court commenced on the next Monday, as the barbacue was on a Saturday, and the candidates for governor and for Congress, as well as my competitor and myself, all attended.

The thought of having to make a speech made my knees feel mighty weak, and set my heart to fluttering almost as bad as my first love scrape with the Quaker's niece. But as good luck would have it, these big candidates spoke nearly all day, and when they quit, the people were worn out with fatigue, which afforded me a good apology, for not discussing the government. But I listened mighty close to them, and was learning pretty fast about political matters. When they were all done, I got up and told some laughable story, and quit. I found I was safe in those parts, and so I went home, and did not go back again until after the election was over. But to cut this matter short, I was elected, doubling my competitor, and nine votes over.

A short time after this, I was in Pulaski, when I met with Colonel Polk, now a member of Congress from Tennessee. He was at that time a member elected to the Legislature, as well as myself; and in a large company he said to me, "Well, colonel, I suppose we shall have a radical change of the judiciary at the next session of the Legislature." "Very likely, sir," says I, and I put out quicker, for I was afraid some one would ask me what the judiciary was; and if I knowed I wish I may be shot. I don't indeed believe I had ever before heard that there was any such thing in all nature; but still I was not willing that the people there should know how ignorant I was about it.

When the time for meeting of the Legislature arrived, I went on, and before I had been there long, I could have told what the judiciary was, and what the government was too; and many other things that I had known nothing about before.

About this time I met with a very severe misfortune, which I may be pardoned for naming, as it made a great change in my circumstances, and kept me back very much in the world. I had built an extensive grist mill, and powder mill, all connected together, and also a large distillery. They had cost me upwards of three thousand dollars, more than I was worth in the world. The first news that I heard after I got to the Legislature, was, that my mills were—not blown up sky high, as you would guess, by my powder establishment—but swept away all to smash by a large fresh, that came soon after I left home. I had, of course, to stop my distillery, as my grinding was broken up; and, indeed, I may say, that the misfortune just made a complete mash of me. I had some likely negroes, and a good stock of almost every thing about me, and, best of all, I had an honest wife. She didn't advise me, as is too fashionable, to smuggle up this, and that, and t'other, to go on at home; but she told me, says she, "Just pay up, as long as you have a bit's worth in the world; and then every body will be satisfied, and we will scuffle for more." This was just such talk as I wanted to hear, for a man's wife can hold him devilish uneasy, if she begins to scold and fret, and perplex him, at a time when he has a full load for a railroad car on his mind already.

And so, you see, I determined not to break full handed, but thought it better to keep a good conscience with an empty purse, than to get a bad opinion of myself, with a full one. I therefore gave up all I had, and took a bran-fire new start.

CHAPTER XI.

HAVING returned from the Legislature, I determined to make another move, and so I took my eldest son with me, and a young man by the name of Abram Henry, and cut out for the Obion. I selected a spot when I got there, where I determined to settle; and the nearest house to it was seven miles, the next nearest was fifteen, and so on to twenty. It was a complete wilderness, and full of Indians who were hunting. Game was plenty of almost every kind, which suited me exactly, as I was always fond of hunting. The house which was nearest me, and which, as I have already stated, was seven miles off, and on the different side of the Obion river, belonged to a man by the name of Owens; and I started to go there. I had taken one horse along, to pack our provision, and when I got to the water I hobbled him out to graze, until I got back; as there was no boat to cross the river in, and it was so high that it had overflowed all the bottoms and low country near it.

We now took water like so many beavers, notwithstanding it was mighty cold, and waded on. The water would sometimes be up to our necks, and at others not so deep; but I went, of course, before, and carried a pole, with which would feel along before me, to see how deep it was, and to guard against falling into a slough, as there was many in our way. When I would come to one, I would take out my tomahawk and cut a small tree across it, and then go ahead again. Frequently my little son would have to swim, even where myself and the young man could wade; but we worked on till at last we got to the channel of the river, which made it about half a mile we had waded from where we took water. I saw a large tree that had fallen into the river from the other side, but it did not reach across. One stood on the same bank where we were, that I thought I could fall, so as to reach the other; and so at it we went with my tomahawk, cutting away till we got it down; and, as good luck would have it, it fell right, and made us a way that we could pass.

When we got over this, it was still a sea of water as far as our eyes could reach. We took into it again, and went ahead, for about a mile, hardly ever seeing a single spot of land, and sometimes very deep. At last we come in sight of land, which was a very pleasing thing; and when we got out we went but a little way, before we came in sight of the house, which was more pleasing than ever; for we were wet all over, and mighty cold. I felt mighty sorry when I would look at my little boy, and see him shaking like he had the worst sort of an ague, for there was no time for fever then. As we got near to the house, we saw Mr. Owens and several men that were with him, just starting away. They saw us, and stop'd, but looked much astonished until we got up to them, and I made myself known. The men who were with him were the owners of the boat which was the first that ever went that far up the Obion river; and some hands he had hired to carry it about a hundred miles still further up, by water, tho'. it was only about thirty by land, as the river is very crooked.

They all turned back to the house with me, where I found Mrs. Owens, a fine, friendly old woman; and her kindness to my little boy did me ten times as much good as any thing she could have done for me, if she had tried her best. The old gentleman set out his bottle to us, and I concluded that if a horn wasn't good then, there was no use for its invention.—So I swig'd off about a half pint, and the young man was by no means bashful in such a case; he took a strong pull at it too. I then gave my boy some, and in a little time we felt pretty well. We dried ourselves by the fire, and were asked to go on board the boat that evening. I agreed to do so, but left my son with the old lady, and myself and the young man went to the boat with Mr. Owens and the others. The boat was loaded with whiskey, flour, sugar, coffee, salt, castings, and other articles suitable for the country; and they were to receive five hundred dollars to land the load at McLemore's Bluff, beside the profit they could make on their load. This was merely to show that boats could get up to that point.—We staid all night with them, and had a high night of it, as I took steam enough to drive out all the cold that was in me, and about three times as much more. In the morning we concluded to go on with the boat to where a great *harricane* had crossed the river, and blowed all the timber down into it. When we got there, we found the river was falling fast, and concluded we couldn't get thro' the timber without more rise: so we drop'd down opposite Mr. Owens' again where they determined to wait for more water.

The next day it rained rip-roriously, and the river rose pretty considerable, but not enough yet. And so I got the boatsmen all to go out with me to where I was going to settle, and we slap'd up a cabin in little or no time. I got from the boat four barrels of meal, and one of salt, and about ten gallons of whiskey.

To pay for these, I agreed to go with the boat up the river to their landing place. I got also a large middling of bacon, and killed a fine deer, and left them for my young man and my little boy, who were to stay at my cabin till I got back; which I expected would be in six or seven days. We cut out, and moved up to the harricane, where we stop'd for the night. In the morning I started about daylight intending to kill a deer, as I had no thought they would get the boat through the timber that day. I had gone but a little way before I killed a fine buck, and started to go back to the boat; but on the way I came on the tracts of a large gang of elks, and so I took after them. I had followed them only a little distance when I saw them, and directly after, I saw two large bucks. I shot one down, and the other wouldn't leave him; so I loaded my gun, and shot him down too. I hung them up, and went ahead again after my elks. I pursued on till after the middle of the day before I saw them again; but they took the hint before I got in shooting distance, and run off. I still pushed on till late in the evening, when I found I was about four miles from where I had left the boat, and as hungry as a wolf, for I hadn't eaten a bite that day.

I started down the edge of the river low grounds, giving out the pursuit of my elks, and hadn't gone hardly any distance at all, before I saw two more bucks, very large fellows too. I took a blizzard at one of them and up he tumbled. The other ran off a few jumps and stop'd; and stood there till I loaded again, and fired at him. I knock'd his trotters from under him, and then I hung them both up. I pushed on again; and about sunset I saw three other bucks. I down'd with one of them, and the other two ran off. I hung this one up also, having now killed six that day. I then pushed on till I got to the harricane, and at the lower edge of it, about where I expected the boat was. Here I hollered as hard as I could roar, but could get no answer. I fired off my gun, and the men on the boat fired one too; but quite contrary to my expectation, they had got through the timber, and were about two miles above me. It was now dark, and I had to crawl through the fallen timber the best way I could; and if the reader don't know it was bad enough, I am sure I do. For the vines and briers had grown all through it, and so thick, that a good fat coon couldn't much more than get along. I got through at last, and went on near to where I had killed my last deer, and once more fired off my gun, which was again answered from the boat, which was still a little above me. I moved on as fast as I could, but soon came to water, and not knowing how deep it was, I halted and hollered till they came to me with a skiff. I now got to the boat, without further difficulty; but the briers had worked on me at such a rate, that I felt like I wanted sewing up, all over. I took a pretty stiff horn, which soon made me feel much better; but I was so tired that I could hardly work my jaws to eat.

In the morning, myself and a young man started and brought in the first buck I had killed, and after breakfast we went and brought in the last one. The boat then started, but we again went and got the two I had killed just as I turned down the river in the evening; and we then pushed on and o'ertook the boat, leaving the other two hanging in the woods, as we had now as much as we wanted.

We got up the river very well, but quite slowly; and we landed on the eleventh day, at the place the load was delivered at. They here gave me their skiff, and myself and a young man by the name of Flavius Harris, who was determined to go and live with me, cut out down the river for my cabin, which we reached safely enough.

We turned in and cleared a field, and planted our corn; but it was so late in the spring, we had no time to make rails, and therefore we put no fence around our field. There was no stock, however, nor any thing else to disturb our corn, except the wild *varments*, and the old serpent himself, with a fence to help him, couldn't keep them out. I made corn enough to do me, and during that spring I killed ten bears, and a great abundance of deer. But in all this time, we saw the face of no white person in that country, except Mr. Owens' family, and a very few passengers, who went out there, looking at the country. Indians, though, were still plenty enough. Having laid by my crap, I went home, which was a distance of about a hundred and fifty miles; and when I got there, I was met by an order to attend a call-session of our Legislature. I attended at, and served out my time, and then returned, and took my family and what little plunder I had, and moved to where I had built my cabin, and made my crap.

I gathered my corn, and then set out for my Fall's hunt. This was in the last of October, 1822. I found bear very plenty, and, indeed, all sorts of game and wild varments, except buffalo. There was none of them. I hunted on till Christmas, having supplied my family very well all along with wild meat, at which time my powder gave out; and I had none either to fire Christmas guns, which is very common in that country, or to hunt with. I had a brother-in-law who had now moved out and settled about six miles west of me, on the opposite side of Rutherford's fork of the Obion river, and he had brought me a keg of powder, but I had never gotten it home. There had just been another of Noah's freshes, and the low grounds were flooded all over with water. I know'd the stream was at least a mile wide which I would have to cross, as the water was from hill to hill, and yet I determined to go on over in some way or other, so as to get my powder. I told this to my wife, and she immediately opposed it with all her might. I still insisted, telling her we had no powder for Christmas, and, worse than all, we were out of meat. She said, we had as well starve as for me to freeze to death, or to get drowned, and one or the other was certain if I attempted to go.

But I didn't believe the half of this; and so I took my woollen wrappers, and a pair of moccasins, and put them on, and tied up some dry clothes and a pair of shoes and stockings, and started. But I didn't before know how much any body could suffer and not die. This, and some of my other experiments in water, learned me something about it, and I therefore relate them.

The snow was about four inches deep when I started; and when I got to the water, which was only about a quarter of a mile off, it look'd like an ocean. I put in, and waded on till I come to the channel, where I crossed that on a high log. I then took water again, having my gun and all my hunting tools along, and waded till I came to a deep slough, that was wider than the river itself. I had crossed it often on a log; but, behold, when I got there, no log was to be seen. I knowed of an island in the slough, and a sapling stood on it close to the side of that log, which was now entirely under water. I knowed further, that the water was about eight or ten feet deep under the log, and I judged it to be about three feet deep over it. After studying a little what I should do, I determined to cut a forked sapling, which stood near me, so as to lodge it against the one that stood on the island, in which I succeeded very well. I then cut me a pole, and crawled along on my sapling till I got to the one it was lodged against, which was about six feet above the water. I then felt about with my pole till I found the log, which was just about as deep under the water as I had judged. I then crawled back and got my gun, which I had left at the stump of the sapling I had cut, and again made my way to the place of lodgement, and then climbed down the other sapling so as to get on the log. I then felt my way along with my feet, in the water, about waist deep, but it was a mighty ticklish business. However, I got over, and by this time I had very little feeling in my feet and legs, as I had been all the time in the water, except what time I was crossing the high log over the river, and climbing my lodged sapling.

I went but a short distance before I came to another slough, over which there was a log, but it was floating on the water. I thought I could walk it, and so I mounted on it; but when I had got about the middle of the deep water, somehow or somehow else, it turned over, and in I went up to my head. I waded out of this deep water, and went ahead till I came to the high-land, where I stop'd to pull off my wet clothes, and put on the others, which I had held up with my gun, above the water, when I fell in. I got them on, but my flesh had no feeling in it, I was so cold. I tied up the wet ones, and hung them up in a bush. I now thought I would run, so as to warm myself a little, but I couldn't raise a trot for some time; indeed, I couldn't step more than half the length of my foot. After a while I got better, and went on five miles to the house of my brother-in-law, having not even smelt fire from the time I started. I got there late in the evening, and he was much astonished at seeing me at such a time. I staid all night, and the next morning was most piercing cold, and so they persuaded me not to go home that day. I agreed, and turned out and killed him two deer; but the weather still got worse and colder, instead of better. I staid that night, and in the morning they still insisted I couldn't get home. I knowed the water would be frozen over, but not hard enough to bear me, so I agreed to stay that day. I went out hunting again, and pursued a big *he-bear* all day, but didn't kill him. The next morning was bitter cold, but I knowed my family was without meat, and I determined to get home to them, or die a-trying.

I took my keg of powder, and all my hunting tools, and cut out. When I got to the water, it was a sheet of ice as far as I could see. I put on to it, but hadn't got far before it broke through with me; and so I took out my tomahawk, and broke my way along before me for a considerable distance. At last I got to where the ice would bear me for a short distance, and I mounted on it, and went ahead; but it soon broke in again, and I had to wade on till I came to my floating log. I found it so tight this time, that I know'd it couldn't give me another fall, as it was frozen in with the ice. I crossed over it without much difficulty, and worked along till I got to my lodged sapling, and my log under the water. The swiftness of the current prevented the water from freezing over it, and so I had to wade, just as I di when I crossed it before. When I got to my sapling, I left my gun, and climbed out with my powder keg first, and then went back and got my gun. By this time I was nearly frozen to death, but I saw all along before me, where the ice had been fresh broke, and I thought it must be a bear straggling about in the water. I, therefore, fresh primed my gun, and, cold as I was, I was determined to make war on him, if we met. But I followed the trail till it led me home, and I then found it had been made by my young man that lived with me, who had been sent by my distressed wife to see, if he could, what had become of me, for they all believed that I was dead. When I got home I wasn't quite dead, but mighty nigh it; but had my powder, and that was what I went for.

CHAPTER XII.

THAT night there fell a heavy rain, and it turned to a sleet. In the morning all hands turned out hunting. My young man, and a brother-in-law who had lately settled close by me, went down the river to hunt for turkeys; but I was for larger game. I told them, I had dreamed the night before of having a hard fight with a big black nigger, and I know'd it was a sign that I was to have a battle with a bear; for in a bear country, I never know'd such a dream to fail. So I started to go up above the harricane, determined to have a bear. I had two pretty good dogs, and an old hound, all of which I took along. I had gone about six miles up the river, and it was then about four miles across to the main Obion; so I determined to strike across to that, as I had found nothing yet to kill. I got on to the river, and turned down it; but the sleet was still getting worse and worse. The bushes were all bent down and locked together with ice, so that it was almost impossible to get along. In a little time my dogs started a large gang of old turkey gobblers, and I killed two of them of the biggest sort. I shouldered them up, and moved on, until I got through the harricane, when I was so tired that I laid my gobblers down to rest, as they were confounded heavy, and I was mighty tired. While I was resting, my old hound went to a log, and smelt it awhile, and then raised his eyes toward the sky, and cried out. Away he went, and my other dogs with him, and I shouldered up my turkeys again, and followed on as hard as I could drive. They were soon out of sight, and in a very little time I heard them begin to bark. When I got to them they were barking up a tree, but there was no game there. I concluded it had been a turkey, and that it had flew away.

When they saw me coming, away they went again; and, after a little time, began to bark as before. When I got near them, I found they were barking up the wrong tree again, as there was no game there. They served me in this way three or four times, until I was so infernal mad, that I determined, if I could get near enough, to shoot the old hound at least. With this intention I pushed on the harder, till I came to the edge of an open parara, and looking on before my dogs, I saw in and about the biggest bear that ever was seen in America. He looked, at the distance he was from me, like a large black bull. My dogs were afraid to attack him, and that was the reason they had stop'd so often, that I might overtake them. They were now almost up with him, and I took my gobblers from my back and hung them up in a sapling, and broke like a quarter horse after my bear, for the sight of him had put new springs in me. I soon got near to them, but they were just getting into a roaring thicket, and so I couldn't run through it, but had to pick my way along, and had close work, even at that.

In a little time I saw the bear climbing up a large black oak tree, and I crawled on until I got within about eighty yards of him. He was setting with his breast to me ; and so I put fresh priming in my gun, and fired at him. At this he raised one of his paws and snorted loudly. I loaded again as quick as I could, and fired as near the same place in his breast, as possible. At the crack of my gun here he came tumbling down; and the moment he touched the ground, I heard one of my best dogs cry out. I took my tomahawk in one hand, and my big butcher-knife in the other, and run up within four or five paces of him, at which he let my dog go, and fixed his eyes on me. I got back in all sorts of hurry, for I know'd if he got hold of me, he would hug me altogether too close for comfort. I went to my gun and hastily loaded her again, and shot him the third time, which killed him good.

I now began to think about getting him home, but I didn't know how far it was. So I left him and started; and in order to find him again, I would blaze a sapling every little distance, which would show me the way back. I continued this until I got within about a mile of home, for there I know'd very well where I was, and that I could easily find my way back to my blazes. When I got home, I took my brother-in-law, and my young man, and four horses, and went back. We got there just before dark, and struck up a fire, and commenced butchering my bear. It was some time in the night before we finished it; and I can assert, on my honour, that I believe he would have weighed six hundred pounds. It was the second largest I ever saw. I killed one, a few years after, that weighed six hundred and seventeen pounds. I now felt fully compensated for my sufferings in going after my powder; and well satisfied that a dog might sometimes be doing a good business, even when he seemed to be *barking up the wrong tree.* We got our meat home, and I had the pleasure to know that we now had plenty, and that of the best; and I continued through the winter to supply my family abundantly with bear-meat and venison from the woods.

CHAPTER XIII.

I HAD on hand a great many skins, and so, in the month of February, I packed a horse with them, and taking my eldest son along with me, cut out for a little town called Jackson, situated about forty miles off. We got there well enough, and I sold my skins, and bought me some coffee, and sugar, powder, lead and salt. I packed them all up in readiness for a start, which I intended to make early the next morning. Morning came, but I concluded, before I started, I would go and take a horn with some of my old fellow-soldiers that I had met with at Jackson.

I did so; and while we were engaged in this, I met with three candidates for the Legislature. A Doctor Butler, who was, by marriage, a nephew to General Jackson, a Major Lynn, and a Mr. McEver, all first-rate men. We all took a horn together, and some persons present said to me, "Crockett, you must offer for the Legislature." I told him I lived at least forty miles from any white settlement; and had no thought of becoming a candidate at that time. So we all parted, and I and my little boy went on home.

It was about a week or two after this, that a man came to my house, and told me I was a candidate. I told him not so. But he took out a newspaper from his pocket, and show'd me where I was announced. I said to my wife that this was all a burlesque on me, but I was determined to make it cost the man who had put it there at least the value of the printing, and of the fun he wanted at my expense. So I hired a young man to work in my place on my farm, and turned out myself electioneering. I hadn't been out long, before I found the people began to talk very much about the bear-hunter, the man from the cane; and the three gentlemen, who I have already named, soon found it necessary to enter into an agreement to have a sort of caucus at their March court, to determine which of them was the strongest, and the other two was to withdraw and support him. As the court came on, each one of them spread himself, to secure the nomination; but it fell on Dr. Butler, and the rest backed out. The doctor was a clever fellow, and I have often said he was the most talented man I ever run against for any office. His being related to Gen'l Jackson also helped him on very much; but I was in for it, and I was determined to push ahead and go through, or stick. Their meeting was held in Madison county, which was the strongest in the representative district, which was composed of eleven counties, and they seemed bent on having the member from there.

At this time Col. Alexander was a candidate for Congress, and attending one of his public meetings one day, I walked to where he was treating the people, and he gave me an introduction to several of his acquaintances, and informed them that I was out electioneering. In a little time my competitor, Doctor Butler, came along; he passed by without noticing me, and I supposed, indeed, he did not recognise me. But I hailed him, as I was for all sorts of fun; and when he turned to me, I said to him, "Well, doctor, I suppose they have weighed you out to me; but I should like to know why they fixed your election for *March* instead of *August?* This is," said I, "a bran-fire new way of doing business, if a caucus is to make a representative for the people!" He now discovered who I was, and cried out, "D—n it, Crockett, is that you?" "Be sure it is," said I, "but I don't want it understood that I have come electioneering. I have just crept out of the cane, to see what discoveries I could make among the white folks." I told him that when I set out electioneering, I would go prepared to put every man on as good footing when I left him as when I found him on. I would therefore have me a large buckskin hunting-shirt made, with a couple of pockets holding about a peck each; and that in one I would carry a great big twist of tobacco, and in the other my bottle of liquor; for I knowed when I met a man and offered him a dram, he would throw out his quid of tobacco to take one, and after he had taken a horn, I would out with my twist and give him another chaw. And in this way he would not be worse off than when I found him; and I would be sure to leave him in a first-rate good humour. He said I could beat him electioneering all hollow. I told him I would give him better evidence of that before August, notwithstanding he had many advantages over me, and particularly in the way of money; but I told him that I would go on the products of the country; that I had industrious children, and the best of coon-dogs, and they would hunt every night till midnight to support my election; and when the coon fur wa'n't good, I would myself go a wolfing, and shoot down a wolf, and skin his head, and his scalp would be good to me for three dollars, in our State Treasury money; and in this way I would get along on the big string. He stood like he was both amused and astonished, and the whole crowd was in a roar of laughter. From this place I returned home, leaving the people in a first-rate way; and I was sure I would do a good business among them. At any rate, I was determined to stand up to my lick-log, salt or no salt.

In a short time there came out two other candidates, a Mr. Shaw and a Mr. Brown. We all ran the race through; and when the election was over, it turned out that I beat them all by a majority of two hundred and forty-seven votes, and was again returned as a member of the Legislature from a new region of the country, without losing a session. This reminded me of the old saw—"A fool for luck, and a poor man for children."

I now served two years in that body from my new district, which was the years 1823 and '24. At the session of 1823, I had a small trial of my independence, and whether I would forsake principle for party, or for the purpose of following after big men.

The term of Col. John Williams had expired, who was a senator in Congress from the State of Tennessee. He was a candidate for another election, and was opposed by Pleasant M. Miller, Esq., who it was believed, would not be able to beat the Colonel. Some two or three others were spoken of, but it was at last concluded that the only man who could beat him was General Jackson. So, a few days before the election was to come on, he was sent for to come and run for the Senate. He was then in nomination for the presidency; but sure enough he came, and did run as the opponent of Colonel Williams, and beat him too, but not by my vote. The vote was, for Jackson, *thirty-five;* for Williams, *twenty-five.* I thought the Colonel had honestly discharged his duty, and even the mighty name of Jackson couldn't make me vote against him.

But voting against the old chief was found a mighty up-hill business to all of them except myself. I never would, nor never did, acknowledge I had voted wrong; and I am more certain now that I was right than ever.

I told the people it was the best vote I ever gave; that I supported the public interest, and cleared my conscience in giving it, instead of gratifying the private ambition of a man.

I let the people know as early as then, that I wouldn't take a collar around my neck.

During these two sessions of the Legislature, nothing else turned up which I think it worth while to mention; and, indeed, I am fearful that I am too particular about many small matters; but if so, my apology is, that I want the world to understand my true history, and how I worked along to rise from the cane-brake to my present station in life.

Col. Alexander was the representative in Congress of the district I lived in, and his vote on the tariff law of 1824 gave a mighty heap of dissatisfaction to his people. They therefore began to talk pretty strong of running me for Congress against him. At last I was called on by a good many to be a candidate. I told the people that I couldn't stand that; it was a step above my knowledge, and I know'd nothing about Congress matters.

However, I was obliged to agree to run, and myself and two other gentlemen came out. But Providence was a little against two of us this hunt, for it was the year that cotton brought twenty-five dollars a hundred; and so Colonel Alexander would get up and tell the people, it was all the good effect of this tariff law; that it had raised the price of their cotton, and that it would raise the price of every thing else they made to sell. I might as well have sung *salms* over a dead horse, as to try to make people believe otherwise; for they know'd their cotton had raised, sure enough, and if the colonel hadn't done it, they didn't know what had. So he rather made a mash of me this time, as he beat me exactly *two* votes, as they counted the polls, though I have always believed that many other things had been as fairly done as that same count.

He went on, and served out his term, and at the end of it cotton was down to *six* or *eight* dollars a hundred again; and I concluded I would try him once more, and see how it would go with cotton at the common price, and so I became a candidate.

CHAPTER XIV.

BUT the reader, I expect, would have no objection to know a little about my employment during the two years while my competitor was in Congress. In this space I had some pretty tuff times, and will relate some few things that happened to me. So here goes, as the boy said when he run by himself.

In the fall of 1825, I concluded I would build two large boats, and load them with pipe staves for market. So I went down to the lake, which was about twenty-five miles from where I lived, and hired some hands to assist me, and went to work; some at boat building, and others to getting staves. I worked on with my hands till the bears got fat, and then I turned out to hunting, to lay in a supply of meat. I soon killed and salted down as many as was necessary for my family; but about this time one of my old neighbours, who had settled down on the lake about twenty-five miles from me, came to my house and told me he wanted me to go down and kill some bears about in his parts. He said they were extremely fat, and very plenty. I know'd that when they were fat they were easily taken; for a fat bear can't run fast or long. But I asked a bear no favors, no way, further than civility, for I now had *eight* large dogs, and as fierce as painters; so that a bear stood no chance at all to get away from them. So I went home with him, and then went on down towards the Mississippi, and commenced hunting.

We were out two weeks, and in that time killed fifteen bears. Having now supplied my friend with plenty of meat, I engaged occasionally again with my hands in our boat building, and getting staves. But I at length couldn't stand it any longer without another hunt. So I concluded to take my little son, and cross over the lake, and take a hunt there. We got over, and that evening turned out and killed three bears, in little or no time. The next morning we drove up four forks, and made a sort of scaffold, on which we salted up our meat, so as to have it out of the reach of the wolves, for as soon as we would leave our camp, they would take possession. We had just eat our breakfast, when a company of hunters came to our camp, who had fourteen dogs, but all so poor, that when they would bark they would almost have to lean up against a tree and take a rest. I told them their dogs couldn't run in smell of a bear, and they had better stay at my camp, and feed them on the bones I had cut out of my meat. I left them there, and cut out; but I hadn't gone far, when my dogs took a first-rate start after a very large fat old *he-bear*, which run right plump towards my camp. I pursued on, but my other hunters had heard my dogs coming, and met them, and killed the bear before I got up with him. I gave him to them, and cut out again for a creek called Big Clover, which wa'n't very far off. Just as I got there and was entering a cane brake, my dogs all broke and went ahead, and in a little time, they raised a fuss in the cane, and seemed to be going every way. I listened a while, and found my dogs was in two companies, and that both was in a snorting fight. I sent my little son to one, and I broke for t'other. I got to mine first, and found my dogs had a two-year-old bear down, a-wooling away on him; so I just took out my big butcher, and went up and slap'd it into him, and killed him without shooting. There was five of the dogs in my company. In a short time, I heard my little son fire at his bear; when I went to him he had killed it too. He had two dogs in his team. Just at this moment we heard my other dog barking a short distance off, and all the rest immediately broke to him. We pushed on too, and when we got there, we found he had still a larger bear than either of them we had killed, treed by himself. We killed that one also, which made three we had killed in less than half an hour. We turned in and butchered them, and then started to hunt for water, and a good place to camp. But we had no sooner started, than our dogs took a start after another one, and away they went like a thunder-gust, and was out of hearing in a minute. We followed the way they had gone for some time, but at length we gave up the hope of finding them, and turned back. As we were going back I came to where a poor fellow was grubbing, he looked like the very picture of hard times. I asked him what he was doing away there in the woods by himself? He said he was grubbing for a man who intended to settle there; and the reason why he did it was, that he had no meat for his family, and he was working for a little.

I was mighty sorry for the poor fellow, for it was not only a hard, but a very slow way to get meat for a hungry family; so I told him if he would go with me, I would give him more meat than he could get by grubbing in a month. I intended to supply him with meat, and also to get him to assist my little boy, in packing and salting up my bears. He had never seen a bear killed in his life. I told him I had six killed then, and my dogs were hard after another. He went off to his little cabin, which was a short distance in the brush, and his wife was very anxious he should go with me. So we started and went to where I had left my three bears, and made a camp. We then gathered my meat and salted, and scaffled it, as I had done the other. Night now came on, but no word from my dogs yet. I afterwards found they had treed the bear about five miles off, near to a man's house, and had barked at it the whole enduring night. Poor fellows! many a time they looked for me, and wondered why I didn't come, for they knowed there was no mistake in me, and I know'd they were as good as ever fluttered. In the morning, as soon as it was light enough to see, the man took his gun and went to them, and shot the bear, and killed it. My dogs, however, wouldn't have any thing to say to this stranger; so they left him, and came early in the morning back to me.

We got our breakfast, and cut out again; and we killed four large and very fat bears that day. We hunted out the week, and in that time we killed seventeen, all of them first-rate. When we closed our hunt, I gave the man over a thousand weight of fine fat bear-meat, which pleased him mightily, and made him feel as rich as a Jew. I saw him the next fall, and he told me he had plenty of meat to do him the whole year from this week's hunt. My son and me now went home. This was the week between Christmas and New Year that we made this hunt.

When I got home, one of my neighbours was out of meat, and wanted me to go back, and let him go with me, to take another hunt. I couldn't refuse; but I told him I was afraid the bear had taken to house by that time, for after they get very fat in the fall and early part of the winter, they go into their holes, in large hollow trees, or into hollow logs, or their cane houses, or the harricanes; and lie there till spring, like frozen snakes. And one thing about this will seem mighty strange to many people. From about the first of January to about the last of April, these varments lie in their holes altogether. In all that time they have no food to eat; and yet when they come out, they are not an ounce lighter than when they went to house. I don't know the cause of this, and still I know it is a fact; and I leave it for others who have more learning than myself to account for it. They have not a particle of food with them, but they just lie and suck the bottom of their paw all the time. I have killed many of them in their trees, which enables me to speak positively on this subject. However, my neighbour, whose name was McDaniel, and my little son and me, went on down to the lake to my second camp, where I had killed my seventeen bears the week before, and turned out to hunting. But we hunted hard all day without getting a single start. We had carried but little provisions with us, and the next morning was entirely out of meat. I sent my son about three miles off, to the house of an old friend, to get some. The old gentleman was much pleased to hear I was hunting in those parts, for the year before the bears had killed a great many of his hogs. He was that day killing his bacon hogs, and so he gave my son some meat, and sent word to me that I must come in to his house that evening, that he would have plenty of feed for my dogs, and some accommodation for ourselves; but before my son got back, we had gone out hunting, and in a large cane brake my dogs found a big bear in a cane-house, which he had fixed for his winter-quarters, as they sometimes do.

When my lead dog found him, and raised the yell, all the rest broke to him, but none of them entered his house until we got up. I encouraged my dogs, and they knowed me so well, that I could have made them seize the old serpent himself, with all his horns and heads, and cloven foot and ugliness into the bargain, if he would only have come to light, so that they could have seen him. They bulged in, and in an instant the bear followed them out, and I told my friend to shoot him, as he was mighty wrathy to kill a bear. He did so, and killed him prime. We carried him to our camp, by which time my son had returned; and after we got our dinners we packed up, and cut for the house of my old friend, whose name was Davidson.

We got there, and staid with him that night; and the next morning, having salted up our meat, we left it with him, and started to take a hunt between the Obion lake and the Red foot lake; as there had been a dreadful harricane, which passed between them, and I was sure there must be a heap of bears in the fallen timber. We had gone about five miles without seeing any sign at all; but at length we got on some high cany ridges, and, as we rode along, I saw a hole in a large black oak, and on examining more closely, I discovered that a bear had clomb the tree. I could see his tracks going up, but none coming down, and so I was sure he was in there. A person who is acquainted with bear-hunting, can tell easy enough when the varment is in the hollow; for as they go up they don't slip a bit, but as they come down they make long scratches with their nails.

My friend was a little ahead of me, but I called him back, and told him there was a bear in that tree, and I must have him out. So we lit from our horses, and I found a small tree which I thought I could fall so as to lodge against my bear tree, and we fell to work chopping it with our tomahawks. I intended, when we lodged the tree against the other, to let my little son go up, and look into the hole, for he could climb like a squirrel. We had chop'd on a little time and stop'd to rest, when I heard my dogs, barking mighty severe at some distance from us, and I told my friend I knowed they had a bear; for it is the nature of a dog, when he finds you are hunting bears, to hunt for nothing else; he becomes fond of the meat, and considers other game as "not worth a notice," as old Johnson said of the devil.

We concluded to leave our tree a bit, and went to my dogs, and when we got there, sure enough they had an eternal great big fat bear up a tree, just ready for shooting My friend again petitioned me for liberty to shoot this one also. I had a little rather not, as the bear was so big, but I couldn't refuse; and so he blazed away, and down came the old fellow like some great log had fell. I now missed one of my dogs, the same that I before spoke of as having treed the bear by himself sometime before, when I had started the three in the cane break. I told my friend that my missing dog had a bear somewhere, just as sure as fate; so I left them to butcher the one we had just killed, and I went up on a piece of high ground to listen for my dog. I heard him barking with all his might some distance off, and I pushed ahead for him. My other dogs hearing him broke to him, and when I got there, sure enough again he had another bear ready treed; if he hadn't, I wish I may be shot. I fired on him, and brought him down; and then went back, and help'd finish butchering the one at which I had left my friend. We then packed both to our tree where we had left my boy. By this time, the little fellow had cut the tree down that we intended to lodge, but it fell the wrong way; he had then feather'd in on the big tree, to cut that, and had found that it was nothing but a shell on the outside, and all doted in the middle, as too many of our big men are in these days, having only an outside appearance. My friend and my son cut away on it, and I went off about a hundred yards with my dogs to keep them from running under the tree when it should fall. On looking back at the hole, I saw the bear's head out of it, looking down at them as they were cutting. I hollered to them to look up, and they did so; and McDaniel catched up his gun, but by this time the bear was out, and coming down the tree. He fired at it, and as soon as it touch'd the ground the dogs were all round it, and they had a roll-and-tumble fight to the foot of the hill, where they stop'd him. I ran up, and putting my gun against the bear, fired and killed him. We now had three, and so we made our scaffold and salted them up.

CHAPTER XV.

IN the morning I left my son at the camp, and we started on towards the harricane; and when we had went about a mile, we started a very large bear, but we got along mighty slow on account of the cracks in the earth occasioned by the earthquakes. We, however, made out to keep in hearing of the dogs for about three miles, and then we come to the harricane. Here we had to quit our horses, as old Nick himself couldn't have got through it without sneaking it along in the form that he put on to make a fool of our old grandmother Eve. By this time several of my dogs had got tired and come back; but we went ahead on foot for some little time in the harricane, when we met a bear coming straight to us, and not more than twenty or thirty yards off. I started my tired dogs after him, and McDaniel pursued them, and I went on to where my other dogs were. I had seen the track of the bear they were after, and I knowed he was a screamer. I followed on to about the middle of the harricane, but my dogs pursued him so close, that they made him climb an old stump about twenty feet high. I got in shooting distance of him and fired, but I was all over in such a flutter from fatigue and running, that I couldn't hold steady; but, however, I broke his shoulder, and he fell. I run up and loaded my gun as quick as possible, and shot him again and killed him. When I went to take out my knife to butcher him, I found I had lost it in coming through the harricane. The vines and briers was so thick that I would sometimes have to get down and crawl like a varment to get through at all; and a vine had, as I supposed, caught in the handle and pulled it out. While I was standing and studying what to do, my friend came to me. He had followed my trail through the harricane, and had found my knife, which was mighty good news to me; as a hunter hates the worst in the world to lose a good dog, or any part of his hunting-tools. I now left McDaniel to butcher the bear, and I went after our horses, and brought them as near as the nature of the case would allow. I then took our bags, and went back to where he was; and when we had skin'd the bear, we fleeced off the fat and carried it to our horses at several loads. We then packed it up on our horses, and had a heavy pack of it on each one. We now started and went on till about sunset, when I concluded we must be near our camp; so I hollered and my son answered me, and we moved on in the direction to the camp. We had gone but a little way when I heard my dogs make a warm start again; and I jumped down from my horse and gave him up to my friend, and told him I would follow them. He went on to the camp, and I went ahead after my dogs with all my might for a considerable distauce, till at last night came on. The woods were very rough and hilly, and all covered over with cane.

I now was compelled to move on more slowly ; and was frequently falling over logs, and into the cracks made by the earthquakes, so that I was very much afraid I would break my gun. However I went on about three miles, when I came to a good big creek, which I waded. It was very cold, and the creek was about knee-deep ; but I felt no great inconvenience from it just then, as I was all over wet with sweat from running, and I felt hot enough. After I got over this creek and out of the cane, which was very thick on all our creeks, I listened for my dogs. I found they had either treed or brought the bear to a stop, as they continued barking in the same place. I pushed on as near in the direction of the noise as I could, till I found the hill was too steep for me to climb, and so I backed and went down the creek some distance till I came to a hollow, and then took up that, till I came to a place where I could climb up the hill. It was mighty dark and was difficult to see my way or any thing else. When I got up the hill, I found I had passed the dogs ; and so I turned and went to them. I found, when I got there, they had treed the bear in a large forked poplar, and it was setting in the fork.

I could see the lump, but not plain enough to shoot with any certainty, as there was no moonlight ; and so I set in to hunting for some dry brush to make me a light ; but I could find none, though I could find that the ground was torn mightily to pieces by the cracks.

At last I thought I could shoot by guess, and kill him ; so I pointed as near the lump as I could, and fired away. But the bear didn't come, he only clomb up higher, and got out on a limb, which helped me to see him better. I now loaded up again, and fired, but this time he didn't move at all. I commenced loading for a third fire, but the first thing I know'd, the bear was down among my dogs, and they were fighting all around me. I had my big butcher in my belt, and I had a pair of dressed buckskin breeches on. So I took out my knife, and stood, determined, if he should get hold of me, to defend myself in the best way I could. I stood there for some time, and could now and then see a white dog I had, but the rest of them, and the bear, which were dark coloured, I couldn't see at all, it was so miserable dark. They still fought around me, and sometimes within three feet of me ; but, at last, the bear got down into one of the cracks, that the earthquakes had made in the ground, about four feet deep, and I could tell the biting end of him by the hollering of my dogs. So I took my gun and pushed the muzzle of it about, till I thought I had it against the main part of his body and fired ; but it happened to be only the fleshy part of his foreleg. With this he jumped out of the crack, and he and the dogs had another hard fight around me, as before. At last, however, they forced him back into the crack again, as he was when I had shot.

I had laid down my gun in the dark, and I now began to hunt for it; and, while hunting, I got hold of a pole, and I concluded I would punch him awhile with that. I did so, and when I would punch him, the dogs would jump in on him, when he would bite them badly, and they would jump out again. I concluded, as he would take punching so patiently, it might be that he would lie still enough for me to get down in the crack, and feel slowly along till I could find the right place to give him a dig with my butcher, So I got down, and my dogs got in before him and kept his head towards them, till I got along easily up to him; and placing my hand on his rump, felt for his shoulder, just behind which I intended to stick him. I made a lunge with my long knife, and fortunately stuck him right through the heart; at which he just sank down, and I crawled out in a hurry. In a little time my dogs all come out too, and seemed satisfied, which was the way they always had of telling me that they had finished him.

I suffered very much that night with cold, as my leather breeches, and every thing else I had on, was wet and frozen. But I managed to get my bear out of this crack after several hard trials, and so I butchered him and laid down to try to sleep.—But my fire was very bad, and I couldn't find any thing that would burn well to make it any better; and so I concluded I should freeze, if I didn't warm myself in some way by exercise. So I got up, and hollered a while, and then I would just jump up and down with all my might, and throw myself into all sorts of motions. But all this wouldn't do; for my blood was now getting cold, and the chills coming all over me. I was so tired, too, that I could hardly walk; but I thought I would do the best I could to save my life, and then, if I died, nobody would be to blame. So I went to a tree about two feet through, and not a limb on it for thirty feet, and I would climb up to the limbs, and then lock my arms together around it, and slide down to the bottom again. This would make the insides of my legs and arms feel mighty warm and good. I continued this till daylight in the morning, and how often I clomb up my tree and slid down I don't know, but I reckon at least a hundred times.

In the morning I got my bear hung up so as to be safe, and then set out to hunt for my camp. I found it after a while, and McDaniel and my son were very much rejoiced to see me get back, for they were about to give me up for lost. We got our breakfasts, and then secured our meat by building a high scaffold, and covering it over. We had no fear of its spoiling, for the weather was so cold that it couldn't.

We now started after my other bear, which had caused me so much trouble and suffering; and before we got him, we got a start after another, and took him also. We went on to the creek I had crossed the night before and camped, and then went to where my bear was that I had killed in the crack. When we examined the place, McDaniel said he wouldn't have gone into it, as I did, for all the bears in the woods.

We took the meat down to our camp and salted it, and also the last one we had killed; intending in the morning, to make a hunt in the harricane again.

We prepared for resting that night, and I can assure the reader I was in need of it. We had laid down by our fire, and about ten o'clock there came a most terrible earthquake, which shook the earth so, that we were rocked about like we had been in a cradle. We were very much alarmed; for though we were accustomed to feel earthquakes, we were now right in the region which had been torn to pieces by them in 1812, and we thought it might take a notion and swallow us up, like the big fish did Jonah.

In the morning we packed up and moved to the harricane, where we made another camp, and turned out that evening and killed a very large bear, which made *eight* we had now killed in this hunt.

The next morning we entered the harricane again, and in a little or no time my dogs were in full cry. We pursued them, and soon came to a thick cane-brake, in which they had stop'd their bear. We got up close to him, as the cane was so thick that we couldn't see more than a few feet. Here I made my friend hold the cane a little open with his gun till I shot the bear, which was a mighty large one. I killed him dead in his tracks. We got him out and butchered him, and in a little time started another and killed him, which now made *ten* we had killed; and we know'd we couldn't pack any more home, as we had only five horses along; therefore we returned to the camp and salted up all our meat, to be ready for a start homeward next morning.

The morning came, and we packed our horses with the meat, and had as much as they could possibly carry, and sure enough cut out for home. It was about thirty miles, and we reached home the second day. I had now accommodated my neighbour with meat enough to do him, and had killed in all, up to that time, fifty-eight bears, during the fall and winter.

As soon as the time come for them to quit their houses and come out again in the spring, I took a notion to hunt a little more, and in about one month I killed forty-seven more, which made one hundred and five bears which I had killed in less than one year from that time.

CHAPTER XVI.

HAVING now closed my hunting for that winter, I returned to my hands, who were engaged about my boats and staves, and made ready for a trip down the river. I had two boats and about thirty thousand staves, and so I loaded with them, and set out for New Orleans. I got out of the Obion river, in which I had loaded my boats, very well; but when I got into the Mississippi, I found all my hands were bad scared, and in fact I believe I was scared a little the worst of any; for I had never been down the river, and I soon discovered that my pilot was as ignorant of the business as myself. I hadn't gone far before I determined to lash the two boats together; we did so, but it made them so heavy and obstinate, that it was next akin to impossible to do any thing at all with them, or to guide them right in the river.

That evening we fell in company with some Ohio boats; and about night we tried to land, but we could not. The Ohio men hollered to us to go on and run all night. We took their advice, though we had a good deal rather not; but we couldn't do any other way. In a short distance we got into what is called the "*Devil's Elbow;*" and if any place in the wide creation has its own proper name, I thought it was this. Here we had about the hardest work that I ever was engaged in, in my life, to keep out of danger; and even then we were in it all the while. We twice attempted to land at Wood-yards, which we could see, but couldn't reach.

The people would run out with lights, and try to instruct us how to get to shore; but all in vain. Our boats were so heavy that we couldn't take them much any way, except the way they wanted to go, and just the way the current would carry them. At last we quit trying to land, and concluded just to go ahead as well as we could, as we found we couldn't do any better. Some time in the night I was down in the cabin of one of the boats, sitting by the fire, thinking on what a hobble we had got into; and how much better bear-hunting was on hard land, than floating along on the water, when a fellow had to go ahead whether he was exactly willing or not.

The hatchway into the cabin came slap down, right through the top of the boat; and it was the only way out except a small hole in the side, which we had used for putting our arms through to dip up water before we lashed the boats together.

We were now floating sideways, and the boat I was in was the hindmost as we went. All at once I heard the hands begin to run over the top of the boat in great confusion, and pull with all their might; and the first thing I know'd after this we went broadside full tilt against the head of an island where a large raft of drift timber had lodged. The nature of such a place would be, as every body knows, to suck the boats down, and turn them right under this raft; and the uppermost boat would, of course, be suck'd down and go under first. As soon as we struck, I bulged for my hatchway, as the boat was turning under sure enough. But when I got to it, the water was pouring thro' in a current as large as the hole would let it, and as strong as the weight of the river could force it. I found I couldn't get out here, for the boat was now turned down in such a way, that it was steeper than a house-top. I now thought of the hole in the side, and made my way in a hurry for that. With difficulty I got to it, and when I got there, I found it was too small for me to get out by my own power, and I began to think that I was in a worse box than ever. But I put my arms through and hollered as loud as I could roar, as the boat I was in hadn't yet quite filled with water up to my head, and the hands who were next to the raft, seeing my arms out, and hearing me holler, seized them, and began to pull. I told them I was sinking, and to pull my arms off, or force me through, for now I know'd well enough it was neck or nothing, come out or sink.

By a violent effort they jerked me through; but I was in a pretty pickle, when I got through. I had been sitting without any clothing over my shirt; this was torn off, and I was literally skin'd like a rabbit. I was, however, well pleased to get out in any way, even without shirt or hide; as before I could straighten myself on the boat next to the raft, the one they pulled me out of went entirely under, and I have never seen it any more to this day. We all escaped on to the raft, where we were compelled to sit all night, about a mile from land on either side. Four of my company were bareheaded, and three barefooted; and of that number I was one. I reckon I looked like a pretty cracklin ever to get to Congress! ! !

We had now lost all our loading; and every particle of our clothing, except what little we had on; but over all this, while I was setting there, in the night, floating about on the drift, I felt happier and better off than I had ever in my life before, for I had just made such a marvellous escape, that I had forgot almost every thing else in that; and so I felt prime.

In the morning about sunrise, we saw a boat coming down, and we hailed her. They sent a large skiff, and took us all on board, and carried us down as far as Memphis. Here I met with a friend, that I never can forget as long as I am able to go ahead at any thing; it was a Major Winchester, a merchant of that place: he let us all have hats, and shoes, and some little money to go upon, and so we all parted.

A young man and myself concluded to go on down to Natchez, to see if we could hear any thing of our boats; for we supposed they would float out from the raft, and keep on down the river. We got on a boat at Memphis, that was going down, and so cut out. Our largest boat, we were informed, had been seen about fifty miles below where we stove, and an attempt had been made to land her, but without success, as she was as hard-headed as ever.

This was the last of my boats, and of my boating; for it went so badly with me, along at the first, that I had not much mind to try it any more. I now returned home again, and as the next August was the Congressional election, I began to turn my attention a little to that matter, as it was beginning to be talked of a good deal among the people.

CHAPTER XVII.

I HAVE, heretofore, informed the reader that I had determined to run this race to see what effect *the price of cotton* could have again on it. I now had Colonel Alexander to run against once more, and also General William Arnold.

I had difficulties enough to fight against this time, as every one will suppose; for I had no money, and a very bad prospect, so far as I know'd, of getting any to help me along. I had, however, a good friend, who sent for me to come and see him. I went, and he was good enough to offer me some money to help me out. I borrowed as much as I thought I needed at the start, and went ahead. My friend also had a good deal of business about over the district at the different courts; and if he now and then slip'd in a good word for me, it is nobody's business. We frequently met at different places, and, as he thought I needed, he would occasionally hand me a little more cash; so I was able to buy a little of "the *creature*," to put my friends in a good humour, as well as the other gentlemen, for they all treat in that country; not to get elected, of course—for that would be against the law; but just, as I before said, to make themselves and their friends feel their keeping a little.

Nobody ever did know how I got money to get along on, till after the election was over, and I had beat my competitors twenty-seven hundred and forty-eight votes. Even the price of cotton couldn't save my friend Aleck this time. My rich friend, who had been so good to me in the way of money, now sent for me, and loaned me a hundred dollars, and told me to go ahead; that that amount would bear my expenses to Congress, and I must then shift for myself. I came on to Washington, and draw'd two hundred and fifty dollars, and purchased with it a cheque on the bank at Nashville, and enclosed it to my friend; and I may say, in truth, I sent this money with a mighty good will, for I reckon nobody in this world loves a friend better than me, or remembers a kindness longer.

I have now given the close of the election, but I have skip'd entirely over the canvass, of which I will say a very few things in this place; as I know very well how to tell the truth, but not much about placing them in book order, so as to please critics.

Col. Alexander was a very clever fellow, and principal surveyor at that time; so much for one of the men I had to run against. My other competitor was a major-general in the militia, and an attorney-general at the law, and quite a smart clever man also; and so it will be seen I had war work as well as law trick, to stand up under. Taking both together, they made a pretty considerable of a load for any one man to carry. But for war claims, I consider myself behind no man except "the government," and mighty little, if any, behind him; but this the people will have to determine hereafter, as I reckon it won't do to quit the work of "reform and retrenchment" yet for a spell.

But my two competitors seemed some little afraid of the influence of each other, but not to think me in their way at all. They, therefore, were generally working against each other, while I was going ahead for myself, and mixing among the people in the best way I could. I was as cunning as a little red fox, and wouldn't risk my tail in a "committal" trap.

I found the sign was good, almost every where I went. On one occasion, while we were in the eastern counties of the district, it happened that we all had to make a speech, and it fell on me to make the first one. I did so after my manner, and it turned pretty much on the old saying, "A short horse is soon curried," as I spoke not very long. Colonel Alexander followed me, and then General Arnold come on.

The general took much pains to reply to Alexander, but didn't so much as let on that there was any such candidate as myself at all. He had been speaking for a considerable time, when a large flock of guinea-fowls came very near to where he was, and sat up the most unmerciful chattering that ever was heard, for they are a noisy little brute any way. They so confused the general, that he made a stop, and requested that they might be driven away. I let him finish his speech, and then walking up to him, said aloud, "Well, Colonel, you are the first man I ever saw that understood the language of fowls." I told him that he had not had the politeness to name me in his speech, and that when my little friends, the guinea-fowls, had come up and began to holler "Crockett, Crockett, Crockett," he had been ungenerous enough to stop, and drive *them* all away. This raised a universal shout among the people for me, and the general seemed mighty bad plagued. But he got more plagued than this at the polls in August, as I have stated before.

This election was in 1827, and I can say, on my conscience, that I was, without disguise, the friend and supporter of General Jackson, upon his principles as he had laid them down, and as "*I understood them*," before his election as President.—During my two first sessions in Congress, Mr. Adams was president, and I worked along with what was called the Jackson party pretty well. I was re-elected to Congress in 1829, by an overwhelming majority; and soon after the commencement of this second term, I saw, or thought I did, that it was expected of me that I was to bow to the name of Andrew Jackson, and follow him in all his motions, and windings and turnings, even at the expense of my conscience and judgment. Such a thing was new to me, and a total stranger to my principles. I know'd well enough, though, that if I didn't "hurra" for his name, the hue and cry was to be raised against me, and I was to be sacrificed if possible. His famous, or rather I should say his in-*famous*, Indian bill was brought forward, and I opposed it from the purest motives in the world. Several of my colleagues got round me, and told me how well they loved me, and that I was ruining myself. They said this was a favourite measure of the president, and I ought to go for it. I told them I believed it was a wicked unjust measure, and that I should go against it, let the cost to myself be what it might; that I was willing to go with General Jackson in every thing that I believed was honest and right; but, further than this, I wouldn't go for him, or any other man in the whole creation; that I would sooner be honestly and politically d—nd, than hypocritically immortalized. I had been elected by a majority of three thousand five hundred and eighty-five votes, and I believed they were honest men and wouldn't want me to vote for any unjust notion, to please Jackson or any one else; at any rate, I was of age, and determined to trust them.—I voted against this Indian bill, and my conscience yet tells me that I gave a good honest vote, and one that I believe will not make me ashamed in the day of judgment. I served out my term, and though many amusing things happened, I am not disposed to swell my narrative by inserting them.

When it closed, and I returned home, I found the storm had raised against me sure enough; and it was echoed from side to side, and from end to end of my district, that I had turned against Jackson. This was considered the unpardonable sin. I was hunted down like a wild varment, and in this hunt every little newspaper in the district, and every little pin-hook lawyer was engaged. Indeed, they were ready to print any and everything that the ingenuity of man could invent against me. Each editor was furnished with the journals of Congress from head-quarters; and hunted out every vote I had missed in four sessions, whether from sickness or not, no matter: and each one was charged against me at *eight* dollars. In all I had missed about *seventy* votes, which they made amount to five hundred and sixty dollars; and they contended I had swindled the government out of this sum, as I received my pay, as other members do. I was now again a candidate in 1830, while all the attempts were making against me; and every one of these little papers kept up a constant war on me, fighting with every scurrilous report they could catch.

Over all I should have been elected, if it hadn't been, that but a few weeks before the election, the little four-pence-ha'penny limbs of the law fell on a plan to defeat me, which had the desired effect. They agreed to spread out over the district, and make appointments for me to speak, almost every where, to clear up the Jackson question. They would give me no notice of these appointments, and the people would meet in great crowds to hear what excuse Crockett had to make for quitting Jackson.

But instead of Crockett's being there, this small-fry of lawyers would be there with their saddle-bags full of the little newspapers and their journals of Congress; and would get up and speak, and read their scurrilous attacks on me, and would then tell the people that I was afraid to attend; and in this way would turn many against me. All this intrigue was kept a profound secret from me, till it was too late to counteract it; and when the election came, I had a majority in seventeen counties, putting all their votes together, but the eighteenth beat me; and so I was left out of Congress during those two years. The people of my district were induced, by these tricks, to take a stay on me for that time; but they have since found out that they were imposed on, and on re-considering my case, have reversed that decision; which, as the Dutchman said, "is as fair a ding as eber was."

When I last declared myself a candidate, I knew that the district would be divided by the Legislature before the election would come on; and I moreover knew, that from the geographical situation of the country, the county of Madison, which was very strong, and which was the county that had given the majority that had beat me in the former race, should be left off from my district.

But when the Legislature met, as I have been informed, and I have no doubt of the fact, Mr. Fitzgerald, my competitor, went up, and informed his friends in that body, that if Madison county was left off, he wouldn't run; for "that Crockett could beat Jackson himself in those parts, in any way they could fix it."

The liberal Legislature you know, of course, gave him that county; and it is too clear to admit of dispute, that it was done to make a mash of me. In order to make my district in this way, they had to form the southern district of a string of counties around three sides of mine, or very nearly so. Had my old district been properly divided, it would have made two nice ones, in convenient nice form. But as it is, they are certainly the most unreasonably laid off of any in the State, or perhaps in the nation, or even in the te-total creation.

However, when the election came on, the people of the district, and of Madison county among the rest, seemed disposed to prove to Mr. Fitzgerald and the Jackson Legislature, that they were not to be transferred like hogs, and horses, and cattle in the market; and they determined that I shouldn't be broke down, though I had to carry Jackson, and the enemies of the bank, and the legislative works all at once. I had Mr. Fitzgerald, it is true, for my open competitor, but he was helped along by all his little lawyers again, headed by old Black Hawk, as he is sometimes called, (alias) Adam Huntsman, with all his talents for writing "*Chronicles*," and such like foolish stuff.

But one good thing was, and I must record it, the papers in the district were now beginning to say "fair play a little," and they would publish on both sides the question. The contest was a warm one, and the battle well-fought; but I gained the day, and the Jackson horse was left a little behind. When the polls were compared, it turned out I had beat Fitz just two hundred and two votes, having made a mash of all their intrigues.

CHAPTER XVIII.

DURING the session of this Congress, I thought I would take a travel through the Northern States. I had braved the lonely forests of the West; I had shouldered the warrior's rifle in the far South; but the North and East I had never seen. I seemed to like members of Congress who came from these parts, and wished to know what kind of constituents they had. These considerations, in addition to my physician's advice to travel a little for my health, induced me to leave Washington on the 25th day of April, 1834, and steer for the North.

I arrived the same evening at Barnum's Hotel in Baltimore. Uncle Davy, as he is often called, was right glad to see me, perhaps because we were namesakes; or may be he always likes to see folks patronize his house. He has a pleasant face, any how, and his acts don't belie it. No one need look for better quarters: if they do, it will be because they don't know when they are satisfied.

Shortly after I arrived I was called upon, and asked to eat supper with a number of gentlemen. I went, and passed the evening pleasantly with my friend Wilkes and others.

Early next morning I started for Philadelphia, a place where I had never been. I sort of felt lonesome as I went down to the steamboat. The idea of going among a new people, where there are tens of thousands who would pass me by, without knowing or caring who I was, who are all taken up with their own pleasures, or their own business, made me feel small: and indeed if any one who reads this book has a grand idea of his own importance, let him go to a big city, and he will find he is not higher valued than a coon skin.

The steamboat was the *Carroll-of-Carrollton*, a fine craft, with the rum old commodore Chaytor for head man. A good fellow he is—all sorts of a man—bowing and scraping to the ladies; nodding to the gentlemen; cursing the crew; and his right eye broad cast upon the "opposition line," all at the same time. "Let go!" said the old one, and off we walked in prime style.

We immediately came past Fort McHenry, justly celebrated for its gallant defence under Armistead, Stewart, Nicholson, Newcomb, and others, during the last war; and shortly after we passed North Point, where the British landed to make, what they never dared, an attack on Baltimore.

Our passage down the Chesapeake bay was very pleasant; and in a very short run we came to the place where we were to get on board of the railroad cars.

This was a clean new sight to me; about a dozen big stages hung on to one machine, and to start up hill. After a good deal of fuss we all got seated, and moved slowly off; the engine wheezing as if she had the tizzick. By and by she began to take short breaths, and away we went with a blue streak after us. The whole distance is seventeen miles, and it was run in fifty-five minutes.

While I was whizzing along, I burst out laughing. One of the passengers asked me what it was at. "Why," says I, "it's no wonder the fellow's horses run off." A Carolina waggoner had just crossed the railroad, from Charleston to Augusta, when the engine hove in sight with the cars attached. It was growing dark, and the sparks were flying in all directions. His horses ran off, broke his waggon, and smashed his combustibles into items. He run to a house for help, and when they asked him what scared his horses, he said he did not jist know, but it must be hell in harness.

At Delaware City I again embarked on board of a splendid steamboat, which ran to Philadelphia.

When dinner was ready, I sat down with the rest of the passengers; among them was the Reverend O. B. Brown of the Post Office Department, who sat near me. During dinner the parson called for a bottle of wine, and called on me for a toast. Not knowing whether he intended to compliment me, or abash me among so many strangers, or have some fun at my expense, I concluded to go ahead, and give him and his likes a blizzard. So our glasses being filled, the word went round, "a toast from Colonel Crockett." I gave it as follows: "Here's wishing the bones of tyrant kings may answer in hell, in place of gridirons, to roast the souls of Tories on." At this the parson appeared as if he was stump't. I said, "Never heed; it was meant for where it belonged." He did not repeat his invitation, and I eat my dinner quietly.

After dinner I went up on the deck, and saw the captain hoisting three flags. Says I, "What does that mean?" He replied, that he was under promise to the citizens of Philadelphia, if I was on board, to hoist his flags, as a friend of mine had said he expected I would be along soon.

We went on till we came in sight of the city; and as we advanced towards the wharf, I saw the whole face of the earth covered with people, all anxiously looking on towards the boat. The captain and myself were standing on the bow-deck; he pointed his finger at me, and people slung their hats, and huzzaed for Colonel Crockett. It struck me with astonishment to hear a strange people huzzaing for me, and made me feel sort of queer. It took me so uncommon unexpected, as I had no idea of attracting attention. But I had to meet it, and so I stepped on to the wharf, where the folks came crowding round, saying, "Give me the hand of an honest man." I did not know what all this meant; but some gentlemen took hold of me, and pressing through the crowd, put me up into an elegant barouche, drawn by four fine horses; they then told me to bow to the people: I did so, and with much difficulty we moved off. The streets were crowded to a great distance, and the windows full of people, looking out, I supposed, to see the wild man. I thought I had rather be in the wilderness with my gun and dogs, than to be attracting all that fuss. I had never seen the like before, and did not know exactly what to say or do. After some time we reached the United States Hotel in Chesnut Street.

The crowd had followed me, filling up the street, and pressing into the house to shake hands. I was conducted upstairs, and walked out on a platform, drew off my hat, and bowed round to the people. They cried out from all quarters, "A speech, a speech, Colonel Crockett."

After the noise had quit, so I could be heard, I said to them the following words:

"Gentlemen of Philadelphia,—

"My visit to your city is rather accidental. I had no expectation of attracting any uncommon attention. I am travelling for my health, without the least wish of exciting the people in such times of high political feeling. I do not wish to encourage it. I am unable at this time to find language suitable to return my gratitude to the citizens of Philadelphia. However, I am almost induced to believe in flattery—perhaps a burlesque. This is new to me, yet I see nothing but friendship in your faces; and if your curiosity is to hear the backwoodsman, I will assure you I am illy prepared to address this most enlightened people. However, gentlemen, if this is a curiosity to you, if you will meet me to-morrow, at one o'clock, I will endeavour to address you in my plain manner." So I made my obeisance to them, and retired into the house.

After night, when I could walk out unknown, I went up street or down, I don't know which, but took good care not to turn any corners, for fear I might get lost. I soon found that the streets were laid off square. This I thought was queer enough for a Quaker city, for they don't generally come up square to nothing; even their coats have a kind of slope, at least so they have cut Mister Penn's coat in the Capitol. This may be wrong, too, for I was told that when the man who made him first knocked off "the kivers" of the house where he worked at him, he had cut out Mister Penn with a regular built continental cocked hat on; and it was so much laughed at to see such a hat on a Quaker, that as soon as Congress rose, he cut off his head, and worked on a new one, with a rale sloped broad brim. Which is the honest George Fox hat I leave for Philadelphia lawyers and persons to decide.

When I went to my room, and got to bed, I could not sleep, thinking over all that passed, and my promise also to speak next day; but at last I composed myself with the reflection that I had got through many a scrape before, so I thought I'd trust again to good luck.

Next morning I had the honour of being called on by some old friends whom I knew at Washington—Judge Baldwin, Judge Hemphill, John Sargeant, and others, and I took it right kind in them to do so.

Early after breakfast I was taken to the Water-works, where I saw several of the gentlemen managers.—This is a grand sight, and no wonder the Philadelphians ask every one that comes, "have you seen the Water-works?" Just think of a few wheels throwing up more than five hundred thousand people can use: yes, and waste, too; for such scrubbing of steps, and even the very pavements under your feet, I never saw. Indeed, I looked close to see if the housemaids had not web-feet, they walked so well in water; and as for a fire, it has no chance at all; they just screw on a long hollow leather with a brass nose on it, dash up stairs, and seem to draw on Noah's flood.

The next place I visited was the Mint. Here I saw them coining gold and silver in abundance, and they were the rale "e pluribus unum;" not this electioneering trash, that they sent out to cheat the poor people, telling them they would all be paid in gold and silver, when the poor deceived creatures had nothing coming to them. A chip with a spit on the back of it is as good currency as an eagle, provided you can't get the image of the bird. It's all nonsense. The President, both cabinets and Congress to boot, can't enact poor men into rich. Hard knocks, and plenty of them, can only build up a fellow's self.

I asked if the workmen never stole any of the coin. They said not; they got used to it. Well, I thought, that was what my parson would call heterdox doctrine; that the longer a man was in temptation the more he would not sin. But I let it pass, for I had heard that they had got "new lights" in this city, and, of course, new and genuine doctrines—so that the Bible-doxy stood no chance. I could not help, barring the doctrine, giving these honest men great credit; especially when I recollected an old sanctimoniouslyfied fellow, who made his negroes whistle while they were picking cherries, for fear they should eat some.

From the Mint I was taken to the Asylum for insane persons, went through different apartments, saw men and women, some quite distracted, others not so bad. This was a very unpleasant sight. I am not able, nor do I wish I was able, to describe it. I felt monstrous solemn, and could not help thanking God I was not one of them; and I felt grateful in their stead to that city for caring for those who could not take care of themselves, and feeding them that heeded not the hand and heart that provided for them.

On returning to the hotel the hour had nearly arrived when I was to visit the Exchange. I asked Colonel Dorrance, the landlord, to go with me. He is a very clever man, and made me feel quite at home in his house. Whoever goes there once will go back again. So he agreed, and off we started.

I had made set speeches in Congress, and especially on my Tennessee land bill, when all my colleagues were against me; I had made stump speeches at home, in the face of all the little office yelpers who were opposed to me; but, indeed, when I got within sight of the Exchange, and saw the streets crowded, I most wished to take back my promise; but I was brought up by hearing a youngster say, as I passed by, "Go ahead, Davy Crockett!" I said to myself, "I have faced the enemy; these are friends. I have fronted the savage red man of the forest; these are civilized. I'll keep cool, and let them have it."

I was conducted to the house of a Mr. Neil, where I met several gentlemen, and took some refreshment, not passing by a little Dutch courage. Of the latter there was plenty; and I observed the man of the house, when he asked me to drink, he didn't stand by to see what I took, but turned away, and told me to help myself. That's what I call genteel.

Arrived at the Exchange, I crowded through, went up to the second floor, and walked out on the porch, drew off my hat, and made my bow; speaking was out of the question, the huzzas for Crockett were so loud and so long.

The time had come when my promise must be kept. There must have been more than five thousand people, and they were still gathering from all parts. I spoke for about half an hour.

Three times three cheers closed the concern, and I came down to the door, where it appeared as if all the world had a desire to shake hands with me. I stood on the doorstep, and, as Major Jack Downing said, shook hands as hard as I could spring for near an hour. After this I returned to the hotel, and remained until night, when I was asked to visit the theatre in Walnut street. The landlord, Dorrance, and others were to go with me, to see Jim Crow. While we were talking about it, one of them said he could go all over the world "Tu crow juicy." Some laughed very hearty, and others did not.—I was among the latter, for I considered it a dry joke, although there was something *juicy* in it. Some of them said it was Latin; and that proved to me the reason why I did not laugh—I was tired of the "old Roman." But these Philadelphians are eternally cutting up jokes on words; so I puts a conundrum to them; and says I, "Can you tell me why the sacking of Jerusalem was like a cider-mill?" Well, they all were stumpt, and gave it up. "Because it made the Jews fly." Seeing them so much pleased with this, says I, "Why is a cow like a razor-grinder?" No one could answer. "Well," says I, "I thought you could find that out, for I don't know myself."

We started for the theatre, and found a very full house, and Jim a playing for the dear life. Jim makes as good a nigger as if he was clean black, except the bandy-legs.

Everybody seemed pleased, particularly when I laughed; they appeared to act as if I knew exactly when to laugh, and then they all followed.

What a pity it is that these theatres are not contrived that everybody could go; but the fact is, backwoodsman as I am, I have heard some things in them that was a leetle too tough for good women and modest men; and that's a great pity, because there are thousands of scenes of real life that might be exhibited, both for amusement and edification, without offending. Folks pretend to say that high people don't mind these things. Well, it may be that they are better acquainted with vice than we plain folks; but I am yet to live and see a woman polished out of the natural feelings, or too high not to do things that a'n't quite reputable in those of low degree.

Their fiddling was pretty good, considering every fellow played his own piece; and I would have known more about it if they had played a tune, but it was all twee-wee-tadlum-tadlum-tum-tum, tadle-leedle-tadle-leedle-lee. The "Twenty-second of February," or the "Cuckoo's Nest," would have been a treat.

I do not think, however, from all I saw, that the people enjoyed themselves better than we do at a country frolic, where we dance till daylight, and pay off the score by giving one in our turn. It would do you good to see our boys and girls dancing. None of your stradling, mincing, sadying; but a regular sifter, cut-the-buckle, chicken-flutter set-to. It is good wholesome exercise; and when one of our boys put his arm round his partner, it is a good hug, and no harm in it.

Next morning I was waited on by some gentlemen, who presented me with a seal for my watch-chain, which cost forty dollars. I told them I always accepted a present as a testimony of friendship. The engraving on the stone represents the great match race, two horses in full speed, and over them the words, "Go ahead." It is the finest seal I ever saw; and when I returned to Washington, the members almost used it up, making copies to send all over the country.

I was hardly done making my bow to these gentlemen, before Mr. James M. Sanderson informed me that the young Whigs of Philadelphia had a desire to present me with a fine rifle, and had chosen him to have her made agreeably to my wishes. I told him that was an article that I knew somewhat about; and gave him the size, weight, &c.

You can't imagine how I was crowded to get through every thing. Colonel Pulaski called to take me in his carriage to the Naval Hospital, where they stow away the old sailors on dry land, and a splendid building it is; all made of marble. I did not like the situation; but I suppose it was the best they could get with so much ground to it.

From there we went to the Navy Yard, and examined the largest ship ever made in the United States. She was what they call "in the stocks."

I then surveyed the artillery, and the balance of the shipping, not forgetting to pay my respects to the officers of the yard, and then returned home with the colonel, where I was kindly treated, both in eating and drinking; and so ended another day.

Next morning the land admiral, Colonel Reeside, asked me to call on him, and take a ride. I did so; and he carried me out to the railroad and Schuylkill bridge. I found that the railroad was finished near a hundred miles into the interior of the state, and is only one out of many; yet they make no fuss about it.

We drove in past the Girard school—that old man that give so many millions to Philadelphia, and cut out his kin with a crumb. Well, thinks I, blood is thicker than water, and the remembrance of friends better than a big name. I'd have made them all rich, and give away the balance. But, maybe, French people don't think like me.

This being my last night in Philadelphia, Dorrance gave me what they call a "pick knick" supper; which means as much as me and all my company could eat and drink, and nothing to pay.

I forgot to say that I had spent part of the evening before this with Colonel Saint.

CHAPTER XIX.

NEXT morning, Wednesday the 29th, I was invited by Captain Jenkins, of the steamboat *New Philadelphia*, to go on with him to New York. I accepted his offer and started. I saw nothing very particular along the Delaware river, except the place where all the hard stone coal comes to, from the interior of Pennsylvania; where, I am told, they have mountains of it. After some time, we got upon a railroad, where they say we run twenty-five miles to the hour. I can only judge of the speed by putting my head out to spit, which I did, and overtook it so quick, that it hit me smack in the face. We soon arrived at Amboy, and took the water again; and soon came in sight of the great city of New York, and a bulger of a place it is. The number of the ships beat me all hollow, and looked for all the world like a big clearing in the West, with the dead trees all standing.

When we swung round to the wharf, it was covered with people, who inquired if I was on board; and when the captain told them I was, they slung their hats, and gave three cheers.

Immediately a committee came on board, representing the young Whigs, and informed me they were appointed to wait upon me, and invite me to the American Hotel. I accepted their offer, and went with them to the hotel, where I was friendly received; conducted to a large parlour, where I was introduced to a great many gentlemen.

I was invited to visit the new and elegant fire engine, and took some refreshment with the managers, and returned in time to visit the Park theatre, and see Miss Fanny Kemble play in grand style. The house was better filled, and the fixings looked nicer, than the one in Philadelphia; but any of them is good enough, if they have such pretty play-actors as Miss Kemble. In fact, she is like a handsome piece of changeable silk; first one colour, then another, but always the clean thing.

I returned home, as I am told all great folks do, after the lady actor was done; and, sitting with my friends, the cry of "Fire, fire!" struck my ear. I bounced from my chair, and ran for my hat. "Sit down, colonel," said one of the gentlemen, "it's not near us."—"A'n't you going to help to put it out?"—"No," said he, laughing, "we have fire companies here, and we leave it to them." Well, to me this seemed queer enough, for at home I would have jumped on the first horse at hand, and rode full-flight bare-backed, to help put out a fire.

I forgot that I was in a city where you may live, as they tell me, years, and not know who lives next door to you; still, I felt curious to see how they managed; and Colonel Jackson went with me. As it was late, the engines were only assembling when we got there; but when they began to spirt, they put out a four-story house that was all in a blaze, in less than no time. I asked the colonel where they got so much water from. He said it was raised by the Manhattan Bank, out of a charter got by Aaron Burr.

. . . . . .

I returned to the hotel, where I found a great many gentlemen waiting to see the wild man from the far West. After spending some time with them, I was taken to Peale's museum. I shall not attempt to describe the curiosities here; it is above my bend. I could not help, however, thinking what pleasure or curiosity folks could take in sticking up whole rows of little bugs, and such like varmints. I saw a boy there that had been born without any hands or arms; and he took a pair of scissors in his toes, and cut his name in full, and gave it to me. This I called a miracle.

From thence I went to the City Hall, and was introduced to the mayor of the city and several of the aldermen. The mayor is a plain, common-sense-looking man. I was told he had been a tanner; that pleased me; for I thought both him and me had clum up a long way from where we had started: and it is truly said, "Honour and fame from no condition rise." It's the grit of a fellow that makes the man.

On my return, I received an invitation from Colonel Draper to dine with him, informing me also, that the rale Major Jack Downing was expected to be there. . . . Sure enough, when I got to Colonel Draper's, I was introduced to the major. We sat down to a splendid dinner, and amused ourselves with some good jokes. But as this was a private party, I don't think it gentlemanly to tell what was said at this time, and especially as this was not the only communication I had with the major. One observation, however, was made by him, and I gave him an answer which could not offend any body. "Colonel," said he, "what d'ye sort o' think about gineral matters and things in purticlur?" Knowing him to be a Yankee, I tried to answer him in his own way. So, says I, "Major, the Ginneral's matters are all wrong; but some purticklar things are very well: such, for instance, as the honour I have in dining with you at Colonel Draper's."—"Good!" says the major, "and we'll talk about them there matters some other time."—"Agreed," says I, "major, always at your sarvice."

I found a large company waiting for me when I got back to the hotel, and invitation to sup with the young Whigs. Well, now, thinks I, they had better keep some of these things to eat for somebody else, for I'm sure I'm as full as a young cub. But right or wrong, I must go in. There I met the Honourable Augustine S. Clayton, of Georgia, and was right glad to see him, for I knew I could get him to take some of the speaking off of me. He speaks prime, and is always ready, and never goes off half-cock.

Upwards of one hundred sat down to supper. They were going to toast me, but I told some of them near me to toast Judge Clayton first; that there should be more rejoicing over one that was lost and found again, than over ninety-and-nine such as me, that had never strayed away. They did so: and he made a speech that fairly made the tumblers hop. He rowed the Tories up and over Salt river.

Then they toasted me as "the undeviating supporter of the constitution and laws." I made a short speech, and concluded with the story of "the Red Cow," which was, that as long as General Jackson went strait, I followed him; but when he began to go this way, and that way, and every way, I wouldn't go after him: like the boy whose master ordered him to plough across the field to the red cow. Well, *he* began to plough and *she* began to walk; and he ploughed all forenoon after her. So when the master came, he swore at him for going so crooked. "Why, sir," said the boy, "you told me to plough to the red cow, and I kept after her, but she always kept moving."

. . . . . .

On the same walk I was introduced to the Honourable Albert Gallatin. He had an old straw hat in his hand, and, like every body else, was "mooving," and said he was sorry not to have more time to be acquainted with me. He pointed to the house he was leaving, and said it and several others were to be torn down to build a big tavern. It was a very fine house, fit for any man to live in; but in a few hours I saw men on the top of it, and before the next evening the daylight was through it. This tavern is to be near the park, and is building by John Jacob Astor. It is to cost seven hundred thousand dollars, and covers a whole square. Mr. Astor, I am told, begun business in New York as a dealer in furs, and is now worth millions. Lord help the beavers and otters! they must have most got used to getting skinned by this time. And what a meeting of friends and kin there must have been in his warehouse. "Farewell," said the otter to the beaver, "I never expect to see you again, my dear old friend." "Never mind, my dear fellow," said the beaver, "don't be too much distressed, we'll soon meet at the hatter's shop."

This day a new flag was to be hoisted, down on the Battery, and I was invited to attend. The artillery, under command of General Morton, paraded; and he invited many of his friends to be present; among the rest, the mayor, Gideon Lee, was there, and addressed the people. Among other things, he told them that that flag-staff was placed where the old one stood when the British evacuated New York; that they left the flag flying, and greased the pole, so that it could not be clim up; but at last a sailor got up and tore it down, and hoisted the American flag in its place; and when he came down, the people filled his hat with money.

General Morton is a revolutioner, and an officer in the society of old soldiers, called the "Cincinnati Society," and wears its badge on his breast. He gave an entertainment to his friends on this occasion; for you must know that nobody thinks any thing well done in this place, without eating and drinking over it.

. . . . . .

Next morning, Colonel Mapes told me he was requested to invite me over to Jersey City, to see some shooting with a rifle. In the mean time, I had been very kindly invited by Captain Comstock to go that day, at half-past three o'clock, with him to Boston. I concluded to go, as I might never have another opportunity, and it took only eighteen hours to go there. . . .

I started to Jersey City, where I found a great many gentlemen shooting rifles, at the distance of one hundred yards, with a rest. One gentleman gave me his gun, and asked me to shoot. I raised up, off-hand, and cut within about two inches of the centre. I told him my distance was forty yards, off-hand. He loaded his gun, and we walked down to within forty yards when I fired, and was deep in the paper. I shot a second time, and did the same. Colonel Mapes then put up a quarter of a dollar in the middle of a black spot, and asked me to shoot at it. I told him he had better mark the size of it and put his money in his pocket. He said, "fire away." I did so, and made slight-of-hand work with his quarter.

It was now time to return, and prepare for my trip to Boston.

CHAPTER XX.

AT three o'clock I left the hotel, and went over to where the steamboat lay. When I went on board, the captain showed me into a splendid state-room, which I was to occupy for the voyage. So, when I had made my toilet (as great folks say), that is, combed my hair and taken a glass of brandy and water, I went on deck. There I saw almost as many people as were when I landed; and they kept gathering until the whole ground was covered; and when we started, they cheered me for some time; and all I could do was to stand and bow to them. This brought me into new trouble; for the passengers found I was on board, and came round me, so that I missed seeing the city until we got past it.

Soon, however, we came to the place called Hell's Gate; so called, I suppose, because the water boils, and foams, and bounces about as if it was in a pot. I don't think, however, that this is a good name for it, because we are told in the good book that hell's gate is a mighty slick place, and easy to get into. Here I first saw a large square-sailed British merchant ship, under full sail. She was coming in through the channel, and I was glad to see that, for when we were voting for an appropriation for a fort to defend this place, I heard it said that no foreign ship ever attempted coming in that way. But these are the kind of arguments used most generally by those who oppose internal improvements, harbours, &c., &c.; they fancy things, and speak them for truth.

We went on very pleasantly till night; and the captain told me, if I would rise at daylight, we would be out of sight of land. So I went to bed, and rose as soon as I could see. I walked out on deck, and sure enough, there was no land to be seen. We were coming near Point Juda, a place where, the captain informed me, people on board was very often sea-sick. So I set myself down for a case, but was disappointed; it was quite calm, and a clear fine morning, and when the sun rose, it came up like a ball of fire out of the water, and looked, for all the world, as if it had been made for the first time. We went round Point Juda, and kept in sight of land on our left hand. There was very little timber to be seen: the whole country appeared to be laid off in fields, divided by stone fences. These were a great curiosity to me, and I could not help thinking that their cattle must be well schooled here; for one of my cows would pitch over a dozen such fences, without flirting her tail.

We went by the great fort at the Naraganset bay, and landed at

Newport for a short time. From thence we took our way again to Providence. There I met a large number of the citizens. They cheered me on my arrival, and wanted me to stay and partake of a dinner with them. I declined, and took my seat in the fast stage. The driver was ordered to go ahead, and sure enough he did. It was forty miles to Boston, and we run it down in four hours.

What mighty hard land it is on this road, and seems as if the whole face of the earth had been covered over with stones, as thick as Kentuck land titles; but they have got them strung up into fences, as many as they can, by picking of them off; but they won't stay picked, for every time they plough, a new crop comes up.

It was somewhere away long here that the pilgrims landed at Plymouth, and begun to people this part of the world; and a hard time they must have had of it in this barren country; and it seems odd that they should come all the way across the sea, and not look out for good land. However, I suppose it was all right, or God would have given them better pilots. If they had had fine land, they would not have ventured so much on the ocean, and would have had less necessity to work hard, and bring up their children to industry and give them such cute teaching as makes them know how to make ducks and drakes of us ou' yonder, when they come among us. . . .

Bvt I must quit philosophy, and tell you where I stopped in Boston—and that was just where any one that has plenty of cash, and plenty of good-will for pleasure, would like—in a clean street, with a tavern on one side, and the theatre on the other, and both called Tremont. Mr. Boyden did not know me, nor me him; but when I told him my name, where they put it on the bar-book, he treated me like an old friend, and continued to do so all the time I was there. He gave me a good room and nice bed; and did not, like many landlords, let a stranger take care of himself, but attended to me the kindest in the world. I had seen a great many fine taverns; but take this out and out, and Tremont-house is a smart chance ahead. It is lately built, and has every new arrangement; and for a house with a couple of hundred people about it, is the quietest I ever was in. His head man of the gap, in the bar, has eyes all round him; and Will Scarlet, as he is called by a friend of mine, has the sound of every bell in the house by heart. When I arrived, I knew no one, but in a short time I made many acquaintances, and, indeed, was very kindly treated by every person I met. There is a great deal of friendly feeling with the eastern people; and folks need not go out of Boston to find rale hospitality.

Next morning I was invited by Mr. Harding to visit his gallery of paintings, where he had a great many specimens of the fine arts; and finally he asked me to sit for him until he could get my likeness, which I did, during my stay, and he has it now, hung up among the rest of the fine arts. From there I went to Fanuell Hall, where General Davis showed me all the accoutrements of war for several companies of infantry and riflemen, that was deposited in it.—These are in snug rooms on each side of the second story; and in the middle is the parade-room, where, summer and winter, the companies meet to drill. This is doing things in true style, that is all for use, and no show about it. So, instead of hearing a great fuss with volunteers, and drilling, and all that, wheeling and marching, handle cartridge, eyes right—you see a squad of fine soldiers coming out of this same place, and squared up as if they were the rale breed.

General Davis informed me this was the house that was called the "cradle of liberty." I reckon old King George thought they were thundering fine children that was rocked in it, and a good many of them; and that no wonder his red-coats were licked, when the children came out with soldier clothes on, and muskets in their hands. God grant that the liberty-tree bough on which this cradle rocks may never break. . . .

After returning home, I was invited over to Roxborough, where they make the Indian-rubber clothing, shoes, &c. This is done by dissolving the rubber, and putting it on silk and other cloth, which entirely turns the rain, and still is pliable, and not heavy. The proprietor made me a present of a hunting coat, which I have tried, and would risk my powder under it for forty days and nights. It was a great curiosity to see the young ladies cutting out the clothes, and sticking them together without sewing them. I went also through the shoe factory, where they make shoes in the same way without stitching them.—I could not help thinking of the Philadelphia girls—thought they ought to have them, to keep their feet dry.

We often wonder how things are made so cheap among the Yankees. Come here, and you will see women doing men's work, and happy and cheerful as the day is long; and why not? Is it not much better for themselves and families, instead of sitting up all day busy about nothing? It a'n't hard work, neither, and looked as queer to me as it would to one of my countrywomen to see a man milking the cows, as they do here.

After I had seen all that was to be seen here, I was taken to Colonel Perkins' carpet factory. There I saw the widest web I ever saw, and they were glossing and stamping it in handsome style. I was quite friendly received by the colonel. He is said to be a very rich man; is quite old, but firm and healthy in appearance; and uses his riches in the best possible way—by keeping a great many people busy. And he is not one of those foolish people, neither, that strive all their days to see how rich they can die; for he gives with his hands open. I saw one house in Boston which he gave to keep the blind in, and was told t was worth fifty thousand dollars.—What a comfort the old gentleman must have when he looks at his great possessions, and is calculating, not how much he can hoard up, but how much he can give away. God never made such men to be envied, or I could begrudge him a few of his blessings from the poor and destitute.

At the invitation of the owners of the Indian-rubber factory, I met a number of the citizens of Roxborough, and passed a short time with them very pleasantly.

. . . . . .

They appear to me to live generally in New England more snugly, and have more kind feelings to one another, and live in more peace and harmony, than any people I ever was among. And another good thing—they don't forget one another when they are among strangers; old New England binds them hard together; and this gives them, as it ought to do, strength, and confidence, and influence; and with us in the South, Yankee cunning is assuming the true name—Yankee knowledge of business, and perseverance in whatever they undertake.

. . . . . .

I did not like the statue of General Washington in the state-house. They have a Roman gown on him, and he was an American; this a'n't right. They did the thing better at Richmond, in Virginia, where they have him in the old blue and buff. He belonged to *this* country—heart, soul, and body: and I don't want any other to have any part of him—not even his clothes. . . .

Here now comes a poser. I was invited to dine out; but if I can mind the gentleman's name I wish I may be shot. He lived near Tremont; and I hope if he has curiosity enough to read this here book, that he will write me a letter, so that in my second edition, I may give his name as large as life: and I beg him to recollect that it an't every one that signs a letter that makes himself known. Let him write it plain—none of your *hiryglifics*—or I won't put him in.

Some would say that they were mortified that they forgot this gentleman's name. I a'n't; I'm sorry—but the truth is, I saw so many folks, and so many new things, that it's no wonder I should not mind every thing. He was a clever fellow, and I know he will forgive me.

When I went home, there I met a young man that was stone blind. "Well," says you, "that's no new thing." Stop, if you please; that puts me in mind of an old parson and a scolding woman that belonged to his church. She told him, in one of her tantrums, that she could preach as well as he could, and he might select the text: "Well," said the old man, "I'll give you one, and you can study over it—'It is better to dwell on the house-top, than in a wide house with a brawling woman.'"—"You good-for-nothing, impudent, old—what shall I say? do you go for to call me a brawling woman?"—"Dear mistress," said the good old man, "you'll have to study a while longer, for you come to the application of the text before you discuss the doctrine."

Now it was not that I met a blind boy in Tremont house that was any curiosity: but it was his errand. He inquired of the bar-keeper for me, as I was standing by him, and said he was sent by the teacher of the blind, to invite me to visit the institution, and that he would show me the way!!

I was told by the gentlemen present, that he could go all over Boston. A gentleman accompanied me, and we went on till we came to a fine house, where the institution was kept. We went, and were introduced to the teacher. He asked me if I wished to hear some of them read. I said I did: and he ordered a little girl, perhaps ten or twelve years old, to get her book, asked her to find a certain chapter in the Old Testament, and read it. She took up the book, and felt with her fingers until she found it. He then told her to read: and she did so, with a clear, distinct voice. This was truly astonishing: but on examining their books, I found that the letters were stamped on the under side of the paper, so as to raise them above the surface of the upper side; and such was the keenness of their touch, that by passing the end of the finger over the word, it served them for sight, and they pronounced the word. There was a little boy learning to cipher in the same way. The teacher put several questions to him aloud; and, putting his fingers together and working with them for a short time, he answered all the questions correctly.

That kind of education astonished me more than any thing I ever saw.

CHAPTER XXI.

I HAD promised next morning to go to Lowell with Mr. Lawrence, Mr. Harding, and others; but when I woke up, it was pouring down rain, so that kept me in the house all day.

I was not idle, for I had a heap of talk with the folks in the house. One gentleman asked me to come and see him; but he gave me so many directions about getting to where he lived, that I asked him to write it down, and told him if ever he came to my part of the country, I hoped he would call and see me. "Well," said he, "how will I find where you live?"—"Why, sir, run down the Mississippi till you come to the Obion river, run a small streak up that, jump ashore any where and inquire for me."

Says I to one of them, "Do you believe in the sea-sarpent?"—"If I don't there's no snakes. I believe it to be as much true as there is lie in our deacon when he says his red face a'n't made by drinking 'New England.'"—"Do you consider him dangerous, or is he peaceable?"—"Well, now, to keep the truth, I never saw him; but Capting Hodijah Folger said as how he considered the critter as a sort o' so, and a sort o' not."—"Had he a long tail?"—"Tail, did you say? You'd a died to hear Didge tell about that thar verming. Didge said he was like skying a copper—head or tail—but you had to guess which. Ses Didge to me, 'Don't you mind,' ses he, 'that are angel what stood with one leg on the sea, and t'other on the dry land?'—'I guess I do.'—'Well,' ses he to me, 'that are sarpint's skin was long enough to 'a' queued his hair.'"

. . . . . .

CHAPTER XXII.

WHEN I arrived in Philadelphia, I put up at the United States, where I felt a kind of being at home.

Next morning I was informed that the rifle gun which was to be presented to me by the young men of Philadelphia, was finished, and would be delivered that evening; and that a committee had been appointed to wait on me and conduct me to where I was to receive it. So, accordingly, in the evening the committee came and I walked with them to a room nearly fornent the old state-house: it was crowded full, and there was a table in the centre, with the gun, a tomahawk, and butcher-knife, both of fine razor metal, with all the accoutrements necessary to the gun—the most beautiful I ever saw, or anybody else; and I am now happy to add, as good as they are handsome. My friend, John M. Sanderson, Esq., who had the whole management of getting her made, was present, and delivered the gun into my hands.—Upon receiving her, I addressed the company as follows:

"Gentlemen,—

"I receive this rifle from the young men of Philadelphia as a testimony of friendship, which I hope never to live to forget. This is a favourite article with me, and would have been my choice above all presents that could have been selected. I love a good gun, for it makes a man feel independent, and prepared either for war or peace.

"This rifle does honour to the gentleman who made it. I must say, long as I have been accustomed to handle a gun, I have never seen any thing that could come near a comparison to her in beauty. I cannot think that ever such a rifle was made, either in this or any other country; and how, gentlemen, to express my gratitude to you for your splendid present, I am at a loss. This much, however, I will say, that myself and my sons will not forget you while we use this token of your kindness for our amusement. If it should become necessary to use her in defence of the liberty of our country, in my time, I will do as I have done before; and if the struggle should come when I am buried in the dust, I will leave her in the hands of some who will honour your present, in company with your sons, in standing for our country's rights.

"Accept my sincere thanks, therefore, gentlemen, for your valuable present—one which I will keep as a testimony of your friendship, so long as I am in existence."

I then received the gun and accoutrements, and returned to the hotel, where I made an agreement with Mr. Sanderson and Colonel Pulaski, to go with them the next day to Jersey shore, at Camden, and try my gun.

Next morning we went out. I had been long out of practice, so that I could not give her a fair trial. I shot tolerable well, and was satisfied that when we became better acquainted, the fault would be mine if the varmints did not suffer.

. . . . . .

Next morning I was introduced to the great powder-maker, Mr. Dupont, who said to me, that he had been examining my fine gun, and that he wished to make me a present of half a dozen canisters of his best sportsman's powder. I thanked him, and he went off, and in a short time returned with one dozen, nicely boxed up and directed to me. I then made my arrangements to start the next morning.

While walking about that evening with a friend, we called in at a China importer's store. I was introduced to him; and after looking at his splendid collection for some time, he told me he had a wish to present me with a pitcher. I thought the gentleman was joking, at first; but he assured me, that if I would accept it, he would pack it up in a box so that it could not break, and I could carry it home safely. I thanked him sincerely for his friendship. It was sent to me, and I carried it home and gave it to my wife, telling her that, when I was away, that pitcher should remind her that folks get thirsty, and the same spirit which prompted the gentleman to give, should make us use it. I am sorry I have forgot his name.

. . . . . .

I arrived in Pittsburg in the night, and early in the morning went down to the wharf to inquire for a steamboat. I soon found Captain Stone, who commanded the *Hunter*. He said he had been waiting a day, thinking that I would like to go with him. That was true, and I found him all sorts of a clever man. We were to start at ten o'clock. I returned to the tavern where I had put up, and a great many gentlemen called to see me, and among others, Mr. Grant, brother-in-law of Governor Carroll, of Tennessee. He invited me to walk through the city, and to visit his house, which I did, and he introduced me to a great many of the citizens. I returned, and prepared for a start.

. . . . . .

All passed off pleasantly, and next day I took the steamboat *Scotland*, commanded by Captain Buckner, a gentleman, every inch of him. After a fine run, we arrived at Mills' Point, on the 22nd day of July. Here I once more touched the soil of Tennessee, and found my son William waiting to carry me home, which was distant thirty-five miles.

When I landed, and took out my fine gun, the folks gathered round me, to see the great curiosity. A large fellow stepped up, and asked me why all the members did not get such guns given them. I told him I got that gun for being honest, in supporting my country, instead of bowing down and worshipping an idol. He looked at me and said, that was very strong. "No stronger than true, my friend," said I.

In a short time I set out for my own home; yes, my own home, my own soil, my own humble dwelling, my own family, my own hearts, my ocean of love and affection which neither circumstance nor time can dry up. Here, like the wearied bird, let me settle down for awhile, and shut out the world. . . .

In the course of a few days, I determined to try my new gun upon the living subject. I started for a hunt, and shortly came across a fine buck. He fell at the distance of one hundred and thirty steps! Not a bad shot, you will say. I say, not a bad gun either. After a little practice with her, she came up to the eye prime, and I determined to try her at the first shooting match for beef.

As this is a novelty to most of my readers, I will endeavour to give a description of this western amusement.

In the latter part of summer our cattle get very fat, as the range is remarkably fine; and some one, desirous of raising money on one of his cattle, advertises that on a particular day, and at a given place, a first-rate beef will be shot for.

When the day comes, every marksman in the neighbourhood will meet at the appointed place, with his gun. After the company has assembled, a subscription paper is handed round, with the following heading.

"A. B. offers a beef worth twenty dollars, to be shot for, at twenty-five cents a shot." Then the names are put down by each person, thus:

D. C.	puts in four	shots	. . . . . .	$1 00
E. F.	,, eight	,,	. . . . . .	2 00
G. H.	,, two	,,	. . . . . .	0 50

And thus it goes round, until the price is made up.

Two persons are then selected, who have not entered for shots, to act as judges of the match. Every shooter gets a board, and makes a cross in the centre of his target. The shot that drives the centre, or comes nearest to it, gets the *hide and tallow*, which is considered the first choice. The next nearest gets his choice of the hind quarters; the third gets the other hind quarter; the fourth takes choice of the fore quarters; the fifth the remaining quarter; and the sixth gets the lead in the tree against which we shoot.

The judges stand near the tree, and when a man fires they cry out, "Who shot?" and the shooter gives in his name; and so on, till all have shot. The judges then take all the boards, and go off by themselves, and decide what quarter each man has won. Sometimes one will get nearly all.

This is one of our homely amusements—enjoyed as much by us, and perhaps more, than most of your refined entertainments. Here each man takes a part, if he pleases, and no one is excluded, unless his improper conduct renders him unfit as an associate.

CHAPTER XXIII.

I BEGIN this chapter on the 8th day of July, 1835, at Home, Weakley county, Tennessee. I have just returned from a two weeks' electioneering canvass, and I have spoken every day to large concourses of people with my competitor. I have him badly plagued, for he does not know as much about "the Government," the deposites, and the Little Flying Dutchman, whose life I wrote, as I can tell the people; and at times he is as much bothered as a fly in a tar pot to get out of the mess. A candidate is often stumped in making stump speeches. His name is Adam Huntsman; he lost a leg in an Indian fight, they say, during the last war, and the Government run him on the score of his military services. I tell him in my speech that I have great hopes of writing one more book, and that shall be the second fall of Adam, for he is on the Eve of an almighty thrashing. He relishes the joke about as much as a doctor does his own physic. I handle the administration without gloves, and I do believe I will double my competitor, if I have a fair shake, and he does not work like a mole in the dark. . . .

While on the subject of election matters, I will just relate a little anecdote, about myself, which will show the people to the east, how we manage these things on the frontiers. It was when I first run for Congress; I was then in favour of the Hero, for he had chalked out his course so sleek in his letter to the Tennessee legislature, that, like Sam Patch, says I, "there can be no mistake in him," and so I went ahead. No one dreamt about the monster and the deposites at that time, and so, as I afterward found, many, like myself, were taken in by these fair promises, which were worth about as much as a flash in the pan when you have a fair shot at a fat bear.

But I am losing sight of my story.—Well, I started off to the Cross Roads, dressed in my hunting shirt, and my rifle on my shoulder. Many of our constituents had assembled there to get a taste of the quality of the candidates at orating. Job Snelling, a gander-shanked Yankee, who had been caught somewhere about Plymouth Bay, and been shipped to the west with a cargo of cod fish and rum, erected a large shantee, and set up shop for the occasion. A large posse of the voters had assembled before I arrived, and my opponent had already made considerable headway with his speechifying and his treating, when they spied me about a rifle shot from the camp, sauntering along as if I was not a party in the business. "There comes Crockett," cried one. "Let us hear the colonel," cried another, and so I mounted the stump that had been cut down for the occasion, and began to bush-whack in the most approved style.

I had not been up long before there was such an uproar in the crowd that I could not hear my own voice, and some of my constituents let me know, that they could not listen to me on such a dry subject as the welfare of the nation, until they had something to drink, and that I must treat 'em. Accordingly I jumped down from the rostrum, and led the way to the shantee, followed by my constituents, shouting, "Huzza for Crockett," and "Crockett for ever!"

When we entered the shantee, Job was busy dealing out his rum in a style that showed he was making a good day's work of it, and I called for a quart of the best, but the crooked critur returned no other answer than by pointing at a board over the bar, on which he had chalked in large letters, "*Pay to-day and trust to-morrow.*" Now that idea brought me all up standing; it was a sort of cornering in which there was no back out, for ready money in the west, in those times, was the shyest thing in all natur, and it was most particularly shy with me on that occasion.

The voters, seeing my predicament, fell off to the other side, and I was left deserted and alone, as the Government will be, when he no longer has any offices to bestow. I saw, plain as day, that the tide of popular opinion was against me, and that, unless I got some rum speedily, I should lose my election as sure as there are snakes in Virginny—and it must be done soon, or even burnt brandy wouldn't save me. So I walked away from the shantee, but in another guess sort from the way I entered it, for on this occasion I had no train after me, and not a voice shouted "Huzza for Crockett." Popularity sometimes depends on a very small matter indeed; in this particular it was worth a quart of New England rum, and no more.

Well, knowing that a crisis was at hand, I struck into the woods with my rifle on my shoulder, my best friend in time of need, and as good fortune would have it, I had not been out more than a quarter of an hour before I treed a fat coon, and in the pulling of a trigger he lay dead at the root of the tree. I soon whipped his hairy jacket off his back, and again bent my way towards the shantee, and walked up to the bar, but not alone, for this time I had half a dozen of my constituents at my heels. I threw down the coon skin upon the counter, and called for a quart, and Job, though busy in dealing out rum, forgot to point at his chalked rules and regulations, for he knew that a coon was as good a legal tender for a quart, in the west, as a New York shilling, any day in the year.

My constituents now flocked about me, and cried "Huzza for Crockett," "Crockett for ever," and finding the tide had taken a turn, I told them several yarns, to get them in a good humour, and having soon despatched the value of the coon, I went out and mounted the stump, without opposition, and a clear majority of the voters followed me to hear what I had to offer for the good of the nation.—Before I was half through, one of my constituents moved that they would hear the balance of my speech, after they had washed down the first part with some more of Job Snelling's extract of cornstalk and molasses, and the question being put, it was carried unanimously. It wasn't considered necessary to tell the yeas and nays, so we adjourned to the shantee, and on the way I began to reckon that the fate of the nation pretty much depended upon my shooting another coon.

While standing at the bar, feeling sort of bashful while Job's rules and regulations stared me in the face, I cast down my eyes, and discovered one end of the coon skin sticking between the logs that supported the bar. Job had slung it there in the hurry of business. I gave it a sort of quick jerk, and it followed my hand as natural as if I had been the rightful owner. I slapped it on the counter, and Job, little dreaming that he was barking up the wrong tree, shoved along another bottle, which my constituents quickly disposed of with great good humour, for some of them saw the trick, and then we withdrew to the rostrum to discuss the affairs of the nation.

I don't know how it was, but the voters soon became dry again, and nothing would do, but we must adjourn to the shantee, and as luck would have it, the coon skin was still sticking between the logs, as if Job had flung it there on purpose to tempt me. I was not slow in raising it to the counter, the rum followed of course, and I wish I may be shot, if I didn't, before the day was over, get ten quarts for the same identical skin, and from a fellow, too, who in those parts was considered as sharp as a steel trap, and as bright as a pewter button.

This joke secured me my election, for it soon circulated like smoke among my constituents, and they allowed, with one accord, that the man who could get the whip hand of Job Snelling in fair trade, could outwit Old Nick himself, and was the real grit for them in Congress. Job was by no means popular ; he boasted of always being wide awake, and that any one who could take him in was free to do so, for he came from a stock that sleeping or waking had always one eye open, and the other not more than half closed. The whole family were geniuses. His father was the inventor of wooden nutmegs, by which Job said he might have made a fortune, if he had only taken out a patent and kept the business in his own hands ; his mother Patience manufactured the first white oak pumpkin seeds of the mammoth kind, and turned a pretty penny the first season ; and his aunt Prudence was the first to discover that corn husks, steeped in tobacco water, would make as handsome Spanish wrappers as ever came from Havana, and that oak leaves would answer all the purposes of filling, for no one could discover the difference except the man who smoked them, and then it would be too late to make a stir about it. Job, himself, bragged of having made some useful discoveries ; the most profitable of which was the art of converting mahogany sawdust into cayenne pepper, which he said was a profitable and safe business ; for the people have been so long accustomed to having dust thrown in their eyes, that there wasn't much danger of being found out.

The way I got to the blind side of the Yankee merchant was pretty generally known before election day, and the result was, that my opponent might as well have whistled jigs to a milestone, as attempt to beat up for votes in that district. I beat him out and out, quite back into the old year, and there was scarce enough left of him, after the canvass was over, to make a small grease spot. He disappeared without even leaving a mark behind; and such will be the fate of Adam Huntsman, if there is a fair fight and no gouging.

After the election was over, I sent Snelling the price of the rum, but took good care to keep the fact from the knowledge of my constituents.—Job refused the money, and sent me word, that it did him good to be taken in occasionally, as it served to brighten his ideas; but I afterwards learnt that when he found out the trick that had been played upon him, he put all the rum I had ordered, in his bill against my opponent, who, being elated with the speeches he had made on the affairs of the nation, could not descend to examine into the particulars of a bill of a vendor of rum in the small way.

CHAPTER XXIV.

AUGUST 11, 1835. I am now at home in Weakley county. My canvass is over, and the result is known. Contrary to all expectation, I am beaten two hundred and thirty votes, from the best information I can get; and in this instance, I may say, bad is the best. My mantle has fallen upon the shoulders of Adam, and I hope he may wear it with becoming dignity, and never lose sight of the welfare of the nation, for the purpose of elevating a few designing politicians to the head of the heap. The rotten policy pursued by "the Government" cannot last long; it will either work its own downfall, or the downfall of the republic, soon, unless the people tear the seal from their eyes, and behold their danger time enough to avert the ruin.

. . . . . .

I come within two hundred and thirty votes of being elected, notwithstanding I had to contend against "the greatest and the best," with the whole power of the Treasury against me. The Little Flying Dutchman will no doubt calculate upon having a true gamecock in Mr. Huntsman, but if he doesn't show them the White feather before the first session is over, I agree never to be set down for a prophet, that's all. I am gratified that I have spoken the truth to the people of my district regardless of consequences. I would not be compelled to bow down to the idol for a seat in Congress during life. I have never known what it was to sacrifice my own judgment to gratify any party, and I have no doubt of the time being close at hand when I will be rewarded for letting my tongue speak what my heart thinks. I have suffered myself to be politically sacrificed to save my country from ruin and disgrace, and if I am never again elected, I will have the gratification to know that I have done my duty.—Thus much I say in relation to the manner in which my downfall was effected, and in laying it before the public, "I take the responsibility." I may add in the words of the man in the play, "Crockett's occupation's gone."——

Two weeks and more have elapsed since I wrote the foregoing account of my defeat, and I confess the thorn still rankles, not so much on my own account as the nation's, for I had set my heart on following up the travelling deposites until they should be fairly gathered to their proper nest, like young chickens, for I am aware of the vermin that are on the constant look out to pounce upon them, like a cock at a blackberry, which they would have done long since, if it had not been for a few such men as Webster, Clay, and myself. It is my parting advice, that this matter be attended to without delay, for before long the little chickens will take wing, and even the powerful wand of the magician of Kinderhook will be unable to point out the course they have flown.

As my country no longer requires my services, I have made up my mind to go to Texas. My life has been one of danger, toil, and privation, but these difficulties I had to encounter at a time when I considered it nothing more than right good sport to surmount them; but now I start anew upon my own hook, and God only grant that it may be strong enough to support the weight that may be hung upon it. I have a new row to hoe, a long and rough one, but come what will I'll go ahead.

A few days ago I went to a meeting of my constituents. My appetite for politics was at one time just about as sharp set as a saw mill, but late events has given me something of surfeit,—more than I could well digest; still habit they say is second natur, and so I went, and gave them a piece of my mind touching "the Government" and the succession, by way of a codicil to what I have often said before.

. . . . . .

I told them moreover of my services, pretty straight up and down, for a man may be allowed to speak on such subjects when others are about to forget them; and I also told them of the manner in which I had been knocked down and dragged out, and that I did not consider it a fair fight any how they could fix it. I put the ingredients in the cup pretty strong I tell you, and I concluded my speech by telling them that I was done with politics for the present, and that they might all go to hell, and I would go to Texas.

When I returned home I felt a sort of cast down at the change that had taken place in my fortunes, and sorrow, it is said, will make even an oyster feel poetical. I never tried my hand at that sort of writing, but on this particular occasion such was my state of feeling, that I began to fancy myself inspired; so I took pen in hand, and as usual I went ahead. When I had got fairly through, my poetry looked as zigzag as a worm fence; the lines wouldn't tally, no how; so I showed them to Peleg Longfellow, who has a first-rate reputation with us for that sort of writing, having some years ago made a carrier's address for the Nashville Banner, and Peleg lopped off some lines, and stretched out others; but I wish I may be shot if I don't rather think he has made it worse than it was when I placed it in his hands. It being my first, and no doubt last piece of poetry, I will print it in this place, as it will serve to express my feelings on leaving my home, my neighbours, and friends and country, for a strange land, as fully as I could in plain prose.

Farewell to the mountains whose mazes to me
Were more beautiful far than Eden could be;
No fruit was forbidden, but Nature had spread
Her bountiful board, and her children were fed.
The hills were our garners—our herds wildly grew,
And Nature was shepherd and husbandman too.
I felt like a monarch, yet thought like a man,
As I thank'd the Great Giver, and worshipp'd His plan.

The home I forsake where my offspring arose:
The graves I forsake where my children repose.
The home I redeem'd from the savage and wild;
The home I have loved as a father his child;
The corn that I planted, the fields that I clear'd,
The flocks that I raised, and the cabin I rear'd;
The wife of my bosom—Farewell to ye all!
In the land of the stranger I rise—or I fall.

Farewell to my country!—I fought for thee well,
When the savage rush'd forth like the demons from hell.
In peace or in war I have stood by thy side—
My country, for thee I have lived—would have died!
But I am cast off—my career now is run,
And I wander abroad like the prodigal son—
Where the wild savage roves, and the broad prairies spread,
The fallen—despised—will again go ahead!

CHAPTER XXV.

IN my last chapter I made mention of my determination to cut and quit the States until such time as honest and independent men should again work their way to the head of the heap; and as I should probably have some idle time on hand before that state of affairs shall be brought about, I promised to give the Texians a helping hand, on the high road to freedom.—Well, I was always fond of having my spoon in a mess of that kind, for if there is any thing in this world particularly worth living for, it is freedom; any thing that would render death to a brave man particularly pleasant, it is freedom.

I am now on my journey, and have already tortled along as far as Little Rock on the Arkansas, about one hundred and twenty-five miles from the mouth. I had promised to write another book, expecting, when I made that promise, to write about politics, and use up "the Government," his successor, the removal of the deposites, and so on, matters and things that come as natural to me as bear hunting; but being rascalled out of my election, I am taken all aback, and I must now strike into a new path altogether. Still I will redeem my promise, and make a book, and it shall be about my adventures in Texas, hoping that my friends, Messrs. Webster and Clay and Biddle, will keep a sharp look out upon "the Government" during my absence,—I am told that every author of distinction writes a book of travels now-a-days.

My thermometer stood somewhat below the freezing point as I left my wife and children; still there was some thawing about the eyelids, a thing that had not taken place since I first ran away from my father's house when a thoughtless vagabond boy. I dressed myself in a clean hunting shirt, put on a new fox skin cap with the tail hanging behind, took hold of my rifle Betsey, which all the world knows was presented to me by the patriotic citizens of Philadelphia, as a compliment for my unflinching opposition to the tyrannic measures of "the Government," and thus equipped I started off, with a heavy heart, for Mill's Point, to take steamboat down the Mississippi, and go ahead in a new world.

While walking along, and thinking whether it was altogether the right grit to leave my poor country at a time she most needed my services, I came to a clearing, and I was slowly rising a slope, when I was startled by loud, profane, and boisterous voices, (as loud and profane as have been heard in the White House of late years), which seemed to proceed from a thick covert of undergrowth, about two hundred yards in advance of me, and about one hundred to the right of my road.

"You kin, kin you?"

"Yes I kin, and am able to do it! Boo-oo-oo!—O! wake snakes, and walk your chalks! Brimstone and —— fire! Don't hold me, Nick Stoval! The fight's made up, and let go at it. —— my soul if I don't jump down his throat and gallop every chitterling out of him, before you can say 'quit!'"

"Now, Nick, don't hold him! Jist let the wild cat come, and I'll tame him. Ned'll see me a fair fight—won't you, Ned?"

"O! yes, I'll see you a fair fight; blast my old shoes if I don't."

"That's sufficient, as Tom Haynes said, when he saw the elephant. Now let him come."

Thus they went on, with countless oaths interspersed, which I dare not even hint at, and with much that I could not distinctly hear.

In mercy's name! thought I, what a band of ruffians is at work here. I quickened my gait, and had come nearly opposite to the thick grove whence the noise proceeded, when my eye caught indistinctly, through the foliage of the dwarf oaks and hickories that intervened, glimpses of a man or men, who seemed to be on a violent struggle; and I could occasionally catch those deep drawn emphatic oaths, which men in conflict utter, when they deal blows. I hurried to the spot, but before I reached it, I saw the combatants come to the ground, and after a short struggle, I saw the uppermost one (for I could not see the other) make a heavy plunge with both his thumbs, and at the same instant I heard a cry in the accent of keenest torture, "Enough! my eye is out!"

I stood completely horror-struck for a moment. The accomplices in the brutal deed had all fled at my approach, at least I supposed so, for they were not to be seen.

"Now blast your corn-shucking soul," said the victor, a lad of about eighteen, as he rose from the ground, "come cuttin' your shines 'bout me agin, next time I come to the Court House, will you!—Get your owl-eye in agin if you can."

At this moment he saw me for the first time. He looked as though he couldn't help it, and was for making himself particularly scarce, when I called to him, "Come back, you brute, and assist me in relieving the poor critur you have ruined for ever."

Upon this rough salutation, he sort of collected himself, and with a taunting curl of the nose he replied, "You needn't kick before you're spurr'd. There an't nobody there, nor han't been nother. I was jist seein' how I could a 'fout." So saying he bounded to his plough, which stood in the corner of the fence about fifty yards from the battle ground.

Now would any man in his senses believe that a rational being could make such a darned fool of himself? but I wish I may be shot, if his report was not as true as the last Post Office report, every word, and a little more satisfactory. All that I had heard and seen was nothing more nor less than what is called a rehearsal of a knock-down and drag-out fight, in which the young man had played all the parts for his own amusement, and by way of keeping his hand in. I went to the ground from which he had risen, and there was the prints of his two thumbs, plunged up to the balls in the mellow earth, about the distance of a man's eyes apart, and the ground around was broken up, as if two stags had been engaged upon it.

As I resumed my journey I laughed outright at this adventure, for it reminded me of Andrew Jackson's attack upon the United States Bank. He had magnified it into a monster, and then begun to rip and tear and swear and gouge, until he thought he had the monster on its back; and when the fight was over, and he got up to look about for his enemy, he could find none for the soul of him, for his enemy was altogether in his heated imagination. These fighting characters are never at peace, unless they have something to quarrel with, and rather than have no fight at all, they will trample on their own shadows.

The day I arrived at Little Rock, I had no sooner quit the steamer than I streaked it straight ahead for the principal tavern, which is nothing to boast of, nohow, unless a man happens to be like the member of Congress from the south, who was converted to Jacksonism, and then made a speech as long as the longitude about his political honesty. Some men it seems, take a pride in saying a great deal about nothing—like windmills, their tongues must be going whether they have any grist to grind or not. This is all very well in Congress, where every member is expected to make a speech to let his constituents know that some things can be done as well as others; but I set it down as being rather an imposition upon good nature to be compelled to listen, without receiving the consideration of eight dollars per day, besides mileage, as we do in Congress. Many members will do nothing else for their pay but listen, day in and day out, and I wish I may be shot, if they do not earn every penny of it, provided they don't sleep, or Benton or little Isaac Hill will spin their yarns but once in a week. No man who has not tried it can imagine what dreadful hard work it is to listen. Splitting gum logs in the dog days is child's play to it. I've tried both, and give the preference to the gum logs.

Well, as I said, I made straight for the tavern, and as I drew nigh, I saw a considerable crowd assembled before the door. So, thought I, they have heard that Colonel Crockett intended to pay a visit to their settlement, and they have already got together to receive him in due form. I confess I felt a little elated at the idea, and commenced ransacking the lumber room of my brain, to find some one of my speeches that I might furbish up for the occasion; and then I shouldered my Betsey, straightened myself, and walked up to the door, charged to the muzzle and ready to let fly.

But strange as it may seem, no one took any more notice of me, than if I had been Martin Van Buren, or Dick Johnson, the celebrated wool grower. This took me somewhat aback, and I inquired what was the meaning of the gathering: and I learnt that a travelling showman had just arrived, and was about to exhibit for the first time the wonderful feats of Harlequin, and Punch and Judy, to the impatient natives. It was drawing towards nightfall, and expectation was on tiptoe: the children were clinging to their mothers' aprons, with their chubby faces dimpled with delight, and asking "What is it like? when will it begin?" and similar questions, while the women, as all good wives are in duty bound to do, appealed to their husbands for information; but the call for information was responded to in this instance, as is sometimes the case in Congress; their husbands understood the matter about as well as "the Government" did the Post Office accounts.

The showman at length made his appearance, with a countenance as woebegone as that of "the Government" when he found his batch of dirty nominations rejected by the Senate, and mentioned the impossibility that any performance should take place that evening, as the lame fiddler had over-charged his head, and having but one leg at best, it did not require much to destroy his equilibrium. And as all the world knows, a puppet show without a fiddle is like roast pork and no apple sauce. This piece of intelligence was received with a general murmur of dissatisfaction; and such was the indignation of his majesty, the sovereign people, at being thwarted in his rational amusements, that according to the established custom in such cases made and provided, there were some symptoms of a disposition to kick up a row, break the show, and finish the amusements of the day by putting Lynch's law in practice upon the poor showman.

. . . . . .

CHAPTER XXVI.

THE public mind having been quieted by the exhibition of the puppet show, and allowed to return to its usual channel, it was not long before the good people of Little Rock began to inquire what distinguished stranger had come among them; and learning that it was neither more nor less than the identical Colonel Crockett, the champion of the fugitive deposites, than straight they went ahead at getting up another tempest in a teapot; and I wish I may be shot, if I wasn't looked upon as almost as great a sight as Punch and Judy.

Nothing would answer but I must accept of an invitation to a public dinner. Now as public dinners have become so common, that it is enough to take away the appetite of any man, who has a proper sense of his own importance, to sit down and play his part in the humbug business, I had made up my mind to write a letter declining the honour, expressing my regret, and winding up with a flourish of trumpets about the patriotism of the citizens of Little Rock, and all that sort of thing, when the landlord came in, and says he, "Colonel, just oblige me by stepping into the back yard a moment."

I followed the landlord in silence, twisting and turning over in my brain, all the while, what I should say in my letter to the patriotic citizens of Little Rock, who were bent on eating a dinner for the good of their country; when he conducted me to a shed in the yard, where I beheld, hanging up, a fine fat cub bear, several haunches of venison, a wild turkey as big as a young ostrich, and small game too tedious to mention. "Well, Colonel, what do you think of my larder?" says he. —"Fine!" says I: "Let us liquor." We walked back to the bar, I took a horn, and without loss of time I wrote to the committee, that I accepted of the invitation to a public dinner with pleasure,—that I would always be found ready to serve my country either by eating or fasting; and that the honour the patriotic citizens of Little Rock had conferred upon me rendered it the proudest moment of my eventful life. The chairman of the committee was standing by while I wrote the letter, which I handed to him; and so his important business was soon settled.

As there was considerable time to be killed, or got rid of in some way, before the dinner could be cooked, it was proposed that we should go beyond the village, and shoot at a mark, for they had heard that I was a first-rate shot, and they wanted to see for themselves whether fame had not blown her trumpet a little too strong in my favour: for since she had represented "the Government" as being a first-rate statesman, and Colonel Benton as a first-rate orator, they could not receive such reports without proper allowance, as Congress thought of the Post Office report.

Well, I shouldered my Betsey, and she is just about as beautiful a piece as ever came out of Philadelphia, and I went out to the shooting ground, followed by all the leading men in Little Rock, and that was a clear majority of the town, for it is remarkable that there are always more leading men in small villages than there are followers.

I was in prime order. My eye was as keen as a lizard, and my nerves were as steady and unshaken as the political course of Henry Clay; so at it we went, the distance one hundred yards. The principal marksmen, and such as had never been beat, led the way, and there was some pretty fair shooting, I tell you. At length it came to my turn. I squared myself, raised my beautiful Betsey to my shoulder, took deliberate aim, and smack I sent the bullet right into the centre of the bull's eye. "There's no mistake in Betsey," said I, in a sort of careless way, as they were all looking at the target, sort of amazed, and not at all over pleased.

"That's a chance shot, Colonel," said one who had the reputation of being the best marksman in those parts.

"Not as much chance as there was," said I, "when Dick Johnson took his darkie for better for worse. I can do it five times out of six any day in the week." This I said in as confident a tone as "the Government" did when he protested that he forgave Colonel Benton for shooting him and he was now the best friend he had in the world. I knew it was not altogether as correct as it might be, but when a man sets about going the big figure, half-way measures won't answer no how; and "the greatest and the best" had set me the example, that swaggering will answer a good purpose at times.

They now proposed that we should have a second trial; but knowing that I had nothing to gain, and everything to lose, I was for backing out and fighting shy; but there was no let-off, for the cock of the village, though whipped, determined not to stay whipped; so to it again we went. They were now put upon their mettle, and they fired much better than the first time: and it was what might be called pretty sharp shooting. When it came to my turn, I squared myself, and turning to the prime shot, I gave him a knowing nod, by way of showing my confidence; and says I, "Look-out for the bull's eye, stranger." I blazed away, and I wish I may be shot if I didn't miss the target. They examined it all over, and could find neither hair nor hide of my bullet, and pronounced it a dead miss; when says I, "Stand aside and let me look, and I war'nt you I get on the right trail of the critter." They stood aside, and I examined the bull's eye pretty particular, and at length cried out, "Here it is; there is no snakes if it ha'n't followed the very track of the other." They said it was utterly impossible, but I insisted on their searching the hole, and I agreed to be stuck up as a mark myself, if they did not find two bullets there. They searched for my satisfaction, and sure enough it all came out just as I had told them; for I had picked up a bullet that had been fired, and stuck it deep into the hole, without any one perceiving it. They were all perfectly satisfied, that fame had not made too great a flourish of trumpets when speaking of me as a marksman; and they all said they had enough of shooting for that day, and they moved, that we adjourn to the tavern and liquor.

We had scarcely taken drinks round before the landlord announced that dinner was ready, and I was escorted into the dining room by the committee, to the tune of "See the conquering hero come," played upon a drum, which had been beaten until it got a fit of the sullens, and refused to send forth any sound; and it was accompanied by the weazing of a fife that was sadly troubled with a spell of the asthma. I was escorted into the dining room, I say, somewhat after the same fashion that "the Government" was escorted into the different cities when he made his northern tour; the only difference was, that I had no sycophants about me, but true hearted hospitable friends, for it was pretty well known that I had, for the present, abandoned all intention of running for the Presidency against the Little Flying Dutchman.

The dinner was first rate. The bear meat, the venison, and wild turkey would have tempted a man who had given over the business of eating altogether; and every thing was cooked to the notch precisely. The enterprising landlord did himself immortal honour on this momentous occasion; and the committee, thinking that he merited public thanks for his patriotic services, handed his name to posterity to look at in the lasting columns of the *Little Rock Gazette;* and when our children's children behold it, they will think of the pure patriots who sat down in good fellowship to feast on the bear meat and venison; and the enthusiasm the occasion is calculated to awaken will induce them to bless the patriot who, in a cause so glorious, spared no pains in cooking the dinner, and serving it in a becoming manner. And this is fame!

The fragments of the meats being cleared off, we went through the customary evolution of drinking thirteen regular toasts, after every one of which our drum with the loose skin grumbled like an old horse with an empty stomach; and our asthmatic fife squeaked like a stuck pig, a spirit-stirring tune, which we put off christening until we should come to prepare our proceedings for posterity.—The fife appeared to have but one tune in it; possibly it miught have had more, but the poor fifer, with all his puffing and blowing, his too-too-too-ing, and shaking his head and elbow, could not, for the body and soul of him, get more than one out of it. If the fife had had an extra tune to its name, sartin it wouldn't have been quite so hide bound on such an occasion, but have let us have it, good, bad, or indifferent. We warn't particular by no means.

Having gone through with the regular toasts, the president of the day drank, "Our distinguished guest, Col. Crockett," which called forth a prodigious clattering all around the table, and I soon saw that nothing would do, but I must get up and make them a speech. I had no sooner elongated my outward Adam, than they at it again, with renewed vigour, which made me sort of feel that I was still somebody, though no longer a member of Congress.

In my speech I went over the whole history of the present administration; took a long shot at the flying deposites, and gave an outline, a sort of charcoal sketch, of the political life of "the Government's" heir-presumptive.

. . . . . .

My speech was received with three times three, and all that; and we continued speechifying and drinking until nightfall, when it was put to vote, that we would have the puppet show over again, which was carried *nem. con.* The showman set his wires to work, just as "the Government" does the machinery in his big puppet show; and we spent a delightful and rational evening. We raised a subscription for the poor showman; and I went to bed, pleased and gratified with the hospitality and kindness of the citizens of Little Rock. There are some first-rate men there, of the real half-horse half-alligator breed, with a sprinkling of the steamboat, and such as grow no where on the face ot the universal earth, but just about the backbone of North America.

CHAPTER XXVII.

THE day after our public dinner I determined to leave my hospitable friends at Little Rock, and cross Arkansas to Fulton on the Red river, a distance of about one hundred and twenty miles. They wanted me to stay longer; and the gentleman who had the reputation of being the best marksman in those parts was most particularly anxious that we should have another trial of skill; but says I to myself, "Crockett, you've had just about glory enough for one day, so take my advice, and leave well enough alone." I declined shooting, for there was nothing at all to be gained by it, and I might possibly lose some little of the reputation I had acquired. I have always found that it is a very important thing for a man who is fairly going ahead, to know exactly how far to go, and when to stop. . . .

Finding that I was bent on going, for I became impatient to get into Texas, my kind friends at Little Rock procured me a good horse to carry me across to Red river. There are no bounds to the good feeling of the pioneers of the west; they consider nothing a trouble that will confer a favour upon a stranger that they chance to take a fancy to; true, we are something like chestnut burs on the outside, rather prickly if touched roughly, but there's good fruit within.

My horse was brought to the door of the tavern, around which many of the villagers were assembled. The drum and fife were playing what was intended for a lively tune, but the skin of the drum still hung as loose as the hide of a fat man far gone in a consumption; and the fife had not yet recovered from the asthma. The music sounded something like a fellow singing, "Away with melancholy," on the way to the gallows. I took my leave of the landlord, shook hands with the showman, who had done more than an average business, kissed his wife, who had recovered, and bidding farewell to all my kind hearted friends, I mounted my horse, and left the village, accompanied by four or five gentlemen. The drum and fife now appeared to exert themselves, and made more noise than usual, while the crowd sent forth three cheers to encourage me on my way.

I tried to raise some recruits for Texas among my companions, but they said they had their own affairs to attend to, which would keep them at home for the present, but no doubt they would come over and see us as soon as the disturbances should be settled. They looked upon Texas as being part of the United States, though the Mexicans did claim it; and they had no doubt the time was not very distant when it would be received into the glorious Union.

My companions did not intend seeing me farther on my way than the Washita river, near fifty miles. Conversation was pretty brisk, for we talked about the affairs of the nation and Texas; subjects that are by no means to be exhausted, if one may judge by the long speeches made in Congress, where they talk year in and year out; and it would seem that as much still remains to be said as ever. As we drew nigh to the Washita, the silence was broken alone by our own talk and the clattering of our horses' hoofs; and we imagined ourselves pretty much the only travellers, when we were suddenly somewhat startled by the sound of music. We checked our horses, and listened, and the music continued. "What can all that mean?" says I. "Blast my old shoes if I know, Colonel," says one of the party. We listened again, and we now heard, "Hail, Columbia, happy land!" played in first-rate style. "That's fine," says I. "Fine as silk, Colonel, and leetle finer," says the other; "but hark, the tune's changed." We took another spell of listening, and now the musician struck up, in a brisk and lively manner, "Over the water to Charley." "That's mighty mysterious," says one; "Can't cipher it out no how," says another; "A notch beyant my measure," says a third. "Then let us go ahead," says I, and off we dashed at a pretty rapid gait, I tell you —by no means slow.

As we approached the river we saw to the right of the road a new clearing on a hill, where several men were at work, and they running down the hill like wild Indians, or rather like the office holders in pursuit of the deposites. There appeared to be no time to be lost, so they ran, and we cut ahead for the crossing. The music continued in all this time stronger and stronger, and the very notes appeared to speak distinctly, "Over the water to Charley."

When we reached the crossing we were struck all of a heap, at beholding a man seated in a sulky in the middle of the river, and playing for life on a fiddle. The horse was up to his middle in the water; and it seemed as if the flimsy vehicle was ready to be swept away by the current. Still the fiddler fiddled on composedly, as if his life had been insured, and he was nothing more than a passenger. We thought he was mad, and shouted to him. He heard us, and stopped his music. "You have missed the crossing," shouted one of the men from the clearing. "I know I have," returned the fiddler. "If you go ten feet farther you will be drowned." "I know I shall," returned the fiddler. "Turn back," said the man. "I can't," said the other "Then how the devil will you get out?" "I'm sure I don't know; come you and help me."

The men from the clearing, who understood the river, took our horses and rode up to the sulky, and after some difficulty, succeeded in bringing the traveller safe to shore, when we recognized the worthy parson who had fiddled for us at the puppet show at Little Rock. They told him that he had had a narrow escape, and he replied, that he had found that out an hour ago. He said he had been fiddling to the fishes for a full hour, and had exhausted all the tunes that he could play without notes. We then asked him what could have

22

induced him to think of fiddling at a time of such peril; and he replied, that he had remarked in his progress through life, that there was nothing in universal natur so well calculated to draw people together as the sound of a fiddle; and he knew, that he might bawl until he was hoarse for assistance, and no one would stir a peg; but they would no sooner hear the scraping of his catgut, than they would quit all other business, and come to the spot in flocks. We laughed heartily at the knowledge the parson showed of human natur.—And he was right.

Having fixed up the old gentleman's sulky right and tight, and after rubbing down his poor jaded animal, the company insisted on having a dance before we separated. We all had our flasks of whisky; we took a drink all round, and though the parson said he had had about enough fiddling for one day, he struck up with great good humour; at it we went and danced straight fours for an hour and better. We all enjoyed ourselves very much, but came to the conclusion, that dancing wasn't altogether the thing without a few petticoats to give it variety.

The dance being over, our new friends pointed out the right fording, and assisted the parson across the river. We took another drink all round, and after shaking each other cordially by the hand, we separated, wishing each other all the good fortune that the rugged lot that has been assigned us will afford. My friends retraced the road to Little Rock, and I pursued my journey; and as I thought of their disinterested kindness to an entire stranger, I felt that the world is not quite as heartless and selfish as some grumblers would have us think.

. . . .

I kept in company with the parson until we arrived at Greenville, and I do say, he was just about as pleasant an old gentleman to travel with, as any man who wasn't too darned particular, could ask for. We talked about politics, religion, and natur, farming and bear hunting, and the many blessings that an all bountiful Providence has bestowed upon our happy country. He continued to talk upon this subject, travelling over the whole ground as it were, until his imagination glowed, and his soul became full to overflowing; and he checked his horse, and I stopped mine also, and a stream of eloquence burst forth from his aged lips, such as I have seldom listened to: it came from the overflowing fountain of a pure and grateful heart. We were alone in the wilderness, but as he proceeded, it seemed to me as if the tall trees bent their tops to listen;—that the mountain stream laughed out joyfully as it bounded on like some living thing; that the fading flowers of autumn smiled, and sent forth fresher fragrance, as if conscious that they would revive in spring; and even the sterile rocks seemed to be endued with some mysterious influence. We were alone in the wilderness, but all things told me that God was there. That thought renewed my strength and courage. I had left my country, felt somewhat like an outcast, believed that I had been neglected and lost sight of; but I was now conscious that there was still one watchful Eye over me; no matter whether I dwelt in the populous cities, or threaded the pathless forest alone; no matter whether I stood in the high places among men, or made my solitary lair in the untrodden wild, that Eye was still upon me. My very soul leaped joyfully at the thought; I never felt so grateful in all my life; I never loved my God so sincerely in all my life. I felt that I still had a friend.

When the old man finished I found that my eyes were wet with tears. I approached and pressed his hand, and thanked him, and says I, "Now let us take a drink." I set him the example, and he followed it, and in a style too that satisfied me, that if he had ever belonged to the Temperance society, he had either renounced membership or obtained a dispensation. Having liquored, we proceeded on our journey, keeping a sharp look-out for mill-seats and plantations as we rode along.

I left the worthy old man at Greenville, and sorry enough I was to part with him, for he talked a great deal, and he seemed to know a little about everything. He knew all about the history of the country; was well acquainted with all the leading men; knew where all the good lands lay in most of the western states, as well as the cutest clerk in the Land Office; and had traced most of the rivers to their sources. He was very cheerful and happy, though to all appearances very poor. I thought that he would make a first-rate agent for taking up lands, and mentioned it to him; he smiled, and pointing above, said, "My wealth lies not in this world."

I mounted my horse and pushed forward on my road to Fulton. When I reached Washington, a village a few miles from the Red river, I rode up to the Black Bear tavern, when the following conversation took place between me and the landlord, which is a pretty fair sample of the curiosity of some folks:—

"Good morning, mister—I don't exactly recollect your name now," said the landlord as I alighted.

"It's of no consequence," said I.

"I'm pretty sure I've seen ye somewhere."

"Very likely you may, I've been there frequently."

"I was sure 'twas so; but strange I should forget your name," says he.

"It is indeed somewhat strange that you should forget what you never knew," says I.

"It is unaccountable strange. It's what I'm not often in the habit of, I assure you. I have, for the most part, a remarkably detentive memory. In the power of people that pass along this way, I've scarce ever made, as the doctors say, a *slapsus slinkum* of this kind afore."

"Eh heh!" I shouted, while the critter continued.

"Travelling to the western country, I presume, mister?"

"Presume any thing you please, sir," says I, "but don't trouble me with your presumptions."

"O Lord, no, sir—I won't do that. I've no ideer of that—not the least ideer in the world," says he; "I suppose you've been to the westward afore now?"

"Well, suppose I have?"

"Why, on that supposition, I was going to say you must be pretty well—that is to say, you must know something about the place."

"Eh heh!" I ejaculated, looking sort of mazed full in his face. The tarnel critter still went ahead.

"I take it your a married man, mister?"

"Take it as you will, that is no affair of mine," says I.

"Well, after all, a married life is the most happiest way of living; don't you think so, mister?"

"Very possible," says I.

"I conclude you have a family of children, sir?"

"I don't know what reason you have to conclude so."

"Oh, no reason in the world, mister, not the least," says he; "but I thought I might just take the liberty to make the presumption, you know, that's all, sir. I take it mister your a man about my age?"

"Eh heh!"

"How old do you call yourself, if I may be so bold?"

"You're bold enough, the devil knows," says I; and as I spoke rather sharp, the varment seemed rather staggered, but he soon recovered himself, and came up to the chalk again.

"No offence I hope—I—I—I—wouldn't be thought uncivil by any means; I always calculate to treat every body with civility."

"You have a very strange way of showing it."

"True, as you say, I ginerally take my own way in these ere matters.—Do you practise law, mister, or farming, or mechanicals?"

"Perhaps so," says I.

"Ah, I judge so; I was pretty certain it must be the case. Well, it's as good business as any there is followed now-a-days."

"Eh heh!" I shouted, and my lower jaw fell in amazement at his perseverance.

"I take it you've money at interest, mister?" continued the varment, without allowing himself time to take breath.

"Would it be of any particular interest to you to find out?" says I.

"O, not at all, not the least in the world, sir, I'm not at all inquisitive about other people's matters; I mind's my own business—that's my way."

"And a very odd way you have of doing it too."

"I've been thinking what persuasion you're of—whether you're a Unitarian or Baptist, or whether you belong to the Methodisses."

"Well, what's the conclusion?"

"Why, I have concluded that I'm pretty near right in my conjectures. Well, after all, I'm inclined to think they're the nearest right of any persuasion—though some folks think differently."

"Eh heh!" I shouted again.

"As to pollyticks, I take it, you—that is to say, I suppose you——"

"Very likely."

"Ah! I could have sworn it was so from the moment I saw you. I have a knack at finding out a man's sentiments. I dare say, mister, you're a justice in your own country?"

"And if I may return the compliment, I should say you're a just ass, every where." By this time I began to get weary of his impertinence, and led my horse to the trough to water, but the darned critter followed me up.

"Why, yes," said he, "I'm in the commission of the peace, to be sure—and an officer in the militia—though between you and I, I wouldn't wish to boast of it."

My horse having finished drinking, I put one foot in the stirrup, and was preparing to mount—"Any more enquiries to make?" said I.

"Why, no, nothing to speak on," said he, "When do you return, mister?"

"About the time I come back," said I; and leaping into the saddle galloped off. The pestiferous varment bawled after me, at the top of his voice,—

"Well, I shall look for ye then. I hope you won't fail to call."

Now, who in all natur do you reckon the critter was, who afforded so fine a sample of the impertinent curiosity that some people have to pry into other people's affairs?

I knew him well enough at first sight, though he seemed to have forgotten me. It was no other than Job Snelling, the manufacturer of cayenne pepper out of mahogany sawdust, and upon whom I played the trick with the coon skin. I pursued my journey to Fulton, and laughed heartily to think what a swither I had left poor Job in, at not gratifying his curiosity; for I knew he was one of those fellows who would peep down your throat just to ascertain what you had eaten for dinner.

When I arrived at Fulton, I inquired for a gentlemen to whom my friends at Little Rock had given me a letter of introduction. I was received in the most hospitable manner; and as the steamboat did not start for Natchitoches until the next day, I spent the afternoon in seeing all that was to be seen. I left the horse with the gentleman, who promised to have him safely returned to the owner; and I took the steamboat, and started on my way down the Red river, right well pleased with my reception at Fulton.

CHAPTER XXVIII.

THERE was a considerable number of passengers on board the boat, and our assortment was somewhat like the Yankee merchant's cargo of notions, pretty particularly miscellaneous, I tell you. I moved through the crowd from stem to stern, to see if I could discover any face that was not altogether strange to me; but after a general survey, I concluded that I had never seen one of them before. There were merchants and emigrants and gamblers, but none who seemed to have embarked in the particular business that for the time being occupied my mind—I could find none who were going to Texas. All seemed to have their hands full enough of their own affairs, without meddling with the cause of freedom. The greater share of glory will be mine, thought I, so go ahead, Crockett.

I saw a small cluster of passengers at one end of the boat, and hearing an occasional burst of laughter, thinks I, there's some sport started in that quarter, and having nothing better to do, I'll go in for my share of it. Accordingly I drew nigh to the cluster, and seated on the chest was a tall lank sea sarpent looking blackleg, who had crawled over from Natchez under the hill, and was amusing the passengers with his skill at thimblerig; at the same time he was picking up their shillings just about as expeditiously as a hungry gobbler would a pint of corn. He was doing what might be called an average business in a small way, and lost no time in gathering up the fragments.

I watched the whole process for some time and found that he had adopted the example set by the old tempter himself, to get the weather-gauge of us poor weak mortals. He made it a point to let his victims always win the first stake, that they might be tempted to go ahead; and then, when they least suspected it, he would come down upon them like a hurricane in a cornfield, sweeping all before it.

I stood looking on, seeing him pick up the chicken feed from the greenhorns, and thought if men are such darned fools as to be cheated out of their hard earning by a fellow who had just brains enough to pass a pea from one thimble to another, with such slight of hand, that you could not tell under which he had deposited it; it is not astonishing that the magician of Kinderhook should play thimblerig upon the big figure, and attempt to cheat the whole nation. . . .

The thimble conjurer saw me looking on, and eyeing me as if he thought I would be a good subject, said carelessly, "Come, stranger, won't you take a chance?" the whole time passing the pea from one thimble to the other, by way of throwing out a bait for the gudgeons to bite at. "I never gamble, stranger," says I, "principled against it; think it a slippery way of getting through the world at best." "Them are my sentiments to a notch," says he; "but this is not gambling by no means. A little innocent pastime, nothing more. Better take a hack by way of trying your luck at guessing." All this time he continued working with his thimbles; first putting the pea under one, which was plain to be seen, and then uncovering it, would show that the pea was there; he would then put it under the second thimble, and do the same, and then under the third; all of which he did to show how easy it would be to guess where the pea was deposited, if one would only keep a sharp look-out.

"Come, stranger," says he to me again, "you had better take a chance. Stake a trifle, I don't care how small, just for the fun of the thing."

"I am principled against betting money," says I, "but I don't mind going in for drinks for the present company, for I'm as dry as one of little Isaac Hill's regular set speeches."

"I admire your principles," says he, "and to show that I play with these here thimbles just for the sake of pastime, I will take that bet, though I am a whole hog temperance man. Just say when, stranger."

He continued all the time slipping the pea from one thimble to another; my eye was as keen as a lizard's, and when he stopped, I cried out, "Now; the pea is under the middle thimble." He was going to raise it to show that it wasn't there, when I interfered, and said, "Stop, if you please," and raised it myself, and sure enough the pea was there; but it mought have been otherwise if he had had the uncovering of it.

"Sure enough you've won the bet," says he. "You've a sharp eye, but I don't care if I give you another chance. Let us go fifty cents this bout; I'm sure you'll win."

"Then you're a darned fool to bet, stranger," says I; "and since that is the case, it would be little better than picking your pocket to bet with you; so I'll let it alone."

"I don't mind running the risk," said he.

"But I do," says I; "and since I always let well enough alone, and I have had just about glory enough for one day, let us all got to the bar and liquor."

This called forth a loud laugh at the thimble conjurer's expense; and he tried hard to induce me to take just one chance more, but he mought just as well have sung psalms to a dead horse, for my mind was made up, and I told him, that I looked upon gambling as about the dirtiest way that a man could adopt to get through this dirty world; and that I would never bet anything beyond a quart of whisky upon a rifle shot, which I considered a legal bet, and gentlemanly and rational amusement. "But all this cackling," says I, "makes me very thirsty, so let us adjourn to the bar and liquor."

He gathered up his thimbles, and the whole company followed us to the bar, laughing heartily at the conjurer; for, as he had won some of their money, they were sort of delighted to see him beaten with his own cudgel. He tried to laugh too, but his laugh wasn't at all pleasant, and rather forced. The barkeeper placed a big-bellied bottle before us; and after mixing our liquor, I was called on for a toast, by one of the company, a chap just about as rough hewn as if he had been cut out of a gum log with a broad axe, and sent into the market without even being smoothed off with a jack plane,—one of them chaps who, in their journey through life, are always ready for a fight or a frolic, and don't care the toss of a copper which.

"Well, gentlemen," says I, "being called upon for a toast, and being in a slave-holding state, in order to avoid giving offence, and running the risk of being Lynched, it may be necessary to premise that I am neither an abolitionist nor a colonizationist, but simply Colonel Crockett, of Tennessee, now bound for Texas." When they heard my name they gave three cheers for Colonel Crockett; and silence being restored, I continued, "Now, gentlemen, I will offer you a toast, hoping, after what I have stated, that it will give offence to no one present; but should I be mistaken, I must imitate the 'old Roman, and take the responsibility. I offer, gentlemen, The abolition of slavery: Let the work first begin in the two houses of Congress. There are no slaves in the country more servile than the party slaves in Congress. The wink or the nod of their masters is all sufficient for the accomplishment of the most dirty work." . . .

The thimble conjurer having asked the barkeeper how much there was to pay, was told that there were sixteen smallers, which amounted to one dollar. He was about to lay down the blunt, but not in Benton's metallic currency, which I find has already become as shy as honesty with an office holder, but he planked down one of Biddle's notes, when I interfered, and told him that the barkeeper had made a mistake.

"How so?" demanded the barkeeper.

"How much do you charge," says I, "when you retail your liquor?"

"A fip a glass."

"Well, then," says I, "as Thimblerig here, who belongs to the temperance society, took it in wholesale, I reckon you can afford to let him have it at half price?"

Now, as they had all notice that the conjurer went what is called the heavy wet, they laughed outright, and we heard no more about temperance from that quarter. When we returned to the deck the blackleg set to work with his thimbles again, and bantered me to bet; but I told him that it was against my principle, and as I had already reaped glory enough for one day, I would just let well enough alone for the present. . . .

One of the passengers, hearing that I was on board of the boat came up to me, and began to talk about the affairs of the nation, and said a good deal in favour of "the Magician," and wished to hear what I had to say against him. He talked loud, which is the way with all politicians educated in the Jackson school; and by his slangwhanging, drew a considerable crowd around us. Now, this was the very thing I wanted, as I knew I should not soon have another opportunity of making a political speech; he no sooner asked to hear what I had to say against his candidate, than I let him have it, strong and hot as he could take, I tell you.

. . . . . .

My speech was received with great applause, and the politician, finding that I was better acquainted with his candidate than he was himself, for I wrote his life, shut his fly trap, and turned on his heel without saying a word. He found that he had barked up the wrong tree. I afterward learnt that he was a mail contractor in those parts, and that he also had large dealings in the Land Office, and therefore thought it necessary to chime in with his penny whistle, in the universal chorus. There's a large band of the same description, but I'm thinking Uncle Sam will some day find out that he has paid too much for the piper.

CHAPTER XXIX.

AFTER my speech, and setting my face against gambling, poor Thimblerig was obliged to break off conjuring for want of customers, and call it half a day. He came and entered into conversation with me, and I found him a good-natured, intelligent fellow, with a keen eye for the main chance. He belonged to that numerous class, that it is perfectly safe to trust as far as a tailor can sling a bull by the tail—but no farther. He told me that he had been brought up a gentleman; that is to say, he was not instructed in any useful pursuit by which he could obtain a livelihood, so that when he found he had to depend upon himself for the necessaries of life, he began to suspect that dame nature would have conferred a particular favour if she had consigned him to the care of any one else. She had made a very injudicious choice when she selected him to sustain the dignity of a gentleman.

The first bright idea that occurred to him as a speedy means of bettering his fortune, would be to marry an heiress. Accordingly he looked about himself pretty sharp, and after glancing from one fair object to another, finally, his hawk's eye rested upon the young and pretty daughter of a wealthy planter. Thimblerig run his brazen face with his tailor for a new suit, for he abounded more in that metallic currency than he did in either Benton's mint drops or in Biddle's notes; and having the gentility of his outward Adam thus endorsed by his tailor—an important endorsement, by-the-way, as times go—he managed to obtain an introduction to the planter's daughter.

Our worthy had the principle of going ahead strongly developed. He was possessed of considerable address; and had brass enough in his face to make a wash-kettle : .and having once got access to the planter's house, it was no easy matter to dislodge him. In this he resembled those politicians who commence life as office holders; they will hang on tooth and nail, and even when death shakes them off, you'll find a commission of some kind crumpled up in their clenched fingers. Little Van appears to belong to this class—there's no beating his snout from the public crib. He'll feed there while there's a grain of corn left, and even then, from long habit, he'll set to work and gnaw at the manger.

Thimblerig got the blind side of the planter, and every thing to outward appearances went on swimmingly. Our worthy boasted to his cronies that the business was settled, and that in a few weeks he should occupy the elevated station in society that nature had designed him to adorn. He swelled like the frog in the fable, or rather, like Johnson's wife, of Kentucky, when the idea occurred to her of figuring away at Washington.—But there's many a slip 'twixt the cup and the lip, says the proverb, and suddenly Thimblerig discontinued his visits at the planter's house. His friends inquired of him the meaning of this abrupt termination of his devotions.

"I have been treated with disrespect," replied the worthy, indignantly.

"Disrespect! in what way?"

"My visits, it seems, are not altogether agreeable."

"But how have you ascertained that?"

"I received a hint to that effect; and I can take a hint as soon as another."

"A hint!—and have you allowed a hint to drive you from the pursuit? For shame. Go back again."

"No, no, never! a hint is sufficient for a man of my gentlemanly feelings. I asked the old man for his daughter."

"Well, what followed? what did he say?"

"Didn't say a word."

"Silence gives consent all the world over."

"So I thought. I then told him to fix the day."

"Well, what then?"

"Why, then he kicked me down stairs, and ordered his slaves to pump upon me. That's hint enough for me, that my visits are not properly appreciated; and blast my old shoes if I condescend to renew the acquaintance, or notice them in any way until they send for me."

As Thimblerig's new coat became rather too seedy to play the part of a gentleman much longer in real life, he determined to sustain that character upon the stage, and accordingly joined a company of players. He began, according to custom, at the top of the ladder, and was regularly hissed and pelted through every gradation until he found himself at the lowest rowel. "This," said he, "was a dreadful check to proud ambition;" but he consoled himself with the idea of peace and quietness in his present obscure walk; and though he had no prospect of being elated by the applause of admiring multitudes, he no longer trod the scene of mimic glory in constant dread of becoming a target for rotten eggs and oranges.—"And there was much in that," said Thimblerig. But this calm could not continue or ever.

The manager, who, like all managers who pay salaries regularly, was as absolute behind the scenes as the "old Roman" is in the White House, had fixed upon getting up an eastern spectacle, called the Cataract of the Ganges. He intended to introduce a fine procession, in which an elephant was to be the principal feature. Here a difficulty occurred. What was to be done for an elephant? Alligators were plenty in those parts, but an elephant was not to be had for love or money. But an alligator would not answer the purpose, so he determined to make a pasteboard elephant as large as life, and twice as natural. The next difficulty was to find members of the company of suitable dimensions to perform the several members of the pasteboard star. The manager cast his eye upon the long, gaunt figure of the unfortunate Thimblerig, and cast him for the hinder legs, the rump, and part of the back of the elephant. The poor player expostulated, and the manager replied, that he would appear as a star on the occasion, and would no doubt receive more applause than he had during his whole career. "But I shall not be seen," said the player.—"All the better," replied the manager, "as in that case you will have nothing to apprehend from eggs and oranges."

Thimblerig, finding that mild expostulation availed nothing, swore that he would not study the part, and accordingly threw it up in dignified disgust. He said that it was an outrage upon the feelings of the proud representative of Shakespeare's heroes, to be compelled to play pantomime in the hinder parts of the noblest animal that ever trod the stage. If it had been the fore quarters of the elephant, it might possibly have been made a speaking part; at any rate, he might have snorted through the trunk, if nothing more; but from the position he was to occupy, damned the word could he utter, or even roar with propriety. He therefore positively refused to act, as he considered it an insult to his reputation to tread the stage in such a character; and he looked upon the whole affair as a profanation of the legitimate drama. The result was, our worthy was discharged from the company, and compelled to commence hoeing another row.

He drifted to New Orleans, and hired himself as marker to a gambling table. Here he remained but a few months, for his idea of arithmetic differed widely from those of his employer, and accordingly they had some difficulty in balancing their cash account; for when his employer, in adding up the receipts, made it nought and carry two, Thimblerig insisted that it should be nought and carry one; and in order to prove that he was correct, he carried himself off, and left nothing behind him.

He now commenced professional blackleg on his own hook, and took up his quarters in Natchez under the hill. Here he remained, doing business in a small way, until Judge Lynch commenced his practice in that quarter, and made the place too hot for his comfort. He shifted his habitation, but not having sufficient capital to go the big figure, he practised the game of thimblerig until he acquired considerable skill, and then commenced passing up and down the river in the steamboats; and managed, by close attention to business, to pick up a decent livelihood in the small way, from such as had more pence in their pockets than sense in their noddles.

I found Thimblerig to be a pleasant talkative fellow. He communicated the foregoing facts with as much indifference as if there had been nothing disgraceful in his career; and at times he would chuckle with an air of triumph at the adroitness he had displayed in some of the knavish tricks he had practised. He looked upon this world as one vast stage, crowded with empirics and jugglers; and that he who could practise his deceptions with the greatest skill was entitled to the greatest applause.

I asked him to give me an account of Natchez and his adventures there, and I would put it in the book I intended to write, when he gave me the following, which betrays that his feelings were still somewhat irritated at being obliged to give them leg bail when Judge Lynch made his appearance. I give it in his own words:

"Natchez is a land of fevers, alligators, niggers, and cotton bales: where the sun shines with force sufficient to melt the diamond, and the word ice is expunged from the dictionary, for its definition cannot be comprehended by the natives: where to refuse grog before breakfast would degrade you below the brute creation; and where a good dinner is looked upon as an angel's visit, and voted a miracle; where the evergreen and majestic magnolia tree, with its superb flower, unknown to the northern climes, and its fragrance unsurpassed, calls forth the admiration of every beholder; and the dark moss hangs in festoons from the forest trees like the drapery of a funeral pall: where bears, the size of young jackasses, are fondled in lieu of pet dogs; and knives, the length of a barber's pole, usurp the place of toothpicks: where the filth of the town is carried off by buzzards, and the inhabitants are carried off by fevers: . . . where the poorest slave has plenty of yellow boys, but not of Benton's mintage; and indeed the shades of colour are so varied and mixed, that a nigger is frequently seen black and blue at the same time. And such is Natchez.

"The town is divided into two parts, as distinct in character as they are in appearance. Natchez on the hill, situated upon a high bluff overlooking the Mississippi, is a pretty little town with streets regularly laid out, and ornamented with divers handsome public buildings. Natchez under the hill,—where, O! where, shall I find words suitable to describe the peculiarities of that unholy spot? 'Tis, in fact, the jumping off place. Satan looks on it with glee, and chuckles as he beholds the orgies of his votaries."

. . . . . .

Thimblerig had also been at Vicksburg in his time, and entertained as little liking for that place as he did for Natchez. He had luckily made his escape a short time before the recent clearing-out of the slight-of-hand gentry; and he reckoned some time would elapse before he would pay them another visit. He said they must become more civilized first. All the time he was talking to me he was seated on a chest, and playing mechanically with his pea and thimbles, as if he was afraid that he would lose the slight unless he kept his hand in constant practice. Nothing of any consequence occurred in our passage down the river, and I arrived at Natchitoches in perfect health, and in good spirits.

CHAPTER XXX.

NATCHITOCHES is a post town and seat of justice for the parish of Natchitoches, Louisiana, and is situated on the right bank of the Red river. The houses are chiefly contained in one street, running parallel to the river; and the population I should reckon at about eight hundred. The soil in this parish is generally sterile, and covered with pine timber, except near the margin of Red river, where the greatest part of the inhabitants are settled on the alluvial banks. Some other, though comparatively small, tracts of productive soil skirt the streams. An extensive body of low ground, subject to annual submersion, extends along the Red river, which, it is said, will produce forty bushels of frogs to the acre, and alligators enough to fence it.

I stayed two days at Natchitoches, during which time I procured a horse to carry me across Texas to the seat of war. Thimblerig remained with me, and I found his conversation very amusing; for he is possessed of humour and observation, and has seen something of the world. Between whiles he would amuse himself with his thimbles, to which he appeared greatly attached, and occasionally he would pick up a few shillings from the tavern loungers. He no longer asked me to play with him, for he felt somewhat ashamed to do so, and he knew it would be no go.

I took him to task in a friendly manner, and tried to shame him out of his evil practices. I told him that it was a burlesque on human nature, that an able bodied man, possessed of his full share of good sense, should voluntarily debase himself, and be indebted for subsistence to such pitiful artifice.

"But what's to be done, Colonel?" says he. "I'm in the slough of despond, up to the very chin. A miry and slippery path to travel."

"Then hold your head up," says I, "before the slough reaches your lips."

"But what's the use?" says he; "it's utterly impossible for me to wade through; and even if I could, I should be in such a dirty plight, that it would defy all the waters in the Mississippi to wash me clean again. No," he added, in a desponding tone, "I should be like a live eel in a frying pan, Colonel, sort of out of my element, if I attempted to live like an honest man at this time o' day."

"That I deny. It is never too late to become honest," said I. "But even admit what you say to be true—that you cannot live like an honest man, you have at least the next best thing in your power, and no one can say nay to it."

"And what is that?"

"Die like a brave one. And I know not whether, in the eyes of the world, a brilliant death is not preferred to an obscure life of rectitude. Most men are remembered as they died, and not as they lived. We gaze with admiration upon the glories of the setting sun, yet scarcely bestow a passing glance upon its noonday splendour."

"You are right; but how is this to be done?"

"Accompany me to Texas. Cut aloof from your degrading habits and associates here, and in fighting for their freedom, regain your own."

He started from the table, and hastily gathering up the thimbles with which he had been playing all the time I was talking to him, he thrust them into his pocket, and after striding two or three times across the room, suddenly stopped, his leaden eye kindled, and grasping me by the hand violently, he exclaimed with an oath, "By ——— I'll be a man again. Live honestly, or die bravely. I go with you to Texas."

I said what I could to confirm him in his resolution, and finding that the idea had taken fast hold of his mind, I asked him to liquor, which he did not decline, notwithstanding the temperance habits that he boasted of; we then took a walk on the banks of the river.

. . . . . .

I descended to the street in front of the inn. The stars were faintly glimmering in the heavens, and the first beams of the morning sun were struggling through the dim clouds that skirted the eastern horizon. I thought myself alone in the street, when the hush of morning was suddenly broken by a clear, joyful, and musical voice, which sang, as near as I could catch it, the following scrap of a song:

"Oh, what is the time of the merry round year,
That is fittest and sweetest for love?
Ere sucks the bee, ere buds the tree;
And primroses by two, by three,
Faintly shine in the path of the lonely deer,
Like the few stars of twilight above."

I turned towards the spot whence the sounds proceeded, and discovered a tall figure leaning against the sign post. His eyes were fixed on the streaks of light in the east; his mind was absorbed, and he was clearly unconscious of any one being near him. He continued his song in so full and clear a tone, that the street re-echoed—

"When the blackbird and thrush, at early dawn,
Prelude from leafy spray—
Amid dewy scents and blandishments,
Like a choir attuning their instruments,
Ere the curtain of nature aside be drawn
For the concert the live long day."

I now drew nigh enough to see him distinctly. He was a young man, not more than twenty-two. His figure was light and graceful, and at the same time it indicated strength and activity. He was dressed in a hunting shirt, which was made with uncommon neatness, and ornamented tastily with fringe. He held a highly finished rifle in his right hand, and a hunting pouch, covered with Indian ornaments, was slung across his shoulders. His clean shirt collar was open, secured only by a black riband around his neck. His boots were polished without a soil upon them; and on his head was a neat fur cap, tossed on in a manner which said, "I don't care a d——n," just as plainly as any cap could speak it. I thought it must be some popinjay of a lark, until I took a look at his countenance. It was handsome, bright, and manly. There was no mistake in that face. From the eyes down to his breast he was sunburnt as dark as mahogany, while the upper part of his high forehead was as white and polished as marble. Thick clusters of black hair curled from under his cap. I passed on unperceived, and he continued his song:—

"In the green spring-tide, all tender and bright,
When the sun sheds a kindlier gleam
O'er the velvet bank, that sweet flowers prank—
That have fresh dews and sunbeams drank—
Softest and most chaste, as enchanted light
In the visions of maiden's dream."

. . . .

The stranger now came to me, calling me by name. I expressed some astonishment at being known to him, and he said that he had heard of my being in the village, and had sought me out for the purpose of accompanying me to Texas. He told me that he was a bee hunter; that he had travelled pretty much over that country in the way of his business, and that I would find him of considerable use in navigating through the ocean of prairies.

He told me that honey trees are abundant in Texas, and that honey of an excellent quality, and in any quantity, may be obtained from them. There are persons who have a peculiar tact in coursing the bee, and thus discovering their deposites of the luscious food. This employment is not a mere pastime, but is profitable. The wax alone, thus obtained, is a valuable article of commerce in Mexico, and commands a high price. It is much used in churches, where some of the candles made use of are as long as a man's arm. It often happens that the hunters throw away the honey, and save only the wax.

"It is a curious fact," said the Bee hunter, "in the natural history of the bee, that it is never found in a wild country, but always precedes civilization, forming a kind of advance guard between the white man and the savage. The Indians, at least, are perfectly convinced of this fact, for it is a common remark among them, when they observe these insects—'there come the white men.'"

Thimblerig came up, and the Bee hunter spoke to him, calling him by name, for he had met with him in New Orleans. I told him that the conjurer had determined to accompany me also, at which he seemed well pleased, and encouraged the poor fellow to adhere to that resolution; for he would be a man among men in Texas, and no one would be very particular in inquiring about his fortunes in the States. If once there, he might boldly stand up and feed out of the same rack with the best. . . .

With the assistance of our new friend, who was a generous, pleasant fellow, we procured a horse and rifle for Thimblerig; and we started for Nacogdoches, which is about one hundred and twenty miles west of Natchitoches, under the guidance of the Bee hunter.

CHAPTER XXXI.

OUR route, which lay along what is called the old Spanish road, we found to be much better defined on the map, than upon the face of the country. We had, in many instances, no other guide to the path than the blazes on the trees. The Bee hunter was a cheerful communicative companion, and by his pleasant conversation rendered our journey anything but fatiguing. He knew all about the country; had undergone a variety of adventure, and described what he had witnessed with such freshness and so graphically, that if I could only remember one-half he told me about the droves of wild horses, buffalo, various birds, beautiful scenery of the wide spreading and fertile prairies, and his adventures with the roving tribes of Indians, I should fill my book, I am sure, much more agreeably than I shall be able to do on my own hook. When he'd get tired of talking, he'd commence singing, and his list of songs seemed to be as long as a rainy Sunday. He had a fine clear voice, and though I have heard the Woods sing at the Park Theatre, in New York, I must give the Bee hunter the preference over all I have ever heard, except my friend Jim Crow, who, it must be allowed, is a real steamboat at the business, and goes a leetle ahead of any thing that will come after him.

He gave me, among other matters, the following account of a rencounter between one of the early settlers and the Indians:—

"Andrew Tumlinson," said he, "belonged to a family which the colonists of De Witt will long remember as one of their chief stays in the dangers of settling those wilds, trod only by the children of the forest. This indefatigable champion of revenge for his father's death, who had fallen some years before by Indian treachery, had vowed never to rest until he had received satisfaction. In order the better to accomplish his end, he was one of the foremost, if possible, in every skirmish with the Indians; and that he might be enabled to do so without restraint, he placed his wife under the care of his brother-in-law, shouldered his rifle, and headed a ranging party, who were resolved to secure peace to those who followed them, though purchased by their own death.

"He had been frequently victorious in the most desperate fights, where the odds were greatly against him, and at last fell a victim to his own imprudence. A Caddo had been seized as a spy, and threatened with death, in order to compel him to deliver up his knife The fellow never moved a muscle, or even winked, as he beheld the rifles pointed at him. He had been found lurking in the yard attached to the house of a solitary and unprotected family, and he knew that the whites were exasperated at his tribe for injuries that they had committed. When discovered he was accompanied by his little son.

"Tumlinson spoke to him in Spanish, to learn what had brought him there at such a time, but instead of giving any satisfaction, he sprung to his feet, from the log where he was seated, at the same time seizing his rifle which was lying beside him. The owner of the house, with whom the Indian had been on a friendly footing, expostulated with him, and got him to surrender the gun, telling him that the whites only wished to be satisfied of his friendly intentions, and had no desire to injure one who might be useful in conciliating his red brethren.

"He appeared to acquiesce, and wrapping his blanket more closely around his body, moved on in silence ahead of the whites. Tumlinson approached him, and though the rest of the party privately cautioned him not to go too nigh, as they believed the Indian had a knife under his blanket, he disregarded the warning, trusting for safety to his rifle and dexterity.

"He continued to interrogate the captive until he awakened his suspicions that his life was not safe. The Indian returned no answer but a short caustic laugh at the end of every question. Tumlinson at length beheld his countenance become more savage, which was followed by a sudden movement of the right hand beneath his blanket. He fired, and the next instant the Caddo's knife was in his heart, for the savage sprung with the quickness of the wild cat upon his prey. The rifle ball had passed through the Indian's body, yet his victim appeared to be no more in his grasp than a sparrow in the talons of an eagle, for he was a man of gigantic frame, and he knew that not only his own life, but that of his little son, would be taken on the spot. He called to the boy to fly, while he continued to plunge his knife into the bosom of his prostrate victim. The rest of the party levelled their rifles, and the victor shouted, with an air of triumph, 'Do your worst. I have sacrificed another pale face to the spirits of my fathers.' They fired, and he fell dead across the body of the unfortunate Tumlinson. The poor boy fell also. He had sprung forward some distance, when his father was shot, and was running in a zig-zag manner, taught them in their youth, to avoid the balls of their enemies, by rendering it difficult for the best marksman to draw a sight upon them."

In order to afford me some idea of the state of society in the more thickly settled parts of Texas, the Bee hunter told me that he had set down to the breakfast table, one morning at an inn, at San Felipe, and among the small party around the board were eleven who had fled from the States charged with having committed murder. So accustomed are the inhabitants to the appearance of fugitives from justice that they are particularly careful to make inquiries of the characters of new-comers, and generally obtain early and circumstantial information concerning strangers. "Indeed," said he, "it is very common to hear the inquiry made, 'What did he do that made him leave home?' or 'What have you come to Texas for?' intimating almost an assurance of one's being a criminal. Notwithstanding this state of things, however, the good of the public, and of each individual, is so evidently dependent on the public morals, that all appear ready to discountenance and punish crime. Even men who have been expatriated by fear of justice, are here among the last who would be disposed to shield a culprit guilty of a crime against life or property."

Thimblerig was delighted at this favourable account of the state of society, and said that it would be the very place for him to flourish in; he liked their liberal way of thinking, for it did not at all tally with his ideas of natural law, that a man who happened to give offence to the straight laced rules of action established by a set of people contracted in their notions, should be hunted out of all society, even though willing to conform to their regulations. He was lawyer enough, he said, to know that every offence should be tried on the spot where it was committed; and if he had stolen the pennies from his grandmother's eyes in Louisiana, the people in Texas would have nothing to do with that affair, nohow they could fix it. The dejected conjurer pricked up his ears, and from that moment was as gay and cheerful as a blue bird in spring.

As we approached Nacogdoches, the first object that struck our view was a flag flying at the top of a high liberty pole. Drums were beating, and fifes playing, giving an indication, not to be misunderstood, of the spirit that had been awakened in a comparative desert. The people of the town no sooner saw us than many came out to meet us. The Bee hunter, who was known to them, introduced me; and it seems that they had already received the news of my intended visit, and its object, and I met with a cordial and friendly reception.

Nacogdoches is the capital of the department of that name, and is situated about sixty miles west of the river Sabine, in a romantic dell, surrounded by woody bluffs of considerable eminence, within whose inner borders, in a semicircle embracing the town, flow the two forks of the Nana, a branch of the Naches. It is a flourishing town, containing about one thousand actual citizens, although it generally presents twice that number on account of its extensive inland trade, one-half of which is supported by the friendly Indians. The healthiness of this town yields to none in the province, except Bexar, and to none whatsoever south of the same latitude, between the Sabine and the Mississippi. There was a fort established here, by the French, as far back as the year 1717, in order to overawe the wandering tribes of red men, between their borders and the colonists of Great Britain. The soil around it is of an easy nature and well adapted to cultivation.

I passed the day at Nacogdoches in getting information from the principal patriots as to the grievances imposed upon them by the

Mexican government; and I passed the time very pleasantly, but I rather reckon not quite so much so as my friend the Bee hunter. In the evening, as I had missed him for several hours while I was attending to the affairs of the patriots, I inquired for my companion, and was directed, by the landlord, to an apartment appropriated to his family, and accordingly I pushed ahead. Before I reached the door, I heard the joyous and musical voice of the young rover singing as usual.

> "I'd like to have a little farm,
> And leave such scenes as these,
> Where I could live without a care,
> Completely at my ease.
> I'd like to have a pleasant house
> Upon my little farm,
> Airy and cool in summer time
> In winter close and warm."

"And is there nothing else you'd like to have to make you happy, Edward?" demanded a gentle voice, which sounded even more musical in my ear than that of the Bee hunter.

"Yes, in good faith there is, my gentle Kate; and I'll tell you what it is," he exclaimed, and resumed his song:—

> "I'd like to have a little wife—
> I reckon I know who;
> I'd like to have a little son—
> A little daughter too;
> And when they'd climb upon my knee,
> I'd like a little toy
> To give my pretty little girl,
> Another for my boy."

"O, fie, for shame of you to talk so, Edward!" exclaimed the same gentle voice.

"Well, my pretty Kate, if you'll only listen, now, I'll tell you what I wouldn't like."

"Let me hear that, by all means."

> "I should not like my wife to shake
> A broomstick at my head—
> For then I might begin to think
> She did not love her Ned;
> But I should always like to see
> Her gentle as a dove;
> I should not like to have her scold—
> But be all joy and love."

"And there is not much danger, Edward, of her ever being otherwise."

"Bless your sweet lips, that I am certain of," exclaimed the Bee hunter, and I heard something that sounded marvellously like a kiss. But he resumed his song :—

" If I had these I would not ask
For anything beside ;
I'd be content thus smoothly through
The tedious world to glide.
My little wife and I would then
No earthly troubles see—
Surrounded by our little ones,
How happy we would be."

I have always endeavoured to act up to the golden rule of doing as I would be done by, and as I never liked to be interrupted on such occasions, I returned to the bar-room, where I found Thimblerig seated on a table practising with his thimbles, his large white Vicksburg hat stuck in a most independent manner on the side of his head. About half a dozen men were looking on with amazement at his skill, but he got no bets. When he caught my eye his countenance became sort of confused, and he hastily thrust the thimbles into his pocket, saying, as he jumped from the table, " Just amusing myself a little, Colonel, to kill time, and show the natives that some things can be done as well as others.—Let us take an ideer." So we walked up to the bar, took a nip, and let the matter drop.

My horse had become lame, and I found I would not be able to proceed with him, so I concluded to sell him and get another. A gentleman offered to give me a mustang in exchange, and I gladly accepted of his kindness. The mustangs are the wild horses, that are to be seen in droves of thousands pasturing on the prairies. They are taken by means of a lazo, a long rope with a noose, which is thrown around their necks, and they are dragged to the ground with violence, and then secured. These horses, which are considerably smaller than those in the States, are very cheap, and are in such numbers that in times of scarcity of game the settlers and the Indians have made use of them as food. Thousands have been destroyed for this purpose.

I saw nothing of the Bee hunter until bed-time, and then I said nothing to him about what I had overheard. The next morning, as we were preparing for an early start, I went into the private apartment where my companion was, but he did not appear quite as cheerful as usual.—Shortly afterward, a young woman, about eighteen, entered the room.—She was as healthy and blooming as the wild flowers of the prairie. My companion introduced me, she courtesied modestly, and turning to the Bee hunter, said, " Edward, I have made you a new deer skin sack since you were last here. Will you take it with you ? Your old one is so soiled."

" No, no, dear Kate, I shall not have leisure to gather wax this time."

" I have not yet shown you the fine large gourd that I have slung for you.—It will hold near a gallon of water." She went to a closet, and producing it, suspended it around his shoulders,

"My own kind Kate!" he exclaimed, and looked as if he would devour her with his eyes.

"Have I forgotten anything?—Ah! yes, your books." She ran to the closet, and brought out two small volumes.

"One is sufficient this time, Kate—my Bible. I will leave the poet with you." She placed it in his hunting bag, saying,

"You will find here some biscuit and deer sinews, in case you should get bewildered in the prairies. You know you lost your way the last time, and were nearly famished."

"Kind and considerate Kate."

I began to find out that I was a sort of fifth wheel to a waggon, so I went to the front of the tavern to see about starting. There was a considerable crowd there, and I made them a short address on the occasion. I told them, among other things, that "I will die with my Betsey in my arms. No, I will not die—I'll grin down the walls of the Alamo, and the Americans will lick up the Mexicans like fine salt."

I mounted my little mustang, and my legs nearly reached the ground. The thimble conjurer was also ready; at length the Bee hunter made his appearance, followed by his sweetheart, whose eyes looked as though she had been weeping. He took a cordial leave of all his friends, for he appeared to be a general favourite; he then approached Kate, kissed her, and leaped upon his horse. He tried to conceal his emotion by singing, carelessly

> "Saddled and bridled, and booted rode he,
> A plume in his helmet, a sword at his knee."

The tremulous and plaintive voice of Kate took up the next two lines of the song, which sounded like a prophecy:

> "But toom cam' the saddle, all bluidy to see,
> And hame cam' the steed, but hame never cam' he."

We started off rapidly, and left Nacogdoches amid the cheering of true patriots and kind friends.

CHAPTER XXXII.

AN hour or two elapsed before the Bee hunter recovered his usual spirits, after parting from his kind little Kate of Nacogdoches. The conjurer rallied him good humouredly, and had become quite a different man from what he was on the west side of the Sabine. He sat erect in his saddle, stuck his large white Vicksburger conceitedly on his bushy head, carried his rifle with as much ease and grace as if he had been used to the weapon, and altogether he assumed an air of impudence and independence which showed that he had now a soul above thimbles. The Bee hunter at length recovered his spirits, and commenced talking very pleasantly, for the matters he related were for the most part new to me.

My companions, by way of beguiling the tediousness of our journey, repeatedly played tricks upon each other, which were taken in good part. One of them I will relate. We had observed that the Bee hunter always disappeared on stopping at a house, running in to talk with the inhabitants and ingratiate himself with the women, leaving us to take care of the horses. On reaching our stopping place at night he left us as usual, and while we were rubbing down our mustangs, and hobbling them, a negro boy came out of the house with orders from our companion within to see to his horse. Thimblerig, who possessed a good share of roguish ingenuity, after some inquiries about the gentleman in the house, how he looked and what he was doing, told the boy, in rather a low voice, that he had better not come nearer to him than was necessary, for it was possible he might hurt him, though still he didn't think he would. The boy asked why he need be afraid of him. He replied, he did not certainly know that there was any reason—he hoped there was none—but the man had been bitten by a mad dog, and it was rather uncertain whether he was not growing mad himself. Still he would not alarm the boy, but cautioned him not to be afraid, for there might be no danger, though there was something rather strange in the conduct of his poor friend. This was enough for the boy; he was almost afraid to touch the horse of such a man; and when, a moment afterward, our companion came out of the house, he slunk away behind the horse, and though he was in a great hurry to get him unsaddled, kept his eyes fixed steadily on the owner, closely watching his motions.

"Take off that bridle," exclaimed the impatient Bee hunter, in a stern voice: and the black boy sprung off, and darted away as fast as his feet could carry him, much to the vexation and surprise of our companion, who ran after him a little distance, but could in no way account for his singular and provoking conduct. When we entered the house things appeared a great deal more strange; for the negro had rushed hastily into the midst of the family, and in his terrified state communicated the alarming tale, that the gentleman had been bitten by a mad dog. He, unconscious all the time of the trick that was playing off, endeavoured, as usual, to render himself as agreeable as possible, especially to the females with whom he had already formed a partial acquaintance. We could see that they looked on him with apprehension, and retreated whenever he approached them. One of them took an opportunity to inquire of Thimblerig the truth of the charge; and his answer confirmed their fears, and redoubled their caution; though, after confessing with apparent candour, that his friend had been bitten, he stated that there was no certainty of evil consequences, and it was a thing which of course could not be mentioned to the sufferer.

As bed time approached the mistress of the house expressed her fears, lest trouble should arise in the night; for the house, according to custom, contained but two rooms, and was not built for security. She therefore urged us to sleep between him and the door, and by no means to let him pass us. It so happened, however, that he chose to sleep next the door, and it was with great difficulty that we could keep their fears within bounds. The ill-disguised alarm of the whole family was not less a source of merriment to him who had been the cause, than of surprise and wonder of the subject of it. Whatever member of the household he approached promptly withdrew, and as for the negro, whenever he was spoken to by him, he would jump and roll his eyes. In the morning, when we were about to depart, we commissioned our belied companion to pay our bill; but as he approached the hostess she fled from him, and shut the door in his face. "I want to pay our bill," said he. "O! if you will only leave the house," cried she, in terror, "you are welcome to your lodging."

The jest, however, did not end here. The Bee hunter found out the trick that had been played upon him, and determined to retaliate. As we were about mounting, the conjurer's big white Vicksburger was unaccountably missing, and nowhere to be found. He was not altogether pleased with the liberty that had been taken with him, and after searching some time in vain, he tied a handkerchief round his head, sprung upon his horse, and rode off with more gravity than usual. We had rode about two miles, the Bee hunter bantering the other with a story of his hat lying in pawn at the house we had left, and urged upon him to return and redeem it; but finding Thimblerig out of humour, and resolved not to return, he began to repent of his jest, and offered to go back and bring it, on condition that the past should be forgotten and there should be no more retaliation. The other consented to the terms, so lighting a cigar with his sun glass, he set off at a rapid rate on his return. He had not been gone long before I presented Thimblerig with his hat, for I had seen the Bee hunter conceal it, and had secretly brought it along with me. It was some time before our absent friend overtook us, having frightened all the family away by his sudden return, and searched the whole house without success. When he perceived the object of his ride upon the head of the conjurer, and recollected the promise by which he had bound himself not to have any more jesting, he could only exclaim, "Well, it's hard, but it's fair." We all laughed heartily, and good humour was once again restored.

Cane brakes are common in some parts of Texas. Our way led us through one of considerable extent. The frequent passage of men and horses had kept open a narrow path not wide enough for two mustangs to pass with convenience. The reeds, the same as are used in the northern states as fishing rods, had grown to the height of about twenty feet, and were so slender, that having no support directly over the path, they drooped a little inward, and intermingled their tops, forming a complete covering overhead. We rode about a quarter of a mile along this singular arched avenue with the view of the sky completely shut out. The Bee hunter told me that the largest brake is that which lines the banks of Caney Creek, and is seventy miles in length, with scarcely a tree to be seen the whole distance. The reeds are eaten by cattle and horses in the winter when the prairies yield little or no other food.

When we came out of the brake we saw three black wolves jogging like dogs ahead of us, but at too great a distance to reach them with a rifle. Wild turkeys and deer repeatedly crossed our path, and we saw several droves of wild horses pasturing in the prairies. These sights awakened the ruling passion strong within me, and I longed to have a hunt upon a large scale; for though I had killed many bears and deers in my time, I had never brought down a buffalo in all my life, and so I told my friends; but they tried to dissuade me from it, by telling me that I would certainly lose my way, and perhaps perish; for though it appeared as a cultivated garden to the eye, it was still a wilderness. I said little more on the subject, until we crossed the Trinidad river, but every mile we travelled I found the temptation grow stronger and stronger.

The night after we crossed the river we fortunately found shelter in the house of a poor woman, who had little but the barest necessaries to offer us. While we were securing our horses for the night we beheld two men approaching the house on foot. They were both armed with rifles and hunting knives, and though I have been accustomed to the sight of men who have not stepped far over the line of civilization, I must say these were just about the roughest samples I had seen anywhere. One was a man of about fifty years old, tall and raw-boned. He was dressed in a sailor's round jacket, with a tarpaulin on his head. His whiskers nearly covered his face; his hair was coal black and long, and there was a deep scar across his forehead, and another on the back of his right hand. His companion, who was considerably younger, was bare-headed, and clad in a deer skin dress made after our fashion. Though he was not much darker than the old man, I perceived that he was an Indian. They spoke friendly to the Bee hunter, for they both knew him, and said they were on their way to join the Texian forces, at that time near the San Antonio river. Though they had started without horses, they reckoned they would come across a couple before they went much farther. The right of ownership to horse flesh is not much regarded in Texas, for those that have been taken from the wild droves are soon after turned out to graze on the prairies, the owner having first branded them with his mark, and hobbled them by tying their fore feet together, which will enable another to capture them just as readily as himself.

The old woman set about preparing our supper, and apologized for the homely fare, which consisted of bacon and fried onions, when the Indians went to a bag and produced a number of eggs of wild fowls, and a brace of fat rabbits, which were speedily dressed, and we made as good a meal as a hungry man need wish to set down to. The old man spoke very little; but the Indian, who had lived much among the whites, was talkative, and manifested much impatience to arrive at the army. The first opportunity that occurred I inquired of the Bee hunter who our new friends were, and he told me that the old man had been for many years a pirate with the famous Lafitte, and that the Indian was a hunter belonging to a settler near Galveston Bay. I had seen enough of land rats at Washington, but this was the first time that I was ever in company with a water rat to my knowledge; however, baiting that black spot on his escutcheon, he was a well behavod and inoffensive man. Vice does not appear so shocking when we are familiar with the perpetrator of it.

Thimblerig was for taking airs upon himself after learning who our companions were, and protested to me, that he would not sit down at the same table with a man who had outraged the laws in such a manner;—for it was due to society that honest men should discountenance such unprincipled characters, and much more to the same effect; when the old man speedily dissipated the gambler's indignant feelings by calmly saying, "Stranger, you had better take a seat at the table, I think," at the same time drawing a long hunting knife from his belt, and laying it on the table. "I think you had better take some supper with us," he added, in a mild tone, but fixing his eye sternly upon Thimblerig. The conjurer first eyed the knife, and then the fierce whiskers of the pirate, and, unlike some politicians, he wasn't long in making up his mind what course to pursue, but he determined to vote as the pirate voted, and said, "I second that motion, stranger," at the same time seating himself on the bench beside me. The old man then commenced cutting up the meat, for which purpose he had drawn his hunting knife, though the gambler had thought it was for a different purpose; and being relieved from his fears, every thing passed off quite sociable.

Early the following morning we compensated the old woman for the trouble she had been at, and we mounted our horses and pursued our journey, our new friends following on foot, but promising to arrive at the Alamo as soon as we should. About noon we stopped to refresh our horses beneath a cluster of trees that stood in the open prairie, and I again spoke of my longing for a buffalo hunt.—We were all seated on the grass, and they tried hard to dissuade me from the folly of allowing a ruling passion to lead me into such imminent danger and difficulty as I must necessarily encounter. At this time, while they were running down my weakness, as they called it, Thimblerig was amusing himself with his eternal thimbles and pea upon the crown of his big white hat. I could not refrain from laughing outright to see with what gravity and apparent interest he slipped the pea from one thimble to another while in the midst of a desert. . . .

The Bee hunter told me, that if I was determined to leave them, he had in his bag a paper of ground coffee, and biscuit, which little Kate of Nacogdoches had desired him to carry for my use, which he handed to me, and proposed drinking her health, saying that she was one of the kindest and purest of God's creatures.—We drank her health, and wished him all happiness when she should be his own, which time he looked forward to with impatience. He still continued to dissuade me from leaving them, and all the time he was talking his eyes were wandering above, when suddenly he stopped, sprang to his feet, looked around for a moment, then leaped on his mustang, and without saying a word, started off like mad, and scoured along the prairie. We watched him, gradually diminishing in size, until he seemed no larger than a rat, and finally disappeared in the distance. I was amazed, and thought to be sure the man was crazy; and Thimblerig, who continued his game, responded that he was unquestionably out of his head.

Shortly after the Bee hunter had disappeared, we heard a noise like the rumbling of distant thunder. The sky were clear, there were no signs of a storm, and we concluded it could not proceed from that cause. On turning to the west we saw an immense cloud of dust in the distance, but could perceive no object distinctly, and still the roaring continued.—"What can all this mean?" said I. "Burn my old shoes if I know," said the conjurer, gathering up his thimbles, and at the same time cocking his large Vicksburger fiercely on his head. We continued looking in the direction whence the sound proceeded, the cloud of dust became thicker and thicker, and the roaring more distinct—much louder than was ever heard in the White House at Washington.

We at first imagined that it was a tornado, but whatever it was, it was coming directly toward the spot where we stood. Our mustangs had ceased to graze, and cocked up their ears in evident alarm. We ran and caught them, took off the hobbles, and rode into the grove of trees;—still the noise grew louder and louder. We had scarcely got under the shelter of the grove before the object approached near enough for us to ascertain what it was. It was a herd of buffalo, at least four or five hundred in number, dashing along as swift as the wind, and roaring as if so many devils had broke loose.—They passed near the grove, and if we had not taken shelter there, we should have been in great danger of being trampled to death. My poor little mustang shook worse than a politician about to be turned out of office, as the drove came sweeping by. At their head, apart from the rest, was a black bull, who appeared to be their leader; he came roaring along, his tail straight on an end, and at times tossing up the earth with his horns. I never felt such a desire to have a crack at any thing in all my life. He drew nigh the place where I was standing; I raised my beautiful Betsey to my shoulder, took deliberate aim, blazed away, and he roared and suddenly stopped. Those that were near him did so likewise, and the concussion occasioned by the impetus of those in the rear was such, that it was a miracle that some of them did not break their legs or necks. The black bull stood for a few moments pawing the ground after he was shot, then darted off around the cluster of trees, and made for the uplands of the prairies. The whole herd followed, sweeping by like a tornado, and I do say, I never witnessed a more beautiful sight to the eye of a hunter in all my life. Bear hunting is no more to be compared to it than Colonel Benton is to Henry Clay. I watched them for a few moments, then clapped spurs to my mustang and followed in their wake, leaving Thimblerig behind me.

I followed on the trail of the herd for at least two hours, by which time the moving mass appeared like a small cloud in the distant horizon. Still, I followed, my whole mind absorbed by the excitement of the chase, until the object was entirely lost in the distance. I now paused to allow my mustang to breathe, who did not altogether fancy the rapidity of my movements, and to consider which course I would have to take to regain the path I had abandoned. I might have retraced my steps by following the trail of the buffaloes, but it had always been my principle to go ahead, and so I turned to the west and pushed forward.

I had not rode more than an hour before I found I was as completely bewildered as "the Government" was when he entered upon an examination of the Post Office accounts. I looked around, and there was, as far as the eye could reach, spread before me a country apparently in the highest state of cultivation. Extended fields, beautiful and productive, groves of trees cleared from the underwood, and whose margins were as regular as if the art and taste of man had been employed upon them. But there was no other evidence that the sound of the axe, or the voice of man, had ever here disturbed the solitude of nature. My eyes would have cheated my senses into the belief that I was in an earthly paradise, but my fears told me that I was in a wilderness.

I pushed along, following the sun, for I had no compass to guide me, and there was no other path than that which my mustang made. Indeed, if I had found a beaten track, I should have been almost afraid to have followed it; for my friend the Bee hunter had told me, that once, when he had been lost in the prairies, he had accidentally struck into his own path, and had travelled around and around for a whole day before he discovered his error. This I thought was a poor way of going ahead; so I determined to make for the first large stream, and follow its course.

I had travelled several hours without seeing the trace of a human being, and even game was almost as scarce as Benton's mint drops, except just about election time, and I began to wish that I had followed the advice of my companions. I was a good deal bothered to account for the abrupt manner in which the Bee hunter had absconded; and I felt concerned for the poor thimble conjurer, who was left alone, and altogether unaccustomed to the difficulties that he would have to encounter. While my mind was occupied with these unpleasant reflections, I was suddenly startled by another novelty quite as great as that I have just described.

I had just emerged from a beautiful grove of trees, and was entering upon an extended prairie, which looked like the luxuriant meadows of a thrifty farmer; and as if nothing should be wanting to complete the delusion, but a short distance before me, there was a drove of about one hundred beautiful horses quietly pasturing. It required some effort to convince my mind that man had no agency in this. But when I looked around, and fully realized it all, I thought of him who had preached to me in the wilds of the Arkansas, and involuntary exclaimed, "God what hast thou not done for man, and yet how little he does for thee! Not even repays thee with gratitude!"

I entered upon the prairie. The mustangs no sooner espied me than they raised their heads, whinnied, and began coursing around me in an extended circle, which gradually became smaller and smaller, until they closely surrounded me. My little rascally mustang enjoyed the sport, and felt disposed to renew his acquaintance with his wild companions; first turning his head to one, then to another, playfully biting the neck of this one, rubbing noses with that one, and kicking up his heels at a third. I began to feel rather uncomfortable, and plied the spur pretty briskly to get out of the mess, but he was as obstinate as the "old Roman" himself, who will be neither led nor driven. I kicked, and he kicked, but fortunately he became tired first, and he made one start, intending to escape from the annoyance if possible. As I had an annoyance to escape from likewise, I beat the devil's tattoo on his ribs, that he might have some music to dance to, and we went ahead right merrily, the whole drove following in our wake, head up, and tail and mane streaming. My little critter, who was both blood and bottom, seemed delighted at being the head of the heap; and having once got fairly started, I wish I may be shot if I did not find it impossible to stop him. He kept along, tossing his head proudly, and occasionally neighing, as much as to say, "Come on, my hearties, you see I ha'n't forgot our old amusement yet." And they did come on with a vengeance, clatter, clatter, clatter, as if so many fiends had broke loose. The prairie lay extended before me as far as the eye could reach, and I began to think that there would be no end to the race.

My little animal was full of fire and metal, and as it was the first bit of genuine sport that he had had for some time, he appeared determined to make the most of it. He kept the lead for full half an hour, frequently neighing as if in triumph and derision. I thought of John Gilpin's celebrated ride, but that was child's play to this. The proverb says, "The race is not always to the swift, nor the battle to the strong," and so it proved in the present instance. My mustang was obliged to carry weight, while his competitors were as free as nature had made them. A beautiful bay, who had trod close upon my heels the whole way, now came side by side with my mustang, and we had it hip and thigh for about ten minutes, in such style as would have delighted the heart of a true lover of the turf. I now felt an interest in the race myself, and for the credit of my bit of blood, determined to win it if it was at all in the nature of things. I plied the lash and spur, and the little critter took it quite kindly, and tossed his head, and neighed, as much as to say, "Colonel, I know what you're after—Go ahead!"—and he cut dirt in beautiful style, I tell you.

This could not last for ever. At length my competitor darted ahead, somewhat the same way that Adam Huntsman served me last election, except that there was no gouging; and my little fellow was compelled to clatter after his tail, like a needy politician after an office holder when he wants his influence, and which my mustang found it quite as difficult to reach. He hung on like grim death for some time longer, but at last his ambition began to flag; and having lost his ground, others seemed to think that he was not the mighty critter he was cracked up to be, no how, and they tried to outstrip him also. A second shot ahead, and he kicked up his heels in derision as he passed us; then a third, a fourth, and so on, and even the scrubbiest little rascal in the whole drove was disposed to have a fling at their broken down leader. A true picture of politicians and their truckling followers, thought I. We now followed among the last of the drove until we came to the banks of the Navasola river. The foremost leaped from the margin into the rushing stream, the others, politician like, followed him, though he would lead them to destruction; but my wearied animal fell on the banks, completely exhausted with fatigue. It was a beautiful sight to see them stemming the torrent, ascend the opposite bank, and scour over the plain, having been refreshed by the water. I relieved my wearied animal from the saddle, and employed what means were in my power to restore him.

CHAPTER XXXIII.

AFTER toiling for more than an hour to get my mustang upon his feet again, I gave it up as a bad job, as little Van did when he attempted to raise himself to the moon by the waistband of his breeches. Night was fast closing in, and as I began to think that I had just about sport enough for one day, I might as well look around for a place of shelter for the night, and take a fresh start in the morning, by which time I was in hopes my horse would be recruited. Near the margin of the river a large tree had been blown down, and I thought of making my lair in its top, and approached it for that purpose. While beating among the branches I heard a low growl, as much as to say, "Stranger, the apartments are already taken." Looking about to see what sort of a bed-fellow I was likely to have, I discovered, not more than five or six paces from me, an enormous Mexican cougar eyeing me as an epicure surveys the table before he selects his dish, for I have no doubt the cougar looked upon me as the subject of a future supper. Rays of light darted from his large eyes, he showed his teeth like a negro in hysterics, and he was crouching on his haunches, ready for a spring; all of which convinced me that unless I was pretty quick upon the trigger, posterity would know little of the termination of my eventful career, and it would be far less glorious and useful than I intend to make it.

One glance satisfied me that there was no time to be lost, as Pat thought when falling from a church steeple and exclaimed, "This would be mighty pleasant, now, if it would only last,"—but there was no retreat either for me or the cougar, so I levelled my Betsey, and blazed away. The report was followed by a furious growl, (which is sometimes the case in Congress), and the next moment, when I expected to find the tarnal critter struggling with death, I beheld him shaking his head as if nothing more than a bee had stung him. The ball had struck him on the forehead, and glanced off, doing no other injury than stunning him for an instant, and tearing off the skin, which tended to infuriate him the more. The cougar wasn't long in making up his mind what to do, nor was I neither; but he would have it all his own way, and vetoed my motion to back out. I had not retreated three steps before he sprang at me like a steamboat; I stepped aside, and as he lit upon the ground, I struck him violently with the barrel of my rifle, but he didn't mind that, but wheeled round and made at me again. The gun was now of no use, so I threw it away, and drew my hunting knife, for I knew we should come to close quarters before the fight would be over. This time he succeeded in fastening on my left arm, and was just beginning to amuse himself by tearing the flesh off with his fangs, when I ripped my knife into his side, and he let go his hold much to my satisfaction.

He wheeled about and came at me with increased fury, occasioned by the smarting of his wounds. I now tried to blind him, knowing that if I succeeded he would become an easy prey; so as he approached me I watched my opportunity, and aimed a blow at his eyes with my knife, but unfortunately it struck him on the nose, and he paid no other attention to it than by a shake of the head and a low growl. He pressed me close, and as I was stepping backward my foot tripped in a vine, and I fell to the ground. He was down upon me like a night-hawk upon a June bug. He seized hold of the outer part of my right thigh, which afforded him considerable amusement; the hinder part of his body was toward my face; I grasped his tail with my left hand, and tickled his ribs with my hunting knife, which I held in my right. Still, the critter wouldn't let go his hold; and as I found that he would lacerate my leg dreadfully unless he was speedily shaken off, I tried to hurl him down the bank into the river, for our scuffle had already brought us to the edge of the bank. I stuck my knife into his side, and summoned all my strength to throw him over. He resisted, was desperate heavy; but at last I got him so far down the declivity that he lost his balance, and he rolled over and over until he landed on the margin of the river; but in his fall he dragged me along with him. Fortunately I fell uppermost, and his neck presented a fair mark for my hunting knife. Without allowing myself time even to draw breath, I aimed one desperate blow at his neck, and the knife entered his gullet up to the handle, and reached his heart. He struggled for a few moments, and died. I have had many fights with bears, but that was mere child's play; this was the first fight ever I had with a cougar, and I hope it may be the last.

I now returned to the tree top to see if any one else would dispute my lodging; but now I could take peaceable and quiet possession. I parted some of the branches, and cut away others to make a bed in the opening; I then gathered a quantity of moss, which hung in festoons from the trees, which I spread on the litter, and over this I spread my horse blanket; and I had as comfortable a bed as a weary man need ask for. I now took another look at my mustang, and from all appearances he would not live until morning. I ate some of the cakes that little Kate of Nacogdoches had made for me, and then carried my saddle into my tree top, and threw myself down upon my bed, with no very pleasant reflections at the prospect before me.

I was weary, and soon fell asleep, and did not awake until daybreak the next day. I felt somewhat stiff and sore from the wounds I had received in the conflict with the cougar; but I considered myself as having made a lucky escape. I looked over the bank, and as I saw the carcass of the cougar lying there, I thought that it was an even chance that we had not exchanged conditions; and I felt grateful that the fight had ended as it did. I now went to look after my mustang, fully expecting to find him as dead as the cougar; but what was my astonishment to find that he had disappeared without leaving trace of hair or hide of him. I first supposed that some beasts of prey had consumed the poor critter; but then they wouldn't have eaten his bones; and he had vanished as effectually as the deposites, without leaving any mark of the course they had taken. This bothered me amazing; I couldn't figure it out by any rule that I had ever heard of, so I concluded to think no more about it.

I felt a craving for something to eat, and looking around for some game, I saw a flock of geese on the shore of the river. I shot a fine fat gander and soon stripped him of his feathers: and gathering some light wood, I kindled a fire, run a long stick through my goose, for a spit, and put it down to roast, supported by two sticks with prongs. I had a desire for some coffee; and having a tin cup with me, I poured the paper of ground coffee that I had received from the Bee hunter into it, and made a strong cup, which was very refreshing. Off of my goose and biscuit I made a hearty meal, and was preparing to depart, without clearing up the breakfast things, or knowing which direction to pursue, when I was somewhat taken aback by another of the wild scenes of the west. I heard a sound like the trampling of many horses, and I thought to be sure the mustangs or buffaloes were coming upon me again; but on raising my head I beheld in the distance about fifty mounted Cumanches, with their spears glittering in the morning sun, dashing toward the spot where I stood at full speed. As the column advanced it divided, according to their usual practice, into two semicircles, and in an instant I was surrounded. Quicker than thought I sprang to my rifle, but as my hand grasped it, I felt that resistance against so many would be of as little use as pumping for thunder in dry weather.

The chief was for making love to my beautiful Betsey, but I clung fast to her, and assuming an air of composure, I demanded whether their nation was at war with the Americans. "No," was the reply. "Do you like the Americans?" "Yes, they are our friends." "Where do you get your spear heads, your rifles, your blankets, and your knives from?" "Get them from our friends, the Americans." "Well, do you think if you were passing through their nation, as I am passing through yours, they would attempt to rob you of your property?" "No, they would feed me, and protect me; and the Cumanche will do the same by his white brother."

I now asked him what it was had directed him to the spot where I was, and he told me, that they had seen the smoke from a great distance, and had come to see the cause of it. He inquired what had brought me there alone; and I told him that I had come to hunt, and that my mustang had become exhausted, and though I thought he was about to die, that he had escaped from me; at which the chief gave a low chuckling laugh, and said it was all a trick of the mustang, which is the most wily and cunning of all animals. But he said that as I was a brave hunter he would furnish me with another; he gave orders, and a fine young horse was immediately brought forward.

When the party approached there were three old squaws at their head, who made a noise with their mouths, and served as trumpeters. I now told the chief that, as I now had a horse, I would go for my saddle, which was in the place where I had slept. As I approached the spot I discovered one of the squaws devouring the remains of my roasted goose, but my saddle and bridle were nowhere to be found. Almost in despair of seeing them again, I observed, in a thicket at a little distance, one of the trumpeters kicking and belabouring her horse to make him move off, while the sagacious beast would not move a step from the troop. I followed her, and, thanks to her restive mustang, secured my property, which the chief made her restore to me. Some of the warriors had by this time discovered the body of the cougar, and had already commenced skinning it; and seeing how many stabs were about it, I related to the chief the desperate struggle I had had; he said, "Brave hunter, brave man," and wished me to be adopted into his tribe, but I respectfully declined the honour. He then offered to see me on my way; and I asked him to accompany me to the Colorado river, if he was going in that direction, which he agreed to do. I put my saddle on my fresh horse, mounted, and we darted off, at a rate not much slower than I had rode the day previous with the wild herd, the old squaws at the head of the troop braying like young jackasses the whole way.

About three hours after starting we saw a drove of mustangs quietly pasturing in the prairie at a distance. One of the Indians immediately got his lasso ready, which was a long rope made of hide plaited like whip cord, with an iron ring at one end, through which the rope was passed so as to form a noose; and thus prepared, he darted ahead of the troop to make a capture. They allowed him to approach pretty nigh, he all the time flourishing his lasso; but before he got within reaching distance, they started off at a brisk canter, made two or three wide circuits around him, as if they would spy out what he was after, then abruptly changed their course and disappeared. One mustang out of all the drove remained standing quietly; the Indian made up to him, threw the lasso, but the mustang dodged his head between his fore legs, and escaped the noose, but did not attempt to escape. The Indian then rode up to him, and the horse very patiently submitted while he put a bridle on him, and secured him. When I approached, I immediately recognized in the captive the pestilent little animal that had shammed sickness and escaped from me the day before; and when he caught my eye he cast down his head and looked rather sheepish, as if he were sensible and ashamed of the dirty trick he had played me. I expressed my astonishment to the Indian chief at the mustang's allowing himself to be captured without an effort to escape; and he told me, that they are generally hurled to the ground with such violence when first taken with the lasso, that they remember it ever after, and that the sight of it will subdue them to submission, though they may have run wild for years. Just so with an office holder, who, being kicked out, turns patriot—shake a commission at him, and the fire of his patriotism usually escapes in smoke.

We travelled all day, and toward evening we came across a small drove of buffaloes; and it was a beautiful sight to behold with what skill the Indians hunted down this noble game. There are no horsemen who ride more gracefully that the Cumanches; and they sit so closely, and hold such absolute control over the horse, that he seems to be part of their own person. I had the good fortune to bring down a young heifer, and as it was the only beef that we killed, the chief again complimented me as being a brave hunter; and while they were preparing the heifer for our supper I related to him many of my hunting exploits, at which he manifested pleasure and much astonishment for an Indian. He again urged upon me to become one of the tribe.

We made a hearty supper, hobbled our mustangs, which we turned into the prairie to graze, and then encamped for the night. I awoke about two hours before daybreak, and looking over the tract of country through which we had travelled, the sky was as bright and clear as if the sun had already risen. I watched it for some time without being able to account for it, and asked my friend, the chief, to explain, who told me that the prairie was on fire, and that it must have caught when we cooked our dinner. I have seen hundreds of acres of mountain timber on fire in my time, but this is the first time that I ever saw a prairie burning.

Nothing of interest occurred until we reached the Colorado, and were following the river to the place where it crosses the road to Bexar, which place the Indians promised to conduct me to. We saw a light column of smoke ascending in the clear sky, and hastened toward it. It proceeded from a small cluster of trees near the river. When we came within five hundred yards of it, the warriors extended their line around the object, and the chief and myself cautiously approached it. When we came within eyeshot, what was my astonishment to discover a solitary man seated on the ground near the fire, so intent upon some pursuit that he did not perceive our approach. We drew nigh to him, and still he was unconscious of our approach. It was poor Thimblerig practising his game of thimbles upon the crown of his white Vicksburger. This is what I call the ruling passion most amazing strong. The chief shouted the war whoop, and suddenly the warriors came rushing in from all quarters, preceded by the old squaw trumpeters squalling like mad. The conjurer sprang to his feet, and was ready to sink into the earth when he beheld the ferocious looking fellows that surrounded him. I stepped up, took him by the hand, and quieted his fears. I told the chief that he was a friend of mine, and I was very glad to have found him, for I was afraid that he had perished. I now thanked him for his kindness in guiding me over the prairies, and gave him a large Bowie knife, which he said he would keep for the sake of the brave hunter. The whole squadron then wheeled off, and I saw them no more. I have met with many polite men in my time, but no one who possessed in a greater degree what may be called true spontaneous politeness than this Cumanche chief, always excepting Philip Hone, Esq., of New York, whom I look upon as the politest man I ever did see; for when he asked me to take a drink at his own side-board he turned his back upon me, that I mightn't be ashamed to fill as much as I wanted. That was what I call doing the fair thing.

Thimblerig was delighted at meeting me again, but it was some time before he recovered sufficiently from the cold sweat into which the sudden appearance of the Indians had thrown him to recount his adventures to me. He said that he felt rather downhearted when he found himself abandoned both by the Bee hunter and myself, and he knew not which course to pursue; but after thinking about the matter for two hours, he had made up his mind to retrace the road we had travelled over, and had mounted his mustang for that purpose, when he spied the Bee hunter laden with honey. The mystery of his abrupt departure was now fully accounted for; he had spied a solitary bee shaping its course to its hive, and at the moment he couldn't control the ruling passion, but followed the bee without reflecting for a moment upon the difficulties and dangers that his thoughtlessness might occasion his friends.

I now asked him what had become of the Bee hunter, and he said that he had gone out in pursuit of game for their supper, and he expected that he would return shortly, as he had been absent at least an hour. While we were still speaking our friend appeared, bending under the weight of a wild turkey. He manifested great joy at meeting with me so unexpectedly; and desiring the conjurer to pluck the feathers of the bird, which he cheerfully undertook, for he said he had been accustomed to plucking pigeons, we set about preparing our supper.

The position we occupied was directly on the route leading to Bexar, and at the crossings of the Colorado. We were about to commence our supper, for the turkey was done in beautiful style, when the sound of a horse neighing startled us. We looked over the prairie, and beheld two men approaching on horseback, and both armed with rifles and knives. The Bee hunter said that it was time for us to be on our guard, for we should meet, perhaps, more enemies than friends as soon as we crossed the river, and the new-comers were making directly for the spot we occupied; but, as they were only two, it occasioned no uneasiness.

As they drew nigh we recognised the strangers; they turned out to be the old pirate and the Indian hunter who had lodged with us a few nights before. We hailed them, and on seeing us they alighted and asked permission to join our party, which we gladly agreed to, as our journey was becoming rather more perilous every mile we advanced. They partook of our turkey, and as they had some small cakes of bread, which they threw into the general stock, we made a hearty supper: and, after a battle song from the Bee hunter, we prepared to rest for the night.

Early next morning we crossed the river, and pushed forward for the fortress of Alamo. The old pirate was still as taciturn as ever, but his companion was talkative and in good spirits. I asked him where he had procured their mustangs, and he said that he had found them hobbled in Burnet's Grant just at a time that he felt very tired; and as he believed that no one would lay claim to them at Bexar, he couldn't resist mounting one, and persuading his friend to mount the other.

Nothing of interest occurred until we came within about twenty miles of San Antonio. We were in the open prairie, and beheld a band of about fifteen or twenty armed men approaching us at full speed. "Look out for squalls," said the old pirate, who had not spoken for an hour; "they are a scouting party of Mexicans." "And are three or four times our number," said Thimblerig. "No matter," replied the old man; "they are convicts, jail birds, and cowardly ruffians, no doubt, who would tremble at a loud word as much as a mustang at the sight of the lasso.—Let us spread ourselves, dismount, and trust to our arms."

We followed his orders, and stood beside our horses, which served to protect our persons, and we awaited the approach of the enemy. When they perceived this movement of ours, they checked their speed, appeared to consult together for a few minutes, then spread their line, and came within rifle shot of us. The leader called out to us in Spanish, but as I did not understand him, I asked the old man what it was, who said he called upon us to surrender.

"There will be a brush with those blackguards," continued the pirate. "Now each of you single out your man for the first fire, and they are greater fools than I take them for if they give us a chance at a second.—Colonel, as you are a good shot, just settle the business for that talking fellow with the red feather; he's worth any three of the party."

"Surrender, or we fire," shouted the fellow with the red feather in Spanish.

"Fire, and be d——d," returned the pirate, at the top of his voice, in plain English.

And sure enough they took his advice, for the next minute we were saluted with a discharge of musketry, the report of which was so loud that we were convinced they all had fired. Before the smoke had cleared away we had each selected our man, fired, and I never did see such a scattering among their ranks as followed. We beheld several mustangs running wild without their riders over the prairie, and the balance of the company were already retreating at a more rapid gait than they approached. We hastily mounted, and commenced pursuit, which we kept up until we beheld the independent flag flying from the battlements of the fortress of Alamo, our place of destination. The fugitives succeeded in evading our pursuit, and we rode up to the gates of the fortress, announced to the sentinel who we were, and the gates were thrown open; and we entered amid shouts of welcome bestowed upon us by the patriots.

CHAPTER XXXIV.

THE fortress of Alamo is at the town of Bexar, on the San Antonio river, which flows through the town. Bexar is about one hundred and forty miles from the coast, and contains upward of twelve hundred citizens, all native Mexicans, with the exception of a few American families who have settled there. Besides these there is a garrison of soldiers, and trading pedlars of every description, who resort to it from the borders of the Rio Grande, as their nearest depôt of American goods. A military outpost was established at this spot by the Spanish government in 1718. In 1721 the town was settled by emigrants sent out from the Canary Islands by the King of Spain. It became a flourishing settlement, and so continued until the revolution in 1812, since which period the Cumanche and other Indians have greatly harassed the inhabitants, producing much individual suffering, and totally destroying, for a season at least, the prospects of the town. Its site is one of the most beautiful in the western world. The air is salubrious, the water delightful, especially when mixed with a little of the ardent, and the health of the citizens is proverbial. The soil around it is highly fertile, and well calculated for cotton and grain.

The gallant young Colonel Travis, who commands the Texian forces in the fortress of Alamo, received me like a man; and though he can barely muster one hundred and fifty efficient men, should Santa Anna make an attack upon us, with the whole host of ruffians that the Mexican prisons can disgorge, he will have snakes to eat before he gets over the wall, I tell you. But one spirit appears to animate the little band of patriots—and that is liberty, or death. To worship God according to the dictates of their own conscience, and govern themselves as freemen should be governed.

All the world knows, by this time, that the town of Bexar, or, as some call it, San Antonio, was captured from the Mexicans by General Burlison, on the 10th day of December, 1835, after a severe struggle of five days and five nights, during which he sustained a loss of four men only, but the brave old Colonel Milam was among them. There were seventeen hundred men in the town, and the Texian force consisted of but two hundred and sixteen. The Mexicans had walled up the streets leading from the public square, intending to make a desperate resistance; the Texians however made an entrance, and valiantly drove them from house to house, until General Cos retreated to the castle of Alamo, without the city, and there hoisted the white flag, and sent out the terms of capitulation, which were as follows:

General Cos is to retire within six days, with his officers, arms, and private property, on parole of honour. He is not to oppose the re-establishment of the constitution of 1824.

The infantry, and the cavalry, the remnant of Morale's battalion, and the convicts, to return, taking with them ten rounds of cartridge for safety against the Indians.

All public property, money, arms, and ammunition, to be delivered up to General Burlison, of the Texian army,—with some other stipulation in relation to the sick and wounded, private property, and prisoners of war. The Texians would not have acceded to them, preferring to storm him in his stronghold, but at this critical juncture they hadn't a single round of ammunition left, having fought from the 5th to the 9th of the month. General Ugartechea had arrived but the day before with three hundred troops, and the four hundred convicts mentioned above, making a reinforcement of seven hundred men; but such rubbish was no great obstacle to the march of freedom. The Mexicans lost about three hundred men during the siege, and the Texians had only four killed and twenty wounded. The articles of capitulation being signed, we marched into the town, took possession of the fortress, hoisted the independent flag, and told the late proprietors to pack up their moveables and clear out in the snapping of a trigger, as we did not think our pockets quite safe with so many jail birds around us. And this is the way the Alamo came into our possession; but the way we shall maintain our possession of it will be a subject for the future historian to record, or my name's not Crockett.—I wish I may be shot if I don't go ahead to the last.

I found Colonel Bowie, of Louisiana, in the fortress, a man celebrated for having been in more desperate personal conflicts than any other in the country, and whose name has been given to a knife of a peculiar construction, which is now in general use in the south-west. I was introduced to him by Colonel Travis, and he gave me a friendly welcome, and appeared to be mightily pleased that I had arrived safe. While we were conversing he had occasion to draw his famous knife to cut a strap, and I wish I may be shot if the bare sight of it wasn't enough to give a man of a squeamish stomach the cholic, specially before breakfast. . . .

My companions, the Bee hunter and the conjurer, joined us, and the colonel appeared to know them both very well. He had a high opinion of the Bee hunter, for turning to me, he said, "Colonel, you could not have had a braver, better, or more pleasant fellow for a companion than honest Ned here. With fifteen hundred such men I would undertake to march to the city of Mexico, and occupy the seat of Santa Anna myself before three months should elapse."

The colonel's life has been marked by constant peril and deeds of daring. A few years ago he went on a hunting excursion into the prairies of Texas, with nine companions. They were attacked by a roving party of Cumanches, about two hundred strong, and such was the science of the colonel in this sort of wild warfare, that after killing a considerable number of the enemy, he fairly frightened the remainder from the field of action, and they fled in utter dismay. The fight took place among the high grass in the open prairie. He ordered his men to dismount from their horses and scatter; to take deliberate aim before they fired, but as soon as they had discharged their rifles, to fall flat on the ground and crawl away from the spot, and reload their pieces.—By this scheme, they not only escaped the fire of the Indians, but by suddenly discharging their guns from another quarter, they created the impression that their party was a numerous one; and the Indians, finding that they were fighting against an invisible enemy, after losing about thirty of their men, took to flight, believing themselves lucky in having escaped with no greater loss. But one of the colonel's party was slightly wounded, and that was owing to his remaining to reload his rifle without having first shifted his position.

Santa Anna, it is said, roars like an angry lion at the disgraceful defeat that his brother-in-law, General Cos, lately met with at this place. It is rumoured that he has recruited a large force, and commenced his march to San Louis de Potosi, and he is determined to carry on a war of extermination. He is liberal in applying his epithets to our countrymen in Texas, and denounces them as a set of perfidious wretches, whom the compassion of the generous Mexicans has permitted to take refuge in their country; and who, like the serpent in the fable, no sooner warmed themselves than they stung their benefactors. This is a good joke.—By what title does Mexico lay claim to all the territory which belonged to Spain in North America? Each province or state of New Spain contended separately or jointly, just as it happened, for their independence, as we did, and were not united under a general government representing the whole of the Spanish possessions, which was only done afterward by mutual agreement or federation. Let it be remembered that the Spanish authorities were first expelled from Texas by the American settlers, who, from the treachery of their Mexican associates, were unable to retain it; but the second time they were more successful. They certainly had as good a right to the soil thus conquered by them, as the inhabitants of other provinces who succeeded against Spain. The Mexicans talk of the ingratitude of the Americans; the truth is, that the ingratitude has been on the other side. What was the war of Texas, in 1813, when the revolutionary spark was almost extinguished in Mexico? What was the expedition of Mina, and his three hundred American Spartans, who perished heroically in the very heart of Mexico, in the vain attempt to resuscitate and keep alive the spark of independence which has at this time kindled such an ungrateful blaze? If a just estimate could be made of the lives and the treasures contributed by American enterprise in that cause, it would appear incredible. How did the Mexicans obtain their independence at last? Was it by their own virtue and courage? No, it was by the treachery of one of the king's generals, who established himself by successful treason, and they have been in constant commotion ever since, which proves they are unfit to govern themselves, much less a free and enlightened people at a distance of twelve hundred miles from them.

But Santa Anna charges the Americans with ingratitude! This is something like Satan reviling sin. I have gathered some particulars of the life of this moral personage from a gentleman at present in the Alamo, and who is intimately acquainted with him, which I will copy into my book exactly as he wrote it.

Santa Anna is about forty-two years of age, and was born in the city of Vera Cruz. His father was a Spaniard, of old Spain, of respectable standing, though poor; his mother was a Mexican. He received a common education, and at the age of thirteen or fourteen was taken into the military family of the then Intendant of Vera Cruz, General Davila, who took a great fancy to him, and brought him up. He remained with General Davila until about the year 1820. While with Davila he was made a major, and when installed he took the honours very coolly, and on some of his friends congratulating him, he said, "If you were to make me a god, I should desire to be something greater." This trait, developed at so early a period of his life, indicated the existence of that vaulting ambition which has ever since characterized his life.

After serving the Spanish royal cause until 1821, he left Vera Cruz, turned against his old master and benefactor, and placed himself at the head of some irregular troops which he raised on the sea-coast near Vera Cruz, and which are called Jarochos in their language, and which were denominated by him his Cossacks, as they were all mounted and armed with spears. With this rude cavalry he besieged Vera Cruz, drove Davila into the castle of San Juan d'Ulloa, and after having been repulsed again entered at a subsequent period, and got entire possession of the city, expelling therefrom the old Spanish troops, and reducing the power of the mother country in Mexico to the walls of the castle.

His manners are extremely affable; he is full of anecdote and humour, and makes himself exceedingly fascinating and agreeable to all who come into his company; he is about five feet ten, rather spare, has a moderately high forehead, with black hair, short black whiskers, without mustachios, and an eye large, black, and expressive of a lurking devil in his look; he is a man of genteel and dignified deportment, but of a disposition perfectly heartless. He married a Spanish lady of property, a native of Alvarado, and through that marriage obtained the first part of his estate, called Manga de Clavo, six leagues from Vera Cruz. He has three fine children, yet quite young.

The following striking anecdote of Santa Anna illustrates his peculiar quickness and management: During the revolution of 1829, while he was shut up in Oxaca, and surrounded by the government troops, and reduced to the utmost straits for the want of money and provisions; having a very small force, there had been, in consequence of the siege and firing every day through the streets, no mass for several weeks. He had no money, and hit upon the following expedient to get it: he took possession of one of the convents, got hold of the wardrobe of the friars, dressed his officers and some of his soldiers in it, and early in the morning had the bells rung for the mass. The people, delighted at having again an opportunity of adoring the Supreme Being, flocked to the church where he was; and after the house was pretty well filled, his friars showed their side-arms and bayonets from beneath their cowls, and closed the doors upon the assembled multitude.

At this unexpected denouement there was a tremendous shrieking, when one of his officers ascended the pulpit, and told the people that he wanted ten thousand dollars, and must have it. He finally succeeded in getting about thirty-six hundred dollars, when he dismissed the congregation.

. . . . . .

Many similar facts are related of him. He is, in fact, all things to all men; and yet, after his treachery to Davila, he has the impudence to talk about ingratitude. He never was out of Mexico. If I only live to tree him, and take him prisoner, I shall ask for no more glory in this life.

CHAPTER XXXV.

I WRITE this on the nineteenth of February, 1836, at San Antonio. We are all in high spirits, though we are rather short of provisions, for men who have appetites that could digest any thing but oppression; but no matter, we have a prospect of soon getting our bellies full of fighting, and that is victuals and drink to a true patriot any day. We had a little sort of convivial party last evening; just about a dozen of us set to work, most patriotically, to see whether we could not get rid of that curse of the land, whisky, and we made considerable progress; but my poor friend, Thimblerig, got sewed up just about as tight as the eyelet-hole in a lady's corset, and a little tighter too, I reckon; for when he went to bed he called for a bootjack, which was brought to him, and he bent down on his hands and knees, and very gravely pulled off his hat with it, for the darned critter was so thoroughly swiped that he didn't know his head from his heels. But this wasn't all the folly he committed; he pulled off his coat and laid it on the bed, and then hung himself over the back of a chair; and I wish I may be shot if he didn't go to sleep in that position, thinking every thing had been done according to Gunter's late scale. Seeing the poor fellow completely used up, I carried him to bed, though he did belong to the Temperance society; and he knew nothing about what had occurred until I told him the next morning. The Bee hunter didn't join us in this blow-out. Indeed, he will seldom drink more than just enough to prevent his being called a total abstinence man. But then he is the most jovial fellow for a water drinker I ever did see.

This morning I saw a caravan of about fifty mules passing by Bexar, and bound for Santa Fe. They were loaded with different articles to such a degree that it was astonishing how they could travel at all, and they were nearly worn out by their labours. They were without bridle or halter, and yet proceeded with perfect regularity in a single line; and the owners of the caravan rode their mustangs with their enormous spurs, weighing at least a pound a piece, with rowels an inch and a half in length, and lever bits of the harshest description, able to break the jaws of their animals under a very gentle pressure. The men were dressed in the costumes of Mexicans. Colonel Travis sent out a guard to see that they were not laden with munitions of war for the enemy. I went out with the party. The poor mules were bending under a burden of more than three hundred pounds, without including the panniers, which were bound so tight as almost to stop the breath of the poor animal. Each of the sorrowful line came up, spontaneously, in turn to have his girth unbound and his load removed. They seemed scarcely able to keep upon their feet, and as they successively obtained relief, one after another heaved a long deep sigh, which it was painful to hear, because it proved that the poor brutes had been worked beyond their strength. What a world of misery man inflicts upon the rest of creation in his brief passage through life!

Finding that the caravan contained nothing intended for the enemy, we assisted the owners to replace the heavy burdens on the backs of the patient but dejected mules, and allowed them to pursue their weary and lonely way. For full two hours we could see them slowly winding along the narrow path, a faint line that ran like a thread through the extended prairie; and finally they were whittled down to the little end of nothing in the distance, and were blotted out from the horizon.

The caravan had no sooner disappeared than one of the hunters, who had been absent several days, came in.

. . . . . .

He stated that he had met some Indians on the banks of the Rio Frio, who informed him that Santa Anna, with a large force, had already crossed the Nences, and might be expected to arrive before San Antonio in a few days. We immediately set about preparing to give him a warm reception, for we are all well aware, if our little band is overwhelmed by numbers, there is little mercy to be expected from the cowardly Mexicans—it is war to the knife.

I jocosely asked the ragged hunter, who was a smart, active young fellow, of the steamboat and alligator breed, whether he was a rhinocerous or a hyena, as he was so eager for a fight with the invaders. "Neither the one, nor t'other, Colonel," says he, "but a whole menagerie in myself. I'm shaggy as a bear, wolfish about the head, active as a cougar, and can grin like a hyena, until the bark will curl off a gum log. There's a sprinkling of all sorts in me, from the lion down to the skunk; and before the war is over you'll pronounce me an entire zoological institute, or I miss a figure in my calculation. I promise to swallow Santa Anna without gagging, if you will only skewer back his ears, and grease his head a little."

He told me that he was one in the fatal expedition fitted out from New Orleans, in November last, to join the contemplated attack upon Tampico by Mehia and Peraza. They were, in all, about one hundred and thirty men, who embarked as emigrants to Texas; and the terms agreed upon were, that it was optional whether the party took up arms in defence of Texas, or not, on landing. They were at full liberty to act as they pleased. But the truth was, Tampico was their destination, and an attack on that city the covert design, which was not made known before land was in sight. The emigrants were landed, some fifty, who doubtless had a previous understanding, joined the standard of General Mehia, and the following day a formidable fort surrendered without an attack.

The whole party were now tendered arms and ammunition, which even those who had been decoyed accepted; and, the line being formed, they commenced the attack upon the city. The hunter continued: "On the 15th of November our little army, consisting of one hundred and fifty men, marched into Tampico, garrisoned by two thousand Mexicans, who were drawn up in battle array in the public square of the city. We charged them at the point of the bayonet, and although they so greatly outnumbered us, *in two minutes* we completely routed them; and they fled, taking refuge on the house tops, from which they poured a destructive fire upon our gallant little band. We fought them until daylight, when we found our number decreased to fifty or sixty broken down and disheartened men. Without ammunition, and deserted by the officers, twenty-eight immediately surrendered. But a few of us cut our way through, and fortunately escaped to the mouth of the river, where we got on board a vessel and sailed for Texas.

"The twenty-eight prisoners wished to be considered as prisoners of war; they made known the manner in which they had been deceived, but they were tried by a court-martial of Mexican soldiers, and condemned to be shot on the 14th day of December, 1835, which sentence was carried into execution."

After receiving this account from my new friend, the old pirate and the Indian hunter came up, and they went off to liquor together, and I went to see a wild Mexican hog, which one of the hunters had brought in. These animals have become scarce, which circumstance is not to be deplored, for their flesh is of little value; and there will still be hogs enough left in Mexico, from all I can learn, even though these should be extirpated.

February 22.—The Mexicans, about sixteen hundred strong, with their President Santa Anna at their head, aided by Generals Almonte, Cos, Sesma, and Castrillon, are within two leagues of Bexar. General Cos, it seems, has already forgot his parole of honour, and is come back to retrieve the credit he lost in this place in December last. If he is captured a second time, I don't think he can have the impudence to ask to go at large again without giving better bail than on the former occasion. Some of the scouts came in, and bring reports that Santa Anna has been endeavouring to excite the Indians to hostilities against the Texians, but so far without effect. The Cumanches, in particular, entertain such hatred for the Mexicans, and at the same time hold them in such contempt, that they would rather turn their tomahawks against them, and drive them from the land than lend a helping hand. We are up and doing, and as lively as Dutch cheese in the dog-days. The two hunters that I have already introduced to the reader left the town this afternoon, for the purpose of reconnoitring.

February 23.—Early this morning the enemy came in sight, marching in regular order, and displaying their strength to the greatest advantage, in order to strike us with terror. But that was no go; they'll find that they have to do with men who will never lay down their arms as long as they can stand on their legs. We held a short council of war, and, finding that we should be completely surrounded, and overwhelmed by numbers, if we remained in the town, we concluded to withdraw to the fortress of Alamo, and defend it to the last extremity. We accordingly filed off, in good order, having some days before placed all the surplus provisions, arms, and ammunition in the fortress. We have had a large national flag made; it is composed of thirteen stripes, red and white, alternately, on a blue ground with a large white star, of five points, in the centre, and between the points the letter TEXAS. As soon as all our little band, about one hundred and fifty in number, had entered and secured the fortress in the best possible manner, we set about raising our flag on the battlements; on which occasion there was no one more active than my young friend, the Bee hunter. He had been all along sprightly, cheerful, and spirited, but now, notwithstanding the control that he usually maintained over himself, it was with difficulty that he kept his enthusiasm within bounds. As soon as we commenced raising the flag he burst forth, in a clear, full tone of voice, that made the blood tingle in the veins of all who heard him:—

"Up with your banner, Freedom,
  Thy champions cling to thee;
They'll follow where'er you lead 'em,
  To death, or victory:—
Up with your banner, Freedom.

Tyrants and slaves are rushing
  To tread thee in the dust;
Their blood will soon be gushing,
  And stain our knives with rust;—
But not thy banner, Freedom.

While stars and stripes are flying,
  Our blood we'll freely shed:
No groan will 'scape the dying,
  Seeing thee o'er his head;—
Up with your banner, Freedom."

This song was followed by three cheers from all within the fortress, and the drums and trumpets commenced playing. The enemy marched into Bexar, and took possession of the town, a blood red flag flying at their head, to indicate that we need not expect quarters if we should fall into their clutches. In the afternoon a messenger was sent from the enemy to Colonel Travis, demanding an unconditional and absolute surrender of the garrison, threatening to put every man to the sword in case of refusal. The only answer he received was a cannon shot, so the messenger left us with a flea in his ear, and the Mexicans commenced firing grenades at us, but without doing any mischief. At night Colonel Travis sent an express to Colonel Fanning, at Goliad, about three or four days' march from this place, to let him know that we are besieged. The old pirate volunteered to go on this expedition, and accordingly left the fort after nightfall.

February 24.—Very early this morning the enemy commenced a new battery on the banks of the river, about three hundred and fifty yards from the fort, and by afternoon they amused themselves by firing at us from that quarter. Our Indian scout came in this evening, and with him a reinforcement of thirty men from Gonzales, who are just in the nick of time to reap a harvest of glory; but there is some prospect of sweating blood before we gather it in. An accident happened to my friend Thimblerig this afternoon. He was intent on his eternal game of thimbles, in a somewhat exposed position, while the enemy were bombarding us from the new redoubt. A three ounce ball glanced from the parapet and struck him on the breast, inflicting a painful but not dangerous wound. I extracted the ball, which was of lead, and recommended to him to drill a hole through it, and carry it for a watch seal. "No," he replied, with energy, "May I be shot six times if I do: that would be making a bauble for an idle boast. No, Colonel, lead is getting scarce, and I'll lend it out at compound interest.—Curse the thimbles!" he muttered, and went his way, and I saw no more of him that evening.

February 25.—The firing commenced early this morning, but the Mexicans are poor engineers, for we haven't lost a single man, and our outworks have sustained no injury. Our sharp shooters have brought down a considerable number of stragglers at a long shot. I got up before the peep of day, hearing an occasional discharge of a rifle just over the place where I was sleeping, and I was somewhat amazed to see Thimblerig mounted alone on the battlement, no one being on duty at the time but the sentries. "What are you doing there?" says I. "Paying my debts," says he, "interest and all." "And how do you make out?" says I. "I've nearly got through," says he; "stop a moment, Colonel, and I'll close the account." He clapped his rifle to his shoulder, and blazed away, then jumped down from his perch, and said, "That account's settled; them chaps will let me play out my game in quiet next time." I looked over the wall, and saw four Mexicans lying dead on the plain. I asked him to explain what he meant by paying his debts, and he told me that he had run the grape shot into four rifle balls, and that he had taken an early stand to have a chance of picking off stragglers. "Now, Colonel, let's go take our bitters," said he;—and so we did. The enemy have been busy during the night, and have thrown up two batteries on the opposite side of the river. The battalion of Matamoras is posted there, and cavalry occupy the hills to the east and on the road to Gonzales.—They are determined to surround us, and cut us off from reinforcement, or the possibility of escape by a sortie. Well, there's one thing they cannot prevent; we'll still go ahead, and sell our lives at a high price.

February 26.—Colonel Bowie has been taken sick from over exertion and exposure. He did not leave his bed to-day until twelve o'clock. He is worth a dozen common men in a situation like ours. The Bee hunter keeps the whole garrison in good heart with his songs and his jests, and his daring and determined spirit.—He is about the quickest on the trigger, and the best rifle shot we have in the fort. I have already seen him bring down eleven of the enemy, and at such a distance that we all thought it would be a waste of ammunition to attempt it. His gun is first rate, quite equal to my Betsey, though she has not quite as many trinkets about her. This day a small party sallied out of the fort for wood and water, and had a slight skirmish with three times their number from the division under General Sesma. The Bee hunter headed them, and beat the enemy off, after killing three. On opening his Bible at night, of which he always reads a portion before going to rest, he found a musket ball in the middle of it. "See here, Colonel," said he, "how they have treated the valued present of my dear little Kate of Nacogdoches." "It has saved your life," said I. "True," replied he, more seriously than usual, "and I am not the first sinner whose life has been saved by this book." He prepared for bed, and before retiring he prayed, and returned thanks for his providential escape; and I heard the name of Catherine mingled in his prayer.

February 27.—The cannonading began early this morning, and ten bombs were thrown into the fort, but fortunately exploded without doing any mischief. So far it has been a sort of tempest in a teapot; not unlike a pitched battle in the Hall of Congress, where the parties array their forces, make fearful demonstrations on both sides, then fire away with loud sounding speeches, which contain about as much meaning as the report of a howitzer charged with a blank cartridge. Provisions are becoming scarce, and the enemy are endeavouring to cut off our water. If they attempt to stop our grog in that manner, let them look out, for we shall become too wrathy for our shirts to hold us. We are not prepared to submit to an excise of that nature, and they'll find it out. This discovery has created considerable excitement in the fort.

February 28.—Last night our hunters brought in some corn and had a brush with a scout from the enemy beyond gun-shot of the fort. They put the scout to flight, and got in without injury. They bring accounts that the settlers are flying in all quarters, in dismay, leaving their possessions to the mercy of the ruthless invader, who is literally engaged in a war of extermination, more brutal than the untutored savage of the desert could be guilty of. Slaughter is indiscriminate, sparing neither sex, age, nor condition. Buildings have been burnt down, farms laid waste, and Santa Anna appears determined to verify his threat, and convert the blooming paradise into a howling wilderness. For just one fair crack at that rascal, even at a hundred yards distance, I would bargain to break my Betsey, and never pull trigger again. My name's not Crockett if I wouldn't get glory enough to appease my stomach for the remainder of my life. The scouts report that a settler, by the name of Johnson, flying with his wife and three little children, when they reached the Colorado, left his family on the shore, and waded into the river to see whether it would be safe to ford with his waggon. When about the middle of the river he was seized by an alligator, and after a struggle, was dragged under the water and perished. The helpless woman and her babes were discovered, gazing in agony on the spot, by other fugitives who happily passed that way, and relieved them. Those who fight the battles experience but a small part of the privation, suffering and anguish that follow in the train of ruthless war. The cannonading continued, at intervals, throughout the day, and all hands were kept up to their work. The enemy, somewhat imboldened, draws nigher to the fort. So much the better.—There was a move in General Sesma's division toward evening.

February 29.—Before daybreak we saw General Sesma leave his camp with a large body of cavalry and infantry, and move off in the direction of Goliad. We think that he must have received news of Colonel Fanning's coming to our relief. We are all in high spirits at the prospect of being able to give the rascals a fair shake on the plain. This business of being shut up makes a man wolfish.—I had a little sport this morning before breakfast. The enemy had planted a piece of ordnance within gun-shot of the fort during the night, and the first thing in the morning they commenced a brisk cannonade, point-blank, against the spot where I was snoring. I turned out pretty smart, and mounted the rampart. The gun was charged again, a fellow stepped forth to touch her off, but before he could apply the match I let him have it, and he keeled over. A second stepped up, snatched the match from the hand of the dying man, but Thimblerig, who had followed me, handed me his rifle, and the next instant the Mexican was stretched on the earth beside the first. A third came up to the cannon, my companion handed me another gun, and I fixed him off in like manner. A fourth, then a fifth, seized the match, who both met with the same fate, and then the whole party gave it up as a bad job, and hurried off to the camp, leaving the cannon ready charged where they had planted it. I came down, took my bitters and went to breakfast. Thimblerig told me that the place from which I had been firing was one of the snuggest stands in the whole fort, for he never failed picking off two or three stragglers before breakfast, when perched up there.

And I recollect, now, having seen him there, ever since he was wounded, the first thing in the morning, and the last at night,—and at times thoughtlessly playing at his eternal game.

March 1.—The enemy's forces have been increasing in numbers daily, notwithstanding they have already lost about three hundred men in the several assaults they have made upon us. I neglected to mention in the proper place, that when the enemy came in sight we had but three bushels of corn in the garrison, but have since found eighty bushels in a deserted house. Colonel Bowie's illness still continues, but he manages to crawl from his bed every day, that his comrades may see him. His presence alone is a tower of strength.—The enemy becomes more daring as his numbers increase.

March 2.—This day the delegates meet in general convention, at the town of Washington, to frame our Declaration of Independence. That the sacred instrument may never be trampled on by the children of those who had freely shed their blood to establish it, is the sincere wish of David Crockett. Universal independence is an almighty idea, far too extensive for some brains to comprehend. It is a beautiful seed that germinates rapidly, and brings forth a large and vigorous tree, but like the deadly Upas, we sometimes find the smaller plants wither and die in its shades. Its blooming branches spread far and wide, offering a perch of safety to all alike, but even among its protecting branches we find the eagle, the kite, and the owl preying upon the helpless dove and sparrow. Beneath its shades myriads congregate in goodly fellowship, but the lamb and the fawn find but frail security from the lion and the jackal, though the tree of independence waves over them. Some imagine independence to be a natural charter, to exercise without restraint, and to their fullest extent, all the energies, both physical and mental, with which they have been endowed; and for their individual aggrandizement alone, without regard to the rights of others, provided they extend to all the same privilege and freedom of action. Such independence is the worst of tyranny.

March 3.—We have given over all hopes of receiving assistance from Goliad or Refugio. Colonel Travis harangued the garrison, and concluded by exhorting them, in case the enemy should carry the fort, to fight to the last gasp, and render their victory even more serious to them than to us. This was followed by three cheers.

March 4.—Shells have been falling into the fort like hail during the day, but without effect. About dusk, in the evening, we observed a man running towards the fort, pursued by about a dozen Mexican cavalry. The Bee hunter immediately knew him to be the old pirate who had gone to Goliad, and, calling to the two hunters, he sallied out of the fort to the relief of the old man, who was hard pressed. I followed close after. Before we reached the spot the Mexicans were close on the heel of the old man, who stopped suddenly, turned short upon his pursuers, discharged his rifle, and one of the enemy fell from his horse. The chase was renewed, but finding that he would be overtaken and cut to pieces, he now turned again, and to the amazement of the enemy, became the assailant in his turn. He clubbed his gun, and dashed among them like a wounded tiger, and they fled like sparrows. By this time we reached the spot, and in the ardour of the moment, followed some distance before we saw that our retreat to the fort was cut off by another detatchment of cavalry. Nothing was to be done but to fight our way through. We were all of the same mind. "Go ahead!" cried I; and they shouted, "Go ahead, Colonel!" We dashed among them, and a bloody conflict ensued. They were about twenty in number and they stood their ground. After the fight had continued about five minutes, a detachment was seen issuing from the fort to our relief, and the Mexicans scampered off, leaving eight of their comrades dead upon the field. But we did not escape unscathed, for both the pirate and the Bee hunter were mortally wounded, and I received a sabre cut across the forehead. The old man died, without speaking, as soon as we entered the fort. We bore my young friend to his bed, dressed his wounds, and I watched beside him. He lay, without complaint or manifesting pain, until about midnight, when he spoke, and I asked him if he wanted any thing. "Nothing," he replied, but drew a sigh that seemed to rend his heart, as he added, "Poor Kate of Nacogdoches!" His eyes were filled with tears, as he continued, "Her words were prophetic, Colonel;" and then he sang, in a low voice that resembled the sweet notes of his own devoted Kate:

> "But toom' cam' the saddle, all bluidy to see,
> And hame cam' the steed, but hame never cam' he."

He spoke no more, and a few minutes after died. Poor Kate, who will tell this to thee!

March 5.—Pop, pop, pop! Bom, bom, bom! throughout the day.—No time for memorandums now.—Go ahead! — Liberty and independence for ever!

. . . . . .

"Here," says the editor of the original edition, "ends Col. Crockett's manuscript." The hand is cold that wrote the foregoing pages, and it devolves upon another to record the subsequent events. Before daybreak, on the 6th of March, the Alamo was assaulted by the whole force of the Mexican army, commanded by Santa Anna in person. The battle was desperate until daylight, when only six men belonging to the Texian garrison was found alive. They were instantly surrounded, and ordered, by General Castrillon, to surrender, which they did, under a promise of his protection, finding that resistance any longer would be madness. Colonel Crockett was of the number. He stood alone in an angle of the fort, the barrel of his shattered rifle in his right hand, in his left his huge Bowie knife dripping blood. There was a frightful gash across his forehead, while around him there was a complete barrier of about twenty Mexicans, lying pell mell, dead, and dying. At his feet lay the dead body of that well known character, designated in the Colonel's narrative by the assumed name of Thimblerig, his knife driven to the haft in the throat of a Mexican, and his left hand clenched in his hair. Poor fellow, I knew him well, at a time when he was possessed of many virtues, but of late years the weeds had choked up the flowers; however, Colonel Crockett had succeeded in awakening in his bosom a sense of better things, and the poor fellow was grateful to the last, and stood beside his friend throughout the desperate havoc.

"General Castrillon was brave and not cruel, and disposed to save the prisoners. He marched them up to that part of the fort where stood Santa Anna and his murderous crew. The steady, fearless step and undaunted tread of Colonel Crockett, on this occasion, together with the bold demeanour of the hardy veteran, had a powerful effect on all present. Nothing daunted he marched up boldly in front of Santa Anna, and looked him sternly in the face, while Castrillon addressed 'his Excellency,'—'Sir, here are six prisoners I have taken alive; how shall I dispose of them?' Santa Anna looked at Castrillon fiercely, flew into a violent rage, and replied, 'Have I not told you before how to dispose of them?' 'Why do you bring them to me?' At the same time his brave officers plunged their swords into the bosoms of their defenceless prisoners. Colonel Crockett, seeing the act of treachery, instantly sprung like a tiger at the ruffian chief, but before he could reach him a dozen swords were sheathed in his indomitable heart; and he fell, and died without a groan, a frown on his brow, and a smile of scorn and defiance on his lips. Castrillon rushed from the scene, apparently horror-struck, sought his quarters, and did not leave them for several days, and hardly spoke to Santa Anna after."

This crowning brutality of Santa Anna is denied by some authorities, who say Crockett and the rest of the garrison perished in the hand-to-hand fight. Santa Anna may be given the benefit of the doubt, without detracting from his bloody laurels in that struggle.

The memory of David Crockett is held in high honour by the citizens of the great empire State, for whose freedom he gave up his life. The anniversary of his birth is celebrated with becoming ceremonies; his deeds have been commemorated in song and story, and even made the theme of a popular drama. Most enduring monument of all, his "motto" has become a household word with sixty millions of people, who know very little, and that little wrongly, about the philosophical filibuster who gave them the watchword—

"Be sure you're right: then go ahead."

THE END.

The Gresham Press,

UNWIN BROTHERS,

CHILWORTH AND LONDON.